Eye of
the Taika

Contemporary Approaches to Film and Media Series

A complete listing of the books in this series can
be found online at wsupress.wayne.edu.

GENERAL EDITOR

Barry Keith Grant
Brock University

EYE
OF THE
TAIKA

NEW ZEALAND COMEDY AND THE FILMS OF TAIKA WAITITI

Matthew Bannister

WAYNE STATE UNIVERSITY PRESS
DETROIT

ISBN (paperback): 978-0-8143-4533-7
ISBN (hardcover): 978-0-8143-4532-0
ISBN (ebook): 978-0-8143-4534-4

Library of Congress Control Number: 2021936464

Cover photo: Taika Waititi (as Alamein) plays *Boy*'s hero Michael Jackson. Image courtesy of Taika Waititi. Cover design by Brad Norr.

The author acknowledges the assistance of School of Media Arts, Wintec (Waikato Institute of Technology) which provided research funding, and Marion Tahana and Robin Cohen, who read parts of the manuscript and provided useful feedback.

Wayne State University Press rests on Waawiyaataanong, also referred to as Detroit, the ancestral and contemporary homeland of the Three Fires Confederacy. These sovereign lands were granted by the Ojibwe, Odawa, Potawatomi, and Wyandot nations, in 1807, through the Treaty of Detroit. Wayne State University Press affirms Indigenous sovereignty and honors all tribes with a connection to Detroit. With our Native neighbors, the press works to advance educational equity and promote a better future for the earth and all people.

Wayne State University Press
Leonard N. Simons Building
4809 Woodward Avenue
Detroit, Michigan 48201-1309

Visit us online at wsupress.wayne.edu

FOR ALICE,

without whom this book would
not have been written.

Whāia te iti kahurangi ki te
tuohu koe me he maunga teitei.

Contents

Introduction: What Is Funny?   1

1. Waititi's Early Life and Work in Aotearoa/New Zealand   19

2. Aotearoa/New Zealand, National Identity, and Film   41

3. Kiwi Comedy: Nobody Takes Us Seriously Anyway   69

4. On/Off-Color? Ethnicity and Comedy   91

5. Quirks and Nerds: *Eagle vs Shark*   115

6. *Boy* as Comedian Comedy   141

7. *What* [Men] *Do in the Shadows* of Globalization   161

8. The Impossible Song of the Huia: Camp, Comedy, and
   Music in *Hunt for the Wilderpeople*   177

9. *Thor: Ragnarok* and Postcolonial Carnival   195

10. Is *Jojo Rabbit* an Anti-Hate Satire?   213

Conclusion   225

Notes   233
Index   295

Introduction

What Is Funny?

A good place to begin Taika Waititi's story is "The Art of Creativity," his 2010 TEDx talk, given just after the *succès d'estime* of *Boy* (2010).[1] This book is primarily about the films Waititi has directed, but "The Art of Creativity" shows how Waititi is firstly a popular performer and a comedian, comparable to directors like Charlie Chaplin and Woody Allen, who were also performers first. More specifically, as comedians, they take a playful attitude toward their audience, even when (as in this case) the situation is not framed as comic. It's no accident that Waititi has made the two most popular New Zealand films ever (*Boy* and *Hunt for the Wilderpeople* [2016]): local audiences love him.[2] When I went to see *Wilderpeople* in my hometown of Hamilton/Kirikiriroa, New Zealand (NZ), people around me were reciting the dialogue. At the end of the film they clapped and cheered, behavior I'd never seen in a local audience. I thought—someone should write about this guy.

Play is central to understanding Waititi specifically, and laughter in general. Gregory Bateson describes animal play as involving a signal indicating that "These actions in which we now engage do not denote what those actions for which they stand would denote," an example being a dog "playfully" nipping another.[3] "Metacommunicative messages mark something as play; actions within the 'play frame' are not to be received in the same way as the same actions when framed as serious."[4] Metacommunicative messages typically take the form of gestures, and I want to argue that in humans the most important play gesture is laughter. We can distinguish different types of play—some is positive and creates order, for example, Huizinga's *ludus*, as in a game, and Erving Goffman's role-playing.[5] But some is disorderly and negative in that it negates the signal it accompanies, specifically the kind that is accompanied by laughter. Some have argued that Bateson's concept of play is still a bit too orderly. Marianna Keisalo argues that it assumes hierarchy—that we know when we're playing, and when we're not.[6] But in a lot of situations, the "frame" is not clear. Perhaps ambiguity ("is this for real?") is an essential part of the play discourse, but it can also give rise to misinterpretation—for example, taking offense. Keisalo cites Don Handelman's concept of Moebius framing—a frame that is reversible, where we are unsure what is in or out of the frame, as part of humor.[7] She applies this model to a Louis C. K. stand-up routine, showing how humor may arise from frame reversal—oscillation between different perspectives. This suggests the idea of comedy as incongruity—that is, as a joke technique, which will be discussed later. But what if the situation is not even framed as comic in the first place? Wouldn't that be a more radical kind of reframing than what occurs within the structure of a joke? The frame's reversibility could include the laughter/play frame itself. Seriousness can also be humorous. The extension of this idea into a comic persona suggests the trickster, because one can never tell when (s)he's playing, just like one can never tell if (s)he's telling the truth.[8]

The situation I have in mind is Waititi's TEDx presentation. The trickster, like the Cretan liar, speaks from a paradoxical position, and is a practical joker—play can emerge at any time, out of the fabric of ordinary life, without the normal cues that accompany humor. TEDx is described on its website as "events . . . organized by passionate individuals who seek to uncover new ideas and to share the latest research in their local areas that spark conversations in their communities."[9] When I searched "creativity," the nominal topic of Waititi's presentation, I found hundreds of TED/TEDx presentations, by such luminaries as Steve Jobs, Frank Gehry, Philippe Starck, and Elizabeth Gilbert. Creativity is clearly a topic that people take seriously. But is Waititi being serious?

Laughter

Why do people laugh? This is a more fundamental question than what humor is, because laughter occurs for many reasons, only some of them humorous.[10] People laugh when tickled. Do they laugh because of sensory stimulation? No, because it is impossible to tickle oneself.[11] This suggests that the association of laughter and tickling comes from its social nature; tickling is a type of play-fighting.[12] Laughter functions to "signal lack of aggressive intentions during mock aggression."[13] Laughter is prior to humor. "Laughter is a precultural signal . . . [whereas] humor . . . is a cultural phenomenon that originated from a behaviour that . . . still includes . . . this signal."[14] The traditional view, that we laugh because something funny made us, is an illusion encouraged by the professionalization of humor, where performers suppress their laughter.[15] The reverse is true in everyday interaction, where laughter is generally shared, underlining its basically social nature. It doesn't really matter where laughter comes from, its function is still the same—even in uncomfortable situations, it still acts to disarm potential aggression. It is "playful self-repudiation," as in "You don't really mean that, do you?"[16] It signals a playful violation of social norms, and also a "neutralizing metarelation" that signals the nonseriousness of that transgression.[17] Humor is "negativistic play."[18] As a child might say, it's about "the way it isn't."[19] Or as the quote, commonly attributed to W. C. Fields, puts it: "The funniest thing a comedian can do is not do it." In "The Art of Creativity," Waititi doesn't give a presentation about what creativity or art is, at least, not by accepted standards. "Art? What is it? Is it important? I have no idea. Move on. I mean, can it . . . save the impoverished? No, it can't, unless it's made of food. Can it bring about world peace? Only if art is actual world peace."

One of the negations of humor is literalization—by reducing the moral to the physical (as noted by Henri Bergson), it deflates pretension, as seen above.[20] Creativity for Waititi is about "having fun and looking at life through the lens of a child," and this sense of fun is enacted or performed, rather than theorized about. Performance "thinks," and Waititi embodies his attitude to creativity by making fun of it, "a performative pragmatic accomplishment."[21] The point about laughter being part of the everyday is enacted in the form and content of Waititi's talk, which encourages different kinds of laughter and makes us ask ourselves—is this funny? What is funny?

Performance

Waititi's talk/routine is apparently a performance. All TEDx talks are performances, in the sense that they have an audience, who evaluate what they see and hear. But performance is not always sequestered from everyday life. Serious, formal play is widespread in human culture as "roles"—parent, child, banker, criminal, as rituals. A performative evaluation of such roles tends to focus on seamless execution. Henri Bergson writes: "life and society require . . . a constantly alert attention . . . elasticity of mind and body . . . to adapt ourselves."[22] Social intelligence is the ability to adapt to and exploit a changing environment, to be flexible, hence society's suspicion of inelasticity, and its response to it—laughter.[23] Performance should not draw attention to itself as a performance. This would be "reversing the frame."[24] To highlight our performance would be to enter into negativistic play, because it would negate the normal interpretation of our actions. It would incite incredulity. Or, looked at from Bergson's perspective, it would reveal inability to adapt, a mechanical, robotic response, which, he argues, can prompt laughter. Laughter breaks the suspension of disbelief that allows us to view fiction as lifelike and everyday life as a serious, absorbing task, as emotionally engaged. It says, "What's the point?" Mary Douglas refers to jokes as "anti-rites"—rituals make life meaningful, whereas in laughter "meaning disappears."[25]

Waititi's talk is, then, an "anti-performance," most obviously in the sense that he acts like he doesn't know what he is doing and continually refers to his own performance as such: "My, uh, name is Taika Waititi, as she said, and the uh . . . time starts now." These redundant statements have the effect of highlighting convention, reversing the frame (we expect competence), and foregrounding his speech as a performance. He is signaling to the audience that he is playing a man giving a talk, and their perhaps slightly uncomfortable laughter signals that they know (but does he, they think?). Even anti-performance is still performance—the presence of a stage and an audience make such an interpretation almost unavoidable. The "anti" in his performance can also be interpreted as teasing or banter, playful combat with the audience. Waititi then presents a slide with a list, with such mundane titles as "Intro"; "Joke" (which could suggest that his anti-strategy is intentional):

[T]his is a quick run through of what I'm going to talk about tonight [audience titters]. First, I thought I'd just introduce myself. So that would be the first thing where I'm—I mean, Taika Waititi [audience titters]. So that—there's that done. I'd like to just break the ice. Maybe start off with a joke. This joke, I'm just going to put it out there, it just involves me telling you that I've just flown into Doha, and as a result, my arms are tired. The aim with that joke is—I've flown into Doha but it was on an airplane in reality. And what I've done there with the joke is I've taken it further and said that my arms are tired, suggesting that I've flown like a bird to Doha [audience titters], so that's the backstory of the joke [scattered audience laughter, applause]. Cool. It's going pretty well.[26]

The audience may be laughing because they find Waititi funny, or because they are embarrassed, encouraged by his frequent self-deprecating comments: "I just really had no idea what to do, or what to say," an ambiguity relevant to a lot of Waititi's performances. By acting out his refusal to play the game by the rules, Waititi is inviting the audience's aggression—when people laugh in disbelief. But Waititi remains consistent to his own fiction, which consists of his lack of a fiction, and the audience goes along with it. This approach is similar to many alternative comedies, which seem to take a quasi-documentary approach, lacking the traditional cues that signal laughter, *The Office*, for example. This underscores the point about reversibility of frames—the most radical reversal is when the serious is presented as the nonserious, without the cues or gestures that signal humor. These cues are not restricted to laughter; they could include the expectation that one is attending a comic performance, formulas such as "did you hear the one about . . . ," nudges, winks, and so on.[27] In contrast, a documentary approach could reflect a postmodern mixing of fiction and life: postmodernism consists centrally of the Warholian "put-on," that is, a joke.[28] But arguably laughter and humor, which are part of everyday life, were performing this mix well before postmodernism.

Practical Joker—NZ Humor

The most extreme example of lack of cues is a practical joke, which can be thought of as a joke without a context.[29] It also connects to comic practices like deadpan or infantilism, which similarly deny or confuse audience cues. There is a general connection here to NZ humor, which is frequently deadpan, addressing a history of representation of New

Zealanders, especially men, as stoic and inexpressive. It can be argued that many NZ male comedians are "practical jokers" ("joker" is an NZ colloquialism for "man") in that their delivery, in the words of a US policewoman in the TV series *Flight of the Conchords*, "sounds like a robot," adding a discomfiting subtext to their jokes.[30] The "secret to Kiwi humo[u]r . . . [is that] when we sound like we're joking, we're being serious, and when we sound like we're being serious, we're just joking," a description that applies well to Conchords Jemaine Clement and Bret McKenzie, both Waititi friends and collaborators.[31] Waititi is literally a practical joker, feigning sleep at the 2005 Academy Awards, when his short film *Two Cars, One Night*, was up for an award (he didn't win).[32] Even when he did win in 2020, he slyly stowed his Oscar under the seat in front of him.[33] Waititi doesn't need a stage to perform. It's a style that some might call "Aotearoa/New Zealand" in its rejection of the pomposity or pretension typically associated with public events, ceremonies, speeches, formal occasions, and TEDx talks. Discussing practical jokes and NZ, Moira Marsh states that they "dramatize a persistent incongruity in their social setting . . . between New Zealanders' aggressive egalitarian ethos and the considerable power held by government bureaucracies," that is, antiauthoritarianism.[34] The other message a practical joke sends is, "Don't get too cocky," and this ties into self-deprecation, or lack of identity, as a form of identity, a very NZ trope, redoubled by Waititi's Māori ethnicity and the associated history of racism toward Māori.

Amusement and Emotion

Throughout his presentation, Waititi never really changes his tone, talking understatedly in an NZ accent. It's a kind of playing that denies its own fictive and humorous nature by appearing to be matter-of-fact, a kind of humor based around nonjokes. What such actions suggest is noncommitment, not becoming emotionally invested or taking seriously what is occurring—another kind of playing. In this vein, John Morreall argues that amusement is not an emotion:

> In emotions . . . bodily changes are caused by beliefs and desires, and those changes, along with the beliefs and desires, prompt adaptive

actions. But none of these elements—beliefs, desires, or motivations for adaptive actions—are required in amusement. . . . Amusement is not, like emotions, a direct adaptation to dangers and opportunities, and so it does not involve the cognitive and practical engagement of beliefs, desires, and adaptive actions.[35]

Indeed, laughter may render us temporarily incapable of speech and action: being "helpless" with laughter.[36] Henri Bergson states that humor requires "anaesthesia of the heart": the man slipping on a banana skin is not funny if we sympathize.[37] Connectedly, comic characters often break the fourth wall and gesture to the audience, which could signal emotional disengagement. Other characters in the narrative are motivated by needs and desires (or fictional representations of such things); they take the action "seriously." In the UK situation comedy *Fleabag*, the central character, a clever but cynical young woman, often looks ironically at the camera, but then falls for a Catholic priest, who, unlike the other characters, can tell when she does it—"Where did you go then?" he asks her. This suggests that the priest understands her in a way that the other characters don't, and indeed, she falls in love with him. The connotation is that if they did have a relationship (unlikely, given his profession), she would no longer need to address the camera. Directly addressing the camera occurs in all of Waititi's films, whether done by him or another character. He also uses it in TV advertisements, and it is a feature of mockumentary, another favored Waititi form. Clearly it has some of the effects already identified—confusing reality and fiction, signaling detachment from onstage action and bantering complicity with audience. It is central to Steve Seidman's model of filmic comedian comedy, in which the comic character breaks the frame, partly because (s)he is often already known to the audience.[38] It is a performative mode (as in film musicals and music videos). The "eye of the Taika," addressing the audience, is at the heart of Waititi's mostly comic vision. (The title is also a pun on Survivor's 1982 hit "Eye of the Tiger," which is the kind of 1980s US pulp machismo that Waititi loves. "Taika" is "tiger" in Māori, also Waititi's father's nickname.)[39] In his talk, Waititi comments on the audience on a number of occasions, in a kind of reverse heckling way, saying "You're wasting my time by clapping," which could suggest emotional distance. He also congratulates the audience "on being there."

Traditional Theories of Humor

Telling jokes is not central to Waititi's act. He makes this clear by telling two very bad jokes in an extremely clunky fashion, one described above, and a later effort that uses the clichéd "knock knock" formula. He was using basically the same jokes in a stand-up performance in 2003.[40] Clearly, he's not looking too hard for material! Waititi's act is a rebuttal to joke-based theories of humor; indeed, this whole introduction critiques the idea that a joke is a means to an end—laughter. Rather, laughter is prior to joking. The three main theories of humor—superiority, incongruity, and relief or release of tension, are all based on the joke model. Aristotle states that "comedy is a representation of inferior people" and audience laughter expresses superiority.[41] In this theory, humor resides in orientation to a particular object. But we have already established that humor is not primarily about orientations toward objects, which is an attitude characteristic of emotional engagement (of which superiority would be an example). Humor can reduce others to objects but this is different from relating to them as objects (as causes for action)—it may seem funny if a person bounces like a ball, but in doing this, they no longer seem human, they have become a playful object. Why in any case should social inferiority be funny? It might equally be found pitiable or contemptible. An example is Waititi's treatment of Hitler in the TEDx talk. It would be easy to make fun of Hitler on grounds of superiority but instead Waititi converts him into a playful object: "What is it about the mustache? . . . you can make anything look like Hitler" (shows images of a Big Mac, daisies, and the Earth, all with Hitler mustaches). Arguably this approach works better than addressing Hitler as inferior (in *Jojo Rabbit*).

Incongruity is not wholly separate from superiority insofar as hierarchical social relations often give rise to anomalies, but it has also been argued to be inherent in the form of a joke, which relies on a perceived disparity between two elements.[42] Jerry Palmer claims that joke narratives balance a probable, commonsense proposition about the world with a second, playful (but not impossible) proposition that emerges at a strategic moment (the punch line, peripeteia, or moment of recognition) and reinterprets the narrative in an unexpected way, which he terms "the logic of the absurd."[43] Waititi uses incongruity in his talk, particularly in the disparity between the images in his slideshow and his commentary (the same device used in the presentation scene of *Boy*). An example is his gloss of a famous Henri Rousseau painting, *The Sleeping Gypsy*: "This is a lion having a talk to his friend, saying *'Hey Jeffrey, uh, can I borrow your guitar?'*" Waititi's reinterpretation of a piece of high art as a conversation between a man and a lion about a guitar is clearly incongruous. The sudden emergence of resolution out of the joke narrative connects to the third theory—relief. Jokes generally depend for their effect on suspense, capped by a surprise, which releases tension.[44] Release of tension also connects to theories about the comic as an expression of freedom or vitality, and the sublimated expression of aggressive instincts, discussed below.

The problem with semantic incongruity theories like Palmer's is that they analyze jokes in isolation. The humor is located in the joke's magical resolution of ambiguity. But many texts are ambiguous without being funny.[45] Attention then shifts to how ambiguity is resolved, but some humor is unresolved—absurdity or nonsense, for example.[46] There is a good deal of nonsense in Waititi's talk: "[My parents] met and then, a few drinks later, they gave birth to a beautiful Asian daughter called Taika"; "usually the people that talk here have invented a brain, or something, or, like, a lady had a stroke and she could suddenly see through walls and became Rainman." The relief theory, associated with Sigmund Freud, argues that humor sublimates repressed unconscious drives, but this release relates only to the psychology of the individual, when I would argue that it relates to the group (who, moreover, do not necessarily need jokes to laugh).[47] All these theories can be understood as special instances of the play thesis: superiority theory focuses on the "game" of humor in the sense of who "wins," incongruity theory focuses on play as subverting or upsetting normative codes, and relief/release theory shares the idea of play as relaxation, of creating levity. But all these theories are based on the model of telling jokes to an audience, when laughter and humor are broader phenomena. Although the main concern of this book is with "professional" humor, the joke model is not typical of all humor, which, as Bergson states, is the art form closest to life, because it also takes place in real life.[48] Similarly, Waititi's humor seems to be threaded throughout his life and art.

In narrative terms, Waititi's films are a bit like his talks, digressive and rambling. He frequently improvises, both on set and when giving speeches. His films tend to lack the tight teleological drive advocated by screenwriting gurus such as Christopher Vogler or Syd Field.[49] It's not unusual for comedies to have a more episodic structure than standard feature films, but even by the standards of film comedy, Waititi's films are relaxed: "Some people are so good at structure, I'm terrible at it . . . structure . . . sort of comes with the edit."[50] Highly articulated gag sequences, of the kind developed in Hollywood silent comedy, which aim at "escalation of comic effect" through a series of interconnected gags, and plot complications, which create hierarchies of awareness (say, a concealed character overhearing a conversation, common in farce or romantic comedy), are unusual in Waititi's work.[51] Histrionic behavior, not unusual in comedy, is avoided, as is the "intensification of affective experience" characteristic of virtuosic comic performance that originated in vaudeville and can still be seen in modern actors like Jim Carrey.[52] Waititi says, "I find comedy can come from mundane things, really. I find that appealing. Coming from New Zealand, I think we all really like that. But I do think it's varied and, when I'm shooting, I try not to force the comedy too much. I'll try to do a few different versions of something. I usually try to do a comedy one, a dramatic one and then something in-between."[53] The humor is likely to be low-key, and this connects to indie film that reacts against Hollywood norms, such as *Eagle vs Shark*. Barry Barclay's Fourth Cinema advocates an indigenous (Māori) approach to filmmaking that eschews many typical Hollywood narrative devices and could have influenced Waititi.[54] But the main point is that Waititi's filmic style is consistent with the kind of public persona he presents, and this persona relates to the directorial persona of the "auteur."

"Don't ever use that word." Waititi—Auteur?

Auteurism is partly about reading films as art, but film comedy is rarely viewed in such a light. Andrew Stott comments that "comedy's denigration . . . is a product of its populism," while John Mundy and Glyn White note that comedy programs and artists are "seldom [considered] culturally prestigious."[55] Andrew Sarris made Charlie Chaplin his top auteur of all time, but this exception seems to prove the rule.[56] Waititi has also expressed skepticism about the term.[57] This may be due to New Zealand's history of anti-intellectualism (discussed in chapter 2) or a riposte to the paradoxical notion of an indigenous auteur. Nevertheless, he has directed and written five feature films (including *What We Do in the Shadows*, cowritten and directed with Jemaine Clement), directed a further film he didn't write (*Thor: Ragnarok*), and also produced three of them. The commercial and artistic reputation of these films is deeply identified with him. Indeed, in auteur style, aspects of his films have some relation to his life—most obviously *Boy*. He has starred in two and costarred in all of his films. As Andrew Sarris said of Charlie Chaplin, "his other self on the screen has always been the supreme object of contemplation."[58]

But Waititi's output is not limited to feature films. There is the question, as Foucault puts it, of where the work begins and ends—does a laundry list by the author count?[59] He has directed, written, and often appeared in dozens of short films, commercials, episodes of TV series, music videos, and so on. I've discussed them when they seem germane to the kind of themes, material, or personnel he uses in his films. A traditional auteur approach focuses on feature films, whereas my intention is to locate Waititi's films in a broader cultural landscape, more of a cultural studies than a film studies approach. A final point is that Waititi collaborates; he uses similar personnel from film to film, including producers, actors, writers or codirectors, and musicians. I've tried to indicate their contributions. He also frequently improvises on set, and his casual approach could seem like the opposite of auteurs like Alfred Hitchcock.

This book is nominally about Waititi's films, not his life, but it is impossible to separate the two entirely. Film directors are generally fairly retiring, but Waititi clearly enjoys public performance: he is a celebrity. Nowadays, "the instantaneity of celebrity images and the ubiquity of our 'search' culture mean that celebrities inhabit a social space closer to us than ever before."[60] Waititi's performance abilities and charisma, combined with his comic ability to play with art and life, are ideal for constructing a public persona in an age of hypermediation. It is also possible that his ethnic background, Jewish and Māori, imparts a heightened awareness of the performativity of identity. Waititi typifies a new breed of film director, "doing duty not only as the (imaginary or real) anchor for presumed, perceived, or projected coherence [of the film], but . . . actively deployed as a brand name and marketing tool, for the commercial film industry as well as in the realm of independent and art cinema."[61] As an initially indie filmmaker who has become increasingly mainstream, he has moved from cult favorite to Hollywood darling. He displays what Thomas Elsaesser calls "double occupancy," like many modern filmmakers, lacking allegiance to any one nation, as a member of an indigenous minority in his own country while also part of the global Jewish diaspora. Double occupancy also refers to the tightrope that film directors walk between artistic autonomy and commercial success, in an industry that demands both, initiating "paradoxes of . . . 'enabling dependency' or 'master-slave dialectic' that . . . [bind] the auteur to the [film] festival and vice versa. . . ."[62] Another type of double occupancy refers to shifting between film and other artistic occupations—Waititi was a visual artist in the 1990s, and his artwork features in his films; he has a history of performance as an actor and stand-up comedian, like Woody Allen, Charlie Chaplin, Mel Brooks, and so on.[63] The tensions between these roles and sets of circumstances give rise to "performative self-contradiction . . . when one makes a claim that contradicts the validity of the means that are used to make it . . . [it] goes back to the logical or semantic paradoxes of the Greek philosopher Epimenides, who famously claimed 'all Cretans are liars,' while being himself a Cretan."[64] Elsaesser's example is the Danish director Lars von Trier:

> A poster ahead of his appearance at the Berlin Film Festival in February 2014 to promote *Nymphomaniac* showed him with duct tape plastered over his mouth, signaling the fact that he had been "silenced" by the Cannes Festival, and was now "vowing silence" after the disastrous press conference for *Melancholia* in May 2011. Yet the very gesture is so eloquent that it contradicts the assertion that he has been silenced.[65]

Waititi's TEDx talk is an example of performative self-contradiction: it apparently turns a "serious" topic into a stand-up routine, displaying exactly the kind of "ritual reversal" used by comedians and tricksters (of which the Cretan liar is an example):

> ritual reversals mean switching to the opposite of what is considered "the normal order." Such reversals can occur, for example, in

terms of social hierarchies in rites of passage, in action in carnival, or in the framing of action as ritual or performance. For comedic figures such as clowns and tricksters, reversals are part of their semiotic technique.[66]

Waititi's pranks at the Academy Awards in 2005 and 2020 are further examples of performative self-contradiction—they display irreverence for the entertainment industry and the audience. Waititi says, "a lot of New Zealanders thought it was embarrassing. . . . One letter said . . . 'Maybe you should have more respect for a Pākehā [white] tradition because I'm sure you wouldn't fall asleep on a marae,' and I said, 'Yes, I would' (laughs), 'I do it all the time!'"[67] Waititi has a history of awards ceremony controversy, including his hosting of the New Zealand Music Awards in 2012 and 2015.[68] At the former he remarked that overseas award winners Mumford & Sons had "felt him up" before continuing, "It's an honor to be here . . . It's a real who's who . . . of people I've never heard of." One gets the impression that Waititi dislikes award ceremonies, but at the same time recognizes (as with von Trier and film festivals) that they are part of the entertainment industry. Hence his ambivalent attitude: "Only losers get awards."[69] It is widely suggested that he improvises his speeches, which fits with his informal attitude.[70] Finally, the very notion of an indigenous auteur is itself a self-contradiction, as indigeneity generally opposes the type of Western individualism that the auteur exemplifies. But that is one of the roles he is cast in.

Waititi is a comedian—his films do many things but fundamentally, they make people laugh. However, accounts of NZ film have tended to overlook comedy. So how does comedy fit in NZ film history? My thesis centers on antipodean camp, which refers to a populist settler narrative of ironic self-positioning in relation to colonization and which continues into Waititi's work.[71] Antipodean camp is about NZ identity, which has traditionally been defined in gendered terms—the Kiwi bloke—and masculinity is central to Waititi's films, too. "Camp proposes a comic vision of the world,"[72] but is also about gender, thus antipodean camp is a way of connecting comedy to gender to say something about Waititi's films and their relation to NZ. Comedy and masculinity connect in his films through banter: "Although the talk within the homosocial space may superficially appear as men 'just joking,' meaningful policing of masculinity occurs in this banter."[73] Waititi's bicultural identity, Māori/Pākehā (white settler, though the latter part is also Jewish), provides a number of ways to think about the relation of his work/identity to bi- and multiculturalism, locally and globally.[74]

In chapter 1, I've sketched Waititi's early life and career, his experience of growing up in NZ (set against the backdrop of NZ history), and offered an overview of his early work, notably his short films *Two Cars, One Night* (2003) and *Tama Tū* (2004), which show some characteristic themes, such as banter, children, masculinity, and Māori culture. But rather than a fixed entity, or inevitable outcome, identity is also thematized in terms of divergent tendencies or "becomings"—different ethnicities (Jewish/Māori/Pākehā), gender positions (hetero/homo, masculine/feminine), ages (child/adult), and careers (painter/actor/comedian/film director) and the intersectional interactions between these categories.[75] The point, as in the next chapter, is to show how identity, whether personal or national, is always in process, and that attempts to fix it usually relate to hegemony.

Chapter 2 discusses the history of Aotearoa/New Zealand and its film industry, arguing that the chimera of "national identity" is a function of NZ dependence on its colonizer, Britain. The leading NZ signifier, the "Kiwi bloke," a Pākehā rural man, implicitly working-class, is testament to Britain's exploitation of NZ's primary produce and manpower, returned as imported culture to reproduce the colonizer's superiority. The "bloke's" tough, supposedly imposing exterior hid the reality of his subaltern status within the empire, leading to cultural cringe and the gender ambiguities engendered by homosociality. In contrast, Māori have always been central to images of NZ, even in films made by Europeans. Pākehā became central to filmic representations of NZ only with the introduction of documentary as government propaganda during World War II, which built a sense of NZ as a modern nation, but to the detriment of its sense of imaginative possibility. *Forgotten Silver*, Peter Jackson and Costa Botes's 1995 mockumentary about a fictional NZ filmmaker, sends up Pākehā realism, suggesting that practical jokes, comedy, and camp constitute NZ identity best, precisely because they don't take it seriously. Now, funny Māori/Pasifika men like Waititi have ousted the Kiwi bloke, although masculinity remains central to discourses of local identity.

Chapter 3 focuses on the history of local comedy, generally under-valued in NZ film histories, which tend to privilege "serious" art. Richard Dyer's concept of entertainment offers an alternative paradigm.[76] Successful local comedy is built around comedians with a history of entertaining live audiences—which is essential to knowing what makes people laugh. So Waititi's background in live performance and stand-up is essential to his filmmaking, along with associated discourses of improvisation and direct address, relating back to Dyer's emphasis on entertainment as a type of performance. One of Waititi's stand-up routines is discussed in relation to the above themes. Comedy's connection to audience can also mean playing on its prejudices, however, and I consider how Waititi uses antipodean homosociality in two TV advertising campaigns with contradictory aims, producing ethical inconsistency.

Chapter 4 continues this ethical theme with a discussion of ethnicity in NZ comedy, using Waititi's own mixed ethnicity and its echo in NZ biculturalism as a starting point. The chapter traces the recent history of ethnicity in NZ in relation to local comedy, combined with a consideration of US influence on local nonwhite popular culture, culminating in the case study of NZ's most successful TV comedy, *bro'Town*, a key precedent for Waititi, and the work of a Polynesian diaspora. Tropes from African American humor and culture continue to signify in Waititi's work. The question of how Māori and Pasifika positioned themselves historically in relation to discourses of US black identity, and its consequences for cultural production with the rise of local biculturalism, is discussed, alongside an ongoing comparison between the careers of black and Jewish US comedians and Waititi in the film industry.

Chapter 5 looks at Waititi's first feature film, *Eagle vs Shark* (2007), through the glasses of the nerd. Geeks or nerds have a history as popular culture intellectuals/comic figures, from Andy Warhol to Waititi's "clumsy, indigenous geeks."[77] More recently, Roger Ebert coined the term "New Geek Cinema" to describe a strain of Sundance indie film, which Waititi interacted with for this "quirky" film.[78] Such films, by directors like Wes Anderson, feature nerdy characters, representational strategies, and film techniques that distinguish them from Hollywood cinema. *Eagle vs Shark* adopts many quirky conventions, from *Napoleon Dynamite* (2004) in particular, cultivating an ambivalent, painfully comic tone. But how does a Māori/Jewish director respond to a discourse that is dominantly white and Anglo-American? Noting how historically nerd culture has often referred to nonwhite culture for validation, I argue that this option is not available for nonwhite nerds, which helps explain the film's uncertain conclusion.

Chapter 6 addresses *Boy* (2010) as an example of "comedian comedy," a genre typically centered around a well-known comedian, who has a peculiar freedom to play with convention, typically directly addressing the camera, making spectacles, as comics do in performance. The comedian character is often at odds with the fictional world, much like Alamein, the character Waititi plays in *Boy*. Seidman also mentions comic acts like the Marx Brothers or comic duos, thus I argue that the comedian function in the film is split, mainly between "the two Alameins," Boy and his father (Waititi), who operate like a comic duo, with Boy playing straight man to his zany, useless Dad. The emphasis on groups rather than individuals, as well as aspects of the narrative structure, can also be read in terms of kaupapa (method) Māori.

What We Do in the Shadows (2014) is the subject of chapter 7. Vampires are the archetypal immigrants: both traditional and modern, human and nonhuman, cosmopolitan and fundamentalist, Same and Other, categories borrowed from Anthony Giddens's work on modernity and globalization. They are a threat and a joke. Thinking about the text as a mockumentary invites consideration of audiences as textual vampires, voyeurs simultaneously under surveillance, desiring and disdaining the spectacle of Otherness, living in the perverse conditions of late capitalism. It also opens up a reading of young men who talk in funny voices, enjoy dressing up in frilly clothes, going nightclubbing, and searching for a "fix" (of human blood). In the film's denouement, vampire and werewolf homosociality provides a means for their assimilation in NZ society via shared discourses of masculinity, framed broadly against the potential effeminacy of the foreign.

In chapter 8, *Hunt for the Wilderpeople* (2016), a populist, nostalgic, reasonably family-friendly rural romp that plays on and ironizes aspects of Aotearoa/New Zealand identity, is discussed as antipodean camp. I argue that the music, unlike conventional film music, actively constitutes narrative, replacing traditional realism with camp aestheticism. The film features camp exaggeration, artifice, intertextuality, and episodic or hackneyed plotlines, while also distinguishing itself from more extravagantly Australian camp films, like *Muriel's Wedding* and *Strictly Ballroom*, by its rural subject matter, folksier tone, and focus on androgynous or childlike masculinity.

Thor: Ragnarok (chapter 9) marks Waititi's Hollywood debut, with a superhero fantasy sci-fi film that is part of the Marvel Comics franchise. Far from being new territory for Waititi, the film allows him to draw on his knowledge and love for US popular culture, complementing Peter Jackson's earlier franchise forays with *The Lord of the Rings*. The film parodies the superhero genre by invoking Bakhtin's "carnival." The world of Sakaar, with its hybrid population, electronic music, sexual fluidity, and love of "trash," inverts the formal Nordic realms of Asgard, introducing a Māori/Pasifika, Oceanic subaltern's perspective on Western superhero ideology, as the hero Thor is forced to reassess his ideals in Sakaar's fleshpots and find allies among its ethnic exiles.

Chapter 10 deals with *Jojo Rabbit* (2020), evaluating the phrase "anti-hate satire" that was used to market the film. Satire is frequently comedy with a political and topical edge, but is the controversy around the film because of its edginess or because it isn't a very good film? Irrespective of its artistic success, the film has succeeded on other levels, partly due to its topicality and timeliness in Hollywood, which is increasingly concerned with acknowledging cultural diversity in challenging times.

So far academic discussion of Waititi's work has been primarily local, with the *MEDIANZ (Media Studies Journal of Aotearoa New Zealand)* special edition on *Boy* being the most sustained discussion—indeed there is far more written on *Boy* than on his other films, understandably, given Waititi's fairly short career.[79] Especially useful is Ocean Mercier's work, which takes a primarily, but not exclusively, Māori perspective.[80] There is a growing literature on Māori indigeneity in media, but so far little that addresses comedy and intertextuality, which are central to Waititi's filmic identity, as is his diasporic Jewishness.[81]

The interpenetration of global and local in modernity is more than a theme, more like the content of Waititi's highly intertextual films. Comedy is one way of providing a more global perspective, while also helping understand his work inclusively, as popular culture or entertainment, as opposed to the exclusivity of filmic art. Viewing Waititi as a "comic auteur" is a way of interrogating both halves of this term—comic undercuts auteur, and vice versa. Most existing discussion of Waititi centers on issues of local-ness, ethnicity, and "coming of age"; in a word, identity.[82] Framing his work as comic is not so much challenging this approach as enhancing it. Ultimately, the two approaches intersect: themes of indigeneity, ethnicity, colonialism, national identity, and gender are nuanced through a comic perspective. They may become sites of play and difference, which can both reinforce (in the case of masculinity) and undermine hegemony. In relation to Waititi as a Māori/Jewish New Zealander, comedy can be seen as a recognition and exploitation of social marginality, of not being taken seriously, as Māori/Jewish within New Zealand and as a New Zealander within the world. However, lack of seriousness activates the resource of humor. Waititi credits Māori filmmaker Merata Mita, who coproduced *Boy*, with this realization: "The first draft of [*Boy*] was pretty dramatic . . . a typical depressing New Zealand film . . . she reminded me that my point of difference . . . was . . . trying to . . . take a serious situation and inject it with irreverence or humor."[83] Humor, in turn, operates as both a confirmation of and a challenge to social norms: "The strength of its attack is . . . restricted by the consensus on which it depends for recognition."[84]

I want to analyze Waititi's work in terms of comic genres and modes, whether play, parody, camp, satire, Bakhtinian carnival, comedian comedy, quirky film, mockumentary, banter, trickery, or stand-up, but also in terms of identity—gender, ethnicity, and nationality—to construct Waititi as an indigenous/diasporic comic auteur whose mixed ethnicity, varied artistic experience, and playful approach invite a range of readings, from performer to indigenous artist, NZ male, ethnic trickster, and pop-culture fan. I don't mean to imply that Waititi is "only a comic." Laughter is ultimately more than comic, and so his work can accommodate a range of readings, but, as Jerry Palmer argues, if we reduce "comedy to the play of serious values (attacking a, promoting b) the nature of the process, the pleasure which is specific to comedy . . . is lost. . . . To evoke values in the mode of humour is to evoke them in a special, unique way, a way which cannot ultimately be reduced to the serious presentation of the same material."[85]

1
WAITITI'S EARLY LIFE AND WORK IN AOTEAROA/ NEW ZEALAND

So, who am I? Well, I kind of don't really know that myself, often. I come from New Zealand, and I come from these two people, who met in the early '70s. The woman is Robin. She's of Russian-Jewish heritage, and she was a schoolteacher. And the guy next to her, his name is Tiger and he's a farmer and an artist. And they met and then, a few drinks later, they gave birth to a beautiful Asian daughter called Taika. And so I come from a very mixed background and as a result, I've always sort of had trouble kind of finding out, deciding really who I was, or what I wanted to do.[1]

With its history of settler colonization, indigenous peoples and a wide range of immigrants arriving not only from the neighbouring islands in the Pacific Ocean but also from as far as the Caspian Sea, the New Zealand context is complex. I believe this complexity demands a rather different approach to the conceptualization of diasporic film and film-making, one rooted in a diasporic consciousness, engendered by the sense and actual experience of displacement and identity (re)construction and negotiation over the course of time.[2]

These two statements, one from Waititi, one from Arezou Zalipour, provide some useful ways of thinking about identity, whether personal or social and cultural. They suggest avoiding being too categorical about labeling ourselves and others.

Waititi's statement can be read on one level as an example of his self-deprecation, and one can argue about how far that is a product of his New Zealand-ness, Māori-ness, or Jewishness, all of which are cultures with a history of being deprecated, by themselves and others. Its humor also masks some important details, as we'll see. Both statements reflect the displacement of modernity—NZ is the product of multiple diasporas: Anglo-Saxon, Polynesian, Jewish, Asian. Identity is a question of tendencies, not absolutes. Waititi mentions his mother's ethnicity, but not his father's (Māori). One can hardly criticize someone for not stating their ethnicity—white people don't usually. In his TEDx talk, Waititi avoids the usual route of talking about the subject, creativity. Instead, he enacts it, approaching the presentation as quirky comedy. The same might be said of his Māori-ness.

A Māori Filmmaker?

Waititi is reluctant to be categorized as a Māori filmmaker, commenting, "Let's just say I'm a filmmaker who is Māori and some of my films are going to have a lot of Māori content and some aren't. Why can't I just be a guy who writes stories and puts them in a film? Why can't I be a tall filmmaker? Or a black-haired filmmaker?"[3] Such comments are ambiguous: the original context, *North & South*, a conservative magazine read mainly by aging Pākehā, could suggest a "postracial" interpretation of the "we're all New Zealanders" type.[4] But Waititi has also spoken frankly about how NZ is "a racist place. People just flat-out refuse to pronounce Māori names properly. . . . They're like, 'Oh, you've done so well, haven't you? For how you grew up. For one of your people.'"[5] Speaking of film, Leonie Pihama stated in 1994, "Maori people struggle to gain a voice, struggle to be heard from the margins, to have our stories heard, to have our descriptions of ourselves validated, to have access to the domain within which we can control and define those images which are held up as reflections of our realities."[6] Is this still true today? Waititi's statement above could also indicate skepticism about the politics of recognition, as "recognition of cultural distinctiveness . . . promises to reproduce the very configuration of colonial power that indigenous demands for recognition have historically sought to transcend."[7] A hazard of biculturalism is that the institutionalization of culture can also mean reification.

Waititi's statement can be interpreted intersectionally: "highlighting differences within an indigenous group or community, not only the differences between indigenous and non-indigenous groups."[8] Finally, Waititi is suggesting, that he is not just a Māori filmmaker. He has other strings to his bow, like identifying as Jewish, being a New Zealander, having creative parents, being an artist, and so on. Waititi saves enacting or performing Māori until the end of his TEDx talk, when he says:

> Back home in New Zealand, we have the saying Tēnā koe. Okay?
> It's a Māori saying, Tēnā koe is how you say hello. What it literally
> means is *"There you are."* If you say that to a group of people: Tēnā
> koutou, *"There you guys are."* Okay? So, the fact that we're here, that
> we're even on Earth in the first place, I think that's success, in itself.
> So, congratulations everyone, on being here. . . .[9]

By enacting his Māoriness in the form of a greeting, Waititi makes his identity invitational rather than confrontational. It becomes a way of including his audience, allowing them to participate. Anyone can say this greeting, and speaking Te Reo makes you just a little bit Māori. Hence this chapter, while discussing Waititi's "identity" in terms of a biographical narrative, set against the backdrop of NZ history, also refers to the divergent tendencies or "becomings" of identity—different ethnicities (Jewish/Māori/Pākehā), sex/gender ambiguity (hetero/homo, male/female, cis/trans), different ages (child/adult), and different careers (painter/actor/comedian/film director)—and the intersectional interactions between these categories.

NZ History

Aotearoa/New Zealand was probably first settled between seven hundred and one thousand years ago by Polynesians from the Pacific islands, who subsequently became known as Māori.[10] In 1769, British explorer Captain Cook landed on the islands and charted them, and soon after European whalers began establishing stations on the coast.[11] In the early nineteenth century, British settlers began arriving, and in 1840 the Treaty of Waitangi was signed by representatives of both groups, in which Māori ceded sovereignty to the British monarch in return for the rights and privileges of British subjects, although Māori have since disputed what was meant by "sovereignty," as the Māori version of the treaty is worded differently than the English version.[12] New Zealand remained a British colony or dominion until 1947 (New Zealanders remained British subjects until 1983, a point we will return to in chapter 2).[13] In theory, the treaty allowed the two groups to coexist peacefully. In fact, increasing pressures on land from white immigration and financial interests led to the New Zealand Wars, after which, from the 1870s, Māori were deprived of many of the rights and possessions the treaty had supposedly guaranteed.[14] Legally, Aotearoa/New Zealand is now a bicultural society, but in pragmatic terms, power continues to be largely in the hands of Pākehā, or white settlers.

Māori suffered through colonization—imported disease reduced their population from 114,800 in 1843 to 42,113 in 1896 and they lost most of their land to government confiscations of dubious legality.[15] Thereafter their population recovered, although they were still subject to prejudice and legal discrimination, including the banning of Māori language (Te Reo) in schools.[16] After World War II, Māori increasingly migrated into urban areas, which had historically been mainly white. At the same time, immigration also brought thousands of Pacific Islanders, both groups in search of work. The 1970s saw a Māori Renaissance (Taha Māori): a rediscovery of Māori art, language, and culture.[17] Māori urban protest movements such as Ngā Tamatoa (Young Warriors) emerged, counting future Māori filmmakers like Merata Mita and Barry Barclay among their members, and this led to significant interactions with ideas of blackness (from the US) and with Pasifika activists (the Polynesian Panthers), as discussed in chapter 4. In 1975 (the year of Waititi's birth), a Māori woman leader, Dame Whina Cooper, led a Land March the length of the North Island to Wellington, the NZ capital, to present a petition demanding return of Māori land. The Treaty of Waitangi Act 1975 established a legal process for investigating historic claims by Māori against the Crown. The Labour government of 1984 initiated reforms that led toward biculturalism, such as the Māori Language Act (1987), which went some way toward establishing Te Reo as an official language alongside English, while simultaneously pursuing a neoliberal economic agenda.

NZ's unusually close economic and cultural relationship with the UK lasted until the latter joined the European Economic Community

(EEC) in 1973, and while NZ is possibly no longer beholden to its colonizer, arguably it has simply switched its affiliations to neoliberal global corporations. Simultaneous with the opening of NZ to global markets from 1984 (the year in which *Boy* is set) came an increasing emphasis on progressive social policy, decriminalization of homosexuality, the adoption of biculturalism, and the banning of US nuclear warships. The government's social agenda was undermined by its economic agenda, however, as privatization and free trade policies transferred public assets into private hands. In an era of commodification, everything was up for grabs—even national identity, which was increasingly viewed as an exploitable asset, a unique selling point in a global marketplace.[18]

After the 1987 Immigration Act, numbers of Asian immigrants rapidly increased, as did the NZ population, rising from approximately 3.3 million in 1987 to 5 million in 2020.[19] The population according to the 2018 census is 70.2% European, 16.5% Māori, 15.1% Asian, and 8.1% Pacific (people can identify with more than one ethnic group, so the percentages do not add up to 100).[20] NZ is in many respects now a multicultural nation, though its legal framework remains bicultural: "demographically multicultural, officially bicultural, and . . . institutionally monocultural."[21]

Taika David Waititi was born on August 16, 1975, in Wellington Hospital, Wellington, to mother Robin Cohen and father Taika Waititi (died February 2015). They were not legally married and separated when Taika was six years old. Robin Cohen was born in Wellington to David Cohen and Mary Edwards, both born in New Zealand. Her paternal grandfather was a Russian Jew whose family left after pogroms began in their area—Novozybkov, Bryansk Oblast—in 1904–5. They probably arrived in New Zealand via Britain between 1910 and 1915. Waititi's iwi (tribe) is Te-Whānau-ā-Apanui, from the west coast of the North Island's East Cape, which includes the settings (Waihau Bay, Raukokore) of *Boy*.

Waititi's paternal grandfather was Eruiti Taika/Edward Waititi (1919–69), the son of Kāinga O Te Ware Waititi and Taupe Waititi. Eruiti fought in World War II in the Twenty-Eighth Māori Battalion, referenced in *Tama Tū* and *Boy*. Māori attach great importance to genealogy (whakapapa): Kāinga was son to Hone Te Ware Waititi and Te Huingamate Pururangi. Taupe was daughter of Parāone Heremia and Te Owai

Wirepa. Taika's paternal grandmother was Matewa Delamere (1926–98), daughter to Hiki Mānawa Delamere and Rongopouri Poihipi. Hiki was son to Kohi/Neri/Ned/Edward Delamere and Ngarori Nikorima. Kohi's father, Samuel/Sam Delamere, a French-Canadian whaler, married Peti/Irihāpeti Te Hā, a Māori woman.[22]

Waititi's parents met when "my mother was going around . . . prisons . . . giving books to inmates and that's how she met my dad . . . he was in jail. . . . This weird . . . middle class . . . Jewish family who were all intellectuals . . . mixed with this farming family who were all . . . criminals . . . and artists."[23] He was named after his grandparents David and Taika, but because he looked Māori, his parents decided his first name would be Taika.[24] Waititi adds, "My dad's a painter, which is also my background, so I started doing that earlier. My mother's an English teacher who forced me to read a lot of books and poetry and encouraged me more towards the drama side of things, like doing the acting and the writing."[25] Subsequently, he added, "She would read all of the essays . . . I was writing, and grade them before I handed them in . . . [she would] say, 'That's not good enough' . . . even at university."[26] An only child, Waititi grew up partly in Wellington, where his mother lived, and partly in Waihau Bay, East Cape, where his father lived.[27] He comments: "Those were long journeys and I would often have to do them by myself."[28] Robin comments that he usually flew most of the way, however.[29] He attended primary schools Raukokore School (seen in *Boy*) and Te Aro School in Wellington, and, for his secondary education, Onslow College in Wellington. "When I was at Onslow College, [my favorite place] was the Johnsonville Mobil [petrol station] forecourt. I grew up drinking in car parks, sitting on car bonnets, hanging out with my mates."[30] This was also the period in which US hip-hop culture became popular locally, and a boom box blasting out rap and Michael Jackson was a frequent accompaniment to street rendezvous.[31] In Wellington, he lived in the Aro Valley, a central suburb with a bohemian reputation. "We used to hassle kids who came from a two-parent house. Growing up in Aro Street, that wasn't normal. It was considered sad when a mum and dad were stuck together."[32] This alternation between city life and the rural, mostly Māori community of Waihau Bay exposed the young Waititi to a range of lifestyles and influences. Waititi's multicultural identity highlights the "complexities of migration and diasporic movement within the bicultural framework of New Zealand society."[33] Accordingly, at school, Waititi was "a social butterfly . . . I'd hang out with the Goths, I'd go and hang out with the . . . math nerds . . . with the artists . . . be in the first fifteen [rugby team], be a jock . . . I just wanted to be liked."[34] To adapt to so many social situations suggests a protean ability to self-transform, to adapt to different "frames," to "play."[35]

Waititi says that his parents "actually discouraged me from doing things like . . . law."[36] He was interested in comedy, staying up to see the 1980s British TV comedy *The Young Ones*, and taping every show.[37] With his mother's encouragement, he started appearing onstage: Wellington is well known in NZ for its theater scene. "The first significant play I did, I was 10. It was this surreal thing these hippies put on at an art festival in Wellington in 1985 and I got a part as a kid running around the stage. The weird thing was I had this girlfriend in the play who was in her mid-20s."[38] Local director Conrad Newport says that Waititi's first stage appearance was a production of *Frankenstein* at BATS Theatre, Wellington, in February 1986. "He was all of 10 and between scenes walked across the stage carrying the name boards describing each scene of the unfolding melodrama."[39] Both Waititi's parents encouraged him, in different ways, to be an artist. His work as a visual artist appears in his films, especially *Boy*, but is also evident in his eye for detail and design in the mise-en-scène. Working in visual art and theater would also have allowed him to view the art world from complementary perspectives, with visual art being, in Bourdieu's terms, relatively autonomous, and theater more heteronomous, that is, more influenced by audiences and commercial considerations.[40]

Waititi studied film and drama at Victoria University, Wellington, in the mid-1990s, where he met Jemaine Clement (later of Flight of the Conchords) and Loren Horsley (later star of *Eagle vs Shark*, who became Waititi's partner for some years).[41] According to Clement, "We were in the capping revue. I remember seeing him and instantly taking a dislike to him, but I would say he is now one of my very best friends."[42] Waititi comments that they would write and put on plays together at Wellington's BATS Theatre.[43] Waititi formed a comedy troupe/show, So You're a Man, with friends from the Drama Club at Victoria University: Clement, Bret McKenzie, Carey Smith, and David Lawrence. Their show was a 1950s-style mockumentary about male etiquette, indicating Waititi's interest in masculinity. Its premier was at the Basement Theatre in Auckland in May 1996.[44] Waititi graduated in 1997, with a bachelor's degree in theater and film.[45]

Subsequently Waititi formed a comedy duo, Humourbeasts, with Jemaine Clement, which won a Billy T. James Award in 1999.[46] Clement sums up the early Humourbeasts as "just trying to do anything we could think of."[47] This seems accurate, based on their 2001 hosting of Starry Eyed, a talent contest based on imitating pop stars, in holiday resort Queenstown, NZ.[48] Dressed as rappers, albeit with curly blond wigs, the pair dance to Chaka Khan's "I Feel for You" and then humorously flirt with women in the audience. The subject matter and style are similar to later Flight of the Conchords videos like "Ladies of the World," although ruder and more energetic. Clement says, "Me plus Bret equals Flight of the Conchords, and me plus Taika equals Humourbeasts. . . . It's those other guys that steer it. The Humourbeasts shows were really lively and the Conchords ones are really slow and deadpan and low-energy."[49] Presenting to the Starry Eyed contest winner (who impersonated Ronan Keating), the pair dress and act like hysterical schoolgirl fans of the singer.[50] With later Humourbeasts shows, Waititi comments, "we tried to centre it more in theatre . . . one-act plays."[51] *The Untold Tales of Maui* (2003), a coproduction with Māori theater troupe Taki Rua cowritten with Andrew Foster, was based on Māui, a legendary hero and trickster who appears in most Polynesian mythologies, comparable to other ethnic tricksters, such as the Signifying Monkey of African American culture.[52] In Māori culture, Māui is credited with the creation of New Zealand, fishing the North Island (Te Ika a Māui) out of the sea with a giant hook fashioned from his grandmother's jawbone. "Maui is invoked by a fantastically dwarfed, beach-dwelling grandmother with a penchant for deadpan irony (Clement), who tells the 'untold tales' as part of an absurdist ploy to get her Michael Jackson look-alike teenage grandson (Waititi) back on the straight and narrow" in a production that is "fast paced, politically incorrect, rough-hewn and often convulsively funny."[53]

Humourbeasts performed in the 2002 Edinburgh Festival, as did the nascent Flight of the Conchords. Waititi plays smooth-talking Conchords manager Larry Pritchard in a mini-mockumentary about their trip, screened on New Zealand's TV3 arts program, *The Living Room*.[54] The style is not dissimilar to the later *Conchords* TV series (of which

Waititi wrote and directed two episodes and directed several more). In 2004, Waititi presented an episode of *The Living Room*, promoting *Taika's Incredible Show*, a one-man theater show, in which he played a range of comic characters such as Gunter Schliemann: Germanic, blond, with goofily bad teeth, alternating whimsy and pseudoprofundity—"He (Waititi) controls all of us, he is like our master but he is our friend as well."[55] He also plays an alien (who resurfaces in a 2010 TV3 sketch comedy series, *Radiradah*), "Derek from stationery," an aggressively ordinary character similar to David Brent in *The Office*, and Diego, a two-hundred-year-old vampire, anticipating *What We Do in the Shadows* (Clement and Waititi shot an early version of the film in 2005).

Exploiting his diasporic identity in his early career, Waititi used his mother's surname "Cohen" for his acting and performing and "Waititi" for his painting: "I was painting all through my 20s."[56] From 1996 to 1998 (approximately), he lived in Berlin, Germany, working as an artist associated with Schliemann 40 House (hence Gunter Schliemann).[57] "I was trying to figure out what I wanted to do . . . be a painter, or an actor, or something completely different." At this point, Waititi could have become a painter.[58] An important turning point was his return to NZ in 1998 for his film acting debut in *Scarfies* (Robert Sarkies, 1999), a dark comedy about student life in Dunedin, a town in the South Island known mainly for its university (Otago) and 1980s music scene, "The Dunedin Sound," which supplies much of the film's soundtrack. Director Sarkies comments: "I guess *Scarfies* gave him that chance to see what average directing looked like and think 'Oh, I could do better than that.'"[59] Cast as the charming but narcissistic and manipulative Alex Parata, Waititi first encountered the typecasting problem that was to dog his early screen acting career. In his next feature film appearance, *Snakeskin* (Gillian Ashurst, 2001), he plays Nelson, a joint-smoking, dub-loving Rasta/hippy, and in the TV series *The Strip* (2002) he played a stripper. This last role especially made Waititi realize that he needed to get behind the camera: "I remember being on that show and just thinking, I don't know if I want to do this acting job much longer. . . . I was in a G-string."[60] He was playing ethnic stereotypes—handsome hunks, sociopaths, or drug users. In his first Hollywood film, *The Green Lantern* (Martin Campbell, 2011), Waititi plays the hero's sidekick, Tom Kalmaku, originally an Inuit, but as a nonwhite actor, Waititi was deemed close enough to "pass," once again demonstrating the fluidity of ethnic identity, and how that can serve (in this case) hegemonic ends, though presumably it also gave Waititi a point of entry into Hollywood.

Early Works—*Two Cars, One Night* (2003)

Waititi has stated that his first well-known film is based on his own experience.[61] Reportedly his father said, "Yeah, I left him outside the pub in the car, but if I hadn't done it he wouldn't be up for an Oscar now."[62] The pub featured in the film, Te Kaha Tavern, was near Waihau Bay, where Waititi (partly) grew up. The film initiates the director's fascination with a child's-eye view of the world, as well as the "child abandoned in car/child in abandoned car" motif, which features in *Boy*, *Hunt for the Wilderpeople*, and the Blazed drug-driving TV ad campaign. It had already featured in films about Māori (*Once Were Warriors*, Lee Tamahori, 1994) and *bro'Town*, and was fast becoming an ethnic stereotype, implying child neglect. Waititi comments, "I don't think it's a bad thing . . . when I have kids, I'm not gonna give them a Playstation, I'm just gonna stick 'em in a car."[63] This quote, along with Waititi's father's quote, exemplifies New Zealand male "practical joker" humor, deadpan and unsentimental. The car motif also demonstrates how Waititi always locates his indigenous characters in modernity. When considering indigenous film, it's tempting to play off the local against the global: "Indigenous films create a sense of presence, and through their presence they refute Hollywood depictions."[64] But the global and local interpenetrate in modernity, which is central to Waititi's films: placing global influences in a local context.

The film was coproduced by Blueskin Films and Defender Films, a production company Waititi formed with producer Ainsley Gardiner in 2003. Ainsley Gardiner, who shares an iwi affiliation—Te-Whānau-ā-Apanui—with Waititi, produced his first two features, *Eagle vs Shark* and *Boy*. The New Zealand Film Commission, a government agency set up in 1978 to assist NZ filmmakers, contributed funding, as it did to all Waititi's local films.[65] "The Film Commission were really great," Waititi comments, and Arezou Zalipour notes, "in the rhetoric of national identity and cultural expression . . . we can observe a favourable investment climate and provision for 'work[ing] with Māori and Pacific Island content and themes,'" although the same assistance may not be provided to

Romeo (Rangi Ngamoki) and Ed (Te Ahiwaru Ngamoki-Richards) in *Two Cars, One Night*, 2003.

diasporic filmmakers.[66] With the NZ government's recent adoption of a creative industries model, opportunities opened up, and Waititi was the right person, in the right place, at the right time, ending a period in which Māori film received more funding from TV and radio funder Te Māngai Pāho than from the NZFC.[67] "Labour instigated an innovative range of policies and programmes to grow New Zealand's arts and cultural sector; no longer was their fate to be left to market forces."[68] Catherine Fitzgerald (producer and founder of Blueskin Films) says, "[Waititi] was incredibly hard-working, organized and original and creative. . . . With *Two Cars, One Night*, Ainsley [Gardiner] and I . . . wanted to put around him the kind of experience . . . that would . . . allow him to try out things. . . . We wanted his actors to be well-rehearsed, so Nancy Brunning and Loren Taylor (Horsley) worked with the young actors."[69] Clearly Waititi benefited from an experienced crew, commenting: "To direct a film you don't need a huge amount of skill or talent . . . all you have to do is have a feeling for . . . what you want. And make a decision very fast."[70] However, he still found it hard work: "It was freaky enough trying to make your first film, alone, and then on top of that, working with kids who'd never acted before . . . and a remote location."[71] The film traces a developing relationship between a Māori boy, Romeo (Rangi Ngamoki), and girl, Polly (Hutini Waikato), who arrive in a pub carpark, at night, in separate cars. As in *Boy*, focusing on child characters helps keep ethnic stereotypes at bay. The characters start by exchanging obscene banter ("Having a good jack?"), interpretable in terms of the model of humor as aggressive play, but this gives way to curiosity and friendship. Gender is always a theme in Waititi's films—at first, male homosociality is enforced by accusations of homosexuality, but then Romeo's bravado is undercut by Polly's experience:

> ROMEO (trying to impress Polly): Hey bro, you're one of them gays, hey?
> EDDIE (not looking up from his book): Probably.
> ROMEO: He is a gay. He likes boys. (To Eddie) Hey bro, who's your favorite boy? Johnny Depp?
> EDDIE (still not looking up): Yeah.
> ROMEO (to Polly): Johnny Depp's a gay, too. Bet you don't know any gays.
> POLLY: Yes, my auntie's a gay.
> ROMEO: No, she's not.
> POLLY: Yes. She's got a girlfriend.

Ethnic ambiguity is thus complemented by gender ambiguity. Moreover, Polly is several years older than the boys, so her relationship to them seems more maternal than romantic, and this sets the tone for male/female relationships in Waititi's films. Normative heterosexuality, in the form of men chasing women, rarely occurs. Notably, Polly gives Romeo the ring—she's the first of a series of "strong female figures" in his work, although often on the periphery.[72] They suggest his mother's influence. The black-and-white film stock, the use of old cars, and references to Johnny Depp combine to create ambiguity about setting in time, characteristic of a number of Waititi films (*Eagle vs Shark, Wilderpeople*). Perhaps this is appropriate given how his films often deal with children acting like adults, or vice versa. The fast-motion footage of clouds at the start suggests passing of time for kids left to their own devices. It could also relate to Māori concepts of time, as "on the marae, time is . . . an elastic . . . concept."[73] The film has also been interpreted using a Māori frame of reference, or a kaupapa Māori approach.[74] Pōwhiri, or the greeting of visitors, is an important ritual, because of the risk of hostility: "Tūmatauenga [the god of war] . . . is awakened when a *pōwhiri*, or ritual encounter is about to take place on the marae [meeting house, home village]."[75] This approach of treating narrative as a ritual encounter is applied more extensively to *Boy* in chapter 6. Ocean Mercier recuperates "Maori time" (formerly a racist term)[76] in relation to *Two Cars*: both it and *Tama Tū* (discussed next) are essentially films about "passing the time," reflecting the episodic nature of Waititi's films, which could connect to Barclay's Fourth Cinema.[77] *Two Cars* can be read in a number of ways, and its themes, of "passing time," friendship between children, or pop culture mash-ups, address a wide audience, as does the use of comedy.[78]

Tama Tū (2004)

Waititi's next major work was a short film based on a historical subject. He has "always loved the Māori Battalion"—his grandfather Eruiti fought with them in World War II, in North Africa and the Mediterranean, and they also feature briefly in *Boy*.[79] Māori fought in both world wars on the side of the British Empire, seventeen thousand in World War II (Māori were not conscripted; they volunteered).[80] NZ participation in two world wars was instrumental to developing national identity. In the film, we follow a group of six soldiers hiding in a ruined building (possibly in Italy, where the Battalion fought), passing the time while they await orders.

The film title's official translation is "Sons of Tū: The God of War."[81] In Te Reo, words often depend on context for meaning, so "tū" can mean to stand, to remain, to fight, to smell something bad (turn up nose), or even to be wounded.[82] Ocean Mercier argues that the title is an ironic play on the whakataukī (proverb) "Tama tū, tama ora, tama noho, tama mate," which translates as, "He who stands up, lives; he who lies around, suffers for it."[83] "Hei tama tū tama" is also the name of a children's game, similar to rock, paper, scissors (which the Waititi character Korg refers to in *Thor: Ragnarok*): "Hand games play an integral part in the development of . . . hand and eye coordination. . . . Recreational games . . . were mostly played . . . just after the crops were harvested and stored. During this harvest festival, Māori gave themselves over to Ngā Mahi ā te Rēhia, a te harikoa—the arts of pleasure and of joyfulness."[84] Physical dexterity is valued in Māori culture, as is the ability to read body language and communicate nonverbally, all relevant to a narrative about soldiers who must communicate silently or die.

The film continues Waititi's theme of time/age ambiguity: children who act like adults (*Two Cars*) and adults who act like children. *Tama Tū*'s tagline is, "Even at war . . . boys will be boys."[85] Play is central, and Waititi clearly took a boyish relish in creating the film setting: "Wellington hospital . . . [was] being knocked down. . . . We got to, like, smash huge hunks of the hospital . . . use pneumatic drills to make bullet holes."[86] Waititi also collaborated with the other enfant terrible of NZ film: "Peter Jackson and his mate have an armory. . . . We managed to borrow these vintage machine guns."[87] Both men enjoy playing soldiers, as we also see in *Boy* and *Thor: Ragnarok*. Peter Jackson recently directed the World War I documentary *They Shall Not Grow Old* (2018).

In narrative and generic terms, the film challenges audience expectations. Although it displays aspects of the modern war/action genre—subdued color palette, rapid alternating POV shots, use of handheld camera to convey urgent, confused motion, off-screen sound to motivate character reactions, all with the aim of building tension—the expected carnage never ensues. Indeed, the only "action," the death of a German soldier, occurs in spite of, rather than because of, the Māori platoon. The lack of dialogue at first creates tension, but once we realize that the situation enjoins silence, a space of possibility opens. As Waititi states, "It is not a film about war . . . it is about the vitality of life,"[88] that is, all the ways the soldiers find to interact with each other and their environment: carving a manaia (Māori mythical creature) out of a wood splinter; placing a toy soldier and a portrait found in the ruins; subtle civilizing gestures that restore order in chaos. Finally, the whispered karakia (prayer) at the end of the film reconfirms the common purpose of these otherwise beleaguered individuals. Arguably the best war films are anti-war films, and Waititi quotes from one of the most famous, *All Quiet on the Western Front* (Lewis Milestone, 1930), with the detail of the German soldier shot by a sniper as he reaches out to touch a living thing: a butterfly in *Western Front*, replaced here by a kitten.

The narrative is also an essay in nonverbal homosocial bonding—the range of information and emotion enacted without words is remarkable. Waititi's theatrical background is relevant, as timing and bodily control

Waititi's World War II film, *Tama Tū* (2004), is all about homosocial bonding.

are essential both to being funny and to nonverbal communication in general. Another shared aspect is the centrality of banter—both this film and *Two Cars* consist largely of a series of practical jokes that the characters play on each other. Some have described banter as typically masculine: "Outwardly banter is aggressive; inwardly however, it depends on reciprocity . . . a way of affirming the bond of love between men while appearing to deny it," which is certainly applicable to *Tama Tū*.[89] But it is also common among children and resembles ritual abuse in African American culture, which has its modern equivalent in rap battles.[90] Admittedly these are verbal contests, but the broad concept of ritual insult as (comic) communication applies to *Two Cars*, *Tama Tū*, and Waititi's films in general. One nonverbal gesture *Two Cars* and *Tama Tū* share is the "raised eyebrow greeting," which Mercier describes as "typically Māori."[91]

Other Early Works

Waititi made several other films in the 2000s, some for 48Hours, a film competition run in NZ since 2004. His 48Hours entries have low production values, are crudely comic and playful, and mostly live up (or down) to his disclaimer for the film *Arab Samurai* (2007): "This film is supposed to be a little bit shit so just relax and enjoy it."[92] They often use shot reverse shot to allow Waititi to play multiple roles, reminding us that he thrives on performing direct to camera, a reflection of his experience in drama and stand-up comedy, and a feature of many of his films. Their narratives usually concern relationships or conflict between men, also the case for his first ever film, *John & Pogo* (2002), a mockumentary about a policeman and his dog, in which dogs are played by male actors, a scenario that gives rise to much homosocial byplay, for example, men licking each other and sniffing each other's crotches. The 48Hours films include *Heinous Crime* (2004), directed by and starring Waititi and Loren Horsley, a crude, surreal satire on the justice system, reminiscent of Spike Milligan's 1970s BBC comedy *Q*, with Waititi playing an obnoxious judge, but also the accused, one Terry Spears, who haltingly laments how "I had it all—I was a male model!" But then, "It all came tumbling down. I got into . . . drug dependency." Horsley, the court stenographer, writes pornography: "his tool was hard and throbbing." The film crudely parodies representations of Māori as either victims of an uncaring system (as in *Once Were Warriors*) or hypersexual "animals." Other films parody Hollywood genres, especially action, and feature associated ethnic stereotypes. In *Falling Leaves* (2005), a vaguely

Men play dogs in Waititi's first film, *John & Pogo* (2002).

Native American "spirit guide" helps a crippled child escape the clutches of a dictatorial father, while *Slade in Full* (2006) (a pun on *Paid in Full* [Charles Stone III, 2002]) and *Arab Samurai* both feature endless bad acting, macho posturing, violent death, conflict between corrupt authority figures and reluctant hitmen, parading of Asian and Arabic stereotypes, and homophobic references.

Intersectionality and the Colonial Gaze

These films play on the representation of Māori/Pasifika men as objects of a sexual gaze, an example of intersectionality, or how different types of discrimination against minorities interact.[93] The Western/colonial gaze reduces subjects to a sexual or an ethnic type, but the gendered binary that equates the gaze with masculinity is complicated when the object of the gaze is also male (or where the gazer is a woman).[94] In the NZ 1971 Rudall and Ramai Hayward film *To Love a Maori* (about a relationship between a Māori man and a white woman), a feminist character, Dierdre, says: "For years Europeans have been romanticizing South Sea island women, now it's our turn to discover the men . . . it's the approved policy of the government to encourage integration." This is an example of a "revenge" narrative, common in interracial narratives, which allows white women the transgressive enjoyment of the Other traditionally reserved for white patriarchy.[95] While early NZ films often featured white men romancing Māori women, with the rise of second-wave feminism in the 1970s, the roles reversed, as in *Sons for the Return Home* (Paul Maunder, 1979), *Kingi's Story* (TV, Mike Walker, 1981), *Other Halves* (John Laing, 1984), *Mark II* (TV, John Anderson, 1986), and *Eagle vs Shark*. By the late 1990s, the sexualization of male Māori/Pasifika actors was so commonplace as to be a joke—a review of *The Untold Tales of Maui* "shamelessly discuss[es] the hotness of the actors," that is, Waititi.[96] Feature film *Jubilee* (Michael Hurst, 2000) plays interracial romance (white woman, brown man) for laughs, as does *Sione's Wedding* (Chris Graham, 2006). This parodic tone also rules *Toy Boy*, a short film directed by Julian Arahanga in 2004, starring Waititi as Jack Hammer, a sex doll that has become a bone of contention between a gay white couple, one of whom (linking to *Heinous Crime*) is a male model called Terry Spears. In Terry's fantasy, the sex doll, Jack Hammer, talks to him:

Stop being such a nancy boy! What are ya, Terry . . . what are ya? You're a male model . . . and that's something to be fuckin' proud of . . . What about me? What about the mighty Jack Hammer? What does it say on my box, Terry? It says, after a good drilling, I'm ready to fill, so unzip me and grab my tool. Satisfaction guaranteed.

The macho tone, combined with a parody of male homosexuality that verges on homophobia, is common in Waititi's early work: his films often reference the machismo of 1980s US popular culture, from comics to action films and video games. At the same time, he "wanted to move away from how we [Māori men] are traditionally typecast in movies in New Zealand, which is like the Jake character in *Once Were Warriors*, who's basically an alcoholic killer."[97] A limited view of Māori masculinity is to some extent repeated in academic literature, which tends to focus on physical prowess, often in sport. Brendan Hokowhitu discusses the Māori sportsman as a "spectacle," but he does not say for whom.[98]

This masculine ambivalence links neatly to Waititi's direction of music videos, mainly for Wellington alternative rock group The Phoenix Foundation, who also contributed music soundtracks to all of Waititi's feature films up until *Thor*. Waititi refers banteringly to the group as "gay" (on the *Boy* DVD director's commentary), implying rejection of machismo and an aesthetic preference for "camp." Group member Samuel Flynn Scott discusses how the music he likes, "isn't in any way macho . . . I never really got into metal . . . I . . . preferred [a] . . . slightly arrogant, slack kind of wimpy guy vibe."[99] Group and director share a preference for retro stylings, usually 1980s, in visual design and musical genre, plus whimsical humor and touches of twee-ness. The video for "Bright Grey," a song from the group's *Happy Endings* album (2007) starts with 1980s synthesizer drones and a tinkling glockenspiel, not dissimilar to the *Boy* and *Wilderpeople* soundtracks, as we see *Tron*-style 1980s computer game graphics and then a DeLorean car, similar to that used in *Back to the Future* (Robert Zemeckis, 1985), driving onto the stage in front of the band. The wing door opens to reveal a suave Waititi in a suit. Other retro visual effects include ghost trails around performers, crude back projections (common in early music videos), and oversaturated videotape color. The band's performance is very understated, which offsets the campy visual effects, and in a final "cute" touch, children clamber over the set. The same kind of twee/retro aesthetic is used in most of Waititi's feature films, and the 1980s is perhaps the key decade in his work, being the setting of *Boy*, and a stylistic reference in many of his films. The futuristic stylings of the 1980s marked it as the last decade when the future still looked bright, making it key for "hauntology," or nostalgia for "lost futures," a perception heightened by the simultaneous rise of neoliberalism and postmodernity, which signaled "the end of history."[100]

A second video for *Happy Endings*, directed by Waititi, "Forty Years," also stars the director. It's a version of the one-shot video, apparently consisting of a single take in which the camera follows the notional singer/performer through a series of scenes/scenarios. In this case, the camera follows a tracksuited Waititi running along a foreshore in the Wellington area. Along the way, he leaps over or crashes through various obstacles, dispatches a group of mail-clad knights with a cardboard sword, "frees" their prisoners, does tag wrestling, plays an acoustic guitar, and ends up leaping onto a life-size model horse. Jean-Michel Gondry has made a number of music videos in this style; however, arguably Waititi's video is exceptional in that it also stars the director. It reminds the viewer that Waititi is a highly physical performer, full of energy, and how some kinds

Waititi emerges from a DeLorean in the video for The Phoenix Foundation's "Bright Grey" (2005).

of comic acting depend on physical presence. Waititi's roles in these videos are a gentler version of the aggressive parody of machismo we see
in the short films—once again he plays a kind of male model, which
obviates the white performers' need to perform. Waititi's self-awareness
as both subject and object of the gaze could suggest Du Bois's "double
consciousness," intersected with an awareness of gender.[101] It shows
how Waititi takes up a series of identity positions and entertains them
simultaneously, moving between them, according to the situation, displaying a fluidity of identity that Paul Gilroy attributes to black culture,
diasporic, continuously in motion, as discussed in *The Black Atlantic*,
except that perhaps here "Black Pacific" is more apt.[102] Both these videos
present a strange inversion of conventional roles by making the director the star. It might be possible to argue that Waititi is performing an
ethnic identity in much the same way as we see Māori performing New
Zealand identity in early NZ film in chapter 2, while Pākehā whiteness
(the band) remains relatively "invisible" and inscrutable.[103]

In this chapter, I've tried to both sketch Waititi's early life and give an
overview of his early work in terms of themes indicated and concerns
faced, as a Māori man, for example. Important points include his mixed
ethnicity and its influence on his life and career, his parents encourag-
ing him to pursue art, his background in live theater and comedy, and
his experience as an actor/performer continuing over into films he has
directed in the way he playfully highlights himself as a performer in his
own work. The addressing of Māori culture in his work may have been
timely in terms of opportunities for indigenous filmmakers in the early
2000s, and continued in *Boy*. Overall, however, his work was to investi-
gate more general issues of racism and stereotypes of ethnicity; gender,
specifically male homosociality, and the intersection of gender and ethnicity. In this endeavor, NZ biculturalism provides a starting point rather
than an overall structure, and Waititi's intertextuality becomes central to
a more globalized interpretation of nonwhite Otherness. However, the
question of why masculinity is so important for understanding Waititi's
work is tied up with Aotearoa/New Zealand's historic role in the British
Empire as subaltern, and the effect of that on national identity, played out
in local culture as the "Kiwi Bloke." Films in NZ have mostly been made

by white people, but NZ's prolonged dependence on the UK affected Pākehā self-representation, resulting in a tendency to either fetishize or demonize representations of indigenous Māori (who performed New Zealand far more authentically), leading toward a parodic style of self-representation, an exaggerated "bloke" masculinity with a queer subtext. In the next chapter, I will flesh out the above arguments and connect them to three metaphors for local film (proposed by Bruce Babington): the interracial romance, the cinema of unease, and antipodean camp, the last being most germane to Waititi's basically comic vision.

2
AOTEAROA/NEW ZEALAND, NATIONAL IDENTITY, AND FILM

The announcement of a biopic on the exploits of Charles Upham, a soldier from Canterbury who earned the Victoria Cross twice during the Second World War, to become the most highly decorated serviceman from the Commonwealth, confirms that New Zealand has reached the point in its history where it has the confidence to celebrate the distinctiveness of its own heroes. No longer do New Zealanders need to seize upon the supposed achievements of a faux national hero like Colin McKenzie in Peter Jackson and Costa Botes' *Forgotten Silver* (1995) to celebrate the accomplishments of its national heroes.[1]

This account of Charles Upham, by New Zealand film historians Alistair Fox, Barry Grant, and Hilary Radner, contrasts strongly with that of NZ historian of masculinity Jock Phillips: "Upham rose through the ranks largely through his spectacular, some would say crazy, acts of courage ... his horrifying disregard for his own safety and his complete denial of pain became legendary."[2] His acts showed "an alienation from his body that was pathological yet it was the basis of his men's respect," hence Upham "illustrates better than any other the mythology of the NZ officer in the Second World War—disrespectful of authority, self-denying, 'one of the boys,'" but also a "'hard man' ... physically ... emotionally."[3] Another account suggests: "He developed these qualities as a musterer in the Canterbury high country, where men had 'to match the ruggedness of nature with their own ruggedness of physique and temperament.'"[4]

All accounts suggest that Upham incarnates a distinctive NZ identity, but Phillips's critical tone undercuts the optimism of Fox et al. Proving masculinity in battle was equally pertinent to Māori men, who regarded their participation in the Second World War as proof of their patriotism and right to NZ citizenship.[5]

Phillips argues that this idealized NZ masculinity is, in fact, toxic. But I want to go further and suggest that its stony, impassive exterior concealed a complex of global power relations, revealing how "identity . . . is always an authoritarian practice."[6] Historically, NZ's national identity of pioneering white masculinity, "the Kiwi bloke," reveals its domination by Britain, for which NZ figured as a "rural hinterland," populated by a docile, economically and culturally subordinate working class.[7] Supplying military manpower to the British Empire was one manifestation of this relationship. War helped define NZ identity; New Zealand soldiers became "aware of differences between men from Great Britain and from the several colonies. They came to consider their identity self-consciously."[8] Masculinities scholar R. W. Connell states: "We must pay attention to very large scale structures . . . the world gender order . . . hegemony . . . connected with patterns of trade, investment and communication . . . in turn historically based on Colonialist expansion of the West."[9] The Kiwi bloke's tough masculine exterior both advertised (in its working-class connotations) and concealed (via local discourses of egalitarianism and geographical isolation) NZ's dependence on Britain, which NZ historian James Belich terms "recolonization."[10] Hence the key aspect of New Zealand identity, for its dominant settler population, was lack, a "cultural cringe" symbolized by masculine defensiveness and ironic self-deprecation, or palliated by appropriation of Māori culture.[11] The historic tie to the colonizer was sundered when the UK joined the EEC in 1973, by which time Māori were also challenging settler appropriation of their land and culture. Given this double blow, the Kiwi bloke rang hollow, a performance of inauthenticity or low mockery, as in antipodean camp, "the lie that tells the truth."[12] Colin McKenzie, the mythical hero of *Forgotten Silver* (Peter Jackson and Costa Botes, 1995) is a prime example, and Jackson and Waititi are practitioners of this populist countertradition. Nevertheless, the emphasis on homosocial masculinity remains, albeit now more identified with Polynesia, as Pacific camp, or as "bush" camp, a reversal of traditional camp in that women parody men, rather than men parodying women.[13] Exaggerated masculinity, as Susan Sontag points out, can be camp, and "man" is also "joker" in NZ slang.[14] In terms of national cinema, "Maoriland" was the leading trope of NZ representation, reflecting Western exoticization of the Pacific, until government creation of the National Film Unit (NFU) in 1941 initiated a shift toward documentary and news as a means of creating national unity. The NFU's realist emphasis resonated with the Kiwi bloke's suspicion of imaginative work as feminine or exotic. The mockumentary *Forgotten Silver* parodies settler reliance on documentary by showing its realism to be conventional, exposing NZ's identity of masculine self-reliance as fabrication, open to a reading as antipodean camp.[15]

National Identity?

This chapter discusses NZ history in relation to NZ film, the latter an example of a "small nation" cinema, the irony being that studies from this perspective coincide with the rise of globalization and its challenges to the nation-state.[16] These issues are not new. NZ has transitioned swiftly from colonial adjunct to one of the most globalized and deregulated economies in the world under the 1980s neoliberal Labour government. In the case of film, one result has been "Hollywood's direct participation in the production sectors" of the NZ film industry.[17] One possible consequence of this is erosion of cultural difference as global economic imperatives trump the local cultural agenda enshrined in the aims of the NZ Film Commission, set up in 1978. But it has also produced opportunities for some NZ filmmakers, for example, Jackson and Waititi, assisted by NZ government adoption of a creative industries model from 2000 onward.

Traditionally, histories of national cinema have offered "coherent images of the nation, sustaining the nation at an ideological level, exploring what is understood to be the indigenous culture."[18] NZ film historian Bruce Babington responds that in the case of NZ, indigenous "in the New Zealand context [has] a double, even triple meaning: Maori, indigenous Pakeha . . . and indigenous New Zealander."[19] The idea of a coherent national identity is troubled from the start by competing definitions. These conflicts are played out in writing history and writing cinema history. Not all film historians seem aware of these contradictions, however, and neither does the NZ government, which argues that local culture "supports and contributes to New Zealander's [sic] distinct and inclusive identity, strengthening our collective sense of identity as a country."[20] Nabeel Zuberi points out that "state support is absolutely vital for the cultural industries, but why make that support on the basis of national identity rather than other aspects of citizenship?"[21] Government film funding depends on "significant New Zealand content," however this is defined.[22]

Recent NZ historians have also been critical of national identity rhetoric, arguing that earlier histories have been teleological narratives aimed at producing NZ as a coherent nation. They contend that colonization, far from being a now completed process of settlement, is a continuing project that seeks to indigenize settlers while ignoring alternative narratives of indigeneity:

> Pakeha historians do not discuss the possibility that colonization itself may be an ongoing process, or ask very often whether colonization might be construed as something more than organized occupation (or "settlement") of discrete parts of the landscape. It seems likely that this situation is at least in part a result of the preoccupation of certain scholars, especially from around the middle of the twentieth century, with issues of "national identity," with what New Zealand seemed to have become, or was believed to be becoming, rather than with the formative influences which may have continued to configure and constrain the historical process.[23]

Preoccupation with national identity led to colonization being placed firmly in the past. It also ignores how "the New Zealand past since Europeans first appeared over the horizon is not sui generis, but a component of a much wider process, the expansion of European power into the global arena from the fifteenth century onwards."[24]

Peter Gibbons argues that colonization was continually reenacted by Pākehā discursive production of nationhood "through . . . various textualizing strategies."[25] These included Pākehā writing about NZ and Māori, but also images, and ultimately film.[26] Settlers indigenized themselves by appropriation. Simultaneously, a lengthy "recolonization" took place, from the late nineteenth century to the 1970s, in the ways that

NZ cultivated its relationship with Britain.[27] "Geographically [NZ] may have been in the Pacific, but structurally it was a part of Britain's rural hinterland."[28] Decisive for NZ development was its role as a supplier of primary produce and labor—meat, dairy, wool, wood, manpower—for the British Empire.[29] It functioned as a rural proletariat, providing primary products and manpower.[30] This identification with rural landscape and labor conflicts with the fact that NZ is one of the most highly urbanized countries in the world.[31] Such instances illustrate Marx and Engels's definition of ideology as "false consciousness": a blindness to the real conditions of existence propagated by hegemonic economic interests.[32] Indeed, my argument here is Marxist, following Immanuel Wallerstein's world systems theory.[33]

Historically, white settlers viewed themselves as "Better Britons," showing "the fundamental weakness of nationalism in New Zealand, a weakness going back to the late-colonial period when its early Pakeha . . . manifestation emerged not as a break with imperial affiliation but as a confirmation of New Zealand's special place within empire."[34] The Kiwi bloke served to confirm British hegemony by dint of his proletarian connotations, disguised in the local context by "the apparent egalitarianism of male mateship."[35] NZ egalitarianism was based on socialist reforms of successive governments as a response to economic depressions in the 1880s and 1930s. These policies also reflected the rise of working men to positions of power, especially trade unionists. Trade unions operated on an ideal of male proletarian solidarity. However, unions were mostly unwilling to oppose the government, instead entering into a compact, "the historic compromise," and helping suppress radical action.[36] On the surface, male egalitarianism seemed continuous with the Utopian project of New Zealand as a worker's paradise, but in practice it was more of a belief in sameness—to be a bloke, you needed to act like other blokes—be practical, scorn intellectuality, and play sport. This belief in sameness is also known as the "tall poppy syndrome."[37]

Underlying the development of NZ was a global economic system that reduced it to a scion of the British Empire. This hegemony extended to culture. Until quite recently, most NZ schools taught First World culture and history at the expense of the local. Most cultural texts New Zealanders consume are from overseas. Local cultural production has thus struggled against the hegemony of imported culture, first from the

UK and more recently from the US, a hegemony often reproduced in the tendency to disparage local cultural production, or not to value cultural texts until they have been valued by someone else.

New Zealand Film and Cultural Cringe

New Zealanders were keen cinemagoers, Gordon Mirams noting in 1945 that "whereas in the US there is one cinema for every 8,700 persons, in NZ there is approximately one for every 3,000."[38] American and British films dominated the local imagination, filmmaker Peter Wells claiming that NZ, "by contrast, hardly existed . . . lacking, it seemed, poetry, magic, reason. . . . Because we were not James Dean, we were nothing. . . . This is an experience of colonialism."[39] Film salesman Lindsay Shelton states: "We didn't think of New Zealand as having any stories worth telling, or any places worth showing."[40] The idea of New Zealanders acting on the big screen seemed absurd, director Jane Campion noting: "New Zealand is a country hysterically concerned with playing yourself down."[41] In 1992, the makers of local TV soap *Shortland Street* feared that local audiences would not accept Kiwi accents.[42] And even today NZ has a very low proportion of local TV programming, apart from Māori Television.[43] Roger Horrocks states that "these symptoms of cultural cringe seem like a crazy dream from which eventually we had to awaken," with the implication that things are different now.[44] But are they? Cringe is also associated with a long history of disparaging comments about NZ: "the safest country in the world," as one character in *Snakeskin* (2001) snidely notes, a sentiment echoed by travel writer Paul Theroux: "one of the dullest places on earth."[45] Waititi puts his own spin on it: "New Zealanders are, like, experts in cynicism. We're good observers, because we come from a place where basically nothing happens."[46]

The Kiwi Bloke and Cultural Nationalism

The hegemony of rural proletarianism, mixed with a puritanical work ethic arising from pioneer aspiration, led to a suspicion of artists and intellectuals.[47] Prominent New Zealand feminist author Sandra Coney writes of her father's generation:

They would be muscled, sinewy and tough; not effete, weak and bookish. They would be practical men; doers not thinkers. They expressed their culture not in theatres, galleries or pomp, but on the rugby field, in the backblocks [sections of rural land] in the great outdoors. It was a culture of the body, rather than the mind.[48]

Pākehā cultural movements, for example the provincial or cultural nationalist writers of the 1930s onward, celebrated the "Kiwi bloke," connecting him to historic discourses of the pioneer: homosocial, white culture based around rural isolation, work, the pub, and rugby.[49] Intellectuals had mixed feelings about this culture but shared the belief that any search for a national imaginary would begin from a robust "grass roots" New Zealand–ness, as opposed to the perceived effeteness of British or imported mass culture: "Whatever is true vision, belongs here, uniquely to New Zealand."[50] Such representations of NZ culture were constructed primarily within a discourse of whiteness and masculinity.[51] However, Māori also participated on the sports field and in the armed forces: "The mimicry of certain aspects of colonial masculinity by Māori men served to assimilate them into the violent, physical, stoic, rugged, and sport-oriented 'Kiwi-bloke' culture."[52] Virtually all of Waititi's films focus on male characters, whether all-male groups such as soldiers (*Tama Tū*), vampires/flatmates (*What We Do in the Shadows*), father and son–type relationships (*Boy, Wilderpeople, Jojo Rabbit*), or "buddy" movie–type "odd couples" (*Thor: Ragnarok*). The bloke's laconic style also seeped into the sensibility of Māori artists like Ralph Hotere: "There are very few things I can say about my work that are better than saying nothing."[53]

NZ has been interpreted as a "gendered culture" where social relations are organized around gender, as opposed to class, as in the UK.[54] Many settler/postcolonial societies share an ideology of male camaraderie and "mateship" experienced on the "frontier," including the American cowboy and the antipodean bushman, but there are also differences: the cowboy is archetypally a loner who saves a community from peril.[55] The Kiwi bloke, in contrast, is usually represented as anti-heroic, "ordinary," and working class, idealizing physical strength and disdaining bourgeois values. There is nothing natural or essential about such connotations—rather they signal incorporation and subordination of such groups into the global hegemony of modernity.[56] Differences in masculine ideologies relate to their relationship to global power—the US won its independence from Britain, but NZ remained essentially subordinate.

Representing and reproducing "manliness" and its ideological equivalents became a norm of local cultural production.[57] The male "discipline" of the sports field or armed forces had its counterpart in a narrow set of stylistic and representational dictates that emphasized primarily masculine subjects, portrayed in a "realistic" and vigorously "masculine style," allied with a suspicion of artifice or pretense.[58] This robust masculine image also deflected criticism, and similarly the "self-sufficiency" of the working man became allied to discourses of isolation and self-sufficiency such as the "man alone," "the solitary, rootless nonconformist, who crops up persistently in New Zealand writing," downplaying overseas influence and emphasizing local autonomy.[59] Men could be together or alone, as the needs of mythology dictated, as long as women were absent. A realist preoccupation with proletarian masculinity is also evident in contemporary modernist UK and US writers like George Orwell, Louis MacNeice, Ernest Hemingway, and Sherwood Anderson, but these influences were rarely acknowledged locally.[60]

Masculinity, Ambiguity, and Queerness

The combination of masculine inscrutability and the realist form of provincial masculine writing often gives rise to ambiguity:

> The technique of presentation . . . is so often the participating "I" who tells his experience—and incidentally serves as a hero—without benefit of comment or chorus. The writer can select experiences for this "I" who does not fully understand what affects him and tells his view from an angle of vision the constriction of which is in itself informative, but negatively so.[61]

Moreover, "the identification of the reader with the narrator, by completing the narrative and supplying the lack in the narrator's speech, forces an affirmation of the realness of uncertainty."[62] So what was going on in the characters' minds? An example can be found in the opening paragraph of canonical NZ writer Frank Sargeson's "The Hole that

Jack Dug," written in the 1940s: "Jack had got a pretty considerable hole dug in the backyard before I knew anything about it. I went round one scorching hot Saturday afternoon, and Jack was in the hole with nothing on except his boots and his little tight pair of shorts."[63] There is simple language, repetition (of the title in the first line of the story), the preoccupation with work. But there is also ambiguity—why is Jack digging a hole? What is the attitude of the narrator to Jack? Readers must answer these questions themselves. This ironic, ambiguous mode is identified with postcolonial writing in settler societies and can be extended to film.[64] New Zealand critics tended to "underread" Sargeson as a realist, ignoring the homoerotic undercurrents of those shorts.[65] Sargeson's ambiguity can be read as a subversion practiced both against (British) dominance and also against blokey homosociality. His homosexuality only became known after his death in 1982, and the practice remained illegal in NZ until 1986.

Irony is prevalent in many local cultural texts: for example, advertising. A 2000s billboard campaign for Tui beer consists of unadorned white text on a black background, articulating statements connoting homosociality: "A guy at the pub told me," "I'll be home straight after the game," "It's getting too cold for a beer," and "Have you been working out?" Under each statement was the formula "Yeah right," which commonly expresses not assent but incredulity. The cover of a book devoted to the phenomenon reproduces a billboard with the text: "28 weeks on the New York Times Bestsellers List. Yeah right."[66] Such texts can be read as paradoxically both asserting and denying local identity. Waititi has made and starred in beer advertisements (see chapter 3).

The Kiwi bloke has proved durable. In 2004, US advertising company FCB conducted an ethnographic, semiotic study on perceptions of national identity in popular culture, such as TV advertising, in NZ, Australia, and the US.[67] The main similarity between Australia and NZ was the ubiquity of masculine national identity, more particularly a "fraternal" model, with male-male relationships perceived as normative, as opposed to the US, where masculinity is identified with individualism. Male homosociality in NZ advertisements takes forms that other cultures find "inscrutable," such as the Speight's beer commercial in which a young "bloke," on receiving two ball tickets from an attractive and solicitous barmaid, immediately gives one to his older mate.

US viewers speculated that the older man was his father.[68] But queer interpretations are possible—a defining feature of the Kiwi bloke is a lack both of the heterosexual desire that is a defining feature of most hegemonic masculinities, and of gender difference altogether in relation to national iconography: "When we looked at all the symbols for . . . New Zealand . . . men and women all brought the same . . . symbols: rugby, All Blacks, barbecues . . . gumboots, tractors. . . . In America . . . the female symbols . . . apple pie, friendship diaries, are different to the men's."[69] Thus, "[T]here is no equivalent feminine myth, not even a term, to partner the 'Kiwi bloke.'"[70] Eve Sedgwick defines homosociality as how men relate while avoiding the possibility of homosexuality, which could compromise patriarchy: "The production and reproduction of New Zealand masculinity, and by extension New Zealandness as such, is underpinned by the crisis of homo/heterosexual definition that Sedgwick describes."[71] White settler anxiety could be about colonial guilt, but could also relate to a "long national tradition of implying that there is a queer underside to everything and saying nothing more about it."[72]

Popular NZ performers have also investigated the paradoxes of compulsory heterosexuality in all-male environments: for example, the Topp Twins, two lesbian performers whose cross-dressing performances as "Ken and Ken" parody local masculinity. Probably the edgiest moment in *Untouchable Girls*, Leanne Pooley's 2009 documentary about the Twins, concerns a visit to Showgirls, an Auckland strip bar, when Lynda Topp, as Ken, joins the male clientele in ogling the girls. No one seems to mind that Ken is a lesbian woman in drag, because "people believe that Ken and Ken exist in real life" (Lynda Topp).[73] In NZ, men are men, and apparently women can be too. Anita Brady argues that in the Southern Man Speight's beer commercial mentioned above, since:

> mediated "New Zealandness" relies simultaneously on its exclusive self-conception as masculinity, and a requisite female adjunct to cast the resultant homosociality in heterosexual terms, New Zealand "femaleness" is primarily recognizable as a misperformed masculinity. The gender binary that functions in the service of national identity is not male/female but masculinity as the gendered, and the transgendered, body.[74]

Here, we might think about the women in Waititi's films, particularly Rachel House's performances of female masculinity, functioning as a "macho" antagonist to the male characters, as in *Boy*:

> **BOY:** Aunty Gracey is my mum's sister. She has lots of jobs. She's the tennis coach, the mailman, the school bus driver and she runs the local shop . . . Hey, Aunty, can I have an ice block, please?
> **GRACEY:** No!
> **BOY:** Oh, it's not fair.
> **GRACEY:** Get a job, man!
> **BOY:** There's none left. You got them all!

House plays similar "ball-busting" roles in all of Waititi's features, except *Shadows*. One might also think of Frau Betzler in *Jojo Rabbit* (Scarlett Johansen), who literally busts Captain Klenzendorf's balls and later dons male drag.

NZ Identity: Bloke, Joke, or Māori?

The foregoing discussion indicates two possibilities for NZ identity—the traditional strong masculine ideal and its transgendered or queer parody. Masculinity becomes the object of a queer gaze; women become valued for their ability to pass as men. The subtext is a historical cultural cringe that deemed local cultural production as embarrassing or unworthy, hiding behind a masculinity that paradoxically invites a "butch" reading, performing New Zealand–ness as a self-conscious imitation or parody of cultural seriousness. This campness has been around for a while. Bill Pearson, who in 1952 wrote "Restless Sleepers," a critique of postwar Pākehā society, argues:

> the ordinary man will not even sing as he feels: he either assumes a mocking rhetorical tone (to let listeners know he does not take his voice seriously) or he consciously imitates the star who popularised the song. . . . He is performing a tepid act of devotion to someone else's performance which is public property and must not be violated.[75]

Parody and mimicry are frequently related to postcolonial cultures.[76] Ashcroft et al. recognize the ambivalent position of settlers: "displaced from their own point of origin . . . [they] may have difficulties in establishing their identity in the new place . . . they are both colonised and colonizer."[77] Unsure of their position, they "camp." But there is also a third possibility: Māori culture. Gibbons argues that Pākehā appropriated Māori culture as a symbol of New Zealand–ness:

> Maori themselves and their cultures were textualized by Pakeha, so that the colonists could "know" the people they were displacing. It is not too much to say that the colonists produced (or invented) "the Maori," making them picturesque, quaint, largely ahistorical, and, through printed materials, manageable.[78]

This can be seen in the history of filmic representations of Māori, which were central to early NZ cinema, whether construed as exotic symbols of Pacific otherness by foreign filmmakers who made most early NZ films, or as "performers" of the nation by local Pākehā, expressing a conviction that they themselves lacked. Indeed, the Kiwi bloke's association with nature is arguably an appropriation of Maori status as *tangata whenua* (people of the land), a usurpation of indigeneity.

Theories of Local Film: "Cinema of Unease"

Local film criticism has "produced not so much theories as generative metaphors" of local identity, the most pervasive being the "cinema of unease," named after actor Sam Neill's 1995 history of NZ film.[79] Its central idea—white settler anxiety—originated in Bill Pearson's *Fretful Sleepers*.[80] This anxiety is manifest in the "cringey" opening of Neill's documentary, in London, with Neill pointing out NZ on a globe, as if his audience need reminding. This tradition of film is indebted to the "man alone," with themes of puritanical repression and alienation leading to sudden violence or madness. A key early film in this vein was John O'Shea's *Runaway* (1964), the director commenting:

> I wrote *Runaway* as a sort of an allegory about the way NZ was going. . . . Britain was no longer home . . . the . . . anti-hero . . .

doesn't quite know where he was going, [and it] seemed to me this was the problem of the country as whole . . . a materialist outlook . . . was the centre of most Pakeha existence . . . it's not a new theme. . . . [it is present in] Alan Mulgan's *Man Alone*.[81]

Later works include Roger Donaldson's *Sleeping Dogs* (1977), starring Sam Neill, who parodied his "man alone" role there in *Hunt for the Wilderpeople*; *Goodbye Pork Pie* (Geoff Murphy, 1980), *Bad Blood* (Mike Newell, 1981), *Smash Palace* (Roger Donaldson, 1981), *Utu* (Geoff Murphy, 1982), and more loosely *Vigil* (Vincent Ward, 1984), *Bridge to Nowhere* (Ian Mune, 1986), *The Quiet Earth* (Geoff Murphy, 1985), and *Heart of the Stag* (Michael Firth, 1984). These films generally shared a negative view of the state (sometimes the British, as in *Utu*, but usually the police) with a mythologization of the aforementioned male rebel (often played by Bruno Lawrence), who "goes bush," living off the land, in a style mythologized by authors like Barry Crump, who supplied the story for *Wilderpeople*.[82] They were influenced by New Hollywood cinema and the 1960s counterculture, although this was not much commented on at the time, in line with the desire to produce a distinctively local cinema.[83]

The top-grossing local film, until *Boy* toppled it in 2012, was *Once Were Warriors* (Lee Tamahori, 1994) (most of the most popular local films have been made by and about Māori, illustrating their preeminence in representations of New Zealand/Aotearoa). Its dark, brooding tone fits broadly into the cinema of unease thesis, the content shifting, however, from rural white masculinity to urban Māori masculinity. It represented a continuation of the National Film Unit Māori social problem documentaries of the 1950s (discussed below), and 1980s films like *Mark II* (John Anderson, 1986) and *Kingpin* (Mike Walker, 1985) that dealt with Māori/Pasifika men and urban crime.[84] *Warriors* "was discussed within NZ almost as a social documentary, as if its representations really were accurate," despite the film being highly stylized.[85] The novelty of *Warriors* was its graphic violence, mostly perpetrated by the central character, Jake the Muss (Temuera Morrison): "Violence [is shown as] . . . one of the few ways in which Māori men can display skill and achievement. . . . The character of Jake became celebrated as an anti-hero."[86] Waititi comments, "We (Māori) get portrayed in two ways, *Once Were Warriors* or the blue people in *Avatar*," alternating noble and ignoble savagery.[87] He continues: "I wanted to show we are novel, awkward, clumsy indigenous geeks," suggesting alternative masculinities, as in *Boy*, a title suggesting youth but also homosexuality.[88] However, I will argue that Waititi does not really challenge the hegemony of masculinity in representations of Aotearoa/New Zealand, as we have observed it in the "cinema of unease" trope.

Māori commentators seized on the "cinema of unease" thesis as evidence that NZ cinema is "white, neurotic."[89] They criticized *Once Were Warriors'* representation of Māori.[90] Merata Mita suggests that the underlying anxiety of white NZ relates to colonial guilt: "What appears on the screen are . . . symptoms of a deeper malaise."[91] Mita and Barry Barclay proposed that Māori take control of film production, in a Fourth Cinema, as in *Ngāti* (Barry Barclay, 1987) and *Mauri* (Merata Mita, 1988), that is "inclusive and slow-paced, with people framed in group shots, talking among themselves, rather than the . . . abrupt, shot-reverse-shot style . . . of classical Hollywood cinema."[92] Barclay also acknowledges the dangers of identifying Māori filmmaking with a particular style.[93] Rather, Fourth Cinema seems to refer to a methodology, more communal and egalitarian than most film production, which may include some Māori rituals, such as karakia (prayer) and kai (communal eating)—for example, Waititi favors a communal approach on set.[94]

Theories of Local Film 2: Race Relations and Interracial Romance

The second key theme of NZ film is the representation of ethnic relations, often through interracial romance.[95] Martin Blythe suggests a psychological/colonial metaphor: the oedipal family. A settler Pākehā father and a Māori mother figuratively produce a child—Aotearoa/New Zealand. "On the surface, New Zealand's . . . story has been a utopian historical romance, subscribing to a belief in the pursuit of progress and modernity and . . . racial harmony in an attempt to transcend its oedipal origins." But there is also a "counter-tradition, which has reminded New Zealanders . . . of their original Fall, their exile . . . and the greater spiritual authenticity of . . . Māori."[96] The story figures NZ as paradise, which Pākehā destroyed but can regain through progress and the embrace of modernity, a common Western colonization myth. Ideas of NZ as "a laboratory in which political and social experiments are every day made," to quote British Prime Minister Herbert Asquith, were key to how NZ identity was imagined.[97]

At the same time, Māori, as a symbol of Otherness, became a privileged sign in early local filmmaking—acting out a colonial fantasy called "Maoriland," "an exotic and utopian synonym" for Aotearoa/New Zealand from the 1880s to the 1930s.[98] Maoriland films were typically precontact, "timeless" romances of Māori life (for example, *The Romance of Hine-Moa* [Gustave Pauli, 1925/1927], *Under the Southern Cross (aka the Devil's Pit)* [Lew Collins, 1928/1929], and *Hei Tiki* [Alexander Markey 1930/1935]), usually by overseas filmmakers. Now dismissed as "downright offensive" in their racial stereotyping,[99] nevertheless they were mainly about Māori, starred Māori casts, and were made locally. "While the mediums of delivery reflected the hegemony of the nonindigenous, the central story and setting emphasized the importance of Māori culture in the formation of a New Zealand identity."[100] Waititi and Jemaine Clement's *The Untold Tales of Maui* was ironically subtitled "Traditional Comedy from Maoriland."[101] Gaston Méliès made three films in NZ in 1912–13, *Hinemoa, How Chief Te Ponga Won His Bride*, and *Loved by a Maori Chieftess* (all lost). A US member of his crew commented, "The Maoris [*sic*] are born actors . . . they knock all the other natives . . . endways."[102] Filming in Rotorua, Méliès worked with Reverend Frederick Bennett, whose Māori concert party were "seasoned performers, expert at interpreting Māori cultural customs for an international audience. . . . They adapted easily to the demands of film-making."[103] Méliès used them in preference to his own professional actors. In 1929, NZ prime minister Joseph Ward wrote, in support of *Under the Southern Cross*: "once again the Maori race has proved 'second to none' in its capability of reaching the highest standard set by the world in Motion picture production. . . . It is a great tribute to their natural genius."[104] These comments show how Māori performance became synonymous with NZ. At the same time, publicity for the films emphasized Māori's "natural" and untrained status: "There are no actors in this picture," said *Hei Tiki* director Alexander Markey.[105] These examples show how essentialized notions of Māori as "natural" performers could be appropriated by Pākehā to "stand in" for a local identity that they themselves lacked.

Māori have always been *symbolically* important to Pākehā imaginings of "New Zealand," long before the so-called bicultural era. Despite the real, material marginalisation of Māori within New Zealand society, in the national *imaginary* Māori culture and symbolism have always been crucial to marking the distinctiveness of "New Zealand" as a nation. . . . Without Māori, Pākehā culture, a colonial settler culture, was just a derivative offshoot of Britain. . . . Pākehā gave their children Māori names, wore pounamu (greenstone) jewellery and created a New Zealand literature that based its distinctiveness on the relation with "Maoriland." . . . When facing . . . the world, Pākehā New Zealand has also always pointed to Māori culture to signify the society's unique national identity.[106]

Marianne Schultz, in detailing the range and variety of Māori forms of performance on overseas stages—tableaux, musicals, operas, variety shows, songs, music hall shows, and films, between 1862 and 1929—argues that "though these works could be characterized as propaganda that

Star-crossed lovers: Manui (Ben Biddle) and Mara (Ngawāra Kereti) in Maoriland romance *Hei Tiki* (1930/1935).

supported colonization and settlement, they were, first and foremost popular entertainments that featured Māori performers" and that "the prevalence of Maoriness on stage, from both Māori and non-Māori contributed to an acceptance and demand for indigenous expression in popular performance."[107] She includes what might be termed minstrelsy in her survey (that is, Pākehā performances of Māori on stage and screen, including, for example, Bathie Stuart, the "Pākehā Māori," who starred in *The Adventures of Algy* [Beaumont Smith, 1925]).[108] To perform "New Zealand" mainly meant performing as Māori.[109]

This changed to some degree with the next phase of filmmaking, which Blythe terms national romances, produced by NZ filmmakers like Rudall Hayward, including *The Te Kooti Trail* (1927) and *Rewi's Last Stand* (made twice, in 1925 and 1940).[110] If the Maoriland romances were mainly set in the timeless fairyland of true love, the latter are "timebound . . . [and] flirt with cross-racial miscegenation . . . to produce national unity."[111] They featured versions of the oedipal national romance between white man and a Māori woman, "easily the most popular story in NZ films and novels, even into the Eighties."[112] Such plotlines ideologically refer to soothing of racial tensions and assimilation via interbreeding. However, the romances almost always end unhappily, which indicates that the theory rather than the practice of integration prevailed (in the US, filmic representations of miscegenation were banned until 1954).[113] The films mostly dealt with incidents in the New Zealand Wars, and represent Pākehā as heroes and Māori as noble but vanquished opponents. O'Shea's *Broken Barrier* (1952), the only NZ feature film made between 1940 and 1964, is an interracial romance that succeeds by compromise—at the end of the film, the Pākehā hero, Tom (Terence Bayler), "goes native," living with the Māori heroine, Rawi (Keita Whakato Walker), and her family in their East Coast rural community. Whereas national romances showed Pākehā culture winning, here, Māori culture assimilates Tom. Why? By the 1950s, white artists and intellectuals like O'Shea were explicitly thematizing Māori authenticity: "the poets . . . (Denis) Glover, [Rex] Fairbairn, they all touch on this idea of New Zealanders as . . . not having their own culture . . . not so the Maoris [sic] of course."[114] In the film, the Māori lifestyle is ahistorical, idealized, and romantic, as if Tom, by marrying Rawi, can drop out of history and live like "the blue

Rawi (Keita Whakato Walker) and Tom (Terence Bayler): interracial lovers
in *Broken Barrier* (1952).

people in *Avatar*."[115] Māori are associated with spirituality, culture, art,
and fiction, Pākehā with realism.

Idealized representations of Māori predominated in film. Representations of Pākehā were also idealized, by being set in the past or
through fantasy and melodrama. Rudall Hayward's first feature, *My
Lady of the Cave* (1922), is "a feminized interpretation of the Tarzan
myth," about a white female orphan raised in "an exotic wilderness,"
although *The Bush Cinderella* (Rudall Hayward, 1928), despite also featuring female orphans, was more realistic.[116] The trend toward realism
continued in Hayward's "community comedies," which, unlike most
early NZ film, were set in urban locations and featured virtually no
Māori, who were predominantly rural.[117] Repeating the same plot and
characters, their main purpose was to allow urban populations to see
themselves on film.[118] In this respect, they were closer to documentary than to comedy, and documentary was central to the next phase
of NZ film. The introduction of sound also stymied local filmmakers,
requiring complex technology, which the government had the means
to supply.

Documentary and NZ Identity

From the late 1930s, the NZ government seized on the propaganda potential of documentary and newsreels to create an "imagined community based upon . . . virile white masculinity and . . . paternalistic . . . governmentality," representing NZ as a modern—that is, white—nation.[119] UK documentary maker John Grierson, visiting in 1940 at the government's request, advised going beyond dairy and tourist propaganda and showing "the native genius of New Zealand" through documentary, but he wasn't referring to Māori.[120] Grierson's definition of documentary as "a creative treatment of actuality" connected to an agenda of social progress:[121] "a homogenizing, typifying, dramatizing and symbolic treatment of worldly events . . . could make 'democracy' work in an increasingly alienated, complex and abstract world in which the ideal of the rational, enlightened and . . . informed citizen could . . . no longer prevail."[122]

The result was the setting up of the National Film Unit in 1941. The NFU "shaped how New Zealanders viewed their country" via its *Weekly Review* newsreels, focusing on the war effort and the "ordinary working New Zealander," typically rural Pākehā.[123] The year of the NFU's formation also saw a government documentary celebrating the Treaty of Waitangi centennial, *One Hundred Crowded Years* (Michael Forlong, 1941). It opens with a dedication: "To New Zealand's pioneers who came forth from Britain's ordered ways to the wildness of an untouched [*sic*] land." Māori mainly feature in the documentary as an obstacle to progress— at the start, when they (eventually) sign the Treaty, in the middle, when they rebel, and at the end, when they are a "problem." At this point Kingi Tahiwi senior, of Ngāti Raukawa and Ngāti Whakaue, addresses the camera directly on behalf of Māori, stating, "we must retain our individuality in some things, in our music, dancing, and arts and crafts, for they are expressions of something deep within us." The only mention of art in the film, it underlines the symbolic role of Māori, identified with an ideal world of performance, art, and culture, in opposition to Pākehā "reality," manifest in the form of the documentary text.

The progressive, nation-building agenda of the NFU newsreels and documentaries tended to exclude Māori, except when the aim was tourism, as in *The Legend of the Wanganui River* (John Feeney, 1952), or when highlighting the Māori "problem," as in *Aroha* (Michael Forlong, 1951), *Tuberculosis and the Maori People of the Wairoa District* (James Harris, 1952), and *The Maori Today* (Oxley Hughan, 1960). Māori were an attraction or a problem, never "normal." This didn't change until the 1970s, when Māori started making their own documentaries, notably *Tangata Whenua* (TV, Barry Barclay, 1974), *Bastion Point Day 507* (Merata Mita, 1980), and *Patu!* (Merata Mita, 1981), on the 1981 Springbok Tour.

Fake It 'Til You Make It—*Forgotten Silver*

Gordon Mirams, writing in 1945, claimed that documentary "is the only branch of film production in which this country has any chance of making a contribution of real value."[124] Pākehā came to identify with local, nonfiction media—they contained the "truth" of NZ life (only three feature films were completed in NZ from 1941 to 1970). This dour realism also reflected the influence of puritanism, with its mistrust of artistic expression.[125] Acting was pretending, and frowned upon. Also, there was the aforementioned "cultural cringe." This sense of white NZ culture as gloomily inexpressive, unimaginative, and repressed connects to the cinema of unease and NZ Gothic[126] manifest in recent films like *Crush* (Alison Maclean, 1992), *Rain* (Christine Jeffs, 2001), *In My Father's Den* (Brad McGann, 2004), *Out of the Blue* (Robert Sarkies, 2006), and *Human Traces* (Nic Gorman, 2017). The Māori documentaries *Bastion Point Day 507* and *Patu!* exposed Pākehā society to a withering gaze, destroying illusions of social harmony in "God's own country."[127] A notorious prank, played by filmmakers Peter Jackson and Costa Botes on the NZ viewing public in 1995, highlighted these issues.

Presenting a romanticized history of early NZ film, *Forgotten Silver* tells the story of Colin McKenzie, a pioneer Pākehā filmmaker, whose films Jackson discovers in a garden shed. But the film was a mockumentary, Jackson recruiting US film luminaries like Leonard Maltin and Harvey Weinstein to string the audience along. It was also staged as a practical joke—screened on TVNZ in 1995 without "warning" and supported by local print media, who "played along" (it showed in a *Sunday Theatre* time slot, however).[128] Its credibility depended on activating myths of national identity, the same ones cultivated by the NFU and the cinema of unease—the practical "bloke" working in rural isolation, ingeniously using minimal resources, a "pioneer" (one sequence purports to show filmed evidence that local aviator Richard Pearse beat the Wright Brothers' first manned flight by several months). Many viewers were incensed when the hoax was revealed, prompting one commentator to later remark that "the people who have dumped on them (Jackson and Botes) are the same who would have dumped on McKenzie."[129] The film may have represented Jackson's revenge on those who doubted his ability to make NZ films—at the same time, the joke is double-edged, as it highlights a very real lack of filmmakers in the country's history. Jackson's career parallels Waititi's—both have made mockumentaries and (jokey) horror films, which Waititi combined in *What We Do in the Shadows*. One local review of *Shadows* parodied the outraged letters written to NZ papers about *Forgotten Silver*.[130] Both directors have moments of clowning, being tricksters, and playing practical jokes.[131] They share subversive humor and commercial instincts that set them apart from dominant traditions of local film.

In the *Boy* DVD director's commentary, Waititi improvises a dialogue with the role he plays in the film, Alamein (Boy's father), commenting of his own on-screen character, "He's lying—that's what acting is. That's why Māori make such good actors. . . . We're good at pretending," a statement echoed by Wassi (Waihoroi) Shortland: "Because we are liars, we are among the best liars, we lie to each other, that's what makes us funny."[132] Māori have been consistently identified with performances of various kinds, and in the national imaginary, played against the dominant discourse of Pākehā documentary "reality." But realism is based on conventions, just like fiction, as *Forgotten Silver* demonstrated. The documentary, the privileged form of narrating NZ, is as much a construction as fiction, and thus NZ is also constructed of media signs and representations, a "dominion of signs."[133] On another level, the mockumentary was the culminating moment of national embarrassment about the lack of Pākehā culture. For by creating a text that promised a hidden cultural tradition that turns out to be a hoax, Jackson and Botes exposed the New Zealand public's ignorance and disparagement of its own history and culture. The procession of luminaries legitimating the story highlighted the ingenuousness of local deference to overseas cultural authority. This brings us to the third theorization of NZ film—Nick Perry's antipodean camp.[134]

Theories of Local Film 3: Antipodean Camp

"Camp" loses its usual connotations, becoming the politically subdominant's repose to politico-cultural rather than heterosexual dominance.... [Nick] Perry ... suggests a formal peculiarity of Australasian art as residing affirmatively in conditions often perceived negatively—lastness, isolation, distance from the centres, powerlessness, reimagined as a creative act of post-modern "bricolage" ... [resulting in] films of a highly hybridic, cross-generic nature.[135]

Many modern films use a postmodern bricolage approach, so how can such an argument be made specific to NZ and Australian culture? The answer is colonial societies' "nominal repudiation [of], but tacit genuflection to European canons of taste,"[136] for example, "audiences' self-conscious embarrassment at hearing NZ accents in the cinema."[137] This inferiority complex was confirmed in the market exchange by which colonies exported raw material to Britain, which sold it back to them as value-added cultural products. Camp is a way of defending antipodean artlessness: either self-deprecation or a bold flaunting of the tacky similar to homosexual camp. These two styles correspond to NZ and Australian camp, a genre that includes most of what Richard Dyer would describe as popular "entertainment."[138] Perry does not make gender central to his definition, but Australian camp, starting with Barry Humphries and exemplified by the films of Baz Luhrmann, *Muriel's Wedding* (P.J. Hogan, 1994), and TV like *Kath and Kim*, revels in its own vulgarity, like a drag queen, melodramatic and extroverted. Aotearoa/New Zealand "bush" camp is more like a drag king—ambiguous, quirkily ironic, like, for example, the Topp Twins, lesbian farm girls who sing, yodel, crack jokes, and tend toward a "butch" aesthetic. One approach plays with femininity, one with female masculinity,[139] one is predominantly metropolitan/urban, one is local and rural. Judith Halberstam's concept of "female masculinity" provides a complementary frame of reference for "a land where blokes are blokes and even women can be blokes," Halberstam noting that "some rural women may be considered masculine by urban standards. . . . They engage in more manual labour . . . or live in a community with different gender standards."[140] Such insights complement

Anita Brady's work on Speight's Southern Man, exploring the paradox of a gendered regime of signs that simultaneously enjoins exclusive heterosexuality and exclusive homosociality, where, for a woman to become an object of desire for a true Southern Man, she also has to *be* a man.[141]

Nick Perry identifies NZ camp's "affinities with either Gothic foreboding or Germanic melancholy," which hark back to the cinema of unease, and discusses its "ability to move between dark drama and banal comedy."[142] Richard O'Brien's *The Rocky Horror Picture Show* (Jim Sharman, 1975) could be the earliest example of NZ camp, incongruously combining horror and sci-fi with comedy and musical.[143] But later texts tend toward more extreme contrasts of horror and comedy, and are viscerally rather than glamorously tacky. Peter Jackson's invention of "splatstick" in *Bad Taste* (1987), *Meet the Feebles* (1989), and *Braindead* (1992) made "bad taste" a central aspect of his early aesthetic, and some critics took him at his word, dismissing his work.[144] In this light, Susan Sontag's comment that "movie criticism (like lists of 'The 10 Best Bad Movies I Have Seen') is probably the greatest popularizer of Camp taste today" seems apt.[145] These early, amateurish, episodic films, full of weak jokes and gross-out spectacle, follow the broad lines of US camp filmmakers like John Waters and Russ Meyer, while generally playing down their overtly sexual elements—as with Waititi, Jackson's films tend to be homosocial. However, *Heavenly Creatures* (1994), with its two charming, murderous schoolgirl protagonists (based on a real case in 1950s Christchurch), departs from the "boy's own" approach, combining Gothic horror (the girls' gruesome murder of one of their mothers) with teen exploitation, arthouse movie values, and lesbian overtones. The girls are "inspired by a campish conception of the sublime, in which Mario Lanza presides over a Paradise fabricated from the detritus of the culture industry," a CGI-generated fairy-tale world called Borovnia, anticipating Jackson's later move into full-blown fantasy with *The Lord of The Rings*.[146] The girls' fantasy promises escape from the dullness of Pākehā society, a simulacrum of British respectability. Intertextual fantasy is also characteristic of Waititi's films and suggests a similar desire to escape local reality.

Camp is about "putting on a show"—that is, "entertainment." Emphasizing form over content and feeling over signification is what aligns entertainment and gay culture and gives rise to camp, "prising the form of something away from its content . . . revelling in the style while dismissing the content as trivial."[147] Additionally, Dyer discusses tonal incongruity; how "a gay sensibility . . . holds together . . . theatricality and authenticity . . . intensity and irony, a fierce assertion of extreme feeling with a deprecating sense of its absurdity," producing extreme (melo-dramatic) contrasts.[148] Combined with emphasis on form over content, tonal incongruity can produce the appearance of narrative incoherence, with continuity being abandoned in search of heightened effects/affects. Favoring spectacle over plot refers back to variety entertainment as a "string of short items."[149]

Both Jackson and Waititi produce "entertainment"—Jackson's early films are a motley of bad jokes and gross spectacle, with a minimum of plot; they are films that "put on a show" rather than aim at "deep meaning." They are playful and bantering, like Waititi's films, and lack a strong narrative drive, preferring "quirky" tonal oscillations, as in *Eagle vs Shark*, awkward comedy, and trivialization of "serious" issues like child neglect, as in *Boy*. Both filmmakers are highly intertextual—*Meet the Feebles* refers to *Casablanca* (Michael Curtiz, 1942), *The Godfather* (Francis Ford Coppola, 1972), *The Deer Hunter* (Michael Cimino, 1978), *Platoon* (Oliver Stone, 1986), *The Muppet Show*, and backstage musicals, in con-trast with the cinema of unease's obsession with local authenticity. Both filmmakers are US pop culture junkies, echoing the way that camp is centrally concerned with art, usually of the past—a redemptive nostalgia for past forms of popular culture.[150]

Not only local film partakes of camp. The Museum of New Zealand Te Papa Tongarewa, which opened in 1998, has been read in a similar light, its displays "putting on, while pointing out, the fabrications of national identity."[151] One display, somewhat archly titled "Exhibiting Our-selves," recreated a series of NZ pavilions at international exhibitions of the past, highlighting NZ identity as performance. "It encouraged an ironic distancing with regard to the public production of national cul-ture and identity, which proceeded through strategies that 'dethroned the serious' through a self-mockery that nevertheless, asserted the national sign."[152] Another local example of camp is Kiwiana—"quirky things that contribute to a sense of nationhood."[153] Kiwiana is camp because it usually originates overseas, is mass produced, and is commercial: fast food, cheap clothing, and plastic souvenirs. Kiwiana references in Jackson include sheep (being blown up with bazookas in *Bad Taste*), number eight fence wire, a Four Square corner dairy, Kiwi bacon, Sunlight Soap, and Buzzy Bees (in *Braindead*). The jokey, horror element in Jackson functions as a camp riposte to the "cinema of unease," turning angst and existential dread into more literal horror, such as mangled bodies and entrails: "a carnivalesque slap in the face of bourgeois culture."[154] The final Kiwiana reference is the NZ landscape, which, in *Lord of the Rings*, Jackson transforms into Middle Earth. This has given rise to many camp moments, notably an Air New Zealand video, directed by Waititi, in which Tolkien fans rubbed shoulders with dwarves and elvish flight hostesses.[155] Kiwiana in Waititi films includes references to local 1980s TV—the *Billy T James Show*, the Goodnight Kiwi, and iconic waiata (Māori songs), such as "Hine E Hine" (in *Boy*). *Wilderpeople* refers to rural Pākehā myths of the bush, the man alone, and his associated regalia—gumboots and Swanndris, as worn by Hec. Also, there are Te Reo expressions such as "Kia ora" ("Hello"); Māori/Pasifika slang, such as "Chur bro" ("Cheers brother") and "Sweet as" ("Fine, okay"); references to the New Zealand Warriors rugby league team; and local place names incorporated into idiomatic-sounding expressions: "This ain't over by a Mangaweka mile" (*Wilderpeople*). Kiwiana symbolizes a New World, naïve but vigorous working class rather than the Old World, sophisticated bourgeois culture of the colonizer. It is fakery, but its "signs nevertheless go on working . . . to call up nationalist sentiments" via "invented traditions," like the Scottish kilt.[156]

Māori share to some degree in these "invented traditions," while also having access to other forms of identity. The Māori Renaissance was about rediscovering that original identity. But alongside "roots" there are "routes," and alongside being there is becoming.[157] Identities change, and Māori identity has appropriated from global culture to produce new hybridized forms, like the "Poi E/Thriller" haka from *Boy*, combining kapa haka (Māori performance) and lyrics in Te Reo with a hip-hop beat and Michael Jackson references. In recent NZ culture, Pākehā men have been increasingly replaced by Māori/Pasifika males—from *Once Were Warriors* to the Warriors rugby league team to the Naked Samoans, responsible for *bro'Town* and the *Sione's Wedding* films (Chris Graham, 2006, Simon Bennett, 2012). The Speight's Southern Man campaign, discussed above, ceased in 2012.[158] TV advertising features more Māori/Pasifika now, predominantly males.[159] This partly reflects demographic change,

Kiwiana: "The Goodnight Kiwi" in *Boy*.

with more advertising for youth products such as energy drinks, fast food, and cell phones, but increasingly Māori/Pasifika feature in advertisements for internet providers, banks, and supermarkets too, demonstrating the ascendancy of Māori/Pasifika representations of NZ. Some actors in these advertisements, like James Rolleston, Julian Dennison, and Darcey-Ray Flavell-Hudson, are familiar from their roles in Waititi's films.[160] Public service advertisements have always featured Māori/Pasifika men, but some recent examples have become Internet memes, such as the drink driving "Ghost Chips" advertisement and the Waititi-directed drug driving "Blazed" advertisement (discussed in chapter 3).[161] Although ethnic diversity in advertising has increased, gender diversity has moved more slowly, an argument relevant to Waititi's work.

All of Waititi's films feature an eclectic cultural mixture, in casting, dialogue, and production design (similar to quirky directors like Wes Anderson, Waititi is fond of busy domestic interiors, which show a collector's itemizing sense of detail, and could also reflect the influence of local artists like Judy Darragh, who work with domestic kitsch);[162] in his eclectic and eccentric music choices (which will be discussed in the chapters on *Wilderpeople* and *Shadows*); and in the range of pop culture slogans, quotes, and allusions in his scripts. Finally, in his ironic, understated sense of humor, we get the sense that Waititi is affectionate toward

Aotearoa/New Zealand without losing sight of its many faults. As Babing-ton states, "there are certain myths of NZ 'difference,' creativity . . . that may, irrespective of their only partial truth . . . need to be sustained . . . in order for a . . . precarious film industry to prosper."[163] Out of these myths come stories and films. Or, as Nick Perry puts it, "the very idea of a national culture . . . [is] artifice."[164] In the next chapter, I use "camp" leader Richard Dyer's concept of "entertainment" as a way of think-ing about local popular culture, and more particularly comedy, which, I argue, works best when based on live performance, thus providing an alternative to film studies or high cultural approaches for studying Waiti-ti's comic oeuvre.

3
KIWI COMEDY

Nobody Takes Us Seriously Anyway

Reviewing *Film in Aotearoa New Zealand*, one of the first books about New Zealand film, Lawrence McDonald argued its emphasis on legitimating local film via high modernism led to its neglect of film as popular art.[1] In this light, he discusses the local filmic pioneer/director John O'Shea's three completed feature films, *Broken Barrier* (1952), *Runaway* (1964), and *Don't Let It Get You* (1966), as "loose lineage models" for later NZ film: *Broken Barrier* deals with Māori/Pākehā relations via interracial romance; *Runaway* with the "quest for Pākehā identity" (which maps onto "cinema of unease"), and finally the comic pop musical *Don't Let It Get You*, which inaugurates "a more diffuse lineage of works using popular genres."[2] These are roughly the same categories (cinema of unease, interracial romance, popular entertainment) discussed in chapter 2, and it is the last, neglected group that is my concern here. The high modernist approach performs several ideological functions. It creates identity out of a rhetoric of autonomy and independence from foreign influence, particularly popular culture.[3] It also downplays film's intertextuality and interaction with other genres such as comedy and popular music. It connects to the perception that NZ comedy is artistically insignificant, or simply not very funny.[4] Waititi characterizes the high modernist discourse in local film as, "Very dark dramas, bad things happening to nice people, very heavy. I didn't want to make a film [*Boy*] about child abuse, or child neglect, which was unwatchable. Also, my background is comedy—I couldn't ignore that."[5] Discussing *Hunt for the Wilderpeople*, Waititi allies himself with popular culture, not art: "all of that crazy shit from the '80s, these chase films and manhunt films . . . It's fucking *entertainment*."[6]

Film as Entertainment

One way of thinking about McDonald's "diffuse lineage" is as "entertainment": popular culture that is critically and academically marginal because of its low cultural capital. Formally, entertainment is "a string of short items . . . [including] popular or vulgar reference . . . implicit sexuality and open sentimentality . . . produced for profit, [for a] generalized audience . . . [with] the sole (conscious) aim of providing pleasure," in forms specific to contemporary Western capitalist culture.[7] Richard Dyer's key idea is that entertainment is Utopian: not necessarily in content but in form and affect—"what utopia would feel like."[8] These "good feelings" are conveyed through an affective rather than a representational code, arising from form rather than content, what Dyer terms nonrepresentational signs—color, texture, movement, rhythm, melody, which, in turn, generate qualities of energy, abundance, intensity, transparency, and community.[9] We see and hear these qualities in *Don't Let It Get You*'s music, its enthusiastic audiences, and the relaxed interactions of the characters. It was until recently NZ's only pop musical, clearly influenced by *A Hard Day's Night* (Richard Lester, 1964). The loose plot concerns a white Australian drummer, Gary Wallace (played by himself), seeking employment at an NZ pop festival in Rotorua from Māori entertainer Howard Morrison. Both play themselves, giving rise to an easy naturalism. The plot is intercut with music performances, mainly by Māori and Māori/Pasifika showbands, but also diva (Dame) Kiri Te Kanawa, who rehearses with a tape recorder in a *wharenui* (Māori meetinghouse). None of the main characters are Pākehā New Zealanders, and perhaps as a result, "there is no reference at any stage to racial groups and integration is taken as a norm."[10] It also shows different generations interacting harmoniously and is generally angst-free in a way that distinguishes it from the "unease" and "racial tension" models described above. It integrates US popular culture, especially music, into NZ settings. The film culminates in a concert, like *A Hard Day's Night*, where the dominant theme is celebration and communal harmony: "the Rotorua . . . audience is repeatedly defined as embracing all ages," contradicting Laurence Simmons's claims that the film represents the birth of an oppositional youth culture.[11] Simmons's critique falls into what Dyer calls the "but also" trap of film studies, "the model of showing how the text makes profound statements despite also being entertaining."[12] In contrast, it is precisely the entertainment affect that animates the film.

Entertainment addresses a popular audience; it aims to be inclusive. Laughter is a key means by which community can be created. Entertainment can create a sense of "carnival," which "is not a spectacle seen by the people: they live in it, and everyone participates because its very idea embraces all the people."[13] Comedy is clearly allied to entertainment, and key for comedy is its relationship to the audience.[14] Henri Bergson states: "Laughter appears to stand in need of an echo. . . . Our laughter is always the laughter of a group."[15] As sometime local comedian Arthur Baysting states, "Jokes don't make people laugh," rather, "stuff that [is] more contemporary and local."[16] Laughter, in other words, has a social function, which is to reinforce group solidarity. The potential costs and contradictions of this will be become clearer as we proceed.

Comedy, Community, Live Performance

Film comedy in NZ dates back to Rudall Hayward's *The Bloke from Freeman's Bay* in 1920, and from 1928–30 he directed a series of short "community comedies": *Tilly of Te Aroha*, *Hamilton's Hectic Husbands*, *A Daughter of Dunedin*, *Winifred of Wanganui*, *Natalie of Napier*, and *Patsy of Palmerston*, among others. They often used a standardized script, but local audiences got a kick out of seeing themselves on-screen. Peter Jackson attempts to recreate their general style in sequences of *Forgotten Silver*.[17] NZ film comedy has a history of connections to local audiences and performance-based arts such as live comedy and popular music. The Māori concert parties, which evolved in the late 1950s into showbands, took a variety entertainment approach, integrating comedy and music in live performance. They spawned comic stars such as Billy T. James (aka William Taitoko), initially a musician in the Auckland pub scene who joined the Maori Volcanics showband in the early 1970s; as a result, he "knew his routines intricately. Every inflection, every pause, every chuckle, every step had been honed in 100s [sic] of performances."[18] James was NZ's best-known comedian until well after his death in 1991, and became a benchmark for subsequent NZ comedy.[19]

The most famous Māori group integrating comedy and music was the Howard Morrison Quartet, "a one-stop variety show that incorporated

Māori concert parties, the Italian songs heard by the Māori Battalion, the sweet harmonies of doo-wop and the comedy of Stan Freberg. As an entertainment entity, their success helped create the infrastructure of an industry."[20] The group produced a series of parodies of UK and US folk songs, typically localizing the lyrics: "The Battle of New Orleans" became "The Battle of Waikato" (1959) with a pointed lyric about the New Zealand Wars, and "My Old Man's An All Black" (1960), based on "My Old Man's a Dustman," commented on Māori exclusion from the 1960 All Black rugby tour to apartheid South Africa. Finally, "George, the Wild(er) New Zealand Boy" (1964, based on "The Wild Colonial Boy") recounted the exploits of George Wilder, an NZ folk hero famous for his multiple prison escapes and a possible influence on Waititi's *Hunt for the Wilderpeople*. "One thing we had in our favour on the New Zealand market was that we had an undeniably down-home, Maori sense of humour," recalled Morrison.[21] They featured in NZ's first TV broadcast on June 1, 1960.[22] Other Māori entertainers of the period included Auckland cabaret king Kahu Pineaha, who "could sing; dance; play piano, guitar and other instruments. . . . One of his more provocative routines was pretending a fly had infiltrated his underwear while he was singing, causing him to writhe, squeal and shriek."[23] The music comedy duo Lou and Simon (Lou Clauson and Simon Meihana) "specialised in broad, bawdy satires, which often parodied contemporary hits. 'Maori Car' used the melody of Leonard Bernstein's 'America,' the Beatles' 'Yellow Submarine' became 'Purple Maori Pa.'"[24] Early NZ entertainment was predominantly a Māori milieu, but was also highly intertextual, as in Waititi's work. The style of Māori entertainers was unabashedly crowd pleasing for the most part, contrasting with the laconic style of later Pākehā comedians—Billy T. had an infectious giggle, while Fred Dagg and company would never crack a smile onstage. Alamein in *Boy* is a hybrid of Pākehā and Māori styles—he can be laconic but he has Billy T.'s snigger.

The 1970s saw the emergence of Fred Dagg (aka John Clarke), a Pākehā comedian: "John is the audience. He comes from the audience . . . the audience know he is representing their views."[25] The following for Dagg "was of a scale that hasn't been witnessed since the Beatles."[26] Clarke's monotonal, deadpan style and propensity for spinning lengthy "yarns" allied him with the Kiwi bloke, as did his stage attire of black vest and gumboots. But he also wrote and sang NZ's comic national anthem, the self-deprecating "We Don't Know How Lucky We Are" (1975) as well as its B-side, "Larry Loves Barry," about a man in love with his pet emu, which contains the lines "Don't you worry, it's not scary, it's just a fairy with his big canary."[27] So, apparently Dagg is not homophobic, by the standards of 1975, anyway. However, his appeal may have been mainly to Pākehā, Billy T. James noting in 1984, "I couldn't identify with a lot of the things he was saying."[28] Clarke voiced the main character Wal in the animated feature of Murray Ball's popular comic strip *Footrot Flat* (Murray Ball, 1986). Like many NZ comedians, he eventually moved to Australia, writing for and appearing in TV comedies, especially political satire. Like Jackson and Waititi, he also made a mockumentary, *The Games* (2000), about the 2000 Sydney Olympics.

Combining Music and Comedy

Starting with the Māori showbands, many local acts combined live music and comedy. It became a NZ entertainment tradition, corresponding to Dyer's values of energy and intensity.[29] It also referenced a pioneer tradition of adaptability—any entertainer was, by necessity, a variety act. Blerta (Bruno Lawrence's Electric Revolutionary Travelling Apparatus) was a 1970s mixed-media group who combined live music, drama, comedy, and film. Affiliated with the hippy counterculture, some of its members (Bruno Lawrence, Ian Watkin, Geoff Murphy) became stalwarts of the burgeoning film industry.[30] Blerta produced TV programs for the BCNZ (Broadcasting Corporation of New Zealand) and a feature film, *Wild Man* (Geoff Murphy, 1977), which were all broadly comic, anarchic, and experimental in the fashion of contemporary UK comedy like Monty Python and the Bonzo Dog Band.[31] Blerta's communal approach, often staging public events or "happenings" and kids' shows, in the form of a traveling road show, brought the group to all parts of New Zealand until it disbanded in 1975. The fact that discussion of Blerta (and the Front Lawn, see below) occurs in a chapter on experimental filmmaking in *Film in Aotearoa New Zealand*[32] underlines McDonald's point about comedy and popular art being subsumed to a high modernist discourse.[33]

Other popular and influential local acts (all duos) that emphasize live performance, combining comedy and music, include the Topp Twins, two lesbian yodelers who honed their skills through extensive busking in the late 1970s before graduating to concerts and eventually TV and a popular documentary, *Untouchable Girls*.[34] The Front Lawn (Don McGlashan and Harry Sinclair) were a 1980s Auckland duo who alternated between live performance, including music, and comic short films: "It was their philosophy that the audience should be the director, and the reactions of the crowd dictated . . . the show."[35] They "developed a fiercely loyal audience" before producing records and short films: *Walk Short* (Bill Toepfer, 1987), *The Lounge Bar* (the Front Lawn, 1988), and *Linda's Body* (Harry Sinclair, 1990).[36] Neither the Front Lawn nor the Topp Twins are mentioned in *New Zealand Film: An Illustrated History* (2011). Harry Sinclair went on to make three comedy features: *Topless Women Talk about Their Lives* (1997) (see discussion below), *The Price of Milk* (2000), and *Toy Love* (2002). *Topless Women* was parodied by the Naked Samoans (who went on to make *bro'Town*, discussed in the next chapter) for their live comedy revue, Naked Samoans Talk About Their Knives (1998). David Fane, from the group, appears in *Eagle vs Shark*. "New Zealand's fourth most popular guitar-based digi-bongo acapella-rap-funk-comedy folk duo,"[37] Flight of the Conchords, moved from the Edinburgh Fringe Festival (2002) to a BBC radio series (2006) and US TV, making two TV series for HBO in 2007. Waititi was involved with this duo, as previously discussed.

Essentially, all of these acts work in a hybrid form—combining music and comedy in a succession of short items, interacting with the audience, ad-libbing, with the aim of producing an entertaining performance, as opposed to the high seriousness of art, which tends toward formalism, long-form or complete narrative arcs, and lack of audience interaction. Many went on to make films and TV, contributing to an already existing tradition of local filmed comedy. This was also Waititi's trajectory—starting in theater and stand-up comedy and moving into film (he is also an accomplished musician).[38]

Improvisation in Local Film Comedy

I can remember someone saying to me when I came off stage . . . who wrote that? and thinking actually nobody wrote that, in the sense that it's never been written down . . . I made up most of it as I went along.[39]

With comedy, the rules are always changing. I don't even know
any of the rules. It's probably better to not even know the rules.[40]

Improvisation is an ideologically loaded term. Spontaneity is a central
discourse of Dyer's entertainment (a combination of intensity and transparency), as well as art more generally, and has connotations of natu-
ralness and unfettered self-expression.[41] A close parallel is the idea of
"liveness" in music, but Philip Auslander argues it is more relevant to see
it as a discourse, rather than a verifiable fact.[42] A possible middle course is
to recognize that the apparent effortlessness of a jazz solo, for example,
is usually the product of years of hard work and experimentation.
Improvisation is also a New Zealand ideology—practical intelligence
that makes the most of limited resources: "the No. 8 wire" mentality, a
reluctance to follow Old World (European) rituals and customs.[43] John
Clarke, discussing influences on his comic creation Fred Dagg, states:

> I worked with a lot of men and women who seemed to have
> a lot of very practical intelligence, to be a bit self-derogatory and a
> bit inclined to be dismissive of anything that didn't have an obvi-
> ous utilitarian purpose, but also to be rather imaginative in the
> way they talked . . . possibly because talk was the form they knew
> best, they weren't writers, they weren't given a forum of any other
> obvious type, so that was it, talk was the canvas.[44]

The resultant form, the yarn, is also coded as the main form of verbal
self-expression of the "pioneer" or Kiwi bloke, of which both Fred Dagg
and author Barry Crump are examples: "I see myself as an entertainer, a
storyteller . . . I don't mind if people call me a bullshit artist, that's not the
point, at least I've amused somebody."[45] Māori culture is traditionally oral,
and oratory (whaiwhaikōrero) and storytelling (kōrero paki) are central
to it. *Wilderpeople* retells Crump's "yarn" *Wild Pork and Watercress* (1985),
integrating Pākehā and Māori storytelling traditions, again corresponding
to Dyer's paradigms of community and transparency.[46]

Certain types of comedy, notably stand-up, are partly improvised—
most comedians work with the audience, so there is bound to be unpre-
dictability. Sometimes improvisational methods can extend into film
and TV comedy: Blerta's *Wild Man* (1977) seems to have been largely

ad-libbed.[47] Improvisation is easier for an experienced group of perform-ers, like Blerta, who can, given the outlines of a situation, basically "wing it." Other examples of group improvisation in NZ comedy films include Peter Jackson's debut, *Bad Taste* (1987): "Much of the film, especially the dialogue, was . . . made up on the spot as Jackson encouraged the actors to think up their own words, if they did not like the ones he had 'scripted.' The actors also filled in as camera operators for scenes in which Jackson was performing."[48]

Another example of comic group improvisation is the film *Topless Women Talk About Their Lives* (1997). The cast had the advantage of hav-ing already produced a TV series of the same name with the same char-acters, so the actors were familiar with each other. Both film and series have a handheld, low-budget, jumpy feel, scenes being written as film-ing occurred, and this reinforces the overall impression of spontaneity, if not haste, in the style of Richard Linklater films like *Slacker* (1991).[49] The Auckland urban setting, the young cast, and the soundtrack by local indie record label Flying Nun all give the impression of immediacy, as does director Harry Sinclair's incorporation of the unplanned pregnancy of lead actress Danielle Cormack (Liz) into the script. Wacky, intertextual humor defines the film, as does its DIY feel. This semidocumentary style combined with group improvisation, intertextuality, and indie music is an approach Waititi has used repeatedly, notably in *Shadows*, as is the film's whimsical, quirky style. Joel Tobeck (Neil in *Topless Women*) appears in *Eagle vs Shark*.

Waititi as Improviser

Waititi's extensive experience in drama and later in stand-up means that he is accustomed to improvising dialogue and action on set: Jemaine Clement, reflecting on his early career, states: "We did lots of shows in big groups, including a couple of times with Bret McKenzie . . . when Taika and I did our first show together, I thought we were going to phys-ically fight. Sometimes when we were onstage, we would ad-lib a lot. And sometimes we would insult each other. . . ."[50] Note again the connection of humor with aggression. Waititi tends to work with similar people (like Clement) from film to film, and this increases possibilities for sponta-neity. Some examples include "Happy Birthday Ricky Baker," a song from

Hunt for the Wilderpeople. Rima Te Wiata, who plays Bella in the film, recounts how she wrote it on set after they discovered that "Happy Birthday" was still in copyright.[51] Much of the action and dialogue in *What We Do in the Shadows* was improvised. Arguably the mockumentary/reality TV style encourages such an approach, as it depends on the illusion of unscripted reality. Jemaine Clement says:

> A lot of people are doing movies and TV shows where they improvise. . . . They just write the structure—the storylines and how they intersect. They make a very basic document that holds the story together then they let the people improvise the scene. But what we did was write all the dialogue and we didn't use it. It was probably quite similar to what we ended up with but we just wanted to know that, if the improvising stuff didn't work, we had the script to go back on.[52]

They shot 150 hours of improvised footage: "We didn't use 148½ hours of it."[53] Waititi says, "In film I've managed to work with usually the same people all the time . . . coming from the theatre you're used to . . . a cooperative mentality where you . . . develop a kind of language . . . with each other. . . . [However, with theatre] I . . . grew tired of doing the same performance every night . . . stand-up's okay because it's one-off performances that you can change every time."[54]

Most of the leads in *Shadows* are local stand-up comedians, says Clement: "Deacon [Jonathan Brugh] was in a comedy show that was very influential to Taika and me, Sugar And Spice . . . Cori Gonzalez-Macuer [who plays Nick in the movie] was playing in the clubs when Bret, me, and Taika were all playing in the clubs too."[55] Even working on *Thor: Ragnarok*, Waititi favors a loose, collaborative approach:

> I figure out who's good at it [improvisation] and who's not, and only allow the people who are good at it to do it. And then I just tried to create an environment. We're all friends on set. We become mates. And that, to me, is the perfect way of creating a free space to be creative. It's a space where we feel like we're family, and we can tell each other anything, and hassle each other, and make fun of each other. No one's afraid to give an idea because it might

be bad, because actually most of the good stuff comes because of bad ideas and big mistakes, like "hey, we never would have thought about that, unless you'd said that really stupid line!" So I just run with that, and then what do you know, we've discovered something even cooler.[56]

This whānau (family)-based approach is a feature of Barry Barclay's Fourth Cinema. Waititi also works with child actors who have little previous experience. This implies a certain faith in "natural" over learned ability. He is also capable of apparently improvised solo performances to a camera or microphone, for example his director's commentary on the *Boy* DVD, which he turns into a stand-up routine.

Direct Address

Repeatedly Waititi uses direct address, performing directly to camera, often as "himself." Clearly this is a mode that connotes live performance. It corresponds to entertainment values of intensity and transparency.[57] Breaking the fourth wall is common in film comedy.[58] It is a convention of "quirky" film, as in *Eagle vs Shark*. The front-on, direct to camera gaze can signal fictional awkwardness and emotional distance or it can connote a direct relationship with the audience, as in nonfiction media, like a newscast. It is this ambiguity between real and performance that Waititi uses to create mostly comic effects. Examples include *Boy*'s opening monologue, in which Boy gives a presentation about himself at his school, and Waititi's appearance as a priest at Bella's funeral in *Wilderpeople*; both are public performances, hence the convention seems apt, plus, the characters are eccentric—in both cases we get reverse shots of indifferent audiences. Thor's opening speech is also delivered direct to camera: "Now, I know what you're thinking. 'Oh, no! Thor's in a cage. How did this happen?'" again to comic effect. The opening scenes of *Eagle* and *Jojo* also feature a character talking into a mirror, which creates the same front-on effect.

Waititi also fronts several TV commercials he has directed—typically mixing connotations of celebrity, endorsing a product or delivering a message (in public service advertisements), with mockery of his implied authority. In a 2012 commercial for NZ beer Steinlager, he appears as a celebrity.[59] The advertisement begins with Waititi addressing the viewer while (apparently) crossing a busy street in a US city, saying, "New Zealand's really special, right? But do I really need to tell you how good we've got it?"—a pullback reveals a Hollywood set with cardboard props. This alienation effect is repeated in other scenarios, which parody Kiwiana tropes used to sell New Zealand products. The advertisement connects to local audiences through Waititi's ironic self-deprecatory gaze to camera—connoting that he is still "one of us"—a real New Zealand celebrity, even as the sets representing NZ collapse around him. His "Give Nothing to Racism" public service advertisement, discussed in chapter 10, also uses direct address. Once again, the text blurs the boundaries of fiction and reality, functioning as a mockumentary. In 2014, in another public service ad for the NZ Transport Agency, TinnyVision, Waititi directed a series of Snapchat videos, which were sent to followers. Snapchat users typically use their phones to create "selfies" and "live streams" that may also be forms of direct address. Waititi appropriated this style to apparently document the marijuana-fueled antics of a group of "mates," the series of short videos culminating in the inevitable car crash. Waititi's other work for the NZTA, known as the "Blazed" advertisement (2013), features child actor Julian Dennison, future star of *Wilderpeople*, as one of three Māori kids in a parked car.[60] The "kids in a car" scenario is reminiscent of Waititi's first short, *Two Cars, One Night*, as is their facing the camera—the main shot is front on, through the windscreen, which creates the comic effect that the kids are driving the car.

The mockumentary format of *Shadows* also uses "interviews" with the main characters (as do the "Team Thor" promos),[61] and Waititi as the main character Viago addresses the camera constantly. On NZ sketch comedy *Radiradirah* (2010), Waititi plays a drooling, child-like alien "out to destroy earth, on a very small budget," using direct address, parodying sci-fi texts like *Star Trek*, in which an alien Other typically addresses "humankind" via a video monitor.[62] The connotation here is of threat, but also of self-delusion—because direct address assumes unmediated communication, it can also connote narcissistic grandiosity, and vanity, as Bergson notes, is definitive of comedy:[63]

> Free thinking people of the planet Earth! (pause) Hello. (Pause) I'm an alien! I just wanted to say "Hi" and introduce myself and let you

Direct address: Waititi as an "ordinary alien" in the TV comedy *Radiradirah* (2010).

know that . . . um . . . pretty soon I'm going to be taking over your planet (pause). When I do eventually get to earth, there's going to be a few changes for you guys . . . um . . . about half of you will be killed instantly . . . some of you will become slaves, some of you will become pets, the rest of you will become my . . . sexual partners.[64]

Waititi Does Stand-Up

Waititi performs in the live stand-up TV series *Pulp Comedy* (2003).[65] His stand-up experience has informed his films. It is useful to think specifically about how he interacts with the audience, as this is the basic assumption of this chapter. He adopts an "ethnic" persona, which is, however, nonspecific, a "substitutable other."[66] Waititi (using his mother's name, Cohen, here) does not want his Māori ethnicity to be a source of humor, for reasons we will explore in the next chapter. Waititi's dress, a short-sleeved sweater, a loud tie, and a shirt with rolled-up sleeves, along with a funny voice, suggest the nerd or geek, which relates to "quirky" film, as in his first feature, *Eagle vs Shark*.[67] So he positions himself as

eccentric in relation to his audience. This is broadly in line with superiority theories of humor. Against this, some comedians wear suits, like
Jerry Seinfeld, which suggests conformity. Such comedians, however, are
broadly verbal—they tell jokes. But other comedians make a lot more of
their physical presence, usually their awkwardness or eccentricity, more
like clowns. Moreover, this awkwardness to the audience typically suggests a puppet—someone who is not in control of themselves, in contrast with the audience, who are in control, in line with Bergson's thesis
about comedy as social control. On another level, however, the audience want to lose control [become eccentric], because that is the pleasure
of laughter, and its transgressive aspect is mitigated by participation.[68]
For example, Waititi/Cohen mimes a failed hug with the departing MC
(Brendhan Lovegrove) and continues apparently random arm motions,
as if the failed hug "lingers," illustrating Bergson's "mechanical" thesis,
in which people become funny when they behave like objects, failing to
"adapt" to social niceties. He establishes a jerky kind of animation (Bergson's metaphor is a Jack-in-the-box, both human-like and mechanical)[69]
that both feeds off and continues the energy and presence established
by the opening ovation, while also signaling a readiness to play and be
played with that is basic to humorous situations. It is as if his reactions
are controlled to some degree by the audience—a pleasing illusion similar to that a child takes in controlling a toy.

The comedian lives because he is animated by the audience, establishing the reciprocity of animation necessary for any successful comic
performance—he moves them, and they move him. He immediately ban-
ters with the audience: "Hi, how you doing? No not you, him."; "What's
your name? (pause) Rion? (pause) No jokes there!" Banter mixes familiarity with insult and illustrates the incompatibility of comic social intelligence with sympathy—its apparent gesture to the individual is really
to the group, and this can also play into colonial discourses of homosocial "mateship." Secondly, these kinds of mild insults illustrate how
comedy depends on emotional disengagement—the audience are material for the comedian, rather than a group of sensitive individuals, and
they give him or her license to "play" with them. The comedian recip-
rocally becomes a toy of the audience. Promising, but not delivering,
jokes, Waititi plays with the audience's expectations. Joke avoidance is
partly a point of difference for Waititi (who is more interested in creating

Taika (Cohen) does stand-up on *Pulp Comedy* (2003).

characters) but it also demonstrates how joke-based theories of humor, based on the professionalization of humor, fall short.[70] Existing theories present a highly formalized account of laughter, which fails to account for its social nature (its "contagiousness").[71]

Bergson states that "a really living life never repeats itself" and alleges that humor arises out of the performance of the failure of that promise, not just because comic performers do silly things but because laughter is itself repetitive, albeit in a vital rather than a deadening way.[72] At the same time, the comic must seem to chance upon laughter—it must seem natural, as it occurs in everyday situations. Absence of mind, when carried through, becomes presence of mind, as with Don Quixote:

> attracted and fascinated by his heroes, his thoughts . . . turn towards them, till one fine day we find him walking among us like a somnambulist. His actions are distractions. But then his distractions can be traced back to a definite positive cause. They are no

longer cases of ABSENCE of mind, pure and simple, they find their explanation in the PRESENCE of the individual in quite definite, though imaginary circumstances.[73]

That is, the comic fantasy takes on a life of its own and the audience are carried along in the delusion. Moreover, they carry the comedian along, by supporting him/her with laughter. The most deluded character can transcend "mechanism" and become "machinic," that is, connecting in unpredictable and novel ways.[74] His very automatism becomes animation. In other words, comedians' highest achievement is to make a mechanical puppet into a living entity, but they can't do this without the animating force of the audience's laughter. This account also refutes the argument that Bergson's comedy is about superiority and punishing vice or social awkwardness—rather this is where it begins.[75]

Out of the simplest material—asking audience members their names, Waititi builds an "world inside-out" of carnival, a fantasy of identity fluidity in which we are no longer ourselves.[76] Playing on audience confusion about who he's pointing to, Waititi raps:

WAITITI: Tim? Dave? All of the above? Hey, shit, me too . . . sometimes I'm Tim . . . sometimes I'm Dave . . . sometimes I'm Jim . . . What do you do for a living?
AUDIENCE MEMBER: Nothing.
WAITITI: Nothing! Hey, shit, what a coincidence, me too! (Audience laughter). How can this be happening, are we the same person? Perhaps we are, I don't know, maybe you are me and I am you, maybe I'm in your body, or maybe you have taken over my body just for a moment . . . it's possible, you kicked me out of my body, I'm up here in some freaky body here, doing this shit—I don't even know what I'm doing, and you should be up here, and I should be down there looking at you, thinking "Fuck, this sucks!" (Audience laughter, applause).

This also exemplifies how comedy uses "frame reversal," which ramifies by a feedback circle and grows exponentially: in this case, the repetition of "body," the perspective alternating between the audience looking at

Waititi, and Waititi looking at the audience, and then Waititi "becoming" the audience member and vice versa.[77] "Many a comic form that cannot be explained by itself, can . . . only be understood from its resemblance to another, which only makes us laugh by its relation to a third, and so on."[78] It works by an associative, machinic logic. Waititi's subject matter, bodies, is also comic. Swearing is almost always based on bodily functions. "The material body is imperfect . . . any incident is comic that calls our attention to the physical . . . when it is the moral side that is concerned," in this case, the mixing up of personalities with bodies, so that the material usurps the psychological.[79] The rest of the act largely consists of Waititi endlessly promising the audience a joke, the same jokes he uses in his TED talk in 2010! In between he constructs a fantasy based on a play on words ("I just flew into Auckland"), which allows him to imitate birds flying (more arm flapping) and a rap on skywriting:

> . . . then I thought I'd put some smoke in my shoes and do draw-ings, you know? . . . I did a circle then I did another circle and then I did what? a box with no lid (audience laughs) 'cos I know, it's annoying isn't it? A box with no lid, what you gonna do?

Waititi's comedy is based on childish, nonsensical fantasy and clownish body movements, unlike that of most of his stand-up contemporaries, who tend to focus on sex or social taboos and be primarily verbal. It is humor of absurdity and nonsense, rather than being structured around the tension and release of Palmer's joke model. This fascination with children and childlike perspectives recurs in his career. He employs a lot of banter, which depends on audience reaction, demonstrating again the "playful" origins of humor. As stated earlier, popular entertainers in NZ usually have a background in local live performance, and perhaps to entertain local audiences it is necessary to interact with them directly. His childish persona also distances him from contemporary society and obviates any reference to local discourses of ethnicity.

Comedy, Audiences, and Moral Ambiguity

If the intent of the first section of the essay was to argue for a comic aes-thetic in NZ culture, and for Waititi's part in extending it, the intent here is to offer a critique of that aesthetic. For to produce comedy assumes complicity with an audience, its ideologies and discourses: it is permitted transgression. Bergson argues that comedy is based on social, not moral, values: comic characters "make us laugh by reason of their UNSOCIA-BILITY rather than of their IMMORALITY."[80] At the very least, comedy may arise out of the tension between what is socially and morally acceptable—for example, "locker room humor" and male homosociality, a key aspect of NZ society. Bruce Babington, reviewing local comedy films such as *Wild Man* (1977), *Skin Deep* (Geoff Steven, 1978), *Carry Me Back* (John Reid, 1982), and *Came a Hot Friday* (Ian Mune, 1985), finds:

> a frontier society's . . . rough-house humor, reflecting the values of a predominantly male society . . . without much female leavening . . . irreverent, anti-authoritarian, targeting pomposity and privilege, egalitarian and crude—the comedy of a "crew culture," to use Jamie Belich's term for semi-nomadic workers living in the mainly male groups of colonial expansionist days.[81]

Homosociality is a key theme in all of these examples. Almost all of the comedy acts discussed so far comprise only men, the exception being the Topp Twins, although they are fond of cross-dressing and "go out with women."[82] *Wild Man* is about two traveling confidence tricksters, one of whom impersonates a wild man as a way of exploiting small-town people, a similar theme to *Came a Hot Friday*. Both films use pubs, traditional sites of masculine camaraderie, as main settings, and in both male-male friendship, exploitation, and conflict are the dominant themes. *Carry Me Back* concerns two brothers who must take their father's corpse home due to a clause in his will. *Skin Deep* concerns the ructions caused by the arrival of a female masseuse in a small NZ town, associating white masculinity with the natural state of "heartland" NZ, and femininity as intrusion.[83] Barry Crump wrote a series of popular semiautobiographical comic novels based on his bushman experience, including *A Good Keen Man* (1960), *Hang on a Minute Mate* (1961), *Bastards I Have Met* (1971), and *Wild Pork and Watercress* (1986). Crump also appeared in local film and TV from the 1960s on (O'Shea's *Runaway*, for example) and a 1980s series of comic TV advertisements for Toyota Hilux utility vehicles.[84] In these advertisements, he plays the Kiwi bloke, "suspicious of emotional and material attachment, tenderness, modernity and cities," like Uncle Hec in *Wilderpeople*.[85] Crump was married a number of times, and his ex-spouses claim that he was physically abusive.[86]

Partly as a response to feminism, more recent comic acts like the Front Lawn "celebrated what it was like to be a bloke in NZ in an intelligent and nice manner."[87] Waititi's "So You're A Man" offered "a 1950s-style mockumentary guide to coping with manhood."[88] Certain features of the early "masculine" style have been retained, however, especially laconicism and understatement, as with Flight of the Conchords' Jemaine Clement: "People are always surprised to hear that I'm a comedian . . . people will say: 'But you're not funny. You don't even talk.'"[89]

Waititi's work in advertising, including the Blazed and TinnyVision public service advertisements and a series of advertisements for Carlton beer (2013) for Australian TV, also tends to feature all-male groups.[90] The mixture of public service and commercial advertisements raises moral issues, as it includes advertisements that are both pro and anti-drugs but are also very similar in format and content. TinnyVision documented a group of four young men "mucking around, smoking weed and doing funny stuff,"[91] while the Carlton advertisements were "brought to life by four inventive house mates . . . kicking back with mates and having a good time."[92] Both sets of advertisements feature a DIY/amateur aspect, either in the sense of doing funny things with common household items (as in the Carlton advertisements) "when mates get together and get a bit inventive"[93] or, with TinnyVision, the use of the Snapchat format. The fact that "tinny" is NZ slang for a marijuana "deal" (wrapped in tin foil) authenticates the advertisements with a local audience.

Of course, there are also differences. The TinnyVision advertisements feature Māori/Pasifika characters, whereas the Carlton flatmates all look white—this reflects how community service advertisements in NZ tend to feature nonwhite ethnicities, and how beer advertisements feature young white men. The TinnyVision advertisements look more informal and tend to feature "random" verbal humor, whereas the Carlton advertisements are more explicitly "staged," generally as visual puns. Moreover, the Tinny advertisements have a time line and hence a narrative, whereas the Carlton ads are a montage of individual, autonomous sequences. Presumably this reflects the difference in the advertisements' ultimate aims—the Tinny narrative leading toward a (sobering) conclusion, whereas the Carlton advertisements aim only for "fun."

However, the similarities are more significant. The "laddish" banter and absurd humor, whether primarily visual (Carlton) or verbal (Tinny), in a domestic context (a flat), represents an egalitarian community available through male bonding. One gets the sense that, as in his other work, Waititi is expert at capturing apparently spontaneous and amusing interactions between men on film. However, the Tinny advertisement ends with the stoned youths running over a woman on a zebra crossing. So, one could argue that Waititi's aesthetics and morality are clearly in contradiction here, with two very similar advertisements that supposedly have opposite meanings. The fact that TinnyVision was intended for a NZ audience and Carlton for an Australian audience doesn't resolve the issue.

The Blazed public service advertisement is also morally ambiguous.[94] Notably it is very long (2′20″), so it seems more like a short film. One gets so much time to identify with the characters and laugh at the jokes that the caption at the end—"Drug driving. Is it really that safe?"—seems like an afterthought. The advertisement reprises the "Māori kids in a parked car theme." Putatively it is the family car; symbolically, the boys take the place of the father. Driving a car is an obvious symbol of power, and for some social groups, one of the few to which they can

The "Blazed Drug Driving" advertisement (2013), featuring Julian Dennison (right).

legitimately aspire. Usually the theme implies drugs—the kids left in the car park while their parents drink in the pub. While the car in this case is at home, the drug idea is presented through the two boys comparing the respective driving behavior of their dads while "blazed"—that is, stoned.

Some criticized Waititi's use of Māori stereotypes in the Blazed ad, especially since children were used, and argued that such campaigns required more extensive consultation with Māori.[95] As pointed out above, the majority of public service advertisements about drugs in NZ feature mainly youthful, nonwhite characters. But no one else has so far pointed out how Waititi's undoubted comic abilities and celebrity status allow him to produce and endorse contradictory messages.

NZ film legitimated itself by reference to high modernist, auteurist art discourse that marginalized genres like comedy, but these can be recuperated by using Dyer's concept of entertainment. Comedy has also been marginalized by the way that film histories of NZ have tended toward an autonomous art model that downplays film's connections to other aspects of popular culture, for example, comedy's close links with live performance and improvisation and the importance of audience contact and interaction (Dyer's community), as opposed to a high art model. Comedy is closer to life than art is, and direct address is a convention that plays on the idea of liveness (or Dyer's transparency), which Waititi has used repeatedly. Bergson's theory of comedy provides a framework to analyze a live stand-up performance by Waititi, focusing on his use of his body and his relationship to the audience, and establishing how his whimsical style is quite different from that of most ethnic comedians, indeed most stand-up comedians. In the final section, noting the idea that comedy is amoral, it is argued that Waititi's focus on homosociality can reproduce rather than challenge local social norms, with particular reference to advertisements directed by Waititi both for and against drugs and how they used basically the same format and themes in the service of opposed causes.

Comic masculinity was to remain a preoccupation in Waititi's later work, but I want to turn away from one aspect of identity politics, gender, and focus on ethnicity in NZ comedy. Arguably, there is no more recurrent association in comedy than ethnicity; for cultural/ethnic difference is an easy road to misunderstanding, amusing or not. So how have nonwhite comedians negotiated this stereotype? I intend to extend the frame of reference beyond NZ, considering specifically how US and more specifically African American and Jewish culture and humor have informed local comedy, specifically Waititi's, and comparing the career trajectories of US comedians with Waititi's (all the more relevant since his entry into Hollywood with *Thor* and *Jojo Rabbit*). More specifically, how does Waititi's own mixed identity as a Jewish/Māori New Zealander inform his work?

4
On/Off-Color?

Ethnicity and Comedy

In New Zealand, there is this idea of being born strangling yourself
if you're from two different worlds . . . because you're dealing with
two different races who're combatting each other. . . . I see it as a
positive thing . . . two cultures that are self-deprecating, got great
senses of humor, and . . . have been oppressed.[1]

This characteristically ambiguous statement from Waititi is a useful
introduction to thinking about ethnicity in NZ society, in comedy and in
his work. It seems to address the bicultural split between Māori and
Pākehā, one that is foundational to ethnic politics in NZ. But Waititi
also conflates Jews with Pākehā, and while Jews may be self-deprecating,
humorous, and historically oppressed, Pākehā are not generally viewed
in the same light. Jewishness is a highly ambiguous marker of ethnicity that can be allied with both dominant and oppressing groups. In a
country where biculturalism is a norm, Waititi might be considered
a model citizen. At the same time, the bicultural model elides the influence of other ethnic groups in NZ, especially of Pasifika cultures, with
their eclectic contribution to ethnic comedy in NZ, a bricolage that
has happily avoided the burden of national identity carried by Māori/
Pākehā.[2] To admit the influence of foreign popular culture also avoids
the danger of NZ "exceptionalism."[3] The struggles of local minority ethnicities for recognition parallel other minority struggles.

In the 1970s and early 1980s in NZ, Māori and Pasifika were negotiating with ideas of blackness mainly imported from the Civil Rights–era
US. Māori gradually moved away from blackness, identifying instead
as an indigenous (rather than diasporic) minority in negotiation with

a settler government, to some extent leaving Pasifika behind. In biculturalism, Māori adopted a strategic essentialism that both consolidated
and reified their position as uniquely local, at the price of their identification with other minorities. A policy of "positive imaging" predominated, tending to avoid humor, which could be misinterpreted.[4] Waititi,
however, warns against "Māori get[ting] pigeonholed . . . [as] serious . . .
we're pretty funny people and we never really have had an opportunity
to show that side of ourselves."[5]

This historical process began to dissipate in the early 2000s, as a
new generation of Māori like Waititi emerged, as well as dedicated indigenous media like Māori Television, which link Māori to "global indigenous political concerns."[6] Pasifika continued to identify with US popular
culture and blackness (partly because of Samoa's US links), which invig-
orated their culture, and inspired Waititi when he moved into film
comedy.[7] One of my main examples is *bro'Town*, the most popular and
successful local TV comedy series, also significant for the way that its
Pasifika (specifically Samoan) emphasis reopened a space in biculturalism for ethnic humor (Pasifika being neither Māori nor Pākehā). Waititi
identifies a Samoan as a comic antagonist to Māori in *Eagle vs Shark* (Eric
Elisi, played by David Fane) and with diverse types of nonwhite ethnicity and US pop culture in *Boy*. It also seems to me useful in this light to
compare Waititi's career with some US comedians (black and Jewish)
to identify similarities and differences between the US and NZ and offer
some possible reasons why Waititi has become a successful Hollywood
director, while many of them (specifically the black ones) have not.

It's worth considering briefly the morality of comedy and how, in
times of social change, humor often becomes the object of censure:

> It is . . . hardly surprising that comedy has so regularly involved
> the representation of what the ruling and "respectable" elements
> in a society might regard as "deviant" classes and their lives, since
> the attitudes, speech, and behaviour associated with such classes
> can be used to motivate the representation of all kinds of impro-
> priety. It is hardly surprising, either, that the position of the ste-
> reotype in comedy is so often highly ambiguous, depending upon
> the extent to which it is used either as a norm to be transgressed
> or as the ready-made embodiment of the unusual, the eccentric,

and the deviant. Thus, while it can be seen why comedy has so often occupied an exceptional position within specific aesthetic regimes and institutions, and why it has so often been regarded as potentially—or actually—subversive, it can also be seen that that potential is severely curtailed by the fact that "subversion" and "transgression" are institutionalized generic requirements.[8]

The rise in the 1980s of identity politics problematized humor about minorities, homosexuals, for example. Similarly, biculturalism interrogated comic stereotypes of Māori, which had been the basis of much NZ humor, including that of Māori comics like Billy T. James. It is possible to think of Māori comedy in terms of Pākehā appropriation (Dick Frizzell's pop art such as "Mickey to Tiki," in which Mickey Mouse morphs into a tiki, for example).[9] Māori were now asking for mana motuhake, or self-determination, meaning the right to control representations of themselves, and clearly comic stereotypes could be regarded in this light.[10] Much "Māori" comedy was written by Pākehā, up to and including the TV series *The Life & Times of Te Tutu*, starring Pio Terei (1999). If there was to be Māori comedy, it would come from Māori, according to Paora Maxwell: "The ideal situation is that the tribe's people are rooted in the culture . . . writing about their own stuff."[11] But who? Following the death of Billy T. James in 1991, there was a perception (discussed below) that local indigenous comedy had died, although such a perception may have also been influenced by a new seriousness in Māori culture as it was recognized and institutionalized in biculturalism.[12]

Ethnic Humor

Some of the best jokes are Jewish. Much has been written about Jewish humor. Why are there so many Jewish jokes? There are many reasons. . . . Jokes are stories that must be cleverly told, and Jewish culture (for profoundly religious reasons) is probably the most verbal in human history. Psychological reasons: jokes relieve suffering, and what people have endured more suffering over the centuries than the Jews? Sociological reasons: through much of their history the Jews have existed on the margins of societies, and marginality makes for a comic perspective.[13]

Ethnic humor/comedy unfortunately implies a mainstream tradition of non-ethnic comedy, when arguably mainstream comedy is mostly derived from ethnic minorities—Jewish US humor, for example. This might suggest that ethnic comedy can be framed in two ways, as the authentic expression of a minority culture, or as one of the ways that ethnic minorities interact with the dominant culture—by being comedians. One possible narrative is that ethnic or racial humor has always been a feature of oppressed cultures, but over time, some of these forms have become mainstream and are shared with broader audiences, which complicates how they are read, but the point is that racial humor doesn't have to be racist humor. However, critical aspects of that humor might have to be excised. Historically in the US, "Minstrelsy and vaudevilles, comedic forms popular with both white and black audiences, spoke directly to the subordination of blacks in their portrayal of blacks as lazy, jovial, musical, gullible, and unsophisticated."[14] That is, black Americans (and sometimes blackface versions of them) became "the ready-made embodiment of the . . . deviant."[15] NZ had racist humor, too, for example, "'Hori,' the slovenly Māori narrator of a series of books written by non-Māori W. Norman McCallum, including *The half-gallon jar* (1962)."[16] As discussed in the last chapter, Māori comedians historically engaged with the discourse of local entertainment and with mainstream, mixed audiences in NZ without falling wholly into the minstrelsy trap—entertainers like Sir Howard Morrison were held in high esteem, made jokes about Pākehā racism, and parodically indigenized popular songs of the day, while spending much of their professional lives in Australia, where they were better treated and could earn a living.[17] Others, like Billy T. James, left an ambivalent legacy, discussed below.

US Comedy, Stand-Up, and Waititi

Waititi draws on diverse traditions of ethnic comedy, notably Māori, Jewish, African American, and Pasifika. Jewish comedy, however, further complicates the discussion of ethnic comedy, because Jews are characterized, rightly or wrongly, as "the adaptive people par excellence," an idea key to Woody Allen's *Zelig* (1983).[18] This isn't just a matter of physiognomy: Jews have always been associated, along with African Americans, with entertainment, and their complex interrelationships with other ethnic groups are key to understanding US popular culture:

> Jews had a cultural religious predisposition toward public forms of entertainment, particularly as compared to Anglo-Saxon Protestants, whose Puritan ancestors had prohibitions against public theatre; the disproportionate presence of Jews in urban centers where new forms of mass media technology, like the motion picture, developed; and the political economy of the time, which structurally limited the labor opportunities of overtly racialized immigrant groups (including American Jews as well as Irish and Italian Americans) and thus conditioned their willingness "to humiliate themselves" in the performing-arts industry.[19]

At the same time their imbrication in so many levels of culture opens them to charges of inauthenticity: "You [Jews] can move out of the position of the 'most oppressed' if you become the public face of oppression to the rest of society, the middle men (and, increasingly, women) who will represent the elites of wealth and power to the powerless."[20]

Bambi Haggins analyzes the careers of some black US comedians—Dick Gregory, Bill Cosby, Richard Pryor, Eddie Murphy, and Chris Rock, all of whom started in stand-up.[21] Her assumption is that stand-up enables a relative frankness about "race" (the term generally used by US commentators). Similarly, Aaryn Green and Annulla Linders note an ideology of "colorblindness" in US society (another related term is "postracial")—the idea that racial differences are no longer important and that the best way to deal with race is to pretend that it doesn't exist.[22] Stand-up comedy, they argue, foregrounds race and conflicts with colorblindness. Haggins compares black comedians' early work as stand-ups with their later career in Hollywood film. In almost every case, albeit to differing degrees, their film work is found wanting in terms of political engagement with ethnic issues, because film necessitates courting a broader (white) audience and engaging with the white-dominated star-making machinery of Hollywood. Compare this case study with Taika Waititi's career: both feature nonwhite performers doing stand-up, moving into film, and eventually into Hollywood. It is relevant to ask the same kind of questions of Waititi as Haggins does of Eddie Murphy.

A complicating factor is TV, which may provide comedians with an intermediate between live and film performance—[Dave] *Chappelle's Show*, for example. However, in the racially charged US atmosphere, "Chappelle reportedly stopped production of the show (in 2005), because he felt that the satire and commentary he was attempting to create only served to perpetuate racial stereotypes when received by white audiences."[23] This suggests both the thin line that black US comedians walk between critique and assimilation and the degree of agency Chappelle could exercise in TV. It also suggests the prominence of racism in the US. Nathan Abrams discusses a trend toward the more explicit identification of Jews in TV comedy: "This shift was illustrated by the advent of the very unapologetically Jewish *Seinfeld* . . . in 1990 that, according to the Nielsen ratings, was the most popular sitcom of the 1990s."[24] But audiences outside the US may have been unaware of this ethnic identification. Jewishness is often "double coded," that is, "a performance can communicate one message to Jewish audiences while simultaneously communicating another, often contradictory message to gentile audiences."[25] Part of this double coding may be that the text is not even read as Jewish, something that wouldn't happen with African American comedy (although much black US TV comedy simply didn't make it to NZ). Similarly, Waititi's Jewish ancestry was not widely known until his promotion of *Jojo Rabbit*. TV is also relevant in the NZ context because *bro'Town*, and most of the examples of Pasifika comedy, are from TV. But TV is frequently ignored because it possesses neither the authenticity of stand-up nor the cultural capital of film.

Comparing Attitudes toward Ethnicity in the US and NZ

There are many differences between US and NZ society and their attitudes to race and ethnicity. For example, NZ biculturalism has no equivalent in the US. But what does biculturalism mean in everyday life? Jessica Harding et al's 2011 study suggests that unlike the US or Australia, where national identity is usually identified as white, New Zealanders, Pākehā at any rate, see NZ as having a bicultural identity.[26] That is, they recognize both settlers and Māori as sharing NZ identity. Interestingly, Māori respondents saw NZ as having a Māori identity, not a bicultural one: "Without Māori, NZ culture would simply be a colonial derivative of Great Britain. The adoption of symbolic aspects of Māori culture allows NZ Europeans to promote a positively distinct national identity on the world stage."[27] This is similar to the conclusion of chapter 2 and has consequences for ethnic comedy in NZ. But this promotion of Māori culture is not simply preference: it is premised on the legal relationship between Pākehā and Māori, "the acceptance that Māori identity, both with iwi and in non-iwi settings, needed official recognition by the state."[28]

NZ is generally regarded in cultural and socioeconomic terms as a small state; however, "a small state is only small in relation to a larger one. . . . Small state should therefore be considered shorthand for a state in its relationship with a larger state."[29] In NZ's case, the larger state is the US, especially given how neoliberalism and globalization have led to "Hollywood's direct participation in the production sectors of other national film industries," including NZ.[30] The development of local film production infrastructure, during and after *The Lord of the Rings* (Peter Jackson, 2001–3), may have provided opportunities that Waititi took early in his film career. Whereas NZ government policy has encouraged and preserved ethnic cultures, allied with state assistance for cultural production,[31] in contrast, Ilana Gershon, writing on the Samoan diaspora in the US and NZ, notes that "in the United States . . . Samoan organizations are fundable not because Samoan migrants might lose their culture but because they are at risk—just as other minorities are at risk."[32] This suggests that the US approach to cultural minorities is assimilationist (and free-market), whereas the NZ model enlists state assistance to help minorities preserve their culture. Moreover, in NZ:

> Māori culture has become a template for defining what counts as significant cultural difference. Pasifika people now invoke practices that Māori use to construct cultural differences when arguing for their uniqueness. They will stress how culturally unique, and thus implicitly culturally distinct from Māori, they are in their rites of passage, funerals, forms of leadership and communities, language, or extended families.[33]

Another key contrast between the US and NZ is terminology: "research from the United States . . . predominantly refers to 'race,' 'mixed race,' 'multiracial' and 'biracial,' rather than New Zealand and the United Kingdom, which favour 'ethnicity,' 'mixed ethnicity' and 'mixed heritage.'"[34] Race is generally seen as a less negotiable category than ethnicity, which, according to official NZ discourse, is voluntary:

> Ethnicity is the ethnic group or groups that people identify with or feel they belong to. Ethnicity is a measure of cultural affiliation, as opposed to race, ancestry, nationality or citizenship. Ethnicity is self perceived and people can belong to more than one ethnic group.[35]

This is reflected in the NZ census, where respondents can choose more than one ethnicity; NZ ethnicity statistics, as a result, do not add up to 100 percent.

While the foregoing could suggest that NZ is less "racist" than the US, this may be because the term "race" is loaded. But so is "ethnicity," which could reflect a neoliberal ideology of choice and consequent depoliticization of racial difference (in this sense, emphasis on ethnicity could be viewed as an assimilatory strategy).[36] Moreover, Harding et al's study makes some questionable claims: for example, that in NZ it is normal to use "Kia ora" as a greeting.[37] As recently as 1984, a Māori woman almost lost her job for doing that (she was saved by the intervention of the then prime minister, Robert Muldoon).[38] "Kia ora" and a few other Te Reo phrases have become common in governmental and institutional discourse, but are not necessarily widespread outside Māori-dom (although probably more common now than in the past).[39] Gershon notes how "both New Zealand and US governments were using culture as justification for increasing decentralization and privatization of government services," arguing that services such as welfare and mental health should be decentralized to the ethnic community.[40] In NZ, this reflected the 1980s Labour government's dual emphasis on bicultural, liberal social policy and neoliberal economics, which left-wing commentators proclaimed contradictory.[41] Hence, "this NZ = bicultural pattern is largely limited to symbolic representations; it does not reflect rhetoric or ideologies governing the allocation of material interests," with the exception of funding for minorities.[42]

Gershon also argues that making ethnic culture an aspect of government policy requires essentialization:

Māori have had to pay a price for their relative success, they have had to engage with [NZ's] politics of recognition. . . . To be properly recognizable, people have to engage with these stereotypes . . . in such a way that does not challenge the most fundamental assumption of a nation's politics of recognition—that people possess ethnicity, race, or culture in an inalienable way. In short, ethnics are asked to perform an essentialist relationship to identity.[43]

Similarly, Brendon Hokowhitu and Vijay Devadas argue that "recognizable or cognizable forms of indigeneity will rapidly be subsumed by the neoliberal state."[44] Waititi's comments about being categorized as a Māori filmmaker (see chapter 1) are one possible reaction to this ethnic double bind.[45] Cultural identity in NZ is contradictory, because it is increasingly key to legal frameworks, which may determine things like access to resources, but also a matter of individual choice. The former could lead to essentialization—to be classified as a culture in a legal framework means corresponding to a linguistic definition—while the latter could potentially lead to anyone claiming resources according to their "self-perceived" identification, although in practice, identifying as Māori officially would require identifying your whakapapa (genealogy). This ambiguity could be due to the attempt to accommodate different value systems, or it could reflect the contradictions of "neo-liberal governance [which] has since sought to assimilate indigenous identity so that 'Māori' becomes only an adjective that describes the outward appearance of the instrumental interest-maximizing individual of market lore."[46] Essentialization can reflect the logic of neoliberalism—once Māori culture is institutionalized, it can be reified as a brand (albeit one that can be used by Māori). Discussing the branding of culture in relation to indigeneity and tourism, however, Maria Amoamo and Anna Thompson suggest that cultural performance can help renegotiate commerce/culture binaries, and comedy could be an example of this.[47]

US and NZ Blackness

Robbie Shilliam traces the history of US blackness in NZ from the 1970s to the early 80s, arguing that "Pasifika activists learnt similar messages to their cousins in Ngā Tamatoa regarding Black Power, yet cultivated, through the Polynesian Panthers, a closer political identification with Blackness."[48] Ngā Tamatoa ("The Warriors") and the Polynesian Panthers were two activist groups responding to post–Civil Rights organizations in the US such as Black Power, the Black Panthers, and the Nation of Islam. Initially, a uniting "Blackness as a Polynesian identity was [seen as] the solution to colonial divide and rule."[49] However, "Māori are *tangata whenua* (peoples of the land) and Pasifika people are, strictly speaking, *manuhiri* (visitors)."[50] To put it another way, the "Polynesian Panthers had already demonstrated a close identification with Blackness; they were, after all, non-indigenous migrants to urban areas in somewhat the same fashion as African Americans."[51] Māori were not. Instead, they were negotiating with the Pākehā government over the setting up of a bicultural framework. For example, in 1983, the Black Women's Movement was split when Māori women held a separate hui (meeting). Māori activist Zena Tamanui later wrote that Māori in the movement traded love for power.[52] By 1984 "blackness" was no longer a central political term for NZ Māori activists: "While Black Power was seminal to the rebirth of radical strategies for mana motuhake, the very terms of these strategies also required the shedding of Blackness as a political identification for the retrieval and renewal of ancestral identifications."[53]

At the 1970 Māori Leaders conference, Taura Eruera, the first chairman of Ngā Tamatoa, had argued that Māori could already lay claim to a whakapapa of radical oppositional politics and therefore should be wary of cultivating deeper relations with Black Power, writing later that Māori had more in common with (indigenous) "natives" than "negroes."[54] However, while touring the US in early 1971, Eruera had a transcendent experience at a black church service in San Francisco, Shilliam commenting, "'Natives' and 'negroes' fail to bind together precisely because they are created as categories of colonial-sociological segregation. . . . But where these categories fail to connect, affective, aesthetic and religious experience exceed and subvert colonial governance."[55] The experience of popular culture (and art?) can dissolve the political categories of power and promote identification across cultures. These themes are played out in *Boy*, with its references to gangs, which, with names like Black Power, hinted at US blackness. Shilliam argues that gangs played a role in the more militant forms of protest against the 1981 Springbok Tour.[56] Moreover, *Boy*'s conclusion, with its ecstatic melding of haka, Michael Jackson, and US hip-hop culture in "Poi E," hints at the kinds of affective experience forging transnational minoritarian alliances discussed by Shilliam and, more loosely, Amoamo and Thompson.

US Pop Cultural Influence

The essentialization of Māori identity that followed from biculturalism could have made Māori humor more politically risky, whether about or by Māori. Screenwriter Riwia Brown asked in 1993, "Are we as Māori really ready to laugh at ourselves? . . . We're still trying to shake off the image of all those happy-go-lucky guitar singers."[57] There may have been an element of small-nation dynamics at work here too—unlike the US, there was no separate black comedy circuit, and little ethnic media, which meant that politicized humor about ethnic difference was unlikely to thrive. NZ audiences were usually mixed and predominantly Pākehā, though this did change with the launch of Māori Television in 2004. Essentialization also risked losing touch with the everyday reality of modernity, in which identities are not unitary but fragmented, subject to a range of influences, as, for example, popular culture's influence on youth. In terms of Stuart Hall's two models of cultural identity,[58] there was potentially an overemphasis on the first model of roots and tradition at the expense of the second, but in fact:

> Maori have been identifying with US culture for a long time, starting with the impact of Hollywood film in NZ: Maoriland was much affected by Hollywood. . . . It produced those young Maori who came to town on Friday nights dressed like their Hollywood film heroes, challenging British codes of behavior (let alone . . . Maori codes). In the Eighties they dressed as street-smart hybrids of Rasta, breakdancing and primitivist exotic. Back in the Twenties and Thirties, they dressed as cowboys and there was much public agonizing over whether Maori parental controls were inadequate, whether Maori sexual attitudes were just plain different, and whether films were liable to encourage youth into criminal behaviour.[59]

A filmic, comic example of hybridization of Māori identity was Billy T. James's Tainuia Kid in *Came a Hot Friday* (Ian Mune, 1985):[60] "a Māori who thinks he is a Mexican cowboy . . . undoubtedly the main attraction of the film," which was a local hit, largely due to James's performance.[61] The fact that

> Westerns and cowboys were not only admired in Oceania but even imitated, cannot be simply dismissed as yet another example of "spectators . . . unwittingly sutured into a colonialist perspective." Instead, the cowboy constitutes a complex site around which political critique, corporeal desire and modern spectacle coalesce.[62]

Then there is African American music and fashion's influence on Māori youth, something especially obvious in *Boy* and *Wilderpeople*.[63]

The Billy T. James character has "much in common with an urban Maori street culture which has rejected the fixed identities of both marae and Pakeha prescription."[64] As Stephen Turner notes, "Precisely because Polynesian culture has always been performed as authentic and indigenous for white settlers and tourists, Polynesians are happy to speak American. It defies a will to be authentic . . . that is more white than brown."[65] US, and more broadly, foreign popular culture offers Māori (and Pasifika) a "third space" in which to escape from the traditional

Billy T. James as a Mexican gunslinger in *Came a Hot Friday* (1985).

dualities of same and other, colonizer and indigenous, which have often defined local discourses about ethnicity and representation.[66] Māori (and Pasifika) are also happy to speak Japanese, as we see in the constant references to Shogun and martial arts in *Boy* and *Eagle vs Shark*, not to mention *Tongan Ninja* (Jason Stutter, 2002), which Clement costarred in and cowrote and Waititi was also involved in: "In the '50s and '60s . . . Māori . . . were punished if you spoke your language at school and . . . so . . . they tried to identify with other cultures . . . so the father character, he's obsessed with . . . Samurais."[67] Denied their own voice, Māori adopted the voices of others who were, like them, subject to racism, in a kind of cultural ventriloquism.

bro'Town—Pasifika Camp

These two strands, of US pop culture influence and Pasifika negotiation around comedy in a bicultural context, came together in NZ's most popular and successful TV comedy of the early 2000s, *bro'Town*. Clearly modeled on the US TV cartoon *South Park*, the show was written and voiced by the Samoan comedy troupe the Naked Samoans (David Fane, Mario Gaoa, Oscar Kightley, Shimpal Lelisi, Robbie Magasiva, and Jerome Leota) and Elizabeth Mitchell. This animated series, with its scatological, adolescent humor, followed a group of Pasifika teenage boys in a semifictional suburb of Auckland (the world's largest Pasifika city). It was popular with children, despite being nominally an "adult" cartoon. Its success paved the way for other Naked Samoans projects—for example, the *Sione's Wedding* films, also very popular in NZ, proving that there was a big audience for Pasifika humor. Being non-Māori but still Polynesian allowed *bro'Town* to use ethnic humor without getting caught up in the politics of biculturalism: "the show skirts questions about what it means to be culturally Samoan, focusing instead on the consequences of being a relatively generic brown minority with Pacific Island markers in this particular ethnoscape."[68] Naked Samoan Oscar Kightley comments: "Because of the place Samoans occupied in New Zealand society, there was a sense that we could say and do whatever we want."[69]

bro'Town continued a vein of mainly 1990s Pasifika TV humor described as "Pacific camp," with reference to TV texts such as *Tali's Angels* (2000), a segment in the Pacific Island current affairs program

Tagata Pasifika; *Milburn Place* (a recurring segment in *Skitz*), which then became a TV series, *The Semisis* (1996–97); and *Eaten Alive* and *Some Like it Hot*, which both featured *fa'afafine* Buckwheat and Bertha (the term refers to "Samoan men who assume female social roles and sometimes dress like women").[70] All the texts featured Māori/Pasifika men in drag (though not exclusively). *Fa'afafine* feature in *bro'Town* as well, as seen in Brother Ken, the principal of the school the boys attend. Furthermore, the character Mack is obviously gay. The shows parodied or pastiched US texts, such as *Charlie's Angels and Melrose Place*, or well-established TV formats, such as cooking shows, an intertextuality shared by *bro'Town*. The style was flamboyant, gaudy, crude slapstick, as might be expected with male drag, but unusual in NZ comedy, which tends to be pretty low-key (likewise, *bro'Town* was notable for its scatology). All drew heavily on stereotyping, for example, of US action heroes (although *Charlie's Angels* was already a camp text), "symptomatic of a trend in which migrant Pacific Islanders . . . localize and adapt global imagery, deploying a camp strategy that simultaneously vilifies and valorizes those images," a practice also relevant to *bro'Town*.[71] Apart from drag, "Camp's constituent elements of incongruity, theatricality, humour . . . irony and aestheticism . . . [are] found in Pacific Island moving image . . . but there are . . . broader arguments for the existence of an Antipodean camp . . . within which Pacific Island variants of camp can be situated."[72] Sarina Pearson points out the "doubled effect of performing camp within a milieu which itself mobilizes critical camp in relation to what it perceives of as its oppressor."[73] This "reflects a symbiotic relationship in which Pacific moving image practice is strongly influenced by local discursive practices."[74] This ongoing cross-fertilization between settler and migrant/indigenous cultural practices is significant for understanding Waititi's films, although antipodean camp is less flamboyant than Pacific camp, and has different gender connotations.[75] You won't see drag queens in Waititi films; drag kings are another matter. Pearson points out that camp is a "mechanism" that creates different effects for different producers and audiences, rather than relating solely to a minority.[76] In its incarnation as "camp lite," its "riot of colours" and low/broad/crude/slapstick humor, combined with exaggerated performance, ally it with mainstream comedy.[77] Susan Sontag comments that the essence of camp is its artificiality—these Pasifika texts were so exaggerated (or caricatured, *bro'Town* being a cartoon) that they formed an ironic counterpoint to authentic Māori.[78]

Racial stereotypes abounded. Oscar Kightley comments, "There was [*sic*] so many [complaints after the first episode of *bro'Town*]. There was comments from Australians who were offended on our behalf, there was comments from people who were offended on behalf of Māori, on behalf of Islanders . . ."[79] It was influential on the younger generation of NZ comedians: "*bro'Town* was my Billy T.," said Samoan/NZ comedian Rose Matafeo.[80] *bro'Town* used stereotypes, extensive intertextual references and code switching to create a distinctive South Pacific bricolage, with its own patois, a mixture of local Pasifika English, Māori, and African American slang, also used by the show's fans, which we hear in Waititi's films.[81] Finally as Pasifika, the program sent up existing representations of Māori as hard-drinking, parentally negligent losers on the one hand and authentic embodiments of indigenous spirituality on the other, the two poles established by *Once Were Warriors* and *Whale Rider* (Niki Caro, 2002). In the episode "Zeelander" (2005), Jeff da Maori, one of the boys, is "discovered" by German fashion designer Hans Wulfmann, who appropriates Jeff's slovenly ways and markets them as *le dernier cri*, commenting obliquely on the fetishization of Māori authenticity by Pākehā, and perhaps also on the precedence of Māori over Pasifika in NZ cultural identity and politics.

Predictably, the show was criticized for its use of Polynesian stereotypes and corporate sponsorship. Melani Anae, author of *Polynesian Panthers*, accused *bro'Town* of promoting stereotypes "we fought against in the 70s. . . . We've moved beyond the stereotype of just being entertainers."[82] Emma Earl states that the show commodifies Polynesian youth culture as "a marketing strategy to tap into a popular ideological shift towards multiculturalism in Aotearoa New Zealand without disrupting the dominant ideology of white, middle-class masculinity from which advertising's capitalist roots derive."[83] The problem with Anae's critique is its assumption of a "real" Polynesian identity that *bro'Town* distorts, a criticism that could also be leveled at Haggins's account of black US stand-up. Earl sets up Western capitalism as an Other to the exoticized fantasy of a Pacific paradise, untouched by commerce. Both Earl and Anae ignore the realities of globalization as they manifest themselves in the everyday lives of media-savvy Polynesian youth who are more likely to listen to hip-hop or metal than to traditional ethnic music, although Earl's insight that under neoliberalism ethnicity becomes a commodity, a "choice," is a useful critique of the NZ government's policy of ethnic voluntarism. Māori commentators later leveled similar criticisms at Waititi's *Boy* and his advertising work (see chapters 3 and 5). These criticisms are in a similar mode to Haggins's critique of the authenticity of African American comedians, the risk being that they essentialize identity and do not factor in audience response, which is complex and not solely determined by the ethnicity of the performers.

Certainly, the history of NZ comedy reveals its close relationship with audience, as we saw in the last chapter. Michelle Keown's study of fan websites for *bro'Town*, like Green and Landers's study of US black comedy, focuses on how audiences relate to media texts about race. One of the key points of these studies is how nonwhite audiences relate ethnic stereotypes to their own experience: "local knowledge possessed by New Zealand fans often affords them deeper insights into the complexities of the racial politics . . . explored in the show."[84] Fans of the show interacting on websites, whom Keown identifies as mainly Pacific Island or Māori (presumably based on their avatars and self-identifiers), find it "a positive source of ethnic identification," drawing personal associations between their experiences and the characters.[85] For them the show's appeal lies in its realism. Yet the fan discussions go beyond simple affirmation and identification. An ongoing debate on the derivation of "ow" (as in Jeff da Māori's "Not even ow!") related the word back to "the Māori term 'e hoa,' meaning friend, which has over time been abbreviated to 'eho' and then 'ow.'"[86] Many schools banned the show's catchphrases; ironically, they were contradicting their own aim of teaching Māori language.[87] This wasn't the first time local comedy had taught NZ children history: Jessica Hansell (aka Coco Solid) credits Billy T.'s sketches about "first contact" between Captain Cook and Māori with "literally teaching you about . . . colonisation, because the school curriculum wouldn't."[88]

Signifying

Most fans appear to find *bro'Town*'s comic invocation of racial stereotypes unproblematically entertaining, with fans applying terms like "coconuts" and "Fobs" ("fresh off the boat") to themselves and the Naked

Samoans.[89] As noted by Fredric Jameson, "stereotypes commonly function as allegorical cartoons that no longer convey the racist contempt of the older imperialism and which often . . . function as affectionate forms of inclusion and solidarity."[90] This suggests political implications in audience responses that go beyond the critiques offered above. Reversing the frame is central to humor and can be extended to the Foucauldian concept of "reverse discourse," where the very terms used to derogate minorities can be turned into badges of identity—bro'Town's "Dumb-ass P-heads" comes to mind.[91]

Reversing the usual meaning of words in this way occurs in African American culture as signifying:

> By supplanting the received term's associated concept, the black vernacular tradition created a homonymic pun of the profoundest sort, thereby marking its sense of difference from the rest of the English community of speakers. Their complex act of language Signifies upon both formal language use and its conventions, conventions established, at least officially, by middle-class white people. This political offensive could have been mounted against all sorts of standard English terms . . . such as down, nigger, baby, and cool, which snobbishly tend to be written about as "dialect" words or "slang."[92]

This combative use of language features in contests of wit, which are further aspects of signifying: the signifier invents a myth to start the banter and then implicates a third party. "The signified person is aroused and seeks that person. . . . Signifying is completely successful when the signifier convinces the chump he is working on, that what he is saying is true and that it gets him angered to wrath."[93] We see an example of both ritual insult and its ternary structure in this exchange of insults from Boy:

> TEACHER: Now, who knows what disease this sheep has got?
> KINGI: AIDS.
> TEACHER: Not AIDS, you dork!
> KINGI: Yes, because it looks like Murray and he's got AIDS.
> TEACHER: Don't be stupid. Kids can't get AIDS . . . only gays.
> KINGI: He's a gay. He goes out with Boy . . .

Kingi the signifier creates a myth (about Murray) and then implicates Boy (who is his real target here). "It is enough to say, 'Your mama' to commence—or to conclude—this ritual exchange."[94] This happens in *Boy*:

> **TEACHER:** Now, who's heard of the plague?
> **KINGI** (to Boy): You. Your mum had it. (Cue fight).

The above example can be read as Waititi adapting elements of African American and US popular humor. *bro'Town* opened up a space for male, adolescent, puerile, ethnic humor that was adaptable to the NZ context. Its characteristically "boy-ish" approach resonated with Waititi, as did its use of animation, "Taika's favorite thing" (*Boy* includes hand-drawn animation, presumably by Waititi).[95]. He had already done some experiments in this vein—notably 2003's *The Untold Tales of Maui*, which gave a comic, "politically incorrect" spin to Māori myth.[96] Perhaps he felt he could try out new forms of Māori humor in the theater that he couldn't get away with (yet) in film and TV?

NZ Biculturalism and Humor—*Funny As*

One possible effect of biculturalism could be to suppress humor about Māori. Waititi states:

> I wanted to move away from how we [Māori] are traditionally typecast in movies in New Zealand, which is like the Jake character in *Once Were Warriors*, who's basically an alcoholic killer. There's that kind of character, or there's this sort of stoic warrior *Dances with Wolves* type of guy. There's more to us than that. We have geeky, dorky guys who are essentially weaklings who pretend to be tough . . . I wanted a degree of comedy.[97]

The self-deprecating, buffoonish humor of 1980s Māori comics like Billy T. James is now seen by some as too close to minstrelsy.[98] In the TV documentary series *Funny As: The Story Of New Zealand Comedy* (2019), NZ comedian Matariki Whatarau comments, "It's kind of . . . messed-up . . . because he [James] was a Māori fulla, poking fun at Māori . . . a tricky bugger."[99] Riwia Brown stated in 1993 that "for many Maori he crossed the line."[100] Another more mundane reason for a historic scarcity of Māori humor could be that comedy is not a career option in NZ, and entertainers, now and in the past, do it for a while, or as one part of their act, and then move on to something else. Māori comedian Mike King is now a men's health advocate, and Pio Terei is host of the TV show *It's in the Bag.* Others moved to Australia (Rima Te Wiata, who plays Bella in *Wilderpeople,* for example). Some Australian writers have suggested that NZ indigenous comedy is healthier than the Australian variety, but this could be due to the talent drain across the Tasman producing that perception.[101] But the underlying point is that Australia, like the US, has a large entertainment industry, which produces more opportunities.

Funny As, specifically episode 3 on ethnic humor, presents the argument that the death of Billy T. James in 1991 produced a comic vacuum, which is attributed to Billy's talent, in the usual manner of popular history privileging individuals over social forces. A series of comments back this up: "When Billy died, comedy died," (James Nokise, Samoan/NZ comedian); "Normally in New Zealand comedy, there is room for brown people, but just one" (Nathan Rarere); "Billy T. seemed to be on his own back then" (Scott Blanks, director of the Classic Comedy Club); "People would say: 'Billy T. is still the funniest,'" (Madeleine Sami). Then we see an image of Waititi, and the focus switches to him for much of the remainder of the episode. Clearly, the program sets up Waititi as the new Billy T. (James has a cameo in *Boy,* performing a skit from his '80s TV show), sidelining comedians like Mike King and Pio Terei. This narrative also elides the previous fifteen minutes of the program focusing on Pasifika. The implication is that real NZ comedy is made by Māori. The second point is that comments like the above seem to evince nostalgia for the time when it was okay to make jokes about Māori, a pre-PC world before biculturalism (Waititi's *Boy,* set in 1984, could also be interpreted in this light). Or it is a narrative of exceptionalism—no one could get away with that humor except Billy, because he was a genius. A more profound conclusion is that biculturalism actually changed the racial politics of NZ and promoted Māori to a point where their association with humor became problematic. The introduction of Waititi resolves this dilemma because he is more than a comedian—he makes films: "He's an example of someone who is just an artistic person, who is just so good at everything."[102] This is also key to his perceived difference from African American comedians, as we shall see. *Funny As* then shows Waititi doing stand-up (in 2003, the same sequence as discussed in the last chapter) but it is presented as "doing experimental characters": "He went through a phase where he would try these characters on the streets of Wellington"; "The first time he did that, I did not know who it was, it was just some weird guy standing next to me." Waititi possesses a "unique sensibility."[103] In a similar vein, Billy T.'s *film* work is "the best thing he ever did . . ." (Danny Mulheron, comedy director/actor).

Stand-Up, Ethnicity, and Cultural Capital

In his stand-up act, Waititi plays down his Māori ethnicity, adopting instead a generalized "ethnic" persona, a "substitutable other."[104] He makes his personal appearance slightly grotesque—false teeth, and a wig of blonde curls, and talks in a "funny" (foreign, possibly German) accent, similar to "the traditional Yiddish theatrical character of the 'schlemiel,' a hapless, insecure, physically undesirable, romantically ineffectual, and sexually impotent male," or in its more contemporary form, the "neurotic nebbish."[105] He also uses his mother's name (Cohen), all of which suggest the influence of Jewish US comedians like Andy Kaufman. Kaufman was known for his "Foreign Man" persona, an eccentric who talked in a high voice and seemed vaguely effete and infantile.[106] He was also known for his avoidance of jokes, instead generating laughs out of nonsense and absurdity, also features of Waititi's routines.[107] Waititi's performance also echoes Viago, the character he plays in *What We Do in the Shadows*, a role in which he was influenced by his mother.[108] Rather than stressing his Māori ethnicity, he stresses his Jewishness (although, as discussed, Jewishness may not be readily recognizable to gentile audiences), demonstrating a characteristic of mixed ethnicity particularly useful for a performer: shifting personae—"the unique positioning of 'mixed race' identities, which do not fit neatly within established classification structures."[109]

In contrast, African American comedians usually (necessarily?) highlight their ethnicity. One reason is historical: with the 1960s rise of civil rights, African American comedians performed less for white audiences and more for African American audiences, often performing politicized material that highlighted issues of discrimination. This brings us back to Haggins's argument, which is based on the perceived authenticity of the performers' "roots" in stand-up. But equally it could speak to the greater segregation of audience by race in the US compared to NZ. An example is the existence of separate charts for popular music (pop and R&B), historically linked to race.[110] The US also has a history of legal segregation and slavery, which NZ lacks. While a hard point to prove empirically, US culture seems to be more individualistic than NZ, viewpoints are more polarized, and there is more literal and metaphorical ghettoization. The US is also marked by extreme economic and cultural differences, although NZ might be catching up in that regard.[111] Representation of ethnicity in film is also relevant. Most mainstream US films starring black comedians portray them in a white world, as "fish out of water"—most of Eddie Murphy's films, for example—effectively they are the exception that proves the rule.[112] In NZ films (including Waititi's), ethnic characters are more likely to be shown as existing in a primarily ethnic, or at least bicultural, world. Biculturalism could be seen as both cause and effect of a more ethnically integrated society, although few would pretend that NZ's ethnic playing field was level.

But precisely because of the more heterogenous, less polarized NZ social field, Waititi can make cultural moves not generally available to African American entertainers. Eddie Murphy and Chris Rock are career comedians. This could be partly down to the degree of specialization in a larger economy, or because, historically, unemployment benefits are more difficult to get in the US.[113] Waititi has always emphasized the importance of not having to get a "real job," practicing as a visual artist through much of the 1990s, eventually transitioning into acting and comedy.[114] In other words, he has been able to be an artist, an option not available to most African Americans. Whereas for Chris Rock and other African American entertainers filmmaking basically meant acting jobs, Waititi transitioned to directing quite quickly. Relatively few African Americans, never mind comedians, have become well-known directors. Because he presented himself as an artist who also did comedy, Waititi's career took a different trajectory. This is similar to Jewish comedians, who frequently move successfully into directing (Woody Allen, Mel Brooks, Billy Crystal, Carl Reiner, Ben Stiller, and the "Jew Tang Clan" of Seth Rogen, Jason Segel, Jonah Hill, Michael Cera, Paul Rudd, and Jason

Schwartzmann).[115] Of course, this also reflects the relative privilege of contemporary US Jews.[116]

But this brings us back to politics—are the kind of expectations on black US comedians to talk race relevant to Waititi in NZ? We have already established that Waititi's stand-up basically avoided his Māori ethnicity, by the available evidence. Waititi's early film work, up to *Boy*, was more Māori-centric, but displayed a lighter, more comic touch than that of other Māori directors. Was it comedy that addressed race? In the chapter on *Boy*, I consider various critiques of its Māori-ness, but the short answer has to be, no, not explicitly. For contrast, Mike King, at one point in his stand-up act, addresses the audience in Māori and comments: "And for all you honkies out there that didn't understand that shit, now you know what school was like for us."[117] A film like *Boy* rarely addresses Pākehā directly, instead using more indirect means such as reverse racism: for example, the Pākehā school principal referring to himself as "a dumb honky." Explicit statements about race are reserved for the director's commentary, where they are voiced not by Waititi but by Alamein, the character he plays on-screen—for example, "Māori have had a pretty rough time over the last 160 years." Alamein's fallibility as a narrator puts a protective layer of irony around his statements. Skits explicitly comparing black and white races are not a feature of Waititi's work, though they are fairly common with US black comedians. For Barry Barclay, "the category of Fourth Cinema does not simply stand for films produced by Indigenous filmmakers, but refers to a distinct politically engaged mode of filmmaking."[118] Waititi's films do not fit this definition in terms of on-screen representation, although they might in terms of their *whānau*-based mode of production.

There are also differences in performing styles. Many male African American comedians have a fairly aggressive, fast-talking, more or less macho style: Mike King provides a local example. US black machismo could be seen as a corrective to earlier black entertainers who pandered to white stereotypes of black simplicity or infantilism, although it might confirm other stereotypes about aggression. Waititi's style is closer to what Abrams describes as the "sissy Jew" who "emerged as the vanguard of a new softer and kinder cinematic multiculturalism and cultural pluralism," a subspecies of the 1980s New Man, who relates to Waititi's "geeks."[119] As suggested above, Waititi plays a range of nonwhite ethnicities, quite often a kind of nonspecific other. Ethnicity becomes a much more ambiguous resource, because of hybridity. Rather than straightforward black/white binaries, we enter a murky world (for example *Eagle vs Shark*) where ethnicity emerges an issue in the course of the narrative, rather than being signaled from the first.

But the most significant difference between Waititi and black US comedians is the additional aura of respectability or flexibility that Waititi derives from his bohemian background, of being an artist and auteur. To connect this back to the argument about biculturalism, Waititi was driven to differentiate himself from the essentialized definitions of Māori-dom prevalent at the time. Jemaine Clement comments, on being in Humourbeasts with Waititi: "There's Māori drama, and that would be very serious, often dealing with abuse, and there's Māori comedy, lots of jokes about being thieves. . . . We don't really relate to being thieves . . . and we were . . . making fun of Māori theatre."[120] Curator James Alexander sums up Waititi's approach: "There shouldn't just be one type of Māori film." Waititi says: "New Zealand hasn't really had a chance to show its funny side in film . . . Kiwis want to see themselves in a more original way."[121] All of this suggests a bigger agenda than telling a few jokes. It might mean the freedom for Māori to not be only Māori: to be E.T., Michael Jackson, vampires, superheroes, or Hitler. The argument about Waititi's cultural capital is also applicable to the NZ context—what gives him "the edge" over other Māori comedians like Pio Terei and Mike King is again the perception that he is more than a comedian—he's a film director.

There is a certain aptness in concluding that Waititi's comic eminence is partly due to the perception that he is more than a comic, as this confirms the proposition advanced at the start of the chapter before this, that comedy has been neglected by NZ critics because of its lowly reputation as popular entertainment and because of its frequent (and problematic) highlighting of ethnicity. However, the legitimacy conferred by "art" is also problematic, albeit useful, as it helped Waititi take his career overseas. The next chapter examines Waititi's first feature film, *Eagle vs Shark*, the script of which was workshopped at the Sundance Director's and Screenwriter's Lab in 2005, thus demonstrating the NZ/US relationship discussed in this chapter. This influence was also manifest in the finished film, which, arguably more than his subsequent work, tapped into a mostly US genre of alternative, quirky film, featuring geeky Jewish-style characters not far removed from Waititi's stand-up days. But in terms of ethnicity, even if the film is apparently an interracial heterosexual romance, some of the romance is arguably more homosexual and intraracial, and this ties into the identity politics of geekdom.

5
QUIRKS AND
NERDS

Eagle vs Shark

Quirky, eccentric and "nerdy" characters proliferate in contemporary American film. . . . These character typologies are . . . evident in the work of smart directors, such as [Wes] Anderson and Todd Solondz, as well as particular smart "one-offs" such as *Ghost World* and *American Splendor*. . . . These films foreground American antiheroes that become special by their very non-specialness; playing on banal, prosaic and conventionally unattractive qualities, apparent in their physical appearance, behavioral traits and enunciation, to create ironic, self-conscious character representations. They are the antithesis of popular Hollywood representations, which tend to conform to American ideals constructed around beauty, success and affluence.[1]

Deborah Thomas identifies "nerds" or "geeks" as central characters in recent US alternative cinema, prefacing her discussion of Wes Anderson's *Rushmore* (1998), which centers on eccentric adolescent Max Fischer (Jason Schwartzmann). But Thomas is not just describing a character type but a set of representational strategies, even a genre, "New Geek Cinema."[2] It has influenced Waititi, who participated in script development of *Eagle vs Shark* (2007) via the US indie film institution the Sundance Institute, and who is frequently compared to Anderson.[3] Cast the net wider, and geekdom pervades virtually every aspect of contemporary Hollywood, from the comic book remakes that dominate box offices to geek/slacker/stoner comedies like *Knocked Up* and *Superbad* (Judd Apatow, 2007; Greg Mottola, 2007).[4]

Thomas reads *Rushmore* as departing from the verisimilitudi-nous characterization of mainstream film, which treats characters as causal agents whose expressiveness is cued through "acting signs"[5] and enhanced through formal techniques such as close up and reaction shots, producing a naturalism "designed to minimise ambiguity . . . communicate information about character interiority and motivation, and encourage . . . affective connection . . . whether it be sympathy, empa-thy or antipathy" (also complemented by mise en scène, etc.).[6] Instead, there is "a minimalism of actor movement and gesture in relation to the camera's field of vision, deadpan or impassive facial expressions, and a relative sparsity of dialogue enunciated with 'flat' vocal intonations."[7] The characters are not sympathetic in the conventional way, and become part of "melancomic" films that mix distance and empathy.

The ultimate aim of this chapter is to provide a reading of Waititi's first feature film, which many compared to contemporary US indie films such as *Napoleon Dynamite* (Jared Hess, 2004) and *Punch-Drunk Love* (Paul Thomas Anderson, 2002).[8] How does Waititi, as a New Zealand Māori director, respond to a discourse that is predominantly white and Anglo-American? Is his film simply an imitation or does it rather par-ticipate in a larger discourse of nerd-dom, and what is that discourse? How are nerds located in relation to discourses of identity, for example gender and ethnicity? My argument is that nerds can be read as popular culture intellectuals, ambivalently associated with various kinds of "low" culture—ambivalent because historically intellectuals associate with high culture or are defined by their ability to make judgments or dis-tinctions between high and low culture.[9] But the popular culture intel-lectual's work consists of legitimizing low culture by reconceptualizing and labeling it through acts of connoisseurship, criticism, collecting, and the like. The low is often associated with minorities—ethnic and sexual subcultures, and low-status genres like comedy, and intellectuals both help "mainstream" such cultures and gain credibility or cultural capital from associating with their rise. A connected point is how intellectuals predict and engage with "new media"—culminating in the rise of the techno-geek or computer nerd. This trend began in the 1960s, with Andy Warhol, a key influence on US indie film:[10] "'hip,' 'camp,' 'bad' or 'sick' taste, and, most recently, postmodernist 'fun' . . . are opportunities for intellectuals to sample the emotional charge of popular culture while guaranteeing their immunity from its power to constitute social identities that are in some way marked as subordinate."[11] Nerd and geek often intersect with Jewish stereotypes like nebbish and schlemiel, and Jewish characters (e.g., Harvey Pekar), actors (Jason Schwartzmann, Adam Sandler, Ben Stiller, and Thora Birch), and directors (Jared Hess, Noah Baumbach, Todd Haynes, Miranda July, and Jason Reitman) recur in this chapter.

At the same time, nerds are subject to similar kinds of stereotyping as low culture and its associated identities. They continually defend their tastes and choices, but unlike traditional intellectuals, cannot shelter behind institutional authority. Moreover, unlike other intellectuals, nerds often get represented in popular culture—because "in the US there is a very powerful, almost ubiquitous (classed discourse) of jocks vs nerds."[12] Nerds have even been described as a subculture.[13] Unlike other intellectuals, they don't get to be invisible mediators. "The history of [US] popular culture is . . . not simply a history of producers . . . and/or a history of consumers. . . . It must also be a history of intellectuals . . . experts in culture whose traditional business is to define what is popular and what is legitimate . . . and who occasionally make their own . . . forays [into popular culture]."[14]

Nerds are positioned between production and consumption, because they are gatekeepers (as intellectuals often are) or because they participate in both production and consumption (and are represented as doing so).[15] The intellectual has an ambivalent relation to popular culture, judging it from above but also longing to participate, an ambivalence returned by popular culture: are they eggheads or experts? Intellectual attitudes toward popular culture are both "strategies of containment" (ways of regulating and taming threats to hegemony) and powerful conduits for expressions of social desire that would otherwise be considered illegitimate: "'hip' and 'camp' . . . are . . . components of the respective cultural politics that preceded . . . the civil rights and gay liberation movements."[16] Nerds have an affinity with identities marginalized by ethnicity or gender/sexuality, but it is a shifting alliance. For example, derogatory terms applied to minorities can be reappropriated by groups they are aimed at, but "nerd" and "geek" lack the taboo force of "faggot," "slut," or "nigger." Thus, nerds are both "abject" and "privileged."[17] Heather Mendick and Becky Francis studied high school nerds, which should remind us that nerds are also associated with childishness.[18]

Mendick and Francis's study only really covers high school, so what happens later? With the rise of digital culture and associated boffin expertise, the nerd is central to modern life. Another aspect of this changing trajectory is nerds as fans—from music connoisseurship, to film watching, to participation in video game and comic/fantasy fiction and of course digital culture. Once characterized as obsessive, fan practices have become central to discussions of online "convergence culture" and "spreadable media."[19] Fan collecting, archiving, and sharing of popular culture has become "curating," and the nerd fan has become a key figure—again demonstrating how nerds can be thought of as avant-garde intellectuals who predict the rise of new forms of media and culture.

Nerds and Identity Politics

Andrew Ross describes how historically white subcultures allied themselves with African American culture, even if the explicit identification with "blackness" gradually became a more general identification with marginality, producing a range of alternative identities, of which nerds could be an example.[20] For example, Jews and African Americans linked through the entertainment industry, the archetypal (and problematic) example being the first sound film, *The Jazz Singer* (Alan Crosland, 1927), in which Al Jolson (himself Jewish) plays a Jew who defies his parents and becomes a singer performing in blackface, revealing the complex accommodations ethnic performers had to make with racism.[21] In the frat comedy *Revenge of the Nerds* (Jeff Kanew, 1984), nerds associate with an African American fraternity to resist jock bullying, which is presented in racist terms, including a burning sign on the nerds' front lawn—both groups suffer from discrimination "based on sight."[22] Such identifications were increasingly mediated through popular culture and only tenuously related to any original social reality, although audiences could always identify with what they saw on-screen. For example, in *American Splendor* (Shari Springer Berman and Robert Pulcini, 2003), comic book writer Harvey Pekar (Paul Giamatti) upbraids his geek friends: "Go to the movies and daydream, but *Revenge of the Nerds* ain't reality. It's just Hollywood bullshit." However, his friends (including his wife, Joyce [Hope Davis]), disagree. In retrospect, Pekar admits, "Okay, maybe I was bein' so harsh . . . on account a' my own problems." Pekar is a record collector, and "curating" African American music, usually vinyl, is a leitmotif of nerdiness in millennial US film, other examples including Seymour (Steve Buscemi) in *Ghost World* (Terry Zwigoff, 2001), continuing the African American connection. In both cases, there is also a feminist theme. Pekar notes that his troubles relate to his wife: "I wasn't even married a month and my old lady was already showin' signs a' trouble. Granted, I tend to get married fast 'cos I'll take any woman that'll have me." Similarly, in *Ghost World*, Seymour's troubles multiply due to his involvement with nerd goth girl Enid (Thora Birch). Geek girls, like femmes fatales, are sexually assertive (Enid is a bit of both). "Harvey, we better skip this whole courtship thing and just get married," says Joyce in *American Splendor*. Similarly, in *Punch-Drunk Love* (2002), Lena Leonard (Emily Watson) pursues protagonist Barry Egan (Adam Sandler). Nerdy men depend on women to initiate sexual relationships (also a theme in *Eagle vs Shark*). The gaze feminizes the nerd in an ironic inversion of Laura Mulvey's model.[23] This also plays into the Jewish male stereotype of the sexually passive schlemiel. All of these models tend to situate the nerd as insufficiently masculine, as effeminate. "Boffin girls and boys tend to be pathologized as homosexual in the case of boys and asexual in the case of girls."[24] Will Straw (in an article on record collecting) describes a continuum of masculinity from the nerd to the brute to the dandy, the brute a traditional aggressive masculinity, with the two alternatives on the fringe:

> The dandy . . . manifests a mastery of the most social of codes, [but] the sense that his persona is frivolous or depthless . . . is the frequent basis of his denigration. Inversely the nerd is noted for a master of knowledges whose common trait is that they are of little use in navigating the terrains of social intercourse. . . . Both the dandy and the nerd are characterized by a relationship to knowledge that is semiotically rich and easy material for parody.[25]

Straw distinguishes two types but then connects them—both provide models for new forms of alternative culture, one around form, one around content, the combination producing a new kind of artist/consumer who both knows and displays his or her knowledge in symbolic forms. A parallel (though not exact) is Andrew Ross's "hip" and "camp" taste, two strategies by which intellectuals engage with popular culture.[26]

Andy Warhol—Silver Screen, Super Nerd

Andy Warhol was a geeky guy with a bad self-image, bullied at school, and mother-fixated, who found in popular culture a means of escape by creating larger-than-life personae, as a dandy, reverencing pop culture stardom, fame, and glamour. He was both an artist and a fan, a new kind of artist/intellectual whose nerdiness was a way of combining these two categories—for example, apparent social dysfunction allowed him to combine intellectualism and childishness. Warhol was frequently described as "simple," nonverbal, childlike, and helpless, even "catatonic," but always by knowledgeable people.[27] This persona of a "blank" or *faux naïf* suggested that Warhol was incapable of doing anything except watching.[28] But his voyeurism created a public space for others to perform—the Factory. His blank gaze created multiple personae, a succession of media "stars," who were famous "for being famous." Connectedly, Warhol envisioned the artist/intellectual as his mass cultural "opposite," the audience/consumer/fan: "his famous mute withdrawal is a devoted fan's attention to his culture."[29] His worship of stardom demonstrated how fans and stars produced each other, just as commerce and art were inseparable: hence pop art.[30]

Warhol's power (cultural capital) came from his gaze, that is, his ability to make people feel they were being watched. Unlike the traditional intellectual, he did not pass judgment; his persona "was neither exactly complicit or dissenting, since it was based on an outright refusal of the act of judgment . . . an attitude of pure *indifference*."[31] He let the audience judge the objects of consumer culture that, like a TV screen, he represented for them. His apparent suspension of judgment was double edged. Its noncommittal passivity was also its claim to superiority, as in Bourdieu's "pure gaze": "a systematic refusal of all that is 'human.' . . . the passions, emotions and feelings which *ordinary* people put into their *ordinary* existence."[32] It does not necessarily imply a free-for-all polysemy; rather, categories of camp and bad taste became institutionalized in a burgeoning alternative discourse, as its "pseudo–aristocratic patrilineage."[33]

Warhol combined the fan and the auteur, passivity and power, low and high culture, to create postmodernism. Its central question was "Is it real?" which Warhol answered in multiple ways. His very art practice was a "put-on," and his documentation of everyday objects and events—soup cans, car crashes, film stars' publicity pics—mimicked televisual "immediacy" and the direct address of "live" TV and TV advertising.[34] TV combines immediacy with hypermediacy—the awareness that everything is mediated.[35] His *Screen Tests* (1964–66) were documents on one level, but also auditions (for would-be Factory stars) and thus fictions, and this ambiguity informs all of Warhol's work, influencing new forms like alternative cinema. Hypermediacy was also conveyed through Warhol's eclecticism: like TV, his art was a collage of different practices and media.

Post-Warhol Cinema

> Pop artists "say neither No nor Yes to the world. They don't accept things as they are, they make fun of them, they make use of them out of context, but they don't rebel against anything. They have made use of every scrap of information . . . that comes their way."[36]

Warhol prophesied many of the forms of alternative culture: he was "committed to setting up an alternative studio system."[37] Accordingly, "post-pop" cinema has moved through and beyond the distancing mechanisms of pop art.[38] It moves from "neither No nor Yes" toward "Maybe."[39] One example is "smart" cinema,[40] characterized by Warholian blank disengagement, irony, dampened affect, and authorial effacement and exemplified by films like Todd Solondz's *Happiness* (1998) and Todd Haynes's *Safe* (1995), which some found "pointlessly and simplistically grim."[41] Other critics point out shared thematic concerns of interpersonal alienation within the white middle class, and within contemporary consumer culture—"smart people in a stupid world."[42] Films like *Ghost World* present characters who, like Warhol, combine nerdy collecting with highly developed taste and judgment: pop culture intellectuals. Their smartness consists not in refusing a "stupid world" but in making selections within it, presenting the "stupid" as potentially "smart." Their practices include "decade blending," combining elements from different decades to create a personal mood,[43] and they practice "the politics of constructing your identity from the products of consumer capitalism."[44] These techniques echo the conventions of post-pop genres more generally, from "smart" to the more recent "quirky" film.[45]

In terms of techniques, Jeffrey Sconce describes frequent use of long shots, static composition, little camera movement, and sparse cutting, resulting in longer shot lengths. In Todd Haynes's *Safe* (1995), camera and characters often remain stationary, resulting in a tableau presentation and static long takes with straight-on, level framing. James MacDowell discusses "static, flat looking, medium long or long shots that feel nearly geometrically even, depicting isolated or carefully arranged characters, sometimes facing directly toward us, who are made to look faintly ridiculous or out of place by virtue of the composition's rigidity,"[46] as in *Punch-Drunk Love, Napoleon Dynamite*, and the films of Wes Anderson. At the same time, the "static tableau" might also include cultural references for the discerning audience: "a culture (or more to the point, an audience) of master semioticians, hyper-aware of how and what objects . . . signify."[47]

Most critics describe the absorption of postmodernism into US alternative film in terms of a movement from "smart" cinema, associated with "shock" and extremity—for example *Happiness*'s representations of pedophilia and mass murder set to library music—toward a gentler kind of post-postmodernism variously related to New Sincerity[48] or metamodernism,[49] which alternate between irony, distance, and a more old-fashioned identification with character: "a knife-edge of judgement and empathy, detachment and engagement, irony and sincerity."[50] Thomas coins the term "melancomic" and MacDowell "quirky": both labels suggest a less confrontational approach. *Me and You and Everyone We Know* (Miranda July, 2005) presents pedophilia, children's sexuality, and online "grooming" in a more nuanced fashion than earlier "smart" films, partly by focusing more on child characters' perspectives—blankness connoting naivety rather than menace, a strategy also used by Waititi. Quirky films often use comic actors, often with stand-up backgrounds: Bill Murray, Will Ferrell, Adam Sandler, Ben Stiller, Steve Carell, and Jack Black (again like Waititi). The comedy is awkward but less likely to be shocking. It's cringy.

Cringe Comedy and Quirk

Much comedy of cringe or embarrassment relates to documentary conventions and thus mockumentary—for example, TV shows like *The Office* (2001) and films like *Borat* (2006)—what has been termed "comedy verité."[51] The awkwardness of the comedy relates to its closeness to "real-life" situations, or the ambiguity of not knowing how to "take" a situation or a person. The postmodern motif— "Is this (for) real?"—takes on a special resonance, demonstrating again how post-pop mixes real and fictive. All comedy has a documentary aspect: "comedy undermines our involvement with the characters, barely maintaining a dramatic illusion . . . and invites us to observe plot machinery as machinery."[52] And, of course, it also takes place in real life.

According to Henri Bergson, "The kind of observation from which comedy springs . . . is directed outwards" and toward the general, as opposed to art, which is concerned with the inward and the unique.[53] Bergson suggests that comedy deals with generalities—with that which does not change. In comedy, nature is a machine, a set of predictable functions. Hence its focus on rigidity in behavior, on characters who are machine-like or who interpret life according to a fixed scheme. Such a definition can embrace both philosophers and clowns: laughter arises from their failure to adapt to the demands of life and social convention. Quirky humor often mocks the vanity of expertise: the (would-be) intellectual or the artist, whose pretensions are played for laughs. In quirky film, child characters behave like adults, displaying a rigidity unbecoming to their age, like Max Fischer, and often balancing out adult characters who behave *childishly*, like clowns or child-men, such as Barry Egan (Adam Sandler) in *Punch-Drunk Love* (2002) and Lars Lindstrom (Ryan Gosling) in *Lars and the Real Girl* (Craig Gillespie, 2007). Both sets of characters feature in films about marital problems, with adults squabbling and children taking responsibility (as, for example, in *Little Miss Sunshine* [Jonathan Dayton and Valerie Faris, 2006], *The Squid and the Whale* [Noah Baumbach, 2005], *Running with Scissors* [Ryan Murphy, 2006], *Rushmore*, *The Royal Tenenbaums* [Anderson, 2001], and *Juno* [Adam Reitman, 2007]). The category of nerd can embrace adult and child, intellectual and clown.

Cringe comedy typically depends on singular, "incorrigible" characters who seem unaware of their social dysfunction and often get away with their behavior, causing audience discomfort, such as the pretentious David Brent (Ricky Gervais) in *The Office* or Larry David in *Curb Your Enthusiasm* (2000-). Whereas conventional comedy is "closed"[54]—the sitcom, for example, recycles a few characters and situations, thus facilitating "corrective" plot machinations by which deluded characters get their comeuppance—in cringe or comedy verité, with their more open or documentary-type narratives, this may not occur. It is this art/life ambiguity that is exploited in quirk—we're not sure whether to laugh (because it's a comedy) or be shocked (because it's like life).

The aural equivalent of Warhol's blank gaze in comic terms is understatement—which could, in nerd terms, be interpreted as an autistic inability to respond appropriately to emotional or melodramatic situations, comic because it highlights automatism and relevant because both nerds and intellectuals can be characterized as socially inept. James MacDowell cites a scene in *Rushmore* where Max Fischer and Herman Blume (Bill Murray) have been attempting to kill each other (not your typical comedy scenario). Max tells Herman: "I was going to have that tree over there fall on you." "That big one?" replies Herman. "That would have flattened me like a pancake."[55] Deadpan delivery gives the scene its quirky edge. Just as Warhol played it straight to incite his wannabes to greater heights of excess, so quirky actors deadpan to make the audience squirm uncontrollably.

Painful slapstick is another comic device used in these films. Slapstick, like all comedy, depends on emotional distance. In these films, however, slapstick tends to occur unexpectedly and suddenly to characters who are not overtly set up as clowns, and thus our experience mixes shock with laughter. For example, Barry Egan (Adam Sandler) in *Punch-Drunk Love* alternates between comic pratfalls and random acts of violence, keeping the audience on edge.

Quirk Conventions

These films are not only about eccentric people, they are also made by and for them, and this can be shown by the range of metafictional devices they use, which combine a blank gaze with camp exaggeration, as in pop art. Quirk has been described as an aesthetic of excessive neatness: a quasi-obsessive compulsive desire to impose order on the filmic world.[56] I have already discussed some of the shot types used, with their emphasis on symmetry; there is also the "God's eye" shot, in which we view objects from directly above, making them look 2D, creating a sense of objectivity and distance from human affairs, as in a map ("planimetric" or "topographic"), as seen, for example, in the title sequences of *The Royal Tenenbaums* (2001) and *Napoleon Dynamite*. Such devices suggest the ordering and curating of reality into boxes, a desire to label and pin life; the use of captions and intertitles throughout Wes Anderson films like *Rushmore* and *The Royal Tenenbaums* continues this trend. It produces a metacinematic or distancing effect. But there is also the semiotic richness of the arrangement of elements in these tableaux, their layers of reference to popular and other culture, usually retro. The combination of distance and retro culture can produce a camp effect: "A celebration . . . of the alienation, distance and incongruity reflected in the very process by which . . . value can be located in some obscure . . . object."[57] Finally, the use of animation and children's drawings (as seen in *Napoleon Dynamite, Eagle vs Shark, Juno*, and *I Heart Huckabees* [David O. Russell, 2004]) creates a complex effect balanced between *faux naif* (the "innocence" of children's art) and knowingness (the heightened sense of artifice that animation, for example, brings to a supposedly adult film).

Another feature of quirky film is the music soundtrack. There are three main approaches. The first is the use of obscure, archival popular music, with no obvious relation to the diegesis, instead suggesting the connoisseurship and discernment of the auteur (as seen in Wes Anderson films like *Rushmore* and *The Royal Tenenbaums*, but also Baumbach's *The Squid and the Whale*, which uses Bert Jansch recordings). This can also be an example of "decade blending,"[58] the popular culture of one era being imposed on another, creating a sense of hybridity and eccentricity. Sometimes the obscure music is diegetic, in which case it indexes the characters' eccentricity (as happens in *American Splendor and Ghost World*). The second approach is soundtrack music with the "tinkling purity of a child's music box,"[59] typically arpeggios or simple melodies, often in waltz time, played on keyboards (glockenspiels, marimbas, celestes and harpsichords), sometimes favoring a high, chiming register (as seen in *Me and You and Everyone We Know, Lars and the Real Girl, I Heart Huckabees*, and *Punch-Drunk Love*). Pianos, arpeggios, and waltz times connote nostalgia for the formal perfection of classical music,

with connotations of middle-class aspiration. Early electronic keyboards and high, tinkly glockenspiel sounds connote quirky childhood,
arrested male adolescence, and possibly gay themes. A third approach is
lo-fi indie music, often acoustic, gesturing toward freak folk and "twee"
genres. Often this is associated with characters (especially women) who
make music themselves (as found in *Juno, Me and You and Everyone We
Know, and Eagle vs Shark*). In terms of effect, the music tends to distance us from the action, and in general adds a quirky, naive, ironic, or
comic tone—as opposed to traditional film music, which tends to make
us identify with the characters' emotional worlds, or creates setting in
place or time. All of these devices create quirky effects, and indeed the
epithet itself underlines the eccentricity of the filmmaker, and by extension the audience.

Eagle vs Shark vs. *Napoleon Dynamite*

Waititi developed the idea for the film with his partner at the time, Loren
Horsley (Lily in the film). After the success of *Two Cars, One Night*, the
Sundance Institute approached them about workshopping a script.
Many reviews pointed out resemblances between *Eagle* and "quirky"
films: "The film's off-putting humor and polarizing anti-hero will remind
many of *Napoleon Dynamite*."[60]

The male protagonists of the two films, Jarrod (Jemaine Clement)
in *Eagle* and Napoleon (Jon Heder) in *Napoleon Dynamite*, resemble
each other: they both wear glasses, are clumsy or maladroit, lack social
skills, avoid eye contact and extended conversations with other characters, have eccentric hobbies, and style themselves as artists but wear
unfashionable clothes and have unflattering haircuts. Both the lead
female characters, Lily in *Eagle* and Deb Bradshaw (Tina Majorino)
in *Dynamite*, have similar presences, although they do smile and are
more sociable. In narrative terms, both films are "odd couple" romantic
comedies.

Cinematography

Dynamite uses the front-on, symmetrically framed, facing-camera
style of presenting characters from quirky and smart film, typified by
its first shot—a long shot of the main character standing center, facing

camera, in front of a plain brick bungalow (putatively his home). Conversations between characters are sometimes rendered by graphically matched reverse shots (for example, doorstep conversations between Napoleon and Deb [11.00] and the conversation of Napoleon's brother Kipling [Aaron Ruell] and Uncle Rico [Jon Gries], set in a fast-food restaurant [24.00]). This device establishes the awkwardness of the characters via the departure from naturalism and the denial of conventional affective cues for the audience, who instead face characters gazing at them.

Eagle uses the same device extensively in its early scenes. The first image of the film is Lily's face centrally framed in a mirror, looking at us. She addresses herself and us in the form of a dialogue between herself and an imagined lover. The device connotes awkwardness—it makes the audience into voyeurs; nevertheless, they are being directly addressed. The device of a female character saying, "I love you" directly to camera is similar to the closing shot of Todd Haynes's *Safe* (1995). There, the connotation is self-delusion. The next scene, in the Meaty Boy fast-food franchise, presents more front-on (medium) shots of Lily, except now we are seeing her as a customer would, behind a counter, wearing a uniform. The connotation is of being "boxed in," and her continual glances toward the clock confirm this. Customers approach her in reverse shots, again front-on, which emphasizes confrontation and alienation. The technique highlights Lily as trapped—but also invisible, as she is merely a means to access food. Her self-deprecating gestures, continually glancing downward, and flat vocal tone highlight her discomfort. Then there is a symmetrical shot (3.22) where Lily seems to address the camera directly, as in the opening scene. As the reverse shot moves into focus, a figure emerges in slow motion, mysterious music begins to play, and we see Jarrod approaching the camera purposefully, but at this point he is a customer—he doesn't know her. The increasing tempo of reverse shots between the two, both directly facing, has connotations of romantic meeting. But then Jared looks to the right and exits shot—he has joined the other queue. This parallels both the above-mentioned scenes from *Napoleon*, one in terms of setting (a fast-food restaurant) and one in terms of narrative function (the doorstep conversation between Napoleon and Deb, an interaction based on a female salesperson/male customer relationship, another inversion of the gender norm, but also the first meeting between the lovers-to-be). In both cases, interaction fails: Lily doesn't establish contact with Jarrod, and Deb runs away after Napoleon fails to respond to her "pitch." Further examples of facing camera in the opening scenes include shots of a TV screen, followed by reverse POV shot of Lily and her brother (4.42–50). This screen reverse shot sequence connotes Lily's identification with media, rather than social interaction, and also her depression, as she has just lost her job. *Dynamite* features similar scenes where the main characters stare at a TV screen, with a similar effect. Back at Meaty Boy, where Lily is working out her notice, the same shot setup is used, except that this time Jarrod (reluctantly) is served by Lily (6.50ff). Introducing Jarrod's character in this format has effect of highlighting his social awkwardness, also connoted through his sneering, monosyllabic responses and perplexity at Lily's apparent enthusiasm—he misreads the situation, using Lily as a go-between to invite one of her coworkers to a party.

A further consequence of the facing camera device, which "flout[s] realist conventions of spatial continuity,"[61] is that when it replaces the establishing shot, additional characters may suddenly appear, creating disorientation—for example, apparently intimate discussions between

Direct address? Lily (Loren Horsley) sees her ideal love.

The reverse shot. Jarrod (Jemaine Clement).

Lily and Jarrod (24.42ff), filmed in close-up, are disrupted by a sudden reverse shot revealing another character (Lily's brother Damon, 26.52). The straight-on format has the effect of restricting information, reproducing a nerdy "tunnel vision" that ignores social context. Damon (who is pleasant and socially adjusted) is "out of place" in this film about "losers." In *Dynamite*, a scene at a chicken farm opens on a front-on medium close-up of two elderly, grotesque farm workers (38.43), addressing the camera, but the addressees, the young farm workers, including Napoleon, are not revealed until the reverse shot, so the context is not immediately clear. The audience's surprise is presumably similar to Napoleon's: "Do the chickens have large talons?" he asks, forlornly. "I don't understand a word you just said," a farm worker replies, putting the seal on the mismatch.

Dialogue

The front-on technique also features in *Eagle*'s party video game contest (12.59ff), but here I shift emphasis to the dialogue. Lily appropriates Jarrod's invitation, intended for her coworker, to go to a fancy-dress party where participants dress up as their favorite animal, developing the theme of awkward childishness and animals common to both films (Lily dresses as a shark, Jarrod as an eagle). Characters interact mainly

through questions and answers rather than more naturalistic dialogue
(11.02ff):

> **JARROD:** Hi.
> **LILY:** Hi.
> **J:** Who are you guys?
> **L:** I'm Lily . . .
> **DAMON:** She gave you free fries.
> **LILY** (embarrassed): Damon!
> **J:** Oh, yeah. (To flatmate) I got some free fries.
> **J'S FLATMATE:** Cool.
> **J:** Oh, yeah. I told you, eh?
> **J'S FLATMATE:** Yeah, you told me.
> **J:** (to Lily) Where's that chick, Jenny (Lily's coworker)? Why
>   isn't she here?
> **L:** She's a lesbian. She went to a lesbian party.
> **J:** Typical.

Likewise, in *Napoleon*, question and answer is the main format for interactions, for example, early in the film where our anti-hero tries to skip
school, to be rebuffed by his brother (7.00ff):

> *[Phone ringing]*

> **KIPLING:** Hi?
> **NAPOLEON:** Is Grandma there?
> **K:** No, she's getting her hair done.
> **N:** [Sighs]
> **K:** What do you need?
> **N:** Can you just go get her for me?
> **K:** I'm really busy right now.
> **N:** Well, just tell her to come get me.
> **K:** Why?
> **N:** 'Cos I don't feel good.
> **K:** Well, have you talked to the school nurse?
> **N:** No, she doesn't know anything. (Pause). Will you just come
>   get me?

K: No.

N: Well, will you do me a favor then? (Pause) Can you bring
me my Chapstick?

K: No, Napoleon.

Jarrod's conversational attempts reveal his over-quickness to judge and
categorize even the most trivial distinctions, travestying the intellectual
role (11.32ff):

J: I like your costume.

L: Thanks.

J: It's pretty much the second-best outfit here. So, your
favorite animal is a shark?

L: Yep.

J: Pretty cool. I almost came as a shark, actually . . . but then I
realized that an eagle is slightly better.

The focus of the party is a video game contest in which characters
battle each other one-on-one. Again, this doesn't seem conventionally sociable—there is no music or drinking at the party, rather a silent

Staring at the screen. Facing the camera here shows characters' primary
engagement with media.

audience for the pairs of battling contestants. The screen reverse shot format again reveals the characters' primary engagement with media, as opposed to face-to-face sociability.

Lily's video game prowess brings her to Jarrod's attention as she challenges him in the final. Here the pattern of facing camera reverse shots is disrupted as Lily turns repeatedly to look at Jarrod rather than the screen, so that she loses. But she gets into Jarrod's bedroom, leading to a courtship scene (more camera-facing reverse shots) where Jarrod tries to impress Lily with his creations—a model plane, painted eggs, a "watch-wallet": "I guess I gotta keep creating or I'll just die" (18.00), he says, parodying the tortured artist. Similarly, in *Napoleon*, Napoleon tries to impress a girl with a portrait he has drawn of her: "It's probably the best drawing that I've ever done," he says, ignoring her obvious distaste at his childlike rendering. Awkward courtship continues in the *Eagle* scene (19.15ff):

> **J:** Do you wanna kiss?
> **L:** Yep.
> **J:** On the lips, though.
> **L:** Yep. (They kiss).
> **J:** Okay. (Pause) Do you wanna have a lie-down on my bed?
> **L:** Yep.
> **J:** Okay. Do you wanna have sex?
> **L:** Yep.

This leads to a sex scene that demonstrates Sconce's typology of "awkward" romance scenes: "the 'awkward couple' shot (a . . . couple shot in tableau form separated by blank space), the awkward coupling shot (a camera placed directly over the bed recording passionless sex)."[62] We also see, in Jarrod's room, some of that semiotic richness of the mise-en-scène important in quirk—a tape recorder, indicating retro hipster culture, Asian Tae Kwon Do paraphernalia, and candles in the shapes of the Twin Towers and Osama Bin Laden. Similarly, Napoleon experiments with Asian martial arts, draws pictures, and uses outdated media technology.

However, the "romantic" atmosphere is punctured when Jarrod, still in bed with Lily, suddenly makes a phone call (21.18ff): "Hello, is Eric there, please? . . . You're fuckin' dead, you fuckin' Samoan . . . fuck." In a later scene, Jarrod explains to Lily (25.15ff):

J: I need to go home. To my hometown.

L: Oh, that sounds cool.

J: No. It's not cool. It's necessary.

L: Why?

J: Because of my mission. It's time to put my training into use.

L: What do you have to do?

J: Kill a man . . . probably.

L: Who?

J: Eric Elisi. He's Samoan.

L: Why? What did he do?

J: Nearly ruined my life, that's all. He's my high school
    nemesis.

Here the jock/nerd discourse is introduced—Jared wants revenge on a high school bully (Napoleon is also bullied at school). This is also the first scene in which race, which gradually becomes a theme, is mentioned. But the scene is mainly notable for Jarrod's macho language, which suggests a Hollywood fantasy world where problems can be solved through violence. Like Jarrod, Napoleon often adopts an "action man" tone (6.00ff):

> **JOCK** (teasing): Hey, Napoleon, what'd you do all last summer
>   again?
>
> **NAPOLEON:** I told you. I spent it with my uncle in Alaska
>   hunting wolverines.
>
> **JOCK:** Did you shoot any?
>
> **N:** Yes, like fifty of 'em. They kept tryin' to attack my cousins.
>   What the heck would you do in a situation like that?
>
> **J:** What kind of gun did you use?
>
> **N:** A frickin' 12-gauge. What do you think?

Even the subject matter of this exchange gets appropriated in *Eagle* when Jarrod invites Lily to "the new Wolverine movie. It's got Hugh Jackman in it. Apparently, I look like him" (22.42ff). Both films feature nerdish anti-heroes given to delusions of grandeur, who get bullied. Like Jarrod, Napoleon is judgmental: "This is pretty much the worst video ever made"; "A liger . . . [is] pretty much my favorite animal" (28.29). He is surrounded by geeky accomplices who use large, outdated computers and video recorders, can't drive, make childlike drawings and other artwork, try to learn Asian martial arts, and get rejected for dates by high-school cheerleaders. The facing camera device gives a superficial resemblance to Seidman's comedian comedy, and the dialogue exemplifies painful comedy in its incongruous, mechanical nature, with the absence of cues that signal levity.

Mise-en-Scène

The two films share a garish aesthetic dominated by consumer culture, fast-food signage, TV advertising, primitive video graphics, violent color clashes, and a midwestern US trailer park and strip mall look that echoes the unattractive lives of the characters. *Eagle* features a lot of kitsch: domestic interiors with floral print upholstery, velvet paintings and hangings with romanticized images of tigers and horses, and a prominent Cassius Marcellus Coolidge print, *Dogs Playing Pool*, a sentimental, anthropomorphic image with Philistine connotations. Characters sell "tacky" goods: "Awesome Apparel" designer tracksuits in *Eagle*, Tupperware and model sailing ships in *Dynamite*.

The range and mixture of pop culture signifiers in both films is an example of decade blending, rendering the films' periods ambiguous. *Dynamite*'s color palette is dominated by '70s brown, orange, and beige: Uncle Rico drives an orange 1975 Dodge Tradesman, for example. But the film is set during 2004–5—we see the year on Napoleon's student ID card in the title sequence. Deb wears a side ponytail and Napoleon wears Moon Boots, 1980s fashions.[63] Anachronistic video, audio, and digital technologies introduce a retro aesthetic into the films—connoting that the characters are "out of time," out of touch, or nostalgic for "past futures" (in one *Dynamite* sequence, Kipling purchases a time machine, which he sets for 1982, echoing *Back to the Future* [Robert Zemeckis, 1985]).[64] Alternatively, it could suggest a postmodern mix and match aesthetic reflecting the collapsing of time and space that characterizes modernity.

Soundtrack

This eclectic approach continues into the music soundtrack. Napoleon's school dance features 1980s music, including Alphaville's "Forever Young" and Cyndi Lauper's "Time After Time" (both 1984); another scene features "The Rose" by Bette Midler (1979) (15.38ff). Napoleon's climactic performance is to "Canned Heat" by Jamiroquai (1999), although the track sounds like 1970s disco (1.17.22ff). *Eagle* features David Bowie's "Let's Dance" (1983) although in an acoustic cover version by M. Ward from 2003. The soundtrack of *Eagle* is mostly by the NZ group the Phoenix Foundation and features tinkling keyboard sounds associated with quirk, as heard, for example, when Jarrod and Lily first meet (3.25ff). A reflective, baroque harpsichord in Gordon's room reflects idealization of his character (32.30ff). Quirky keyboard tinkles feature occasionally in *Napoleon* (e.g., "Bus Rider" [John Swihart]). Both films have naive musical moments—*Dynamite*'s opening credits are set to a childish acoustic love song, "We're Going to Be Friends" by The White Stripes (2001), whereas *Eagle* features an out-of-tune ukulele ("I Love You, Awesome"). Lily's own attempts to write songs ("Apples and Tangerines") on an out-of-tune guitar also connotes whimsy. "Twee" indie folk/pop tracks ("The Body Breaks," Devendra Banhart [2004]; the Bowie cover) fit the melancholy mood of the latter part of *Eagle*, as opposed to *Napoleon*'s more upbeat tone.

The Differences between the Films

Napoleon is resourceful: he makes friends, notably with Mexican schoolmate Pedro (Efren Ramirez), helping Pedro become class president. He symbolically allies himself, in nerd fashion, with nonwhite culture, and this becomes his redemption. He purchases a video, "D-Qwon's Dance Grooves," and learns hip-hop dance, which leads to the climactic scene where he impresses the high school with his dancing skills. In a related subplot, his brother Kipling finds love online with an African American woman. This bears out Andrew Ross's thesis about intellectuals aligning themselves with African American culture, and to lesser extent a feminist thesis about the power of women characters who are not bound by Western ideals of beauty but exercise agency, albeit in the service of a conventional end. Napoleon appropriates from feminine culture as well, his dancing symbolically set against the cheerleaders who have preceded his performance on the school stage. Of course, Napoleon's dancing is ludicrous, but it shows initiative, unlike Jarrod.

Jarrod as a character seems stuck, and this may be why some reviewers disliked the film: one quotes Waititi saying that Jarrod represents "all the very worst traits of every male you've ever known, including myself, plonked into one package."[65] The action climax of *Napoleon* (his dance) may be ambiguously affirmative, but *Eagle's* is wretched humiliation—Jarrod arranges a public showdown with his Samoan nemesis, Eric (David Fane), only to find him confined to a wheelchair. In a scene of gruesomely painful slapstick (1.13.45ff), Jarrod attacks him but Eric still beats him. The fight unfolds to the unlikely soundtrack of a gently strummed ukulele (The Phoenix Foundation's "Wholly Molly"), underlining the audience's distance from the characters and making Jarrod even more unlikeable.

Jarrod is stuck is because he mourns his mother and especially his brother Gordon, and this is why he dumps Lily. His "revenge mission" is an attempt to change the world back to when "my brother would help out and then we'd kick some serious ass" (29.00), hence his desire to "restore honor to the family name" (39.50). But how can he do this? Does he have the same symbolic resources as Napoleon?

How Gender and Ethnicity Intersect in *Eagle*

Eagle is the only Waititi film in which the central character is female. Her POV is established with the first shot, where Lily talks to herself in the mirror. A female fantasy of impossible love—the dowdy heroine infatuated with an unattainable man—it echoes Australian films like *Strictly Ballroom* and *Muriel's Wedding*, which can be read as camp.[66] The film is dominated by a female gaze, which connects to a "queer" gaze. Lily desires Jarrod, but Jarrod desires his dead brother Gordon (whom we only ever see in photographs and videos); this confirms the gaze as queer/impossible. Gordon is idealized; he is an artist (Lily admires a portrait of Jarrod, which is Gordon's work). In the same scene (in Gordon's room), Lily finds a family portrait where Gordon smiles in easy mastery, symbolically presiding over his once-happy family. He died "saving a kid from a fire at the school" (33.58), says Jarrod, but it's later revealed that he committed suicide; similarly, Jarrod lies about his mother dying. Also in the portrait is Gordon's fiancé, Tracy, a conventional Pākehā netballer, whom Jarrod unsuccessfully courts after dumping Lily. He also unsuccessfully appeals to his father, who is distracted by melancholy and anger at Gordon's death—we see his father weeping over a video of Gordon

winning a running race. So, the structure of the gaze in the film is basically queer—the men all desire the dead brother, and the women are
trapped in this vicious circle, based around loss, melancholia, and queerness. Judith Butler "identifies a culture of 'gender melancholy,' whereby
the gender binary and heteronormativity are established through 'prohi-
bitions which *demand the loss* of certain sexual attachments and demand
that those losses *not* be avowed, and not be grieved."[67] Butler config-
ures "masculinity" and "femininity" as incorporating the excluded and
ungrievable same-sex love-object through heightened gender identification.[68] Jarrod is stuck, being a man.

This gender reading intersects with a reading about ethnicity. The
family portrait suggests that Jarrod's mother is Māori, and Lily appears
to be Pākehā, and although this is never referred to in the film, race is a
factor in the differences between the two. So, *Eagle vs Shark* is an interracial romance, a prominent theme in early NZ film, where it connoted
the possibility of a racially integrated nation. Usually the relationship
was between a Māori woman and a Pākehā man, which mapped onto
a colonized/colonizer binary. The assertion of cultural difference and

Jarrod's family portrait with dead brother Gordon (Taika Waititi) at top.

emergence of identity politics from the 1970s onward tended to make such equations of personal and national romance look dated, however. Here we start to see how *Eagle* and *Napoleon* diverge, and how Waititi approaches the problem of being a nonwhite nerd, which is what Jarrod is. Unlike for Napoleon, escape into a world of "magical" ethnic Otherness is not an option for Jarrod, as he is already Other.

The projection of an erotic, implicitly white, gaze onto Māori/Pasifika cultures has been ongoing since the earliest NZ films. Masculinity is the main symbol of NZ identity in media, at first mainly Pākehā, but Māori/Pasifika men have become more prominent to the point where they are starting to displace Pākehā, in advertising, for example, Waititi himself being an example of this trend. This could be seen as progressive, as positive discrimination, but it is also linked to commodification of the gaze, including female/queer gazes. *Queer Eye for the Straight Guy* (2003), for example, explicitly links a queer/female gaze with commodification of masculinity. It is also linked to eroticization of nonwhite men, who are already marked as Other. As discussed, young brown men are frequently eroticized in visual media, and female characters and the audience often ogle them. We are more likely to see Māori/Pasifika bodies dancing, making love, and fighting on-screen than Pākehā.

Waititi is familiar with stereotypes of eroticized nonwhite masculinity (see chapter 1). Narcissism also features prominently in Waititi's early short films, sometimes explicitly, as in *A Perfect Love* (2008), in which he plays a character who falls in love with his own reflection. This relates back to a key theme of *Eagle*, which is that everybody's in love with Waititi, who plays the dead brother, Gordon. Loren Horsley was also in a relationship with Waititi at the time. So, in a sense, the film features a woman who is in love with Waititi, and who is in love with a man who is also in love with Waititi, in a kind of eternal triangle. But perhaps the point of this mischievous piece of self-casting was to send up the objectification of nonwhite masculinity as an idealized erotic Other. It also shows how Waititi, engaging with the white intellectual discourse that idealizes nonwhite cultures, offers a critique along the lines of the difficulties of being a nonwhite nerd. Unlike for white hipsters, the option of identifying with or desiring an exotic culture is not available for him, nor for his male protagonist, Jarrod, because he is already exotic himself. To buy into the New Zealand integration myth of white/nonwhite intermarriage is also difficult, as nonwhite masculinity is not liberated by representation, but rather subject to another set of gazes. There is no "unmarked" position, that which the intellectual aspires to. Like all geeks, he will always be visible, but especially as a nonwhite. Few of Waititi's other films offer the easy resolution of heterosexual romance, except as a joke (as in Viago's betrothal to a geriatric woman in *What We Do in the Shadows* and Jojo and Elsa's unlikely relationship). Finally, the manner of Gordon's death could also be a commentary on the status of young nonwhite men in Aotearoa/New Zealand, who dominate suicide statistics.[69] Aotearoa/New Zealand has one of the highest suicide rates in the English-speaking world, just behind the US.[70] The film evinces nostalgia for a type of masculinity, physically powerful and accomplished, that is also threatened. Jarrod may be a geek, but at least he's alive. The time of the nerds beckons.

In this chapter I used the "nerd" as a way of investigating gender and ethnic identities in relation to US and NZ film, arguing for its association with alternative cultures such as quirky film, and with a history of popular culture intellectuals. Such intellectuals act to legitimize popular culture but also to gain "cool" by associating with its perceived marginality, and this is reflected in the ambivalent representation of nerds. Andy Warhol is a case study in how a nerd can predict and help create new cultural movements like postmodernism, in turn influencing US indie films and NZ film, producing quirky films that combine comic and avant-garde conventions with socially awkward characters in "painful comedy." But I also argued that the implicit model of the intellectual is of a white man, and that this introduces problems when the nerd is, as in this case, not white. The Māori geek "comedian" character is one that Waititi explores in greater depth, playing the part himself, in *Boy*.

6
BOY AS COMEDIAN COMEDY

Most discussions of *Boy* have overlooked the fact that the film is comic entertainment, instead focusing on the film's representation of Māori, criticizing the use of stereotypes and avoidance of "realities" from child neglect to postcolonial trauma. But stereotypes and fantasy are also generic comic tropes. This chapter reads the film as an example of Steve Seidman's "comedian comedy," a type of film centered around a charismatic comic performer, often with previous experience in nonfilm comedy, a "star" with an extradiegetic presence that intrudes on the film narrative.[1] Waititi's performance as Boy's father, Alamein, can be viewed in this light. Even if he was not initially well known, the film made him a star (and this can be seen in the way that later iterations of the film and paratexts around it increasingly featured Waititi's character). Waititi also "stars" as Michael Jackson in the film. Seidman notes that the comedian can be a disruptive influence both in the mise-en-scène and at the metafictional level: he can explode the "hermetic," closed structure of film narrative via direct address or by referring to other films or texts.[2] At the level of plot and character, the comedian figure is often childishly narcissistic, living in a fantasy world. His comic skills mark him as special but also abnormal.

Waititi's character may not seem as central as we might expect in comedian comedy—after all, the film is called *Boy*, after the character played by James Rolleston. However, comedian comedy may also be based around groups of performers—as with the Marx Brothers and "buddy" duos such as Bob Hope and Bing Crosby—and the comedian figure may have multiple identities in a single film or even a split personality. This device generates dramatic conflict, typically between conformist and nonconformist "halves," just as a comic duo typically features a "straight" and a funny role: the "inflexible straight man [who] fails to perceive the evident absurdity of his adversary and the crimes he perpetrates against language and logic."[3] So, the comedian role can be split between two or more characters. Waititi's character and Boy share the same name, Alamein, are father and son, and are both childish (figuratively or literally), and the narrative concerns their conflict and reconciliation. Furthermore, Waititi's character is constructed as much through Boy's fantasy as through his "real" role—the two characters are interdependent. Boy represents normality and Waititi's character eccentricity, as Boy is the acting matua, or parent, for his family, whereas Waititi's character neglects his parental role. Thus, the comic protagonist is "split" between father and son—Boy's frequent direct address of the camera (a key comedian comedy device) generally presages fantasy sequences about his father, who presents comic spectacles, playing superheroes and media celebrities, like Michael Jackson. Finally, Boy's brother, Rocky (Te Aho Aho Eketone-Whitu, surely named after the *Rocky Horror Show*) also participates in this persona to the degree that he has magical powers, another aspect of Seidman's model.[4] This interpretation of a shared persona could also relate to Māori valuation of family (whānau) and communality or group solidarity (kotahitanga) over individuality, especially when considering the film's ending: "All Maori initiatives have attempted to organize the basic decision making and participation within and around the concept of whanau. . . . The whanau, in pre-colonial times, was the core social unit, rather than the individual. . . . The whanau remains as a persistent way of living and organizing the social world."[5] Finally, reading the film as to some degree autobiographical, in line with auteur theory, all three characters dramatize aspects of Waititi. One is played by him, and has some relation to Waititi's father, who lived in Waihau Bay (the film's setting); Boy is the obvious candidate for Waititi as a child, until we consider Rocky's artistic proclivities and age (nine, the same as Waititi's in 1984).

Typically, the comedian comedy narrative tends to culminate with the comedian's assimilation into the conventional social world, but *Boy* can also be interpreted as a pōwhiri, or ritual encounter between manuhiri (Waititi's character, the visitor) and haukāinga (the residents, Boy and his siblings).[6] A pōwhiri doesn't necessarily involve the sacrifice of individuality; rather it is a managed meeting with the Other.[7] *Boy's* narrative could follow a pōwhiri structure: Boy's initial presentation is a karanga (call), followed by a whaikōrero (discussion of issues), which is the body of the film; a koha (gift or sacrifice), which is the death of Leaf, the goat; a harirū (touching, physical contact), which is Rocky's healing touch on Alamein, and finally a kai (feast, celebration), which is the entire credits sequence.[8] The pōwhiri structure also addresses the underlying plot matter (the death of Boy's mother, who is connected to Leaf). Rocky's "magical powers" are instrumental in reuniting the family. The pōwhiri is also magical as it removes tapu from the visitor, which Rocky's touch accomplishes.[9] Magic is also present in the film's credit sequence, a performative spectacle typical of comedian comedy, which, by mashing up Michael Jackson's "Thriller" video with the Patea Māori Club's "Poi E" in a kapa haka performance, led by Waititi but featuring all of the film's main characters, reconciles real and fantasy worlds, father and sons, and Māori with modernity. At the same time, because the kapa haka sequence occurs outside the film narrative, it is an ambiguous space, where shared fantasy supersedes reality. The kapa haka sequence could demonstrate how communal Māori culture negotiates with the individualistic conventions of comedian comedy. Peter Kramer insists that in comedian comedy, "by the end of the film, the comic character . . . has become an adult," but this individuation is less important in *Boy*.[10] It's more about finding a balance between the main characters, based on their shared love/grief. As *Boy* is a film about children, and takes a child's perspective, it also questions adult "reality."

Academic Assessments

Boy is Waititi's most discussed film; it was early in his career and the most locally successful NZ film ever (until displaced by *Hunt for the Wilderpeople*).[11] Popularity invites varied reactions, especially when indigeneity is highlighted, and the "burden of representation" comes into play.[12] Although Ella Shohat and Robert Stam argue that the "burden" can be lightened by minority groups producing and starring in their own films, *Boy*'s reception suggests a more complex picture. In the *MEDIANZ* issue on the film in 2012, most contributors criticized the film's representation of indigeneity: "participants spoke of the discomfort of watching the film among strangers and the ambivalent effects of the audiences' laughter. Some asked: were these people laughing with or at Māori?"[13]

Māori academic Leonie Pihama objected to Boy's guardian/grandmother attending a funeral at the start of the film, leaving him in charge: "Earlier reflections of *Once Were Warriors* came flooding back. I had entered into the world of lame stereotypes yet again and felt an instant disappointment."[14] "Parental neglect" is a frequent theme, although the editors' aim is "historicising and contextualising the prevalence of this theme in media depictions of things Māori."[15] The fact that many comedies about children have negligible parent presence was overlooked. Misha Kavka and Stephen Turner observe how

> in *Boy* . . . deprivation is signalled everywhere, but it appears as a "natural" part of the landscape, encompassing impoverished homes . . . derelict houses, ruined cars, collective unemployment, missing mothers, deadbeat fathers, and numerous references to the fantasised wealth of the "rich," as opposed to local people's lack of money.[16]

However, writing elsewhere, Barry Barclay suggests:

> Maori tradition tells us there is a time for some things to be left in peace to die . . . often . . . a disused house is left in the field to quietly fall down . . . there are . . . spiritual reasons for a leaving a house that way, and no amount of sneering . . . about "typical untidy Maoris" will persuade a family to dismember an old family building. It even applies to cars.[17]

By the editors' own admission, the issue "does not address the perpetual 'boy-ish'-ness of Waititi's body of work"; there is little discussion of comedy, in which ethnic stereotypes may serve different purposes.[18] David Geary discusses how *Boy* "make[s] a comedy from material that is not ostensibly funny," although this raises the question of what funny material is.[19] Many comedies feature "highly traumatic" environments.[20]

Other commentaries stress the role of comedy in mediating serious issues, Barry Barclay stating that: "a Maori filmmaker has the marae tradition to draw on . . . that makes use of humour and anecdote more freely than other New Zealanders do in situations which are potentially confrontational."[21] Ocean Mercier suggests that comedy in a pōwhiri can mediate issues like parental neglect.[22] Alistair Fox, however, reads *Boy*'s comedy from a Freudian perspective, as a smokescreen for "trauma," an example of the "but also" approach critiqued by Richard Dyer.[23] Waititi distances himself from the "traumatic" approach:

> **Q:** Did you feel pressured at all to like, make a teen commit suicide or have the dad hit the son or something?
>
> **Waititi:** [Laughs] Yeah, well, there was never any interest in that. But I definitely wanted to make something different, just to show a brighter side . . . I don't want to make an "issue" film.[24]

Most relevant to a comic/entertainment reading of the film is Ocean Mercier's article on how Waititi's director's commentary on the *Boy* DVD incorporates Waititi's character in the film in an apparently improvised "dialogue," which is actually a comic monologue.[25] "Waititi's delivery of a feature-length conversation between Taika the director and Alamein the star . . . has a novelty value that is inherently entertaining."[26] It is a remarkable improvisation, which in turn corresponds to Dyer's entertainment values of intensity and transparency, and highlights how "multiple role-playing is a feature of Waititi's on-screen and off-screen work."[27] Alamein is an unreliable, childish character, a trickster, an archetype that Seidman sees as central to comedian comedy (and Gates as central to African American humor).[28] The reality/fiction binary breaks down as Alamein insists that the film is a documentary about himself, although not consistently, as in some places he talks about acting. Is this confusion intentional on Waititi's part and a comment on Alamein's self-delusion, or an error? There's no way of knowing. The African American trickster, the signifying monkey, is relevant when Alamein's comments on the action reference racial stereotypes: "That's why Māori make such good actors . . . We're good at pretending." The trickster is paradoxical, a Cretan liar, a mask for criticism, like a Shakespearean fool or Erasmus's Folly (who speaks, like Alamein, in her own praise), a character we start by laughing at but then find ourselves laughing with.[29] Alamein also offers "political" criticism of the type that Kavka and Turner find the film lacking in: "so many years of oppression and resentment, because, you know, the Māori have had a pretty rough time over the last 160 years," so much that Waititi "tells" Alamein, "Let's not make it political."[30] Alamein is also more likely than Waititi to talk about "traditional Māori ways . . . How we used to do it before the white man came," although the information that there are thirteen months in the year and about the traditional Māori way of giving yourself a hickey (love bite) does not seem reliable. Waititi uses signifying to mock all understandings of Māori culture. The "duo" banter, continually striving to one-up the other, and this style of comic conflict is probably more significant than the veracity of any of the statements made. This stream of "patter" gives Waititi's films their playful tone. Mercier also comments that the packaging and presentation of the enhanced *Boy* DVD emphasizes the character of Alamein.[31] The commentary allows Waititi to comment on the film's reception and to parody, through Alamein, its judgmental tone, as well as giving Alamein a central position. Finally, Alamein's interference in the commentary conforms to Seidman's definition of comedian comedy, in the way that he freely moves in and out of the fiction, producing a performance that disrupts the narrative (both the film and Waititi's director's commentary).

Comedian Comedy

Steve Seidman's "comedian comedy" is "a cinematic hybrid of presentational and representational processes that mediates between a tradition of modular entertainment spectacle . . . and the classical narrative protocols that Hollywood adapted from nineteenth century fiction and drama."[32] The genre centers on a gifted comic performer, sometimes already a "star." Starting with silent film, which frequently centered on performers like Charlie Chaplin or Buster Keaton, comedian comedy continued through the Marx Brothers, W. C. Fields, Bob Hope, and Jerry Lewis (and the various duos they participated in), to more recent examples like Woody Allen, Steve Martin, Eddie Murphy, Jim Carrey, and Mike Myers and (outside the US) Peter Sellers, Norman Wisdom, Jacques Tati, Rowan Atkinson, Steve Coogan, and Sacha Baron-Cohen, among others. The featured comedian's performance may take the form of spectacles that disrupt the narrative flow, like "numbers" in a musical.[33] He is "an anomalous and privileged figure within the world of the film . . . able to step outside its boundaries . . . [and] play with its . . . conventions."[34] This could include performing direct to the camera and stepping out of the narrative to comment on the action, as with Groucho Marx, Bob Hope, Woody Allen, and Waititi/Alamein in the DVD commentary.[35] At the level of plot and character, he is "a child in a world of adults, comically misplaced in the role of the adult hero."[36] His comic skills mark him as special but also abnormal. "The signs of the comedian's creativity are thus simultaneously configured as indicators of the character's aberrance."[37] Of course, the fact that the children are a source of humor in the film is also relevant here. Finally, comedian comedies are highly intertextual, incorporating "references to the self-ness of the film . . . references to other films . . . 'quotes' derived from specific films or film styles."[38] *Boy* is packed with intertextual references, and Boy and Alamein are fans of Michael Jackson, E.T., The Hulk, and Shogun. Seidman argues this relates to the comedian's liminal position between film and real life, and in *Boy* this intertextuality is linked to both the main characters, which supports the idea that they both incarnate aspects of the comedian comedy protagonist.[39] Waititi had reasonably extensive experience as an actor and a stand-up comic before *Boy*, though he wasn't a star. But neither were Charlie Chaplin and Harold Lloyd, whom Seidman discusses, before they made films. Reading *Boy* retrospectively, it is hard to suppress the knowledge that Waititi is playing Alamein and that that character became well known to the public. Indeed, Waititi has appeared in all of his films, and as 2017 New Zealander of the Year, is clearly now a star. Thus, it is possible to argue that comedian comedy is relevant to Waititi's oeuvre.

The Film

Boy is set in 1984 in Waihau Bay, New Zealand, the place and time where Waititi partly grew up, in the house featured in the film.[40] Although Waititi has insisted that the film is not directly autobiographical, he has recently stated that his father did spend time in jail, and was a gang member.[41] Boy, Rocky, and Alamein can all be read autobiographically, but, more importantly, address aspects of the comedian protagonist. The film opens with a brief montage of local locations to the strains of "Poi E," which thus brackets the film. But the first character we see is Boy, addressing the camera directly, thus establishing his centrality. His opening karanga calls specifically to his father, the manuhiri, or visitor. Waititi first appears in a series of comic live action cutaways that represent Boy's narrated fantasies about his dad, presented in the context of a classroom presentation: "He's a busy man. He's a master carver, deep-sea treasure diver, the captain of the rugby team and he holds the record for punching out the most people with one hand." In succession we see brief shots of Waititi carving, posing in a scuba outfit, single-handedly scoring a try, and "punching out" the entire opposing team. A reverse shot reveals a classroom of kids, indifferent to Boy's tale. In response to classmate Kingi's whispered taunt: "Your dad's not overseas. He's in jail for robbery!" Boy responds: "Not anymore, he escaped." Another cutaway reveals Waititi, dressed in comical prison stripes, emerging from a tunnel, wielding the spoon he has used to dig his way out to overcome a guard. These cutaways have a cartoonish quality: they are silent slapstick or parodies of genre texts. They establish Waititi as a comic fantasy figure, as in Seidman's model: "By creating a fantasy existence, the comic figure demonstrates his imaginative powers . . . Many of these fantasy projections take the form of familiar genre films, which permit the comic figure to assume the dimensions of 'real' movie heroes," the complicating factor being, of course, that they are Boy's fantasies, not Alamein's, though this fact also tends to link the two characters together.[42] It would be possible to dispense with these inserts if the film was not a comedy, underlining how comic spectacle may be superfluous to exposition, and could be viewed as "a counter-tendency" to traditional Hollywood narrative.[43] Humor is also generated through the incongruity between Boy's words and the accompanying visuals (listing his school subjects, "social studies" is illustrated by a brief scene in which bullies throw water on Boy's pants). The playful nature of this opening montage of images, comic or childish (Rocky's animated crayon pictures), and Boy's colorful narration (Michael Jackson "lives in a castle with a snake and a monkey") encourages the audience to identify with a child's perspective. Waititi comments:

> I had a really amazing childhood. I grew up half in the city, half in the country. In the country, you know, where *Boy* was set, it was pretty different times from now, like where kids were brought up to look after each other and given a lot more freedom. A difference from now where children's whole lives are organized, regimented.[44]

Accordingly, much of *Boy*'s comedy is childish and playful, even infantile ("Kingi shat his pants!"), again characteristic of comedian comedy.[45] The humorous use of children offsets to some degree the representation of Māori stereotypes: a tight shot of Boy's grandma framed in the window of a departing car, saying "Goodbye, my mokos" (mokopuna, or grandchildren) is followed by a shot of the mokopuna—pushing the car. Another gag addresses racism, although "reverse racism," a characteristic Waititi technique:

> **SCHOOL PRINCIPAL:** People call me a dumb honky all the
>   time. I don't go around punching them out.
> **BOY:** Why not?
> **PRINCIPAL:** Because they're usually children.

Boy's opening presentation can also be read as a "gag sequence," another convention of comedian comedy, featuring various kinds of humor, some of it slapstick, much of it premised on the gap between Boy's awareness and the audience's. He plays the "straight man," unaware of the buffoonery of Waititi's character and his own comedy. Nevertheless, Alamein is dependent on Boy for his visualization.[46]

The Film's Comic Style

However, not all of the film's humor is conventional. Seemingly innocent details in Boy's narration: "My friends are Dallas and her sister Dynasty. They also have a sister called Falcon Crest," strike the audience as incongruous, but the film cleverly changes tack as the theme of names continues: "My real name is Alamein. I'm named after my dad and he's named after some place where the Māori battalion fought during World War II. Dad's brothers and sisters are Faenza, Tunisia, Libya . . ." The funniness is undercut by the reference to war and to real life—it is not unusual for Māori to take such names. Throughout the film, Waititi/Alamein's antics are amusing or interesting to Boy alone, partly because they are often his fantasies. When Alamein attempts a gag in real life, spectators appear indifferent. This deadpan style is a major factor in the film's comic style, as in conventional comedies, laughs are generally signaled by the over-reactions of the supporting cast: "spectators . . . react . . . in astonishment, as if they are committed to the conventions of classical realism."[47] But when Alamein attempts a cool Dukes of Hazzard–style jump into his car, he gets stuck in the window. The onlooking kids offer no reaction, making Alamein's predicament as embarrassing as it is amusing. Nevertheless, the overall effect of these deadpan reactions is to further isolate the Boy/Alamein dyad as comic outsiders: "the outlaw/fugitive and the loner/reject," in line with Seidman's theory.[48]

The key trope that establishes Alamein's centrality is Boy's enraptured gaze, which frequently also directly addresses the camera (as occurs at the beginning of his karanga), contrasting with the looks of other characters toward Alamein, which are generally skeptical or indifferent. It sets the stage for Alamein/Waititi's performance. In his initial meeting with his Dad, Boy is front-on, center frame in a reverse shot sequence, which juxtaposes his expectant gaze with Alamein's avoidance of it, a juxtaposition echoed in the dialogue:

> **ALAMEIN** (impatiently): Who are you?
> **BOY** (smiling): Boy.
> **ALAMEIN** (impatiently): What boy?
> **BOY:** Alamein.
> **ALAMEIN:** Yeah (pauses). Alright, I'm your dad.
> **BOY:** (surprised, excited) Oh! Hey, Dad!

Alamein's laconic responses reference guarded, impassive "Kiwi bloke" masculinity, which seems incongruous in the context of a long-delayed family reunion.[49] Boy's offer of a cup of tea, clearly intended as an invitation, is comically misunderstood, as the next shot reveals Waititi and his mates (Chuppa and Juju, named for local varieties of children's candy) drinking tea, still in the car. As Alamein becomes gradually more animated, he adopts a characteristic rising inflection that Mercier describes as "rural Māori" and often carries comic connotations, as in the work of Billy T James.[50] The following sequence in the house also features a comic symmetry of reverse shots where Alamein and his mates are framed front-on on one side of the kitchen table, with Boy and his siblings on the other. Waititi now starts to perform the child/man persona, characteristic of comedian comedy:

ALAMEIN: Seen *E.T.* yet, the movie?
BOY: No. What's it about?
ALAMEIN: Spaceman. Oh, space kid, really. He gets trapped on Earth and him and this kid fly around everywhere on a bicycle. I seen it four times.

"Direct address . . . [and] quotes from, or references to, other films, and references to the world of showbiz . . . [are] all endemic to comedian comedy."[51] Waititi then takes center stage and performs direct to camera, using a sparkler, at first awkwardly, but encouraged by Boy's admiring looks, eventually using it to draw images and words. Seidman comments: "the subjective world of the comic figure . . . becomes magical. . . . It is generally the magic of the movie medium (e.g., special effects, sound, elliptical devices) that produces . . . these powers."[52] Clearly, Alamein's sparkler images are CGI-enhanced (and Rocky's drawings are animated). Some anomalous details offset his quasi-magical evocation: Alamein turns to reveal a gang "patch" on the back of his jacket; the words he writes are "Fuck the world" (but inverted as a mirror image); and at the end of his show, he moves a painting to reveal swastika graffiti on the wall. "I did that. Don't get into the Nazi stuff," he tells Boy, conspiratorially. This presentational sequence demonstrates how "the comedian . . . [is] not simply a misfit-hero, but deviant with respect to the more general 'rules' of identity and 'adult' maturity."[53] Indeed, it seems likely that many of Alamein's later flights of fancy are due to marijuana.

The Two Alameins

Having established the main relationship in the film between the two Alameins, Waititi brings them into conflict. A key moment is when Alamein attempts to renounce his paternity:

ALAMEIN: And can you stop calling me "Dad"? It sounds weird. Besides, we're more like bros, you and me.
BOY: Then what shall I call you?
ALAMEIN: I don't know. What do you reckon?—Alamein?
BOY: Maybe.
ALAMEIN: What about "Shogun"? I like that.

BOY: What's Shogun?
ALAMEIN: Samurai master. Like a commander. He rules the
  samurais.
BOY: Like ariki [high chief, lord]?
ALAMEIN: Yeah, but he's a samurai. Samurais are better.
BOTH: Shogun.
ALAMEIN: Yeah. Oh, that sounds good!
BOY: So what should we call me?
ALAMEIN: I don't know. "Little Shogun"? That'd be funny.

This exchange shows Alamein refusing to play the role ascribed to him by society and by Boy. Mercer describes it as the nub of the whaikōrero: to deny your whakapapa (genealogy, links to your whānau), is deeply problematic in Māori culture.[54] Alamein resists fatherhood, instead imagining himself as a Japanese martial arts hero (referencing James Clavell's novel and its 1980 TV dramatization). Henceforth, Boy's attitude to Alamein changes. He starts to imitate Alamein, attempting to repeat his sparkler trick to his friends in front of the store, and later borrowing his gang jacket and boasting to his friends in a macho style, literally trying to take his father's place. Increasingly, his fantasies compensate for Alamein's shortcomings, in that they temporally coincide with and fill in for Alamein's behavior. Rather than imagining Alamein as his father, he imagines him as Michael Jackson. In his karanga, Boy explains that Michael Jackson is his favorite person, repeating this information three times, also claiming that "When [Dad] comes home, he's taking me to see Michael Jackson live." When Alamein gets drunk and obnoxious at a party, Boy transforms his father's behavior into a sequence from the "Billie Jean" video, enabling him to maintain his idealized view. "Fantasies provide an opportunity for the comic figure to accomplish what he is unable to do in his real environment, which is presented as highly traumatic," comments Seidman, though again the situation is more complex as two characters are involved, one setting the scene via direct address, and one performing.[55] Boy plays the "straight man" or audience to Alamein's performance. Both this and the following example demonstrate how aggression is transformed into play by Boy, which then becomes humor for the audience, thus demonstrating the humor as mock-aggression thesis.

Boy transforms his father's drunken antics into a sequence from Michael Jackson's "Billie Jean" video.

Boy transforms a gang brawl into a sequence from Michael Jackson's "Beat It" video.

The second Jackson homage sequence also occurs at a traumatic moment—when Alamein is confronted by Dynasty's dad's gang about stealing their marijuana. Once again, Boy transforms the scene into a Jackson video—this time "Beat It," aptly enough. Gang warfare is the link between song and filmic action: in both sequences violence is choreographed into dance moves, but in real life, Alamein's gang, the Crazy Horses, are getting a beating. In both sequences, Boy's enraptured gaze to camera signals the movement into a fantasy space. "As with the musical, a convention of comedian comedy is the placing of diegetic enclosures within narrative to provide space for ostentatious performance."[56] This observation is peculiarly pertinent as Waititi/Alamein performs dance moves, demonstrating his physical expertise, while at the same time the situation is humorous (he is imitating someone else, and his performance is inappropriate, given the real circumstances). Philip Drake comments how "comedian performers . . . represent a character in the fictional narrative while at the same time signifying a star, outside of that character."[57] Drake is referring to the character as a real-life star, in this case Waititi, but this example has additional "star" connotations arising from Waititi's Jackson impersonation. Notably, the sequence of Jackson homages in the film parallels the actual historical sequence of the videos: "Billie Jean," "Beat It," then "Thriller." They are a microcosm of Jackson's evolution on *Thriller* from a relative innocent, to a street fighter, to a werewolf, possibly also a metaphor for his changing public image, which became increasingly controversial, also paralleling Boy's developing awareness of his father's flaws, indeed his split personality. At the same time, the relationship of the two Alameins remains close, even codependent in the sense that Boy's fantasy compensates for his father's deficits. Seidman notes how "the comic figure is . . . capable of taking on the traits of another," including "the portrayal of dual and multiple roles. . . . This grouping underscores the threat of madness."[58]

Split Personality

In comedies like *The Nutty Professor* (Jerry Lewis, 1963/Tom Shadyac, 1996), *Me Myself and Irene* (Peter and Bobby Farrelly, 2000), and *Liar Liar* (Tom Shadyac, 1997), Drake notes the "frequent use of a narrative conceit whereby the protagonist suffers from a split personality which helps to emphasise the disjunction between social conformity and eccentricity."[59] Typically, there is a normal, unobtrusive, perhaps socially awkward or reticent character and an eccentric, outrageous, sociopathic incarnation, underlining the conformity/nonconformity theme. For example, in *The Nutty Professor* (1996), Eddie Murphy plays a brilliant though shy and overweight scientist, Sherman Klump, whose magical formula transforms him into smooth-talking, manipulative Buddy Love. The device allows the comedian to display his virtuosity, what Drake calls "a hyperbolic justification of the gag sequence."[60] In other words, it allows the comedian to perform in more modes and be funnier. But it also provides a key plot point as, sooner or later, the two halves meet.

Clearly splitting also applies to Waititi's character. On the one hand, he plays the "normal," real-life Alamein, while on the other, in Boy's fantasies, he is a superhero, capable of hyperbolic acts of heroism, violence, and rebellion on the sports field, in family life, and in war: "And once, when he was a soldier, all these commies pinned him down to the ground, so he leapt out of his foxhole and just did this mean-as haka and all them commies got scared and ran away." But one of these incarnations is actually Boy's wish fulfillment (a common theme in the split personality trope, the difference being that in these sequences, Waititi is acting out someone else's wish, not his own). *Boy* is not the only comedian comedy in which a father acts out his son's fantasies—in *Liar Liar*, Jim Carrey plays a fast-talking lawyer who is compelled by his son Max to tell the truth for one day. Like Boy, Max represents the normality of family life as opposed to his father's antics when he finds himself unable to lie. So there is a similar split between normality and eccentricity. The difference is that Boy's fantasy has no apparent effect on Alamein's real-life situation; Max's does, but it is achieved through magic.

The Magical Resolution

Magic is part of comedian comedy, relating to wish fulfillment, but it can also be a narrative device, as in *Liar Liar*.[61] It can help bring about resolution, such as the ending of *The Nutty Professor*, when, with the help of CGI, Klump reemerges out of Buddy Love's body to shocked onlookers. Here we also see the confrontation of the two halves of the comedian character. In *Boy*, this confrontation is between the two Alameins. The resolution of comedian comedy works to

> divest the comic figure of his creativity—his difference—so that he can be incorporated into the culture depicted in the films. . . . The comedian figure's difference sets him in conflict with the community, resolved when he either learns to relinquish eccentricity—by "evolving a coherent identity" . . . or chooses to remain an outsider by resisting cultural assimilation.[62]

Klump gets back with his girlfriend and receives a research grant, and Carrey is reunited with his family. But the climax of *Boy* is a disaster for Alamein; he is beaten up, and driving home, accidentally kills Leaf, Boy's pet goat. His gang deserts him, humiliating him as they leave.

Alamein is not only split between himself and Boy but also within himself: first he plays Shogun, and later E.T. and the Incredible Hulk. However, these latter roles suggest character development: "E.T. is one of the ugliest buggers I've ever seen . . . big googly eyes, long neck. But you know what . . . on his home planet, he probably looks normal." This could be read as a comment to Boy, implying that his father is not as bad as he looks, a theme continued later when he compares himself to the Hulk: "I'm sorry I am like I am sometimes. I get angry. A bit like the Hulk. He gets angry. He's usually helping people, but sometimes he loses control, but he's not a bad guy." These fantasies make some attempt to reform the superhero, renegade image that he adopts earlier in the film. They suggest that rather than Alamein ultimately facing reality, as in comedian comedy, he changes through engaging with modes of fantasy that acknowledge the possibility of relationship with others, like Boy, which becomes important in the film's resolution.

Throughout the film, Boy's fantasies about Alamein are complemented by a parallel set of flashbacks about his mother, which the audience assumes, through their noncomic tone, to be true. But the key one, a memory of Alamein grieving at his dead wife's bedside (she died giving birth to Rocky) turns out to be another fantasy. Disillusioned, Boy attacks his father, who does not retaliate, acknowledging that Boy is right. Why? Because immediately preceding this, Rocky also encountered his father, touching him on the forehead and saying, "Sorry about Mum." In these two encounters, the different aspects of the comedian comedy figure are united: the "normal" Boy, whose direct address created Alamein's performance; and Alamein, the clown, via Rocky, the magician. Rocky's "magic finger" benediction works because of his father's fantasy identification with E.T. In this, Rocky follows the advice of Weirdo: "You gotta use them [your powers] to do good, eh? Just like in the comic books." But it also represents another stage in the pōwhiri. The koha (gift or sacrifice) is the goat Leaf's death.[63] Boy's friend and confidante, Leaf takes a maternal role; while Boy plays father, sitting in the driver's seat of the wrecked car, talking about his day, Leaf listens. The inscription on Boy's mother's grave reads, "A leaf has fallen from the tree," sealing the identification. Leaf's sacrifice leads to the reconciliation that makes the ending possible—Boy and Rocky share the work of burying Leaf, symbolically burying their mother properly and their differences with it, doing what Alamein failed to do—be present at her death, and thus grieve. Harirū is the next stage in the pōwhiri, where visitors and residents make physical contact—Rocky's touch (which is also the first time Rocky speaks to his father in the film).[64]

Barry Barclay's comments on Māori cinema suggest that other kinds of film endings are possible than the fulfillment of individual desire. Barclay states that "individualism is eschewed in the Maori world" and

Rocky heals the family's psychological scars with his magical E.T. finger.

with it, the implied teleological, quest-focused mode of Hollywood narrative.[65] "The Pakeha linear style is reflected in much film-making where the argument is thrust forward with punch. . . . Viewers will say 'I never felt lost. I knew exactly where I was going.' Nothing could be further from what Maori people will say."[66] The mythical, magical ending of *Boy* is testament to the effectiveness of an approach that doesn't simply realize the desire of a driven individual but focuses on reconciliation of a family, which is also a shared comic persona. Moreover, Alamein doesn't entirely renounce his fantasy—almost the last shot of the film shows him as a samurai warrior, and it is left ambiguous as to whether this is another of Boy's fantasies, or indeed Rocky's (hence Rocky's "So how was Japan?" which is the last line in the script). It points toward the credits sequence, which features a return to full-blown magic and fantasy.

"Poi E"/"Thriller" Sequence

The final Michael Jackson sequence occurs in the credits sequence, and effectively supplies the film with an alternative ending, almost as if the comedian character was writing the script, as in comedies like *Wayne's World* (Penelope Spheeris, 1992). The sequence is set to "Poi E," which frames the film, as it also plays over the opening. "Poi E" is significant in its own right—the first record in Te Reo to incorporate hip-hop electronic beats, it was a number-one hit in NZ in 1984. It is rendered in a kapa haka version of the "Thriller" video, which also incorporates elements from the "Poi E" video, for example hip-hop dance moves like "locking."[67] Rocky even attempts a Jackson crotch grab. Kapa haka is the Māori art of performing waiata (song) and haka (ritual dance). Te Rita Papesch and Sharon Mazer term it "an artificial form of Māori repertoire that preserves cultural memory, reo, ritual, and protocol through performance—a living, performative means to restore, transmit and value Māori culture through performance for all Māori people regardless of iwi."[68] By "artificial" they mean syncretic, that is, uniting formerly separate elements (waiata and haka), and incorporating non-Māori elements, like melodies of popular songs, and in this case, contemporary electronic rhythm. Unlike the other Michael Jackson homage scenes, all characters are included, so it is no longer presented as Boy's fantasy about Alamein—everyone performs as a community. At the same time, the sequence is not part of the "story world," so it presents a kind of magical solution, much like the Jackson video homages function elsewhere in the film. Finally, by focusing on Waititi, who leads the haka and performs straight to camera, the film confirms his centrality as a comic figure who can step across the borders of the narrative. At the same time, he cannot perform without the cooperation of the other characters. Indeed, as a kind of all-cast musical number it represents celebration, the final stage of pōwhiri, which Mercier describes as kai (food, feast).[69] It also represents the survival of fantasy—unlike the ending of comedian comedy, where the hero must give up his eccentric persona, the kapa haka presents a space where not just Alamein but all of the characters can go on dreaming. Through its foregrounding of fantasy, the focus of the film finally rests on the children, not the adults, and thus offers the possibility of change: "Cultural identity . . . is a matter of 'becoming' as well as 'being.' It belongs to the future as much as the past."[70] By emphasizing the close links between Māori culture and performance, it helps integrate performance into the everyday—no longer a special place for eccentrics, but a communal place. The credits sequence also has a special significance for Māori, as it shows the film's whakapapa, acknowledging everyone involved—given that Waititi made the film in his ancestral hometown, with the help of his iwi, Te Whānau ā Apanui, this would be

The "Thriller" kapa haka scene, set to "Poi E" that concludes the film. Finally, everyone is included in this fantasy. James Rolleston (Boy) is far left at front.

doubly important, also corresponding to Barclay's definition of Fourth Cinema as community-based filmmaking.[71]

In showing that *Boy* can be read in terms of "comedian comedy," I have emphasized how the film draws on comic convention, while giving them a distinctive indigenous twist, emphasizing how the comic mode and the Māori subject matter work together, rather than against each other, as many commentaries have implied. In *What We Do in the Shadows*, Waititi's next film, we see *Boy*'s hybridization of Māori identity being extended. Waititi's vampires are Eurasian immigrants (presumably illegal). Like Borat, another Eurasian, they are a "substitutable other," fitting the general template of non-white-ness. A further link for Waititi is his Russian Jewish ancestry, which he channels in this film.

Missing from this chapter has been a discussion of masculinity. The comedian comedy tradition is almost exclusively masculine, and *Boy* tends to shore up the traditional NZ emphasis on masculinity, present in all of Waititi's films up to *Jojo Rabbit*. It is not so much that women are fetishized as objects in Waititi's films, more that they are insignificant: *Boy*'s desire for Chardonnay is presented as a joke, and Waititi's character, in line with his "child-man persona," professes no interest in the opposite sex, showing how the key relationships in his films are almost always homosocial. Most of Waititi's plots are structured around the death or disappearance of a mother figure. The only adult woman present in *Boy* is Aunt Gracey, who, ironically, is the voice of paternal authority and responsibility. In Waititi's films, the women act like men, and the men act like boys, running around in gangs, and this emphasis continues into *Shadows*, with its competing gangs of foreign vampires and local werewolves, adumbrating the possibility of granting the immigrant vampires entry into NZ society, albeit on homosocial terms.

7

WHAT [MEN] DO
IN THE SHADOWS OF
GLOBALIZATION

The vampire is the dark side of modernity. Just as the gothic horror of Bram Stoker's 1897 novel *Dracula* represented late Romanticism's final protest against the Enlightenment, so more recent versions of the vampire constitute reactions to a modernized world marked by the collapsing of time and space and the dominance of global capitalism. For Marx, the vampire is capitalism, feeding on the worker's labor; for Rob Latham, it symbolizes the "pathological" consumption of postwar youth.[1] For Richard Dyer and many other writers on gay or queer themes, the secret life of the vampire, feeding on his own kind, parallels the closeted (usually male) homosexual,[2] while woman writers like Anne Rice, Stephenie Meyer, or Charlaine Harris (whose novels have been adapted into films and TV series: *Interview with the Vampire* [Neil Jordan, 1994], *Twilight* [Catherine Hardwicke, 2008], and *True Blood* [2008–14]) see them as: "elegant, tragic, sensitive people,"[3] another minority culture like blacks or gays, struggling for their rights. At the same time, vampires are usually male. This combination of exotic Otherness and masculinity is significant in *What We Do in the Shadows* (2014), written and directed by Waititi and Jemaine Clement, insofar as integration of vampires into NZ society requires suppression of Otherness and confirmation of masculinity.[4]

The way that vampires have moved from monstrous to quasi-human echoes the way that fiction and fact have mingled in contemporary society and culture. Vampires have also become amusing: old horror films are now routinely read as camp, and a long list of films, including *Vamps* (Amy Heckerling, 2012), *Vampires Suck* (Jason Friedberg and Aaron Seltzer, 2010), *Vampire's Kiss* (Robert Bierman, 1988), and *Love at First*

Bite (Stan Dragoti, 1979) and TV shows (notably Joss Whedon's *Buffy the Vampire Slayer* [1997–2003]), play bloodsucking primarily for laughs. This polysemy also informs *Shadows*, as does the fact that vampires are also typically immigrants. Waititi's character in the film, Viago, is based on his Jewish mother, Robin Cohen.[5] "In my previous film, *Boy*, I'm playing my dad. But I didn't want my mum to feel left out, so in this film, I'm playing a version of her, but as a vampire man."[6] Another Cohen influence on the film is *Borat* (Larry Charles, 2006), for, like that character, the vampires function as an easily "substitutable other," a generalized Eastern European stereotype of "funny foreigners."[7] Also, "the vampire Jew reflects a long history of anti-Judaism in European culture."[8] The movement of vampires and coffins by sea is a key element in Stoker's novel and in film adaptations such as *Nosferatu* (F. W. Murnau, 1922) and *Bram Stoker's Dracula* (Francis Ford Coppola, 1992), where it also symbolizes the spread of infectious disease, specifically the plague. The sea voyage is also key to modernity, beginning with the European explorers of Renaissance Europe.[9] And sea voyages are also mentioned in *Shadows*, although, as Viago points out, his servant put the wrong postage on his coffin.

More broadly, *Shadows* is about globalization and modernity. Anthony Giddens argues that modern life, which was supposed to be controlled by science and technology, "seems out of our control—a runaway world."[10] Globalization is "shaking up our existing ways of life . . . emerging in an anarchic, haphazard, fashion. . . . It is not settled or secure, but fraught with anxieties, as well as scarred by deep divisions. Many of us feel in the grip of forces over which we have no power."[11] Likewise, Ulrich Beck and Natan Sznaider write, "'Society' no longer appears under anyone's control."[12] The "juggernaut" of modernity, one of Giddens's key metaphors, refers to a Hindu idol who inspires blind devotion and human sacrifice.[13] Elsewhere, he paraphrases Weber's "disenchanted world": "can we live in a world where nothing is sacred? . . . I don't think we can,"[14] arguing that the abolition of religious certainty has created ontological insecurity. The triumph of reason has a "dark side":[15] terrorism, fundamentalism, environmental disaster, "the end of nature,"[16] global inequality, and, in everyday life, addiction, alienation, and anomie. Many of these themes are directly relevant to vampires, but *Shadows* subjects these dark themes to a light treatment, by showing vampires to be as lost and helpless as ordinary humans in the face of modernity. Far from the supernatural monsters of yore, *Shadows'* denizens are mostly laughable. What they share with the locals is homosociality, which ultimately aids their assimilation into NZ society.

Mockumentary

The humorous approach extends to *Shadows'* format: mockumentary, marked by its parodic use of documentary conventions such as archival images, direct address, and handheld camera. Waititi follows Peter Jackson, who has also made mockumentaries and comedy horror films, albeit not at the same time. Like *Shadows*, Jackson's comic horror films—*Bad Taste, Braindead*, and *The Frighteners* (1996)—were filmed in or around Wellington, making it NZ's capital of (joke) horror, while his mockumentary *Forgotten Silver* lampooned myths of New Zealand identity. Craig Hight and Jane Roscoe, however, note how "instead of mockumentary retaining a . . . subversive edge . . . it has become just one part of a broader reflexivity towards factual forms within visual culture as a whole."[17] Given the scenario of four flatmates living in seclusion (necessarily, considering they're vampires), most reviewers read the film as a parody of reality TV shows such as *The Real World* (1992–) and *Big Brother* (2000–): "Clement and Waititi have got the reality-show format just right: the direct-address interviews, the confessional voice-overs, the zoom-in reaction shots."[18] At the same time, J. R. Jones also identifies it as a horror comedy, noting the makers' obvious affection for and knowledge of the genre: "The genial Viago (Waititi), a 17th-century dandy, affects the frilly shirts and jewelry of the Hammer horror movies; Vladislav (Clement), a 12th-century hypnotist and impaler, favors the swarthy pop-star look of Gary Oldman in *Bram Stoker's Dracula*; Petyr (Ben Fransham), apparently even older, is a mirror image of the rodentlike bloodsucker in *Nosferatu*. . . ," the last being another Jewish stereotype.[19] This kind of reflexive awareness, which treats all media, "fact" or fiction, as no more than the sum of its conventions, is important to interpreting the film. Also, the film continues Waititi's fascination with direct address, already discussed in relation to comedy performance, "quirky" film, and documentary (as Viago, he is effectively the documentary presenter). As a convention signaling both "real" and "performance," serious and nonserious, direct address is part of the fact/fiction game that Waititi's films play with their audiences.

Reality TV, allied to emergent forms of "diversionary" documentary ("a primary viewing activity of onlooking or overhearing"),[20] can be
thought of as surveillance, linking to Giddens's reflexivity—the constant
monitoring and adjusting of identities according to modernity's feedback
eddies and information flows via media technologies.[21] But who controls
these technologies? Is the difference between *Big Brother* now and in
George Orwell's *1984* that we "watch him," rather than being watched
by him: rather than being spied on by the State, we are spying on each
other? Have we chosen to participate in our own surveillance, by install-
ing screens and cameras in our homes? Mark Andrejevic discusses how
late (digital) capitalism is marked by a complex relationship between the
promise of participatory interactivity (digital media as democratization,
as community, as fulfilment) and productive surveillance (how global
capitalism harvests and sells the information from our interactions).[22]
In terms of different modalities of observing and being observed, Andrejevic discusses voyeurism, an example of the above conundrum—are
voyeurs empowered by their gaze, or helpless bystanders? He draws a
parallel with the "savvy" viewer of postmodern culture who knows that
he or she is being exploited and derives enjoyment from that knowledge.
This "perverse" (vampiric?) logic characterizes the position of the consumer in late capitalism.[23] To recap a central theme, the viewing subject
is in a playful relation to the medium, aware that he is being lied to by
a medium that repeatedly reminds him of this fact: "To say 'I am lying'
is to tell the truth about not telling the truth and is thus both true and
untrue," which applies specifically to mockumentary and more generally
to comedy.[24]

Reality TV and associated formats thrive on identifying and exploiting Otherness, that is, creating and representing situations in which
identities are examined or judged in terms of degrees of conformity
to a norm, an imagined, omniscient gaze, which derives its coherence
from the very transgression that it condemns, like Zizek's "big Other."[25]
Of particular interest are identities that resist surveillance, the aforementioned "dark side" of modernity, although the fact of appearing on
TV suggests that they are already co-opted. Sometimes they are people
trying to adapt to modernity: flatmates, the overweight, even hopeful
inductees for talent quest, but given the neoliberal individualist logic
of winner takes all, they are already also "losers." This could include

documentaries about sects, religious cults (*Wild Wild Country* [2018]), "catfish," white racists, spiritualists, and conspiracy theorists, on the one hand, and reality programs based on enforcement agencies on the other. Vampires in *Shadows* are another minority group. "Vampires have had a really bad rap, we're not these moldy old peaches who live in castles. We participate in modern life." Viago's rather pathetic appeal exemplifies the superiority theory of comedy—we laugh at those who are simpler than us. But vampires are also like a fundamentalist sect or a terrorist group—their existence is supposed to be secret (belying the camera's presence), their practices abhorrent. However, as a film like *Four Lions* (Chris Morris, 2010) demonstrates, even fundamentalist terrorism can be comic.

Vampires, Tradition, and Modernity

Giddens argues that modernity challenges tradition: beliefs and actions once considered customary or timeless are now subject to revision.[26] The vampires are apparently traditionalists, living in an unchanging world outside time and hence comically intractable. This idea is humorously addressed in the film's first shot: an alarm clock ringing and a hand emerging from a coffin to switch it off. Early in the film, a "flat meeting" occurs, where Viago, the "modern" vampire. berates his flatmates: "You have not done the dishes for five years!" reemphasizing the incompatibility of modern clock time and the eternal, traditional vampiric mode of existence. Vampires are patriarchally negligent ("Vampires do not do dishes!"; "We should get some slaves"), whereas the more modern (hence effeminate) Viago fusses about "putting down towels, if you're going to eat a victim on my nice clean couch." They are ignorant of contemporary culture (when it makes for a funny line): when Viago is asked what he wants to "search" the Internet for, he says, "I have lost a really nice silk scarf in about 1912." Later, this conflict between tradition and modernity leads to disaster as new vampire Nick (Cory Gonzalez-Macuer) goes public about his status, yelling, "I'm Twilight!" on a city street and showing vampire tricks to bystanders. For him, vampirism is a form of celebrity, but his indiscretion leads to an attack on the flat by vampire hunters.

"Cosmopolitans welcome . . . cultural complexity. Fundamentalists find it disturbing and dangerous . . . they take refuge in . . . purified tradition—and

"You have not done the dishes for five years!" Flat meeting, a reality TV convention, with vampires Vladislav (Jemaine Clement), Deacon (Jonathan Brugh), and Viago (Taika Waititi).

quite often, violence."[27] Beck and Sznaider discuss how, "In the cosmopolitan constellation sociology is then concerned with the formation of post-national and cross-national bonds, or who belongs and who does not, and how inclusion and exclusion arise."[28] The vampires are split between tradition (Petyr), and a more modern progressive group, who, *Twilight*-like, consider the possibility of peaceful coexistence with humans, symbolized by their friendship with Nick's human friend, Stu (Stu Rutherford), a male parody of Bella Swan. Humor arises from the vampires' (cosmopolitan) attempts to attenuate their violence for their presumptive TV audience: "One of the most unfortunate things about being a vampire is that you have to drink human blood . . . I like to make a real evening of it . . . it's their last moment alive, so why not make it a nice experience?" (Viago). What follows starts as a dating sequence familiar from countless reality shows—the victim talks blandly about how she plans to go overseas (cue telling glance from Viago to the camera), but the scene degenerates into Grand Guignol bathos as Viago accidentally severs her carotid artery, showering himself with gore. Elsewhere he introduces Vlad as "a really great guy . . . a bit of a pervert" and Vlad explains: "I was quite tyrannical, I was known for torturing," then apologizes, "I tended to torture when I was in a bad place."

In *The Transformation of Intimacy*, Giddens discusses how, in modernity, private life becomes public property—loving another person becomes a "relationship"; "partners" share "experiences" and "realise potential."[29] Identities become self-reflexive and this is reflected in the development of a formal vocabulary, parodied in *Shadows*: for example, "a nice experience" and "living in a flatting situation." Viago says, "One of the unfortunate things about not having a reflection is that you don't know exactly what you look like, but we can give each other feedback." The statement highlights both vampires' lack of reflexivity (they can't see themselves, they are tradition-bound) and their attempt to overcome it, while "feedback" is part of that modern, formalized "relationship" vocabulary. In a related vein (joke), Jackie (Jackie van Beek) urges vampire Deacon (Jonathan Brugh) to make her a vampire: "I feel like I've reached my potential . . . the best version of myself that I can be." Giddens discusses how psychoanalysis reinvents self-identity for a "de-traditionalising culture."[30] However, Deacon does not see their relationship as "negotiable": "Begone!" he cries.

New vampire Nick reflects on his new companions' maladjustment to modern life, using the familiar metaphor of youth and age: "I know they're old and stuff but they're kind of naïve when it comes to the real world . . . I can probably teach them a few things," and uses the modern language of "relationships" which transcends the old bonds of blood: "I've got a whole new family . . . they accept me for who I am, and I accept them for who they are." These platitudes parody reality TV show breakouts when participants are asked to reflect on their "experience"—they typically adopt a prolix, redundant style. Thus, Nick discusses his changing "relationship" with nonvampire Stu: "I've been going through a few changes lately . . . I don't want to break that friendship . . . I'm expecting him to be angry, scared . . . expecting a lot of things to bubble to the surface." Sometimes the redundancy is in the narrativization of on-screen events: "Vladislav has just had a reaction to the information that the guest of honor is the Beast." (Viago). The total effect of these conventions is humorous, because they seem incongruous when applied to such otherworldly phenomena as vampires. They highlight the absurdity of a documentary about mythical figures. They reveal the awkwardness of vampires' relationship to modernity.

Vladislav engages with modern media technology, with the help of human Stu (Stu Rutherford).

Reverse Colonization

Giddens's "reverse colonization" refers to how the West, historically the colonizer, is now being "colonized" by immigration from the East, a contemporary manifestation of an old Western fantasy about Eastern takeover, of which the vampire is an example.[31] In the film, the vampires' exoticism is emphasized through Orientalism—stereotypical representations of "Eastern" culture.[32] The backstories of the vampires, presented through montages of archival images (a documentary technique), and the music, used throughout the film, have strong Eastern connotations. Vampires are generally identified with Eastern Europe. Vladislav "the Poker" (Jemaine Clement) is a comic echo of Vlad the Impaler, a fifteenth-century Romanian prince, the source of much vampire mythology. It is ironic that two indigenous Māori actors (Clement and Waititi) play foreigners, demonstrating how stereotypes of non-Western, nonwhite characters tend to blend into a generalized Otherness. The accents and styles of the main vampires are a simulacrum of exoticism, which means Eastern (as in the character of Borat), "an absurdly grotesque spectre of the Dark or Other Europe in the Western imagination."[33] It underlines continuities between the experiences of indigenous and diasporic groups: "At some point in their history, indigenous people have faced forced dislocations, a form of exile in their own land."[34] It highlights the need for "new ways of thinking about the complexities of migration and diasporic movement within the bicultural framework of New Zealand society as it engages with and is challenged by diasporic formations."[35]

The soundtrack exemplifies Orientalization. Contemporary group Black Ox Orkestar play Jewish folk music that features minor scales, exotic acoustic instrumentation—cimbalom (zither or hammered dulcimer) and saz (a type of lute)—odd time signatures, and hollow timbres that often connote Eastern or exotic, similar to the soundtrack of *Borat*. Two tracks by Armenian opera singer Armenak Shahmuradyan— "Alagyaz" and "Khunki Tsar"—recorded in 1912 feature in the scene where Nick and another victim visit the vampires' flat, the crackly, remote tones of the recording emphasizing the awkwardness of the situation and the discomfort of the victims. The following sequence where the vampires chase Nick features the music of Iqbal Jogi: "recorded live in the interior desert region of Pakistan. The instrument 'Been' also called 'Murli' . . . is essentially a snake charmers' instrument."[36] The nasal, drony tones of multiple beens, playing rapid, descending patterns, accompanied by clattering percussion, connote macabre confusion and alarm. But not all of the music produces a jarring effect. More Iqbal Jogi music accompanies Deacon's exotic dance, and here the effect is humorous. "Dance of Maria" (1974) by Elias Rahbani, a Lebanese composer, plays in a sequence in the vampires' nightclub, registering as relaxing, slightly exotic background music. Its more contemporary, rock-influenced style makes it less obtrusive. Finally, Wellington group Niko Ne Zna add "Balkan Brass," vaguely redolent of the circus.

Vampires as Modern and Queer

Vampires are not always maladjusted outsiders, being superhuman in some respects. Giddens notes that "in conditions of modernity, place becomes increasingly *phantasmagoric* . . . locales are thoroughly penetrated by . . . influences quite distant from them."[37] Vampires can fly, transform themselves, and potentially exert paranormal influence, and their powers echo the "uncanny" power of technology and globalization to collapse time and space. CGI enhances the magical scenes, underlining the alliance between new technologies and old-fashioned "wonder." Another aspect of vampires' superior adaptation is their physical attractiveness: "When you are a vampire you become very sexy" (Deacon); "We are trying to attract victims . . . we are the bait but also the trap" (Vladislav). At the same time, their vanity is amusing, because men are not supposed to think about their appearance. Most vampire stories emphasize sexual attraction and exchange of bodily fluids. Vampires are also "modern" individualists—relationships, as in Giddens, are freed from reproductive obligations. Quite often vampire sexuality implies homosexuality: "Sexuality which has no content is by definition no longer dominated by heterosexuality."[38] *Interview with the Vampire*, clearly an influence on the film,[39] stars Hollywood "hunks" Tom Cruise and Brad Pitt as two vampires whose relationship has a gay subtext—Cruise bites Pitt and turns him into a vampire, just as Petyr bites both Deacon and Nick in *Shadows*, the difference being that in *Shadows*, the act takes place off-screen, so the homoerotic connotations remain fairly subtle. Vampire homosexuality remains a subtext throughout *Shadows*. Jackie, Deacon's servant, frustrated at his indifference to her pleas to make her a vampire, comments bitterly: "If I had a penis I would've been bitten years ago . . . It's this big homo-erotic dick-biting club and I'm stuck here ironing their fucking frills." Jackie's speech highlights that all the main characters are male, but also how the latent queerness of the vampire

Deacon and Petyr: blood brothers, but the biting stays off-screen.

scene is denied by its participants. As Eve Sedgwick argues, just as patri-archy depends on maintaining a strict division between male homo-sociality and homosexuality, so feminist or queer critiques will tend to break it down.[40]

The homosexual theme is generally played for laughs in *Shadows*, which tends to confirm heteronormativity. It mainly relates to Stu, the rather unprepossessing human friend of Nick, whom the vampires adopt as a mascot (like Bella Swan, with the ironic difference of gender, again emphasizing the centrality of homosociality in the NZ context). Stu is referred to as a potential meal, coinciding with delectation of his body. Nick says, "He's the reddest guy I know . . ." (mimes biting him), while Viago comments, "Well of course he looks delicious with his big red cheeks." Stu is also the occasion for double entendres: "It really, really sucks that I can't eat him," says Nick, and "No matter how much I'd want to eat him, I'd never eat him 'cos he's my mate." Supposedly Waititi and Clement got the blank performance they wanted by not telling the actor, whose name really is Stu (Rutherford), what his role in the film was. "When we wrote the script and made him a big part of it," says Clement, "we let him think he was going to be our IT guy, and told him he'd just be in a little bit. Every day he'd go, 'So when do I help with the computers?' and we'd say, 'Oh, just put that costume on first.' Because we almost keep him silent, I think, the whole time he thinks he's just being made fun of."[41] The secrecy (or foolery) surround-ing Stu's true "part" parallels that surrounding homosexuality—he is unwitting beefcake. Under the jokes lurk two subtexts: the first equates vampirism with homosexuality and implies that it is a curse. It would be wrong to eat one's "mates." In *Interview with the Vampire*, Louis's (Pitt's) rage at Lestat (Cruise) for turning him into a vampire can be read as denial of homosexuality: Lestat keeps telling Louis to "accept his own nature" (in the novel, Lestat asks Louis to sleep with him). But Louis's refusal ties in with another discourse: by refusing to drink human blood, he is a prototype modern vampire who can coexist with humans. So, the implication is that to live with humans, to "set-tle" in NZ, would also be embracing heteronormativity. Moreover, vampirism is an addiction: to fight one's "nature" could be seen as the attempt to renounce not only antisocial (homosexual) behavior but also an addictive substance—human blood.

Addiction

Giddens claims that as tradition loses its grip on people's lives, they must choose for themselves, rather than being dictated to: "Living on the other side of nature and tradition . . . calls for decision making," but "the dark side of decision making is the rise of addictions and compulsions . . . now any area of activity can become invaded. . . . One can be addicted to work, exercise, food, sex—or even love."[42] He continues, "Like tradition, addiction is about the influence of the past upon the present; and . . . repetition has a key role" (for example, ritual).[43] The difference is that the past is now that of an individual, not a collective, and repetition is driven not by shared custom but by individual anxiety: "I would see addiction as frozen autonomy. . . . The addict is . . . in thrall to the past . . . he or she cannot break away from what were originally freely chosen lifestyle habits. . . . This explains why therapy and counselling . . . have become so popular in Western countries."[44] The addiction discourse features in many contemporary vampire texts, like *True Blood*, where technological advances like artificial human blood are seen as steps toward vampire/human integration, thus equating progress with freedom from addiction. However, apart from their devotion to Stu, the *Shadows* vampires show little interest in being "cured." Nevertheless, the "mechanical," repetitive nature of addiction makes it easy to mock when the vampires' attempts to snare humans go awry.

In contrast, werewolves actively engage in "therapy," their leader (Rhys Darby) telling his charges to "do the breathing" when incited by vampire insults. Again, this detail seems to parody *Twilight*'s werewolves, who protect humans from vampires. Later in the film, the vampires come across the werewolves chaining themselves to trees—again, an organized intervention with the aim of fighting their condition. In contrast with the vampires, the werewolves are a hierarchy. This may be one reason for their emphasis on discipline and self-restraint. However, the untimely appearance of the moon leads to them attacking and apparently killing Stu. The denouement reveals that Stu has been transformed into a werewolf, and this leads to a rapprochement between the vampire and werewolf groups. So, although there is little integration with the human world, there is between different nonhuman groups, up to a point. For both vampires and werewolves are all-male groups. Stu says, "Those werewolf guys, they eventually found me, and they lent me some pants. So, those guys have been supporting me because I was quite confused." Confused about what? The discovery scene shows a semiclothed Stu confronted by naked werewolves, the scene playing the homosocial/homosexual continuum as a joke.

Red-Blooded Kiwi Vampires

The NZ Breweries Lion Red 1993 beer campaign had a theme song that went, "We're red-blooded, blood brothers."[45] Similarly, the final scene of *Shadows* shows all the "boys," vampires and werewolves alike, celebrating together—homoerotic giving way to homosocial mateship. The only women we see are the ninety-six-year-old Catherine, whom Viago has made into a vampire, so they can be a couple ("some people called me a cradle-snatcher," he wryly notes); Jackie, reminding her human husband, "I love you . . . but I am your master"; and Vladislav's girlfriend, The Beast, although they are shown (as ever) fighting. So, the social harmony achieved at the end of this comedy marginalizes women, like most of Waititi's films. The werewolves have strong NZ accents and act and dress conventionally, so by integrating with them, the vampires are also integrating with local masculinity, which symbolizes national identity. The vampires are becoming "Kiwis," sharing a beer and some banter over the closing credits. The broader context here is the suspicion of foreign influence that often surfaces in local discourses, manifest in NZ exceptionalism.[46] If the local equates with heterosexual masculinity, then the foreign is feminine or homosexual. Of course, this formation is not unique to NZ—it is common, historically, in the West, "to protect the nation as an ideological formation from the threats of non-Whites, homosexuality, and feminism."[47] At the same time, vampirism is not always necessarily imagined as Other. The film *Vampires* (Vincent Lannoo, 2010) is another mockumentary about a family of vampires living in Belgium. Far from being immigrants, however, the family are Belgian citizens who live off the state, fed a diet of illegal immigrants by the authorities. "I'm tired of eating black people," one of them complains. Eventually they emigrate to Canada. "They're . . . not scary. Not sexy. Not trendy. Just Belgian," reads the tagline, so here vampires are identified with the nation, albeit satirically, whereas in *Shadows*, they start off as outsiders but are homosocially integrated into NZ by the end of the film. The European text shows a self-critical, reflexive construction of the nation, lacking in NZ culture. At the same time, the contrast highlights how, historically, settler societies like NZ are based on immigration from European colonizers, and the ambivalent relations between the Old and New Worlds.

The vampires of *Shadows* lead generally frivolous lives, lacking any kind of emotional commitment. Their main interests are self-gratification and fighting. They typify a male gang, homosocial sensibility. But they're also witty. Given that comedy is a kind of play fighting or mock aggression, does it follow that it is more socially acceptable for men? Joanna Rapf quotes Freud to the effect that in humor, the "highest of defensive processes," the ego "refuses to be hurt . . . or to be compelled to suffer. It insists that it is impervious to wounds dealt by the outside world, in fact that these are merely occasions for affording it pleasure. Humour is not resigned, it is rebellious. It signifies the triumph of not only the ego but the pleasure principle."[48] Freud's definition of humor has strong connotations of masculine invulnerability, which finds its correlate in the vampires' immortality. Moreover, the divorce of humor from emotion discussed earlier could exclude "women, traditionally 'longsuffering,' self-sacrificing and ego-effacing."[49]

Mockumentaries often deal with an aspect of the "real" world that is heavily mythologized—for example, the image of the US in *Borat* (2006), or rock music in *This Is Spinal Tap* (Rob Reiner, 1984). *Shadows*, instead, deals with an aspect of the mythical that is heavily "real"-ized, but the overall effect is similar. In both, the characters dwell in a netherworld where fiction and reality blur, not dissimilar to the experience of the viewer. Intertextual references are rife, and a potential source of audience pleasure, mixing superiority (spot the reference) and the familiarity of recognition. Throughout *Shadows*, the vampires move in and out of "character," marveling at the novelty of the Internet at one moment, while name-dropping at the next: "We stole that idea from *The Lost Boys*," says Deacon of the spaghetti/worms joke they play on their victims. Viago discusses the costumes he has worn to the Unholy Masquerade: "One year I went . . . dressed as Whoopi Goldberg from *Sister Act* . . ."; "You can't go to the ball dressed as Blade," counsels Deacon. "But vampires love Wesley Snipes," responds Viago. They play the truth/fiction game both ways, like the audience. They are aware of the conventions of the fiction they participate in—in this sense the film truly is an Unholy Masquerade.

Looked at through the lens of comedy rather than of reality TV, these vampires are not old at all, but ultramodern hipsters pretending to be old fogies because it's the latest thing. Waititi says that they based their vampire look on the 1980s retro-androgynous Prince and the Revolution.[50] Today, it would not be unlikely to see a group of people dressed like vampires walking down the street. However, as Clement notes, when they made the first version of the film in 2006, "People were yelling out homophobic slurs constantly. It probably happened like fifty times in an hour, and it was terrifying."[51] When they refilmed the scene, nine years later, they didn't receive a single insult: "The kid who yells it here had to be convinced to say it" (see DVD commentary).[52] Vampire masculinity is clearly less of a threat now than in 2005. This reflects a new cosmopolitanism in NZ that makes some New Man masculinities—the hipster, the nerd—comparatively normal: "a slightly arrogant, slack kind of wimpy guy vibe."[53] How far these new masculinities challenge traditional heteronormativity is questionable, however: "hipster masculinity claims . . . to possess an enlightened social politic," but it functions mainly "to insulate and expand his own social privilege."[54]

Shadows can be read as an example of how gender interacts with globalization. Vampires are foreign, and their Otherness is identified with homosexuality, which is a threat—they see themselves and others as "meat," and comment on male desirability, which breaks the heterosexual code of silence about male sexuality. Their masculinity is also demonstrated through their humor, which can be read as male "invulnerability" or vampire immortality. Flip the lens and you have a bunch of hipsters who demonstrate masculinity through their cosmopolitan visual style and connoisseurship of popular culture—a newer, "alternative" masculinity. Finally, there is the local version of masculinity—of homosocial mateship, which brings the boys together at the end of the film. The precarious position of women in the film's ending connotes the normativity in the NZ context of male-male friendship, to the point (as discussed in chapter 2) of ironically almost normalizing queerness. This illustrates how masculine hegemony doesn't have to be consistent—the homosexual taboo is not necessarily against homosexual practice but more against what is seen as effeminate.[55]

Giddens discusses, in *Runaway World*'s conclusion, the idea that globalization is an opportunity to globalize democratic values; yet in the conclusion of *Shadows*, we mainly see confirmation of dominant NZ values of mateship, a democracy of men. Many critics argue that Giddens is too optimistic, that globalization typically benefits the already powerful, and the conclusion of the film bears this out.[56]

Waititi's next film would focus on a different kind of minority—New Zealanders marginalized by their own culture. Ricky Baker, Māori orphan and ward of the state, and Hec, a convicted criminal, star in a classic chase movie that shows how "New Zealand film is rooted in narratives of travel, migration, emotional displacement and social and cultural (un)settlement" and how "indigenous people have faced forced dislocations, a form of exile in their own land."[57] At the same time, camp (and this film really is about camping), reveals how exile is more fun, and in its own way more authentic, than any amount of staying at home. The film's music is used as a means to open up the text to a camp reading, which problematizes, along with the chase narrative, fixed notions of national identity.

8

THE IMPOSSIBLE SONG
OF THE HUIA

Camp, Comedy, and Music in
Hunt for the Wilderpeople

Music and comedy are often linked, as in the genre "musical comedy." "The rhythm of comedy is connected to the rhythm of music. They're both about creating tension and knowing when to let it go. I'm always surprised when somebody funny is not musical."[1] *Hunt for the Wilderpeople* (2016) is a hybrid text that references many different genres—comedy, indie, "quirk," and family entertainment. One symptom of that hybridity is the way that the music functions in the film: rather than complementing the narrative, music actively produces the story world. The film's subversion of standard narrative techniques extends to the subject of that narrative—Aotearoa/New Zealand. The NZ "story," or the typical NZ stories that have been told, are shown to be fictions, created in the act of narration. New Zealand becomes a spectacle, a performance. "Camp . . . is the difference . . . between the thing as meaning something, anything, and the thing as pure artifice."[2] The film exemplifies antipodean camp,[3] which works by an analogy between postcolonial and other kinds of marginal sensibilities (most obviously queer), questioning existing local identities (e.g., the man alone, nature, and even Māori) just as queerness questions heteronormativity. Camp emphasizes form over content, affect over representation, and music, as a "nonrepresentational sign," contributes to this camp spectacle of entertainment.[4] I also consider "invented traditions" as examples of the artifice of the "natural." The emphasis is on how music contributes to campness rather than simply supplying "familiar comic cues" (for example, the humorous connotations of solo tubas, and "Mickey Mousing," or exact synchronization of image with score).[5] Such approaches include "songs performed within the . . . diegesis that are perceived as comic" ("Ricky Baker Birthday Song" is a possible candidate); musical quotation, and "nondiegetic music comically juxtaposed" with the action (there are plenty of such juxtapositions in the film, but they are bemusing rather than straightforwardly comic).[6] With obvious music/comedy cues mostly absent, we are thrown back on a looser, more ironic, "weirder" relationship of music to action, closer to "quirky" film.

Wilderpeople is a rural romp about a misfit Māori boy, Ricky (Julian Dennison), transplanted from the city to a rural backwater, who goes bush with his adoptive Pākehā "Uncle" Hec Faulkner (Sam Neill) after the death of Ricky's adoptive "Auntie" Bella (Rima Te Wiata). The pair are pursued by the authorities, personified by Paula Hore (Rachel House), take refuge briefly with a young Māori girl, Kahu (Tioreore Ngatai-Melbourne), and her dad, but are finally captured in a *Thelma & Louise/ Smash Palace*–style showdown with massed police cars. The film has a happy ending, however, as Hec and Ricky return to the bush to seek the elusive huia, a supposedly extinct native bird that they sighted during their sojourn. The film's subject matter and characters draw on traditional local narratives of settler identity—the "man alone" rebelling against authority and "going bush," as in Barry Crump's source novel *Wild Pork and Watercress* and many films discussed in Sam Neill's 1995 documentary *Cinema of Unease, including Smash Palace* (1981), *Goodbye Pork Pie* (1981), *Bad Blood* (1982), *Vigil* (1984), and Crump's Toyota Hilux TV advertisements.[7]

Music and Time

In Waititi's earlier film *Boy* (2010), the use of preexisting popular music (diegetic and nondiegetic) set the film firmly in 1980s New Zealand. Crump's novel was published in the 1980s, and *Wilderpeople* briefly features a 1985 track by NZ artist Dave Dobbyn ("Magic What She Do") and a 1980s Cadbury Flake TV advertisement. The film soundtrack (composed by members of the NZ group The Phoenix Foundation) continues the retro theme with analogue synth sounds similar to film scores by John Carpenter and Giorgio Moroder, 1980s synth-pop acts, and late-1970s soft rock (the Alessi Brothers' "Seabird" [1976]). Other 1980s references include *Miami Vice*–like "chase" music at the film's action climax. But the other prerecorded songs used (Leonard Cohen's "The Partisan" [1969] and Nina Simone's "Sinnerman" [1965]) are not in period. Indeed, the film is ostensibly set in the present day, with references to current TV programs and presenters, models of car, cellphone use, hip-hop artists, urban and local slang ("skux," "koretux"), and so on.[8] So, the film music does not denote a clear period—if anything, it suggests a fairy-tale "once upon a time," a hauntological nostalgia for lost futures.[9] Waititi says: "I . . . usually . . . try not to set anything in any real time . . . *Eagle vs Shark* could . . . be set anywhere between 1989 and 2005."[10] However, Waititi's fascination with the 1970s and 1980s could be because of their campiness—the former popularly known as "the decade that taste forgot" and the latter's androgyny, artifice (think big hair and shoulder pads), futurism, and crass materialism all lending themselves to ironic reappropriation.[11] "Many of the objects prized by Camp taste are . . . démodé. It's not a love of the old as such. It's simply that the process of aging . . . provides the necessary detachment—or arouses a necessary sympathy."[12]

Usually film music establishes time and place, defines character, and shapes emotional tenor.[13] These functions are based on the diegetic/nondiegetic distinction, which in turn depends on the idea that the diegesis or narrative is real, preexisting the addition of nondiegetic music. Music is simply a means to an end (telling the story). Anahid Kassabian suggests that film music, rather than complementing a preexisting story, can actually create narrative.[14] The opening of *Hunt for the Wilderpeople* sets familiar visual signs of New Zealand-ness—aerial views of pristine mountains and bush—to a soundtrack that combines operatic voices chanting in a mixture of Latin and Te Reo with the deep, resonating drums that nowadays connote "historic fantasy video game" in a kind of baroque medieval ethnic hybrid, like *The Lord of the Rings* (*LOTR*) gone native. But there is an abrupt cut to a police car on a country road, and then to its Māori/Pasifika occupants, whose urban apparel seems incongruous in the light of their destination—a remote broken-down farmhouse—but no less incongruous than the sickeningly retro analogue synthesizer squelch that heralds the movie title's appearance. The music playfully suggests that we are watching neither a *Deliverance*-style tale of white people gone mad in the bush, nor an urban Māori/Pasifika crime drama, nor a fantasy epic, but some bizarre amalgam of all of them, while also implying that none of these representations of NZ is to be taken at face value. The film, says Waititi, is "entertainment . . . a fantasy tale told in a real-world setting . . . disbelief is part of the way that you enjoy this film."[15] The way the music functions to create the film-world exemplifies Waititi's playful and irreverent approach to classic Hollywood narrative's naturalistic suspension of disbelief, bemusing NZ film critics in the process. Helene Wong notes "a tonally odd music choice in the choral work over the titles,"[16] which another local critic found "hilariously overwrought."[17] Steve Newall states, "After watching a quarter hour . . . you may be wondering if the pic has more going for it."[18] But perhaps this confusion is deliberate on Waititi's part.

Waititi's approach can be compared to that of the auteur who is more interested in creating a distinctive mood than in authenticity of time and place. Many film auteurs have a distinctive approach to music—for example, Alfred Hitchcock, Stanley Kubrick, Woody Allen, or Wes Anderson, the latter an influence on Waititi.[19] As discussed earlier, "quirky" films are often ambiguous in time setting and use music idiosyncratically. Arguably this ambiguity has become a feature of "millennial" film and TV, reflecting a suspicion of the progress-oriented narrative implied by a contemporary setting.[20] Such an approach could suggest the postmodern "death of history,"[21] where distinct times and places collapse with the click of a computer mouse, resulting in texts that are more about intertextuality than traditional narrative. Violence, danger, and confrontation are immediately transformed into movie quotes: "Shit just got real!" as Ricky says in one scene where he subdues feuding bounty hunters (the line is from *Bad Boys II* [Michael Bay, 2003]). Ricky even risks capture by whispering to Hec as they hide down a bank: "I was trying to tell you it was like *Lord of the Rings*," he says afterward. As with *Shadows'* vampires, one sometimes feels that Ricky is participating in a mockumentary about the making of a film. His reactions are often so far out of sync with the "chase narrative" that he almost seems like Seidman's comedian (his clothes don't even get dirty). So, in places, intertextuality literally trumps narrative as the focus. When Paula Hore confronts Ricky in the bush, they wrangle, not physically but textually, over different readings of *The Terminator* (James Cameron, 1984): "I'm more like the Terminator than you"; "You're more like Sarah Connor";

"Come on, Sarah Connor, don't be a fool!" Much of the film's exuberantly silly tone arises from such bantering exchanges. Indeed, the film's dense web of references to other films, TV, music, and media arguably sustains audience interest more than its episodic and (according to some) incoherent narrative.[22]

Invented Traditions

Place in NZ film is generally associated with nature, and a much-used aural denotation in this respect is birdsong, which in *Wilderpeople* also supplies a key moment in the narrative—Hec and Ricky's discovery of the supposedly extinct huia. Narratives of national identity have frequently included native birds, used to connote prelapsarian innocence: "New Zealand was a land of birds and in this island paradise there were no animals to harm them."[23] NZ has only one native mammal, a tiny bat. The kiwi is seen as incarnating a unique, local identity, and there is a well-developed native conservation discourse in NZ—producing national identity as vulnerable indigeneity threatened by overseas influence. Birdsong features prominently in NZ music as a distinctively local voice, as in in Larry Pruden's scores for National Film Unit bird documentaries such

The extinct huia. Birdsong is a metonym for New Zealand identity.

as *Legend of Birds* (Oxley Hughan, 1962), quoted above.[24] In popular culture, state broadcaster Radio New Zealand has, since 1974, incorporated local birdsong into its on-air identity.[25] Birdsong in NZ music and culture is metonymic for the natural landscape, which functions as a privileged sign of local identity. It also underlines the normative function of music in film—to emphasize place.

But the association of native birds with NZ identity is an "invented tradition."[26] Like the Scottish kilt, it relates to the response of modernity and the historic colonizer to a market demand for authenticity and tradition. In NZ, this takes the form of Kiwiana. But most Kiwiana originates overseas and is mass-produced; nevertheless "the signs . . . go on working . . . to call up nationalist sentiments."[27] The kiwi is another example—it only became a national symbol after becoming associated with an Australian brand of boot polish popular with Commonwealth armed forces in two world wars.[28] In the case of Radio New Zealand's use of birdsong, "former broadcaster Robert Taylor says the first bird call which aired [in 1974] was a fake morepork [ruru] call which he recorded with a technician by making noises with their hands cupped over their mouths."[29] After a couple of months, conservationist John Kendrick spotted the fakes and offered his own recordings, which are still in use today. The huia is extinct and there are no recordings of its song, only human recreations.[30] The bird in the film is obviously CGI-generated. But the huia is also at the heart of the narrative—it is the central discovery that the protagonists make that brings them together at the end, two blokes tramping off into the bush, incarnating the archetypal NZ settler myth of mateship or shared purpose in the natural landscape. So, the most natural-seeming myth (native birdsong) is also the most artificial.

Another example of invented tradition in the film is the appropriation of reggae music, particularly that of Bob Marley, in NZ by Māori/Pasifika cultures. Reggae music became associated with ethnic political protest in 1980s NZ, a seemingly natural association arising out of its original status as "rebel" music in Jamaica.[31] But *Wilderpeople* mocks this idea: when Kahu pulls out a guitar to play to Ricky, she first says, "Wanna hear a song I wrote?" but then comments "can't lie, it's not an original." The song is Bob Marley's "Turn Your Lights Down Low" (1977). The homology of Jamaican and Māori culture naturalizes reggae in the

South Pacific. Waititi has said that as a child, he "thought that that Bob Marley was from Ruatoria"[32] (an East Cape town with a strong Rastafarian presence in the 1980s), which shows the ubiquity of representations of Marley in Māori culture. But Waititi could also be commenting ironically on Marley's "natural" association with NZ. One final example of invented tradition is the pattern of *Lord of the Rings* allusions in the film music, script, and action, which show how easily New Zealand can be transformed into Middle Earth, underlining the lack of an original, true identity. Just as there is no film narrative that precedes the music, so there is no NZ narrative, no true or universal history of the nation that antedates the various acts of creation, appropriation, and expression by which Aotearoa/New Zealand is brought into being.

Music and Character/Emotional Tenor

The film's central character is Māori boy Ricky Baker—appropriately, he has a theme song, "Ricky Baker Birthday Song," performed in the film by Bella on a Casiotone keyboard. The use of cheap electronic keyboards connects to the soundtrack's corny 1970s/1980s synth sounds on the one hand, while also gesturing toward "quirky" indie films, with their frequently *faux naïf*, "tinkling" soundtracks,[33] and children's films (e.g., Giorgio Moroder's score for *The Neverending Story* [Wolfgang Petersen, 1984]) and early computer game music. Such sounds connote quirky childhood, arrested male adolescence, and possibly even queer themes, discussed later in the chapter. However, in other respects the music soundtrack doesn't define Ricky's character at all. For example, he wears a Tupac Shakur hoodie and calls his dog Tupac, but there is no hip-hop music in the film. Once again, realism is not the aim. Ricky "goes bush" after Bella's death, torching his effigy to put pursuers off his scent. It seems like a tense, dangerous scenario, but the music accompanying his flight, "Ocean Blue," is cheesy 1970s soft rock, with gently strummed acoustic guitars, Fender Rhodes piano, a warm Moog lead, and "ultra-sensitive vocal delivery."[34] Quasi-poetic lyrics suggest blissful solitude: "Out alone in the middle of the ocean blue" and a chorus that insists, "don't you worry about me." It seems Ricky has gone on a stroll rather than a perilous journey. So, the music often cuts against the grain of conventional audience identification, being so incongruous as to be amusing. Ricky's

Uncle Hec conforms to the NZ "man alone" stereotype, a solitary, self-sufficient, laconic, rural rebel, not dissimilar to Barry Crump (Hec's first words to Ricky are "Leave me alone"). This Kiwi bloke stereotype is often musically accompanied by lonely harmonica, bottleneck guitar, or blues/country motifs, as in the Southern Man Speight's TV commercials.[35] Yet this music is virtually absent from *Wilderpeople*. Uncle Hec seems like a figure of fun (one of the characters mistakes him for Australian bushman Crocodile Dundee) and the music provides little support for his traditionally hegemonic white masculinity. The last character I want to discuss is Bella, who is associated with the aforementioned "Ricky Baker Birthday Song"—as far as the audience can tell, she wrote it.[36] So, rather than the music defining the character, in a sense, the character is defining the music, which fits my general thesis about music coming out of rather than following the narrative. But to the extent that the song says something about Bella, it emphasizes her quirky humor and emotional warmth. This contrasts with Bella's other big scene that uses music—pig hunting. The urgent, insistent, loud, and bassy percussion connoting primal violence seems like a rather conventional association. But consider that the supposedly gentle, maternal Bella is the prime perpetrator of the violence, single-handedly dispatching a wild pig with a pocketknife: "That's dinner sorted!" So conventional music is offset by the incongruity of its association with an unexpected character (indeed, the two scenes, the birthday party and the pig hunting, are contiguous). Such extreme tonal contrasts are also characteristic of camp.

Son and father, odd couple, or new and old New Zealand? Ricky (Julian Dennison) and Hec (Sam Neill).

The maternal Bella (Rima Te Wiata) kills a wild pig.

Blurring Distinctions: Diegetic vs. Nondiegetic and Pop Music vs. Soundtrack

Comedy often plays with the diegetic binary, with the result that the audience find themselves wondering where the music in the film is coming from—is it diegetic or "in the mind" of the character—in outer or inner space? In one scene in *Wilderpeople* we see Ricky, apparently alone in the bush, dancing to music (Dave Dobbyn's "Magic What She Do").[37] The scene is confusing because the music has no obvious on-screen source, and characters cannot dance to nondiegetic music unless they are hallucinating. In this case, a cut to a longer shot reveals Hec staring at Ricky—simultaneously the music is silenced, and we see Ricky wearing headphones. This example also highlights how playing with the diegetic binary can relate to comedy, which shares with alternative film a tendency to feature unconventional sound/image relationships.

Kassabian argues that prerecorded popular music can give audiences more choice about how to interpret visuals (affiliative identification) whereas the purpose-written score (the traditional Hollywood approach) tends toward a coercion that the diegetic binary implicitly supports, much like the object/subject distinction can be used to insist on a unitary definition of reality.[38] By the same token, prerecorded pop songs have a life outside the diegesis, and so defy, to some degree, the diegetic binary—they emphasize the power of the audience to create its own reading. Does the music in *Wilderpeople* support Kassabian's contention?

Preexisting music need not relate to audience affiliation—it could also relate to film music's defining time/place. In *Boy*, the main character's obsession with Michael Jackson would seem to demand a Jackson song in the film, but Waititi comments: "We started off exploring the rights thing and . . . we did have it in the budget . . . But actually in the edit we realized that . . . it took away from . . . what the film was about . . . You can't have a tiny film set in the middle of nowhere and suddenly . . . kick into 'Beat It' . . . the audience would just go, 'How did you afford this?'"[39] The quote suggests that Waititi is sensitive to local readings of his film, that arguments based on US film culture may not be applicable in Aotearoa/ New Zealand, and that since Kassabian wrote her book, new(ish) genres such as "quirk" have employed music in ways that challenge alternative/ mainstream and preexisting/purpose-composed binaries.

Wilderpeople consistently blurs distinctions between preexisting pop music and composed soundtrack. Waititi has worked with NZ rock band The Phoenix Foundation and its various offshoots (in this film, Moniker) throughout his film career, just as Wes Anderson worked with founder of 1970s rock band Devo, Mark Mothersbaugh, for many of his film soundtracks (Mothersbaugh wrote the *Thor: Ragnarok* soundtrack, and his funky synthesizers help distinguish the film from standard fantasy blockbuster fare). The use of purpose-composed pop songs for a film soundtrack (e.g., "Ocean Blue") further blurs the distinction, such songs tending to blend with preexisting tracks in the audience's ears. Moreover, the preexisting songs are fairly obscure, so audience recognition, important for Kassabian's argument about "affiliative identification," is compromised. "Ocean Blue" sounds very similar to the Alessi Brothers' "Seabird" (1976), which plays over the credits. The Dave Dobbyn example features only the song's introduction, with no vocals, and is similarly hard to identify. My interpretation of this is that the quirky auteur may choose obscure music to display superior taste, a strategy also used by Wes Anderson. At the same time, Waititi's film has also been successful with mainstream audiences, so his music choices, whether existing pop/rock or soundtrack music, while "quirky" in some respects, are not so jarring or obscure as to alienate audiences. They work on more than one level.

Camp

To summarize, often the music in this film does not work in the traditional way, but neither does it necessarily work in the alternative way described by Kassabian. I would suggest a third model, camp, which refuses the mainstream/alternative or assimilative/affiliative binary. Camp is characteristically slippery, more of a sensibility than an identity, more style than content, more perspective than style, neither overtly oppositional nor wholly co-opted.[40] Camp can be a minority reading of a mainstream text—US culture read in an NZ, indeed Māori, context, but a pastiche rather than an oppositional reading. Antipodean camp shows how Australian and NZ cultural identities have developed as ironic responses to their perceived "lack" in relation to First World discourses of first UK and then US cultural imperialism, the former dominating high culture and the latter dominating popular culture.[41] Just as homosexuality reveals the lack of original gender identity, so camp reveals the lack of an "original" antipodean identity, but also how it can be created through reiterated performances, masquerades and camp acts.[42]

Wilderpeople reviewers could not agree on the film's genre—indie or mainstream, colonial critique or "crowd-pleasing" family film.[43] Its music is subtly disorienting or slyly subversive, but the overall tone is upbeat and lighthearted—we never feel that the central characters are in serious trouble. This tone is consistent with camp. Richard Dyer's definition of camp relates on the one hand to formal definition of a genre—variety entertainment—and on the other to a queer sensibility.[44] So let us apply these ideas to *Wilderpeople*.

Dyer discusses "entertainment" formally as episodic or spectacular, with the primary aim of giving pleasure, conveyed through an affective rather than a representational code, using nonrepresentational signs, which include music, creating, in this case, an occasionally quirky, to some degree nostalgic, but basically lighthearted mood.[45] Emphasizing feeling over signification aligns entertainment and gay culture and gives rise to camp. Tonal incongruity arises because feeling is more important than narrative coherence—affect counts for more than logic. Finally, camp, as a mode of aestheticism, is centrally concerned with art, usually of the past—a redemptive nostalgia for past forms of popular culture, sometimes called Camp Lite.[46]

Narrative Incoherence

The plot of the film is episodic, picaresque rather than a tightly structured character study. Some incidents seem to have a primarily comic rather than narrative purpose—Ricky's burning of his own effigy, for example, which makes no narrative sense but leads to spectacle (the burning barn) and a punch line (Paula Hore's "This ain't no charred foster kid!"). Critics frequently find the plot implausible, clichéd, and lacking continuity, or they note sudden, awkward oscillations in tone: "hugely likeable but not always coherent";[47] "alternately conventional and peculiar";[48] "the proceedings grow increasingly more far-fetched";[49] "you can probably guess what happens next."[50] But the overall exuberance of tone and humor allows them to skip over minor points of logic and predictable subject matter: the "pic's sheer good-naturedness pulls off a not particularly inspired crusty-old-coot-thawed-by-young-scamp concept."[51] In a phrase, they find the film to be a triumph of style over content, which is camp. Additionally, critics find it basically affirmative (that is, "fun"), which is important for both camp and entertainment: "Camp is generous. It wants to enjoy," especially things that might be thought corny.[52] The film's episodic character is emphasized by a metafictional device (also a feature of Wes Anderson's films)—the use of chapter headings. These work together with short musical interludes to bookend scenes of dialogue and action. Metafictional devices clearly have a camp aspect—they highlight artifice, and the use of incidental music relates to the variety format, where music maintains continuity while separating individual acts.

Tonal Incongruity

Wilderpeople lurches between sentiment and bawdy humor, tragedy and farce. An example is Bella's story, which changes tone continuously: one moment she's cracking jokes about Ricky's weight, the next coddling him like a baby and singing him a birthday song, then she gleefully dispatches a pig. Her death is sudden and totally unexpected, devastating Hec and Ricky. But her funeral is played as a farce: the minister (Waititi in a comic turn, which one reviewer found "misjudged," that is, in bad taste, which can be camp)[53] rambles about Bella's soul as "a sheep caught in a maze made by wolves" and mentions "two doors." Behind the first door lies "all the nummiest treats you can imagine . . . Fanta, Doritos, L&P, Burger Rings . . . [junk food]. But what lies behind the second door?" he asks rhetorically.[54] "Vegetables?" answers Ricky. The script parodies media representations of Māori/Pasifika budgeting and diet—for example, a notoriously racist cartoon widely published in NZ newspapers in 2013.[55] The film also features two of the corniest plot devices imaginable—the "father/son" reconciliation, combined with the "odd couple" motif—but the script is also full of un-PC banter and double entendres about pedophiles, death, obesity ("Who ate all the pies?"), and race ("Cauc . . . Asian? Well they got that wrong 'cos you're obviously white") and a haiku about maggots: "There's heaps of maggots/ Maggots wriggling in that sheep/ Like moving rice. Yuck." The haiku demonstrates tonal incongruity in the clash of high culture (poetry) with local popular culture; musical examples include "Makutekahu" in the opening scene, and "Carol of the Bells (Shchedryk, shchedryk)," a traditional Ukrainian carol, arranged by Mykola Leontovych, which introduces the action climax. In both cases, the music could suggest a *LOTR* fantasy blockbuster, although the climactic sequence itself features *Miami Vice*–style, jaggedly rhythmic synthesizer sequences and MIDI drums accompanying a mass police pursuit on a desert plain, visually referencing *Thelma & Louise* (Ridley Scott, 1990), a film frequently read as queer.[56] The climax also references Barry Crump's Toyota Hilux advertisements, which are Kiwiana, another "invented tradition"—imported commodities that paradoxically come to symbolize local authenticity, while also demonstrating the high/popular culture oscillation typical of camp (Crump as novelist and TV celebrity). The Hilux "ute" (utility vehicle, pickup truck) advertisements featured Crump showing off hair-raising driving stunts to his epicene city sidekick (played by Lloyd Scott). Dialogue from the original ("Sorry, mate, she's a bit of a bumpy ride!") is quoted in the movie, but by Ricky, not Hec (who is the obvious ringer for Crump). The advertisement is partly about different versions of masculinity—rural bloke/ man alone vs. urban "wowser" (yuppie)[57]— so urban underage Māori boy Ricky grabbing the wheel reverses the tropes, emphasizing who's really "driving" the film: young, not old, NZ. The film consistently champions youth over age: "The camp insistence on not being 'serious,' on playing, connects with the homosexual's desire to remain youthful."[58] The chase culminates in a *Smash Palace* standoff (the supposed kidnapper and his victim, trapped in a car scrapyard, in the same location as both *Smash Palace* and *LOTR's* climaxes—the North Island Central Plateau). So, the action scene is also a trainspotter's paradise, paradoxically uniting dense intertextuality with edge-of-the-seat thrills.

The diverse music in *Wilderpeople*, whether Latinate, Ukrainian, Māori, pop, classical, folk, synthetic, or natural, is thus part of a dense mesh of intertextual references, which also encompasses TV and film, mostly US 1980s and 1990s, but also NZ. The more dramatic the action, the more freely the references flow. This relates to camp's aestheticization of the natural (think art nouveau), also reflected in the way Ricky continually "textualizes" his experience (writing a journal, composing haiku, engraving a headstone in the bush for his deceased dog, coining the term "Wilderpeople" based on a book he finds in a hut about migrating wildebeest). Throughout, his wordplay denaturalizes his surroundings: even "bush" takes on a new meaning, as when Bella corrects his pronouncement about his new surroundings as a "jungle," he replies, "Ha-ha, made you say 'bush.'" The double entendre reminds us how nature is never innocent; it is always open to camp ironization, as in the Topp Twins' "bush camp."[59] Ricky's urban frame of reference (fast food, Tupac, "skux," *LOTR*, the *Terminator* franchise) has the effect of civilizing or urbanizing nature, which would seem ludicrous if the film's fantasy-like aura and narrative discontinuities didn't consistently back up Ricky's comic-book worldview—an ironic contrast with the senior white male, Hec, who is illiterate. Art triumphs over nature, another camp definition, although, ironically, in this case, the "native" represents the former and the colonizer the latter. Characters are judged by the kinds of references they make: the villain, Paula Hore, is the only character to get called out for her name-dropping.[60] This is because her references are to authoritarian, clichéd discourses: "no child left behind" refers to a law passed in the US in 2002, inapplicable in NZ.[61] On apprehending Ricky in the final showdown she screams: "You have the right to remain silent!" to which her sidekick, policeman Andy (Oscar Kightley) responds: "That's an American thing. Police in New Zealand don't really say that." *Wilderpeople* champions a version of Māori indigeneity that is at home with itself, freely mixing jokey

historical references ("I'm imagining I'm a Māori warrior, and that bot-
tle over there is a British soldier, and I'm defending all my wives," says
Ricky) with contemporary styles. Particularly touching is the scene
when renegade Ricky is sheltered by father TK and daughter Kahu (Troy
Kingi and Tioreore Ngatai-Melbourne), who, far from concerned, are
totally in awe of his outlaw status:

> **Kahu:** Relax, bro. I know who you are. I've seen your picture
> in the paper. Except you're skinnier in real life.
> **TK** (after posing for numerous "selfies" with Ricky): Chur, my
> bro. Chur. Thank you, my bro. Been awesome meeting
> you, Ricky. Just keep doing what you're doing, man. Keep
> striving. Stay Māori, bro. We need a couple more Māori
> like you.

NZ may have no "original" identity, but Waititi's representations of
Māori life in this film make it clear where his sympathies lie.

Queer Themes

The final aspect of *Wilderpeople*'s campiness is in its queer themes,
present in the plot (the assumption that Hec is a pedophile who has
kidnapped Ricky to sexually abuse him) and in the ambiguous homosociality of the film in general (the women dress like men, and antagonist Paula Hore seems more masculine than her male counterparts, a
role that she repeats in *Eagle*, *Boy*, and *Thor: Ragnarok*).[62] This links to
the androgynous style of New Zealand camp.[63] Additionally, the use of
1980s synthesizer music in the soundtrack can link to gender—UK synth
pop acts such as The Human League, Eurythmics, and Yazoo all represented themselves androgynously, and in some cases were openly gay,
as with Soft Cell and the Pet Shop Boys.[64] In the director's commentary
on the *Boy* DVD, Waititi refers to The Phoenix Foundation as "openly
gay" and makes further reference to their "weird, arty-farty, gay music"
over the closing credits. Problematically, Waititi loves homosocial banter, but he may also be referring primarily to the sensibility of the music.
Waititi's characteristic elusiveness and ambiguity lead toward a refined
definition of camp specifically located in NZ culture. This involves

defining antipodean camp in terms of not just similarities but differences between Australian and New Zealand culture.

Australian and NZ Camp

Whereas the Australian variant of antipodean camp, as in the films of Baz Luhrmann, is more typically gay—predominantly urban(e), metropolitan, and associated with a flamboyant visual and musical style that generally involves or invokes stereotypical concepts of femininity as masquerade, transvestism, and the like, New Zealand camp is predominantly rural, folksy, and androgynous in a "drag king" rather than "drag queen" fashion.[65] Exuberance is mainly at the level of intertextuality rather than personal or visual style.[66] Paula Hore is an example, but then so is Bella. Both women dress androgynously, and both can behave in a tough or masculine manner, Paula more consistently, although Bella kills a pig with evident relish. Another possible term is "butch," a style that Dyer did not recognize as camp, but commentators have subsequently suggested otherwise.[67] A final point is Waititi's use of child actors and children's stories, producing a fairy-tale, presexual atmosphere, which can also be read as camp.[68] For example, Ricky is quite androgynous at the start of the film; his gender identity is ambiguous, especially since he doesn't speak for several minutes.

There is little in the music of *Wilderpeople* that says "New Zealand," just as there is little in the music of *Strictly Ballroom* that says "Australia," and it is this very disjunction of sound and image that is both camp and revealing of how the cultural identities of these countries are actively created fictions or invented traditions. *Wilderpeople* uses music that confuses space and time, obscures character, questions emotional tenor, and confuses traditional film score with contemporary pop score. Music is highlighted, it "sticks out," and thus continually reminds us of its active role in creating the story world.

Hunt for the Wilderpeople, to an even greater degree than Waititi's other films, is a variety entertainment that highlights its own performativity, with Ricky as emcee, commenting on the action with bemused detachment. New Zealand identity and culture is a spectacle, a creation of smoke, mirrors, and music, with music used to mystify and delight, rather than in a traditionally realistic manner. The film's ability to address multiple audiences—family, mainstream, quirky, art, New Zealand, and overseas—reflects its status as entertainment while also suggesting the ways in which identity arises from audience readings, or indeed hearings, rather than from setting or authorial intention. Music choices defamiliarize the dominant NZ myths of "blokes in the bush," creating NZ as neither a natural paradise nor a heart of darkness but rather a place of intertextual, multicultural possibility, while comic elements create NZ as a world that is simultaneously real and laughable. Although Susan Sontag claims that "Nothing in nature can be campy,"[69] this reading of *Wilderpeople* suggests otherwise, and music, simultaneously the most natural and artificial of arts, underlines that paradoxical claim.

On a more mundane level, *Wilderpeople* became NZ's highest-ever grossing local feature, and also did well in Australia and the US. It seemed a matter of time until Waititi directed a Hollywood film.

9
THOR: RAGNAROK AND POSTCOLONIAL CARNIVAL

In this chapter I consider how Waititi has "reverse colonized" the super-hero genre by recreating the Marvel Cinematic Universe from a post-colonial perspective.[1] Specifically, the use of Sakaar as a complementary, multi-ethnic, "carnivalesque" world allows him to parody the white, imperialist world of Asgard and suggest a postcolonial critique of the superhero genre's values. This critique is delivered through various modes of play, often humorous.

Since *Iron Man* (Jon Favreau, 2008), "the Marvel Cinematic Universe (MCU) films have established themselves as the template for the con-temporary blockbuster movie."[2] Phase one of the project involved films about individual superheroes (including *Thor* [Kenneth Branagh, 2011]), who then joined forces for *The Avengers* (Joss Whedon, 2012). The Thor story continued in *Thor: The Dark World* (Alan Taylor, 2013). "The pre-Avengers MCU films slowly built up a series of mythic films that could reference one another. As a result, Marvel has created a cinematic uni-verse with its own continuity, one that stands apart from the (often con-voluted) continuity of comics, a continuity that rewards cinema-goers for being cinema-goers, rather than just rewarding comic fans for going to the movies."[3]

The MCU is viewed as creating a film world, with each film con-tributing to the ongoing narrative. This world is not limited to film; it includes a range of other tie-in texts and products, most obviously the comics on which the films are based, but also video games, toys, and so on, producing "transmedia storytelling."[4] At the industrial level, corpo-rate mergers bring together entertainment with other financial inter-ests, while at the audience end, the agency of fans and other participants uses, "spreads," and adapts these products in what has become known as "convergence culture."[5] Secondly, the films are viewed individually and taken together as "blockbuster" phenomena. Of course, neither of these phenomena are entirely new.

Historically, blockbusters can refer to any film using spectacular or extravagant imagery and orchestral soundtrack; Geoff King argues that spectacle can also mean "heightened levels of visual stimulus," rapid editing and camera movement, and montage with an "impact aesthetic."[6] More loosely, it can mean any film that makes a lot of money quickly or has a large or lasting media impact. Richard Maltby, in his history of Hollywood cinema, notes that "since 1970, attendance and profit have been concentrated on a relatively small number of blockbuster movies."[7] Whereas in the earlier studio system, studios made a lot of films returning modest profits or losses to feed the moviegoing habit of audiences, the rise of TV, the loss of studio monopolies over film distribution, and New Hollywood, a group of auteur directors such as George Lucas and Steven Spielberg who understood the growing youth market, eventually resulted in the production of smaller numbers of "big" movies, also known as "event" films, High Concept, or blockbusters. Such films were designed to be media "events" with a strong brand identity, tied in with other kinds of merchandising, and generally spawning sequels to capitalize on existing media awareness (that is, they became franchises): *Star Wars*; *Indiana Jones*; *Back to the Future*.

Derek Johnson notes that the idea of interconnecting media texts or transmedia narrative is not new: animated television series such as *Marvel Superheroes* (syndicated, 1966), *Spider-Man and His Amazing Friends* (NBC, 1981–83), *X-Men* (Fox, 1992–97), and *Spider-Man* (Fox, 1994–98) had "leveraged interactions among different characters in a shared Marvel Universe to multiply audience appeals."[8] Classical Hollywood cinema, too, has long relied on installment narratives, not only in cheap serials but also in studio films like *Frankenstein* (James Whale, 1931) and *Dracula* (Tod Browning, 1931), both of which spawned many sequels. What is not in dispute is the way that Marvel marketed the MCU as if it were innovative, also bolstering its cultural capital by drawing on the services of a range of indie or prestigious directors, from Kenneth Branagh for *Thor* to Joss Whedon for *The Avengers*, and now Waititi.[9]

Waititi and Marvel

Only having directed independent, small-budget, New-Zealand-based features previously, Waititi seemed like an unlikely choice, but that he is clearly a fan of both US pop culture in general and Hollywood blockbusters in particular is evident from references in his earlier work: *E.T.* in *Boy*; *The Terminator* films, *The Lord of the Rings* films, and John Carpenter's soundtrack work in *Wilderpeople*; and the vampire genre in *Shadows*. *Eagle vs Shark* also refers to the Marvel Comics character Wolverine. Waititi "obsessively" collected comic books as a child.[10] Moreover, the MCU films rely heavily on self-reference, both as a continuity device and as strategy to reward fan knowledge: for example, Marvel Comics creator Stan Lee's cameo roles in virtually every MCU film until his death in 2018 (he played a barber in *Thor: Ragnarok*). Waititi uses self-referencing in his own films, appearing in all of them and using recurring scenarios, such as the "boy abandoned in car" motif in *Two Cars, One Night* and *Boy*. In 2018 he produced an NZ TV spin-off of *What We Do in the Shadows*, *Wellington Paranormal*, and in 2019, a US TV spin-off series to *Shadows* itself, in which he and Jemaine Clement write and/or direct some episodes. In relation to *Thor*, he produced three promotional mockumentary shorts, collectively named *Team Thor*, showing Thor flatting in Australia with a human called Darryl, who then goes on to flat in LA with the Grandmaster (Jeff Goldblum) ("Team Darryl"). These zany spin-offs functioned like trailers to create interest in *Thor: Ragnarok*, anticipating its comic, improvisatory tone, while also referencing the first *Thor* (2011), in which the superhero is a fish out of water in a human world. Integration of intertextuality into the narrative is part of Waititi's modus operandi. To audition for the job of directing *Thor*, Waititi created a "sizzle reel" that drew heavily on the 1986 John Carpenter action blockbuster *Big Trouble in Little China*, synced to '70s classic-rock band Led Zeppelin's "Immigrant Song."[11] The song, which alludes to Norse mythology, also features in the finished film. Moreover, Waititi's ongoing relationship with Peter Jackson, director of *The Lord of the Rings*, one of the most lucrative film franchises ever,[12] is a fitting precedent for a New Zealander creating a fantasy blockbuster based on Nordic mythology.

> "In the pre-Avengers films, familiar echoes of Greco-Roman demi-gods, Norse gods, Celtic heroes, and Arthurian legends commingle

with Lee and Kirby's post-atomic superheroes. . . . *The Avengers* succeeds where other mythologically inspired one-shot films (the many Beowulfian warriors, Arthurian kings, and Grecian earners that have paraded across the marquees of late) comparatively fail, because Marvel managed to integrate ancient (Western) and modern (American) mythologies throughout the pre-Avengers solo films."[13]

Thor: Ragnarok takes its basic plot and characters from Norse mythology via its retelling in Marvel comics: briefly, Odin (Anthony Hopkins), ruler of Asgard, home of the gods, and father to Thor (Chris Hemsworth) and possibly Loki (Tom Hiddleston) faces Ragnarok, the destruction of Asgard, by Odin's disowned eldest daughter, Hela (Cate Blanchett), the goddess of death.

Waititi's Post-colonial Carnival

Blockbuster sci-fi has frequently been condemned as a Western neocolonial fantasy. Sci-fi writer Ursula Le Guin comments:

> most SF has been incredibly regressive and unimaginative. All those Galactic Empires, taken straight from the British Empire of 1880. All those planets—with 80 trillion miles between them!—conceived of as warring nation-states, or as colonies to be exploited, or to be nudged by the benevolent Imperium of Earth towards self-development—the White Man's Burden all over again.[14]

Even as a fan of US pop-SF, Waititi would be unlikely to endorse Eurocentric, Aryan, and possibly racist myths. Humor is not alien to the Marvel universe: MCU characters tend to be more ordinary and self-deprecating than their DC Comics counterparts such as Superman.[15] And although Thor is a god, after being stripped of his hammer and exiled to Earth in *Thor* (2011), the comic aspects of his predicament come to the fore, which Waititi develops in *Ragnarok*. Joss Whedon, creator of the TV series *Buffy the Vampire Slayer* and director of *The Avengers*, also routinely combines action with comedy, one critic noting that: "'The Avengers,' 'Guardians of the Galaxy' and their various offshoots are basically punchy, predictable sitcoms in comic-book drag."[16] In *Thor: Ragnarok*, Waititi uses comedy, among other devices, to poke fun at some of the more portentous aspects of the mythology he has to work with. At the same time, this doesn't mean the film is only a parody—here, as throughout his oeuvre, Waititi ably alternates lighter and more serious dramatic moments. Critique is delivered obliquely by inhabiting characters and situations and pushing them to the point of absurdity rather than reducing them to easily denounceable cutouts. Waititi's approach to a topic like racism is to perform it in an absurd fashion—for example, nonwhite characters mouthing racist sentiments (see chapter 10). This comic inversion calls to mind Bakhtin's carnival, a ritual that reverses normal social roles to produce a "world inside out" where laughter reveals "the gay relativity of prevailing truths and authorities" and mocks hierarchy.[17] Moreover, a carnival text may take the form of a "fantastic voyage" to an antipodean world that inverts normal values, just as the planet Sakaar in the film reverses Asgard. In such a world, the ruler swaps places with the jester—indeed, Loki finds himself at home in Sakaar. Loki, who in typical trickster fashion may or may not be Thor's brother, is one of Waititi's avatars in the film. He can produce multiple virtual versions of himself, simulacra, if you like, just as filmmakers use CGI. Indeed, Bakhtin describes carnival as "spectacle."[18] A repeated joke concerns Thor throwing things at Loki to check if he's real, which could be read as poking fun at the illusion of the film itself. Finally, Loki is about as nerdy and cynical as a male superhero gets, relying on wits rather than brute force, a masculine type familiar from other Waititi films. "A kind of low-level trickster god of indie cinema himself, Waititi lets his film go a little crazy: He's outfitted it with garish colors and costumes and set designs, some not-entirely-perfect special effects, and a synthesized Mark Mothersbaugh score that sounds like it was lifted from an early period Jean-Claude Van Damme flick."[19] The score debunks the high seriousness of the typical orchestral blockbuster soundtrack, which tends to batter audiences into ideological submission.[20]

Play and Western Culture in Asgard

Loki and Waititi's trickery starts early in the film when Thor arrives back in Asgard to discover a play in progress, in which an actor playing Thor cradles an actor playing the dying Loki, reprising *Thor: The Dark World*, in which Loki apparently dies (but subsequently returns to Asgard to impersonate their father, Odin). Waititi comments: "I thought if I was Loki and I was ruling Asgard, I would write a play about myself and force everyone to go and see it."[21] Although most reviews distance *Thor: Ragnarok* from its "Shakespearean" antecedent (the Branagh-directed *Thor*), the play-within-a-play device functions broadly as it does in Shakespeare, to remind the audience of the illusory nature of the play (or film) they are watching, but also to suggest that life itself is play, comparing theatrical roles to life roles, such as being a king. For a start, film viewers might be surprised to see "high culture" in a Marvel Comics film. Additionally, the play, along with other details of Asgardian mise-en-scène such as such as classical-style clothing and architecture, suggests European, Renaissance culture, a hegemonic discourse that the film soon subverts. It also presents an opportunity for cameos, which are part of the intertextuality of the Marvel Comics Universe, and a chance for fans to spot filmic references: Matt Damon plays the fake Loki (he also played Loki in Kevin Smith's *Dogma* [1999]); Chris's brother, Luke Hemsworth (star of *Westworld*), plays the fake Thor; and Sam Neill (Uncle Hec in *Wilderpeople*) plays their fake father, Odin. The cameos distance viewers by reminding them of the extradiegetic world, while also rewarding fans' inside knowledge. But these fan in-jokes are also echoed in the diegesis, because the "real" Odin watching is actually Loki (Tom Hiddleston). One fake king watches another fake king. Reality is just as illusory as the play.

The return of Hela further reveals the deceptive nature of Asgard. Odin, who up to this point has conformed to the familiar patriarchal stereotype of the Christian God, an apparently benevolent, wise, old, bearded man, reveals to Thor and Loki that he has deceived them—they did not know that Hela, their sister, still exists. Moreover, her return means that Ragnarok (the destruction of Asgard) is inevitable. This pattern of father-son relations is familiar from other Waititi films—the mother is dead (Friga died in *Thor: The Dark World*) and the father counsels despair. The younger generation must learn from him but not give in to hopelessness, often in the process fighting a phallic female figure who is the violent opposite of the self-sacrificing mother (as with Paula Hore and Bella in *Wilderpeople*, or, more loosely, Aunt Gracey and Boy's mother in *Boy*). Once again, the homosociality of Waititi's films (and the source material) is highlighted, with women's roles polarized, although this polarity breaks down in Sakaar. Hela's address to Asgard highlights how Asgardian (Western) culture is a facade. "Does no one remember me? Has no one been taught our history?" she asks, surveying the Sistine Chapel–style ceilings of the palace, with their Christian iconography of benevolent, sainted figures. "Look at these lies. Goblets and garden parties? Peace treaties? Odin . . . Proud to have it, ashamed of how he got it!" She smashes the false ceiling to reveal an earlier, medieval Hieronymus Bosch–style vision of apocalyptic violence, presided over by marauding Hela and Odin figures. "We were unstoppable. I was his weapon in the conquest that built Asgard's empire." Thus, the audience is reminded "of the centuries-long tendency to sweep colonial history under a gilded rug and refuse to learn from it."[22] Just as European civilization was built on violent conquest, so is Asgard's, and that legacy of violence is incarnated in the dead warrior army, buried beneath the palace, whom Hela resurrects. She hearkens back to the European Dark Ages, the rampaging Vikings of "Immigrant Song": "We come from the land of the ice and snow / From the midnight sun where the hot springs blow / The hammer of the gods . . . We are your overlords." Led Zeppelin's lyrics are echoed in Hela's speech: "Our destiny is to rule over all others." Hela casts Thor and Loki out of Asgard, and they find themselves stranded on the planet Sakaar, Thor bereft of his hammer.

Odin (Anthony Hopkins) and Thor (Chris Hemsworth): The father-son relationship is a recurrent theme in Waititi films.

Renaissance Christian imagery in Asgard (*Thor: Ragnarok* [2017]).

Sakaar and Carnival

Sakaar is like Bakhtin's world inside out, where, as the character Korg says, "the only thing that does make sense is that nothing makes sense." It is a carnivalesque party planet, where appearances are reality (mirrors repeatedly feature in the decor), ruled over by the Grandmaster (Jeff Goldblum), a reference to US hip-hop pioneer Grandmaster Flash—indeed, we see him DJ-ing. Thor's entry to the Grandmaster's palace alludes to the hallucinatory boat ride in *Willy Wonka and the Chocolate Factory* (Mel Stuart, 1971) and is set to "Pure Imagination," from the same film. A soothing female voice intones:

> Fear not, for you are found. You are home, and there is no going back. No one leaves this place. But what is this place? The answer is Sakaar. Surrounded by cosmic gateways, Sakaar lives on the edge of the known and unknown. It is the collection point for all lost and unloved things. Like you. But here on Sakaar, you are significant. You are valuable. Here you are loved.

The monologue blends maternal reassurance—Sakaar is safe, like "the maternal womb"[23]—with an acknowledgment that it is the place of the "lost and unloved." "To degrade an object does not imply merely hurling it into the void . . . but . . . the reproductive lower stratum . . . in which conception and new birth take place."[24] Inhabited mostly by nonwhite people, Sakaar is also a kind of ghetto, in contrast to the "First World" of Asgard, a "folk world," as Bakhtin states of carnival. Grotesquerie is another aspect of Bakhtin's inverted world, in the mixture of types of beings in Sakaar, from people made out of rocks (Korg) to what look like Sand People from *Star Wars*. Finally, Bakhtin's world is abject "degradation": rubbish, detritus, bodily fluids, and bodily functions.[25] Like the Earth in *Wall-E* (Andrew Stanton, 2008), Sakaar is a garbage planet, where the trash of the universe accumulates, ejected there through a giant wormhole called the Devil's Anus.

The action on Sakaar is also superfluous: "most of the film . . . can charitably be called a subplot. But it's a fun subplot, which is all that really matters."[26] As the Grandmaster says, "Time works real different around these parts." This part of the story is based on the *Planet Hulk* comic series and 2010 animated film, featuring the Incredible Hulk, centering on a gladiatorial contest between Thor and Hulk, inconsequential in terms of its outcome (no one wins). Mainly the Sakaar sojourn is an opportunity for Waititi to do what he does best: show a group of mostly male characters passing the time by playing tricks and jokes on each other, engaging in badinage, and generally "bonding." Thor also has to find allies against Hela, but his difficulties are initially compounded by his Asgardian sense of entitlement and by the "anything goes" atmosphere of Sakaar.

Space Camp and Postcolonialism

Sakaar is a place where nothing matters, because everything is a game. It is the place that loves trash, which is camp: "committed to the marginal with a commitment greater than the marginal merits,"[27] a place of "gay relativity."[28] The Grandmaster (GM) is also camp: he calls Asgard "Ass-berg," he calls Thor "Sparkles," and he ogles Thor's "wonderful" physique like Frankenfurter eyeing up Rocky in the *Rocky Horror Picture Show*. On Sakaar, Thor is not a god but an object for female and possibly queer gazes—first Scrapper 142, the woman who captures him, then the Grandmaster himself, a "lord of misrule" surrounded by nonwhite female servants who indulge his predilection for "trash talk" and word games:

GM: Whenever we get to talking, Topaz, about Scrapper 142, what do I always say? "She is the . . ." And it starts with a "B."

TOPAZ: Trash.

GM: No, not trash. Were you waiting just to call her that? It doesn't start with a "B."

TOPAZ: Booze hag.

GM: I'm so sorry. No, "best." I was thinking about "best" . . . She brought me my beloved champion, you know.

This doesn't mean the GM is not dangerous; he executes his cousin with a "melt stick," which, in line with the inverted world theme, literally reduces bodies to smelly fluids:

GM: Oh, my God! I'm stepping in it. I'm stepping in it. Look! The smell. What does it smell like?

TOPAZ: Burnt toast.

Thor becomes a contender in what GM refers to as "a little harlequinade called the Contest of Champions," another of the games that define Sakaar, which in turn parody the main action, as carnival parodies official ritual. Thor clowns with the other competitors, notably

The camp triumvirate of Sakaar: Topaz (Rachel House), the Grandmaster (Jeff Goldblum), and Scrapper 142 (Tessa Thompson).

Korg (a CGI rock monster, voiced by Waititi) and later the Hulk and Scrapper. The extended banter that occurs between Thor and Hulk is both typical of Waititi's films but also a particular kind of intimate communication enabled by carnival: "the form of . . . verbal intercourse changes abruptly; they address each other informally; abusive words are used affectionately, and mutual mockery is permitted. . . . The abuses were ambivalent: while humiliating . . . they at the same time revived and renewed."[29] Thus Thor is revived and renewed through ritual abuse, and he gains new allies. Bodily references are part of this "billingsgate," continuing the language of abjection; gladiatorial conflict is a messy business.[30] Korg: "Yuck! There's still someone's hair and blood all over this. Guys, can you clean up the weapons once you finish your fight? Disgusting slobs." This combines with salacious banter, as in the following joke, which plays on the phallic properties of Thor's hammer and reveals his narcissism:

> **KORG:** You rode a hammer?
> **THOR:** No, I didn't ride the hammer.
> **KORG:** The hammer rode you on your back?
> **THOR:** No. I used to spin it really fast, and it would pull me off the . . .
> **KORG:** Oh, my God. A hammer pulled you off?
> **THOR:** The ground. It would pull me off the ground, up into the air, and I would fly. Every time I threw it, it would always come back to me.
> **KORG** (rapidly and tonelessly): Sounds like you had a pretty special and intimate relationship with this hammer and that losing it was almost comparable to losing a loved one.

Sakaar and the South Seas

Like Topaz and Scrapper 142, Korg is coded as ethnic, voiced by the director himself in tones copied from nightclub bouncers on Auckland's K-Road.[31] In his surreal satire of Pasifika social hierarchies, *Kisses in the Nederends*, Epeli Hau'ofa identifies in Pasifika culture the same kind of "billingsgate" that Bakhtin identified in carnival:

White man Thor enlists the quasi-Māori/Pasifika Incredible Hulk as an ally.

> Uppertuks called Lowertuks arseholes, arselickers, buggers, bums, bullshitters, cocksuckers, cunts, fart faces, fuckwits, fucking this, fucking that, greedy guts, shitheads, turds, wankers, and other luridly offensive expressions. They characterised the mental and moral capacities of Lowertuks as piss weak and shit awful and their achievements as cockups.[32]

The Hulk is also identified with Māori/Pasifika. His quarters feature Māori/Pasifika designs on the walls, cushions, and bedspread, in the mainly black and brown tones of tapa cloth. An obvious reference point is the character Maui in *Moana* (Ron Clements, John Musker, 2016), a film for which Waititi wrote an early version of the script.[33] The Hulk's key characteristic is his rage, which sets him apart from the other, more rational, white superheroes such as The Illuminati. *Planet Hulk* is driven by their decision to exile the Hulk to Sakaar.[34] The Illuminati further explain "that they are sending [the Hulk] to a planet full of vegetation but lacking in intelligent life," like the South Seas idyll imagined by European colonizers.[35] On Sakaar, the Hulk remains the Hulk—that is, "primitive," an example of "the Savage slot . . . a structural repository integral to organizing the project of global legitimation referred to as 'the West' . . . a colonial space inhabited by others."[36] There is no need on Sakaar for the Hulk's human alter-ego (Bruce Banner). The Hulk is identified with a "natural" world where ethnic cultures can "be themselves." As the Grandmaster's champion, he seems happy with his lot. Why should he return to "civilization"? The Hulk and the other ethnic characters are employed on Sakaar for their physical strength and fighting prowess—they're a kind of nonwhite proletariat. They make their living as sportspeople or soldiers of fortune. The Hulk embodies a violent, physical Māori/Pasifika masculinity that Waititi has rejected elsewhere, but its mediation here through comic books makes the ethnic stereotype seem less problematic. Elsewhere than Sakaar, however, the familiar stereotype would still apply, which the Hulk recognizes:

> **THOR:** You're gonna love Asgard. It's big. It's golden. Shiny.
> **HULK:** Hulk stay.
> **THOR:** No, no, no. My people need me to get back to Asgard. We must prevent Ragnarok.
> **HULK:** Ragnarok?
> **THOR:** The prophesied death of my home world. The end of days, it's the end of . . . (Hulk yawns). If you help me get back to Asgard, I can help you get back to Earth.
> **HULK:** Earth hate Hulk.

Thor needs allies to prevent the destruction of Asgard, but "the end of the world just doesn't feel as important as it used to in the movies— we see it threatened several times a year by Marvel product alone— which is why Waititi's decision to treat it as a foregone conclusion in *Ragnarok* feels so novel. Nothing's going to stop the calamitous third-act destruction, so we might as well sit back and laugh as it approaches."[37] Waititi refers to Thor as "a rich kid who's . . . trapped in the ghetto . . . trying to get home."[38] For colonized or oppressed peoples, the end of the world is nothing new; indeed, it was brought about by Western culture. Hence the Hulk's utter indifference to Thor's plea, echoed by Scrapper 142:

> **THOR:** I'm putting together a team. It's me, you, and the big guy.
> **HULK:** No. No team. Only Hulk.

> **THOR** (to Scrapper 142): It's me and you.
> **SCRAPPER:** I think it's only you.

When Thor discovers that Scrapper 142 is a Valkyrie, he tries to persuade her to join him, but his patronizing sexism scuppers his attempts:

> **THOR:** I used to want to be a Valkyrie when I was younger,
>   until I found out that you were all women. There's
>   nothing wrong with women, of course. I love women.
>   Sometimes a little too much. Not in a creepy way, just
>   more of a respectful appreciation. I think it's great that
>   there is an elite force of women warriors. It's about
>   time!
> **VALKYRIE:** Are you done?

Much like the Māori Battalion fought for the British Empire, Valkyrie fought for Asgard, a colonial power reluctant to recognize the contribution made by colonized people in its armed forces. Thor's attitude to Valkyrie's gender is another aspect of his sense of colonial entitlement. Even when she changes her mind, he still can't stop patronizing her:

> **VALKYRIE:** Sakaar seemed like the best place to drink and
>   forget, and to die one day.
> **THOR:** I was thinking that you drink too much, and that
>   probably was gonna kill you.
> **VALKYRIE:** I don't plan to stop drinking.

Sexual ambiguity is a big part of Sakaar's "inverted world." Tessa Thompson, who plays Valkyrie, comments that:

> When I first sat down with Taika to talk about the role, he pitched
> Valkyrie as the Han Solo of the movie. I loved it. That character
> obviously occupies such an incredible space of film iconography,
> but also that it should be a male role was really exciting. The phys-
> ical reference for her was Sarah Connor in the second *Terminator*
> movie, which is incredible because she's in the best shape ever and
> is just, like, all muscle.[39]

A scene alluding to Valkyrie's bisexuality (as in the comics) was cut from the film, however.[40] Siddhant Adlakha comments that "Thompson's Valkyrie is given perhaps the film's most complete and resonant character arc, returning to a nation—traveling on a ship bearing the red, yellow, and black of the Aboriginal flag—she has every reason to hate, in order to save its people."[41]

So, the force Thor assembles against Hela is mainly nonwhite—indeed, the main protector of the Asgardian people, Heimdall (Idris Elba), is also nonwhite. Now in dialogue with ordinary "folk," another of the lessons of the Bakhtinian carnival of Sakaar, Thor comes to question the abstract ideal of Asgard as a nation, realizing that he cannot save the city, only its inhabitants: "Asgard is not a place. It is a people." Ultimately, this leads to an evacuation, a tactical retreat rather than a victory. Korg comments, parodying the standard Hollywood ending, "The damage is not too bad. As long as the foundations are still strong, we can rebuild this place. It will become a haven for all peoples and aliens of the universe. [Surtur destroys Asgard]. Nope, those foundations are gone. Sorry!"

The evacuation is an ambiguous ending—on the one hand, it echoes recent blockbusters like *2012* (Roland Emmerich, 2009) and *Interstellar* (Christopher Nolan, 2014), in which humankind, or selected parts of it, leave a polluted or postapocalyptic Earth and colonize space, which seems to confirm rather than challenge colonial, imperialist narratives. On the other hand, Polynesia is based on the historical, diasporic dispersal of Pasifika people around the South Pacific—voyaging is part of the culture, so much so that Epeli Hau'ofa has suggested the concept of Oceania to replace "Pacific Islands":

> "Oceania" denotes a sea of islands with their inhabitants. The world of our ancestors was a large sea full of places to explore, to make their homes in, to breed generations of seafarers like themselves. People raised in this environment were at home with the sea. They played in it as soon as they could walk steadily, they worked in it, they fought on it. They developed great skills for navigating their waters—as well as the spirit to traverse even the few large gaps that separated their island groups.[42]

Such a liminal identity has the potential to change the Western view of the Pacific Islands as small, isolated, impoverished island nations, and to reimagine Pasifika identity as diasporic and fluid. Waititi's ethnic intervention in the superhero franchise adumbrates a view of space exploration that is potentially decolonizing.

Accordingly, the film's ending is also ambiguous for Thor—he loses both his hammer and an eye. This makes him more like his father, Odin, but it's also a sacrifice, leading one to wonder if the days of the male, blond, Nordic superhero are numbered. In the wider comics universe, there are now more films featuring nonwhite superheroes (for example, *Black Panther* [Ryan Coogler, 2018]) and women heroes (for example, *Wonder Woman* [Patty Jenkins, 2017]). There is also less emphasis on the "monomyth," very much part of the *Star Wars* films, which emphasized the individual hero's journey. In contrast, Thor is part of the Avengers "team," like the Hulk. But is teamwork an advance on the old myth of heroic individualism, or rather a kind of corporate update? Do MCU heroes mark the culmination of a development from individual superheroes to organization workers, corporate employees, a move that approximately coincides with when the franchise was bought by Disney (2009)?[43] Increasingly, Marvel heroes tend to discuss their activities as "teamwork" (Thor, meeting the Hulk in the gladiatorial ring, remarks that "He's a friend from work"). They all act on behalf of a large government organization, SHIELD, although Thor finds his colleagues reluctant to endorse the team ethos, which is a fairly transparent smokescreen for neoliberal corporatism. Finally, is Waititi also now part of the corporate behemoth of Hollywood? Bruce Babington states that "Peter Jackson's unprecedented position as a Hollywood director in Wellington is too freakish to be more than an unrepeatable exception."[44] The implication is that Jackson's success has disqualified him as a true NZ director. Such an argument repeats the idea of a commerce/art split, criticized by Thomas Elsaesser in his work on the modern auteur.[45] Jackson, and now Waititi, have proved the film historians wrong and shown that New Zealanders can make good films that are popular overseas while still incorporating distinctively local themes and perspectives. And, in Waititi's case, he has done it by using comedy. But does leaving the familiar territory of New Zealand and comic books mean that Waititi is moving out of his depth? *Jojo Rabbit,* with its historic European setting and themes, might prove a challenge. On the other hand, it might be an opportunity for Waititi to engage more explicitly with his Jewish heritage. And in terms of a world in which violence against ethnic minorities seems to be becoming more common, does the film represent an opportunity to comment on, or at least exploit, the filmmaker's own mixed ethnicity?

10

Is *Jojo Rabbit* an Anti-Hate Satire?

Although (because?) superhero films make a lot of money, they're not culturally prestigious and generally get passed over by the Oscars. However, stung by accusations of racism, the Academy finally offered some overdue recognition to nonwhite superhero film *Black Panther*, which won three Oscars in 2018.[1] Given that the Academy was becoming more open to nonwhite filmmakers, it could be seen as a canny move on Waititi's part to produce a film starring children, aimed at a broad audience, with an unambiguous moral message addressing a historically significant event (like the Holocaust), and release it in "Oscar season," (that is, late in the year).[2] Waititi's films have been male-oriented, but here was a chance to court a broader audience with an adaptation of a book recommended by his mother.[3] In fact, Waititi had written *Jojo Rabbit* earlier, but it had languished until the success of *Thor* lent him the opportunity to make the film.[4]

Jojo Rabbit was a PR coup. The film's 2020 Oscar win (for best adapted screenplay) seemed to consolidate a new era of Hollywood recognition for ethnic diversity, complementing the Korean *Parasite* (Bong Joon-ho, 2019) becoming the first foreign language film to win best film. In his acceptance speech, Waititi dedicated his win to "all the Indigenous kids all over the world who want to do art and dance and write stories."[5] In a world increasingly blighted by racism and intolerance, surely it's important, Waititi suggests, "to educate our kids about tolerance and continue to remind ourselves that there's no place in this world for hate."[6] And the best way to do that is to go and see his latest movie, the themes of which are, by accident or design, ideally positioned for a US film industry seeking to distance itself from present US government policies. If Waititi's statement above seems platitudinous by his standards, we should bear in mind that publicity for this film was carefully orchestrated, given its potentially controversial theme and the adverse reactions of some critics.[7]

Satire

I want to focus on the term "anti-hate satire" that was used to characterize and market the film.[8] Satire is (usually) comic, which fits my focus, but also implies something more current, political, and edgy than comedy.[9] How far is this true of *Jojo*? Or is the term merely a marketing ploy, as one reviewer suggested: "Loudly calling a movie an 'anti-hate satire' strikes me as caution masquerading as boldness, in the marketing department at least."[10] Adding a sheen of political relevance to a sentimental story can be viewed as the ideal recipe for Oscar success: "It's this year's model of Nazi Oscar-bait showmanship: 'Life Is Beautiful' made with attitude."[11]

On the other side of this argument is the contemporary rise in far-right extremism, exemplified in NZ by the Christchurch mosque shootings on March 15, 2019, when a white Australian terrorist, Brenton Tarrant, killed fifty-one Muslim people in a racially and religiously motivated attack,[12] described by New Zealand prime minister Jacinda Ardern as an "extraordinary and unprecedented act of violence."[13] There is also global concern at the number of democratically elected governments with nationalistic, right-wing agendas, such as Donald Trump's in the US. Trump's autocratic, populist style of demagoguery has been compared to that of Hitler.[14] In this sense, an anti-fascist satire might seem timely. However, calling it an "anti-hate satire" suggests condemnation less of a political movement than of a type of rhetoric. "Hate speech" is defined in NZ law by the Human Rights Act 1993 as publishing or distributing "threatening, abusive, or insulting . . . matter or words likely to excite hostility against or bring into contempt any group of persons . . . on the ground of the colour, race, or ethnic or national origins of that group of persons."[15] Such a law could potentially be used against anyone, irrespective of their politics or ethnicity. The vagueness of "anti-hate" led one reviewer to suggest that "[T]he actual target of 'Jojo Rabbit' isn't really the haters, it's those who would presume to hate the haters."[16] In other words, the movie is aimed at an apolitical mainstream, its message that "there's good and bad in everyone."

The method of satire, however, is precisely to ridicule a social group or person: "For all the satirist's high-minded aims, he [*sic*] works with tools—the lash, the pointed pen, the flaying knife—that inflict pain."[17] "Othering is the essence of satire and humor."[18] Some might say that satire is different from hate speech in that it uses the weapons of wit—irony and double entendre. However, irony and double entendre are also used by alt-right groups, who have appropriated "innocent" signs such as the curled finger "okay" sign, so that viewers can no longer know if the sign is used naively or knowingly (a probable example of the latter was Brenton Tarrant's use of it in a court appearance in April 2019).[19]

The object of satire should be contemporary, but parallels between historic and contemporary fascism are implicit in *Jojo*, the closest being the opening montage of Nazi crowds "sieg-heil"-ing Hitler to the strains of the Beatles' German-language version of "I Want to Hold Your Hand."[20] But Beatlemania is hardly contemporary, so the equation of pop music fans with Nazis seems more amusing than pointed. In contrast, another recent "Nazi comedy," the German-language *Look Who's Back!* (David Wnendt, 2015) placed a miraculously revived Hitler in present-day Germany, which made the link between periods more compelling. A further aspect of satire is that while it paints with broad strokes, using stereotyping to present complex realities, its targets must be believable: "Satire . . . is a rhetorical means to the production of difference in the face of a potentially compromising similarity, not the articulation of differences already securely in place."[21] Satire must convince audiences of their potential culpability—for example, in *Look Who's Back*, crowds mobbing Hitler to get a "selfie" do not seem far removed from contemporary behavior. There is nothing like this in *Jojo*. Nevertheless, Waititi notes, "I experienced a certain level of prejudice growing up as a Māori Jew," and parallels have been drawn between postcolonial trauma of indigenous peoples and the Holocaust.[22] US anti-Semitism was satirized in a 2004 *South Park* episode about Mel Gibson's *The Passion of the Christ* (2004). In the episode, Stan and Kenny ask Mel Gibson for their money back, not because the film was anti-Semitic but because it was "a crappy film." This mixing of moral and aesthetic standards is something that Waititi has perpetuated in the marketing of *Jojo*.

Critical Reception

Waititi has suggested the film had been "divisive" on account of its subject matter, Nazism, implying that controversy had arisen from the film's bold confrontation of racism and hate speech. "I never wanted to make something that was very easy, because for me, if it's too easy, then what's the point? . . . People say, 'Oh, it's divisive,' but where I come from, 'divisive' is not a swear word. It's a means to create discussion."[23] However, the film's reviews suggest that the controversy was not over the film's subject matter but its artistic merit. Most reviewers didn't question the film's ostensible aims, but rather its success in achieving them: "the finished film . . . although clearly sincere in its intentions, is neither sharp nor funny enough to cut to the heart of its subject matter"; "If the premise is risky, the execution is depressingly not so."[24]

According to many reviewers, the intertextuality that features in all of Waititi's films seems to function here as a substitute for diegetic reality rather than an enhancement of it. Waititi's knowledge of Nazism seems based largely on fiction. He even suggests himself, perhaps flippantly, but pertinently in the light of the present argument, that "I didn't do any research. I didn't base him on anything I'd seen about Hitler before. I just made him a version of myself that happened to have a bad haircut and a shitty little mustache. And a mediocre German accent."[25] The casting of Jojo as a small, blond-haired, blue-eyed boy recalls, some reviewers point out, the protagonist Oskar of Volker Schlöndorff's *The Tin Drum* (1979), another film about Nazism set primarily in Germany leading up to and including WWII.[26] The difference is that Oskar, a stunted child-man, is a mute witness to the horrors of Nazism and war, while Jojo is a conventional protagonist who renounces politics, somewhat predictably, for love. Intertextuality is also implicit in the characterization of the film as "the first hipster Nazi comedy," implying a (self-consciously) anachronistic approach, with Waititi playing a "stylized goof-head version of Adolf Hitler, who speaks in aggressive anachronisms ('That was *intense!*' 'I'm stressed out!' 'Correctamundo!' 'That was a complete bust!' 'So, how's it all going with that Jew thing upstairs?'), sounding like a petulant mean-girl version of the Führer."[27] Similarly, another review suggests that Jojo's Germany:

looks like a theme park reproduction, and its inhabitants are like costumed cartoon mascots (Sam Rockwell and Rebel Wilson are Hitler Youth leaders, Stephen Merchant a *Raiders of the Lost Ark*–esque Gestapo agent). Jojo's antisemitic beliefs are all cod-Borat non-sequiturs—at one point, he asks Elsa where "the Jew Queen lays her eggs"—while Waititi's Hitler won't feel particularly outrageous to anyone who remembers the pure, deranged gusto of Dick Shawn's similar turn in *The Producers* 52 years ago.[28]

Jay Nilsson notes, "During the 1990s irony became a source of contention in American culture. For some it came to be defined—in opposition to honesty and sincerity—as apolitical, as synonymous with apathy, and as an expression of moral relativism."[29] Implicit here is the characterization of hipster youth irony as universal, and hence meaningless—hence *Jojo*'s ironies are both too broad and too crude to offer genuine critique.

Another reason alleged by Waititi for the film's controversy is its comic treatment of Nazism—but as suggested above, Nazis have been screen comedy fodder since Charles Chaplin's *The Great Dictator* (1940).[30] A BBC TV *Smith & Jones* sketch from 1989 displays many of the Nazi stereotypes from Waititi's film, prefiguring Captain Klenzendorf (Sam Rockwell) almost exactly.[31] Many reviewers suggest that the film's comic tone is incongruous, forced, or superficial: a "smug surface-level audacity" in a film "that employs a repetitive wink as it proudly trots out its central gimmick, recasting Hitler as a buffoonish imaginary friend for maximum lols":

> There is no suggestion that anything on screen remotely impinges on the real world: Nazism and the Holocaust specifically are presented as goofy can-you-ever-believe-they-went-for-this-rubbish? one-offs. As satire it's a dismal dereliction of duty; as comedy, a one-note joke that wears out fast.[32]

The comedy, rather than satirically reinforcing the message, almost seems to exist separately from the more serious part of the film. Critics commented on the film's "uneven" tone and awkward mixture of humor and sentiment.[33] One possibility would be to read this as camp (as in *Hunt for the Wilderpeople*), but in a satire the expectation is that humor should reinforce rather than detract from the central theme. One reviewer suggests that "Waititi is not, at his core, a satirist. A comic filmmaker with some serious ideas, sure, but that isn't really the same thing as satire."[34] Indeed, Waititi's feature films tend, in his self-referential fashion, to poke fun at themselves rather than at an external target. Parody (which takes aesthetics as its object) is more Waititi's style than satire.[35] Satire is often marked by a strong moral tone, condemning particular social groups or personages—not something particularly apparent in Waititi's mostly affable oeuvre. *Jojo Rabbit*, in contrast, has been accused of didacticism.[36]

Reverse Racism

However, Waititi has previously used satire in his nonfilmic work, and usually the subject is racism. "Give Nothing to Racism," the NZ Human Rights Commission TV advertisement he fronted in 2017, and "Drive By," a *Flight of the Conchords* episode he wrote and directed in 2007, share with *Jojo Rabbit* the satiric device of role reversal, in this case a nonwhite person playing a racist, a device used in a modified form in Chaplin's *The Great Dictator*.[37] Another precedent is African American comedian Dave Chappelle's 2004 skit about a blind white supremacist, Clayton Bigsby—the joke being that he was played by Chappelle himself.[38] Despite the whole *Conchords* series being set in New York, Waititi avoids African American race discourse, alluding to it by a joke:

> **DAVE:** You're [i.e., New Zealanders are] pretty much the most hated people in America right now.
> **JEMAINE:** What about black people?
> **DAVE:** They don't like you either.

Waititi partly depoliticizes the issue by playing down links to blackness. An Indian fruit stall owner named Sinjay (Aziz Ansari) refuses to serve the Conchords because they are New Zealanders. Much humor derives from the fact that the Conchords are so unassertive ("New Zealanders all mumble, I can't understand you!" is one of Sinjay's taunts) that they are frequently confused with people from other English-speaking countries, which their American friend Dave conflates with "the redcoats, the oppressors." Deliverance comes when Sinjay oversteps: "Too bad

New Zealanders are a bunch of cocky a-holes descended from criminals and retarded monkeys . . . riding round on your kangaroos all day." Bret replies: "You're thinking of Australians." Sinjay eventually apologizes for having confused them with other white people (of course, white racists commonly confuse nonwhite ethnicities; ironically, Clement is Māori). Situating the series in the US means that the Conchords experience a "crisis of identity" as their national identity is no longer transparent or self-assured. They experience a mild version of "otherness," though nothing like the kind of racism directed toward, say, African Americans.[39]

In the second example, "Give Nothing to Racism," Waititi fronts the public service advertisement himself, drawing on his (real) status as 2017 Kiwibank New Zealander of the Year. Black-and-white film, a suit (for most of the advertisement), a rigid posture, use of direct address, and classical music all add further gravitas to his appeal: "I'm calling on . . . my fellow Kiwis to support a very important cause. Racism [pause] needs your help to survive. You may not be in a position to give much to racism . . . you don't have to be a full-on racist, just being a tiny bit racist is enough . . ." The advertisement parodies a charity appeal, asking the audience to give "just a little" to racism. Like the Conchords example, the humor of the text is based on a nonwhite person apparently being racist. Identifying the audience as "my fellow Kiwis" suggests that Waititi thinks the joke is one that New Zealanders will get, but the subtext is that Waititi is serious, because he really does think that "Kiwis" are racist. The term "Kiwi" is often identified with the dominant ethnic group—Pākehā.[40] NZ Labour MP Tāmati Coffey recently compared news coverage of Waititi's Oscars win with another article in which a Māori filmmaker was sued. Waititi was described as Kiwi, the filmmaker as Māori. Coffey stated, "Negative stories involving Māori call the person out for being Māori. If the individual attains success, Māori are escalated to 'Kiwi.'"[41]

The "Give Nothing to Racism" commercial is clearly satirical, but is Waititi satirizing institutional racism or institutional anti-racism? No one uses the term "racism" more than anti-racists, and after a while its repetition starts to sound parodic. On the other hand, white supremacist groups also claim to be victims of racism.[42] The ambiguity of Waititi's performance strongly suggests the trickster. This takes us back to the definition of comic play as an action that negates conventional meaning. The problem about the trickster is that you can't tell what he or she means. In

"Give Nothing to Racism" TV advertisement for Human Rights Commission (NZ), featuring Taika Waititi, 2017.

contrast, Chappelle's character is racist toward blacks, so the evidence of the absurdity of his stance is irrefutable, highlighting the problem with reverse racism as used by Waititi: if you choose to ignore the irony, it can simply look like black people being racist to whites.

In *Jojo Rabbit*, Waititi is also playing a racist. As noted above, however, he makes little attempt to play Hitler realistically; it's a buffoonish parody. Another point of difference from the above examples is that New Zealanders are not the focus—Waititi is venturing into unfamiliar territory, and this could affect the success of his satire. A lack of familiarity with the source material could affect the quality of the film, and other Pasifika/NZ directors have adapted more easily to working with European stories and settings (Toa Fraser's *Dean Spanley* [2008], for example).

Jojo in Relation to Waititi's Other Films

Waititi is playing a father figure to a boy character, as he did in *Boy*. In terms of "comedian comedy," the Hitler character is also a comic performance that is in places (like the opening scene of the film) played directly to camera (via a mirror), and Jojo is also involved in this direct address. This convention breaks the fourth wall and throws the fictional premise of the film into relief (the risk is that it also trivializes the subject matter of the film, which could be counterproductive if the film is a satire). It opens a fantasy space (as in *Boy*) which the father-son duo share and cocreate to some degree. Notably, though, *Boy*'s father is also a real character, which opens up narrative possibilities (interactions with other characters, for example) lacking here because of Hitler's imaginary status. The narrative of both films is to some degree about the child becoming disillusioned with the father figure. However, *Boy* also features an intermediary figure—child/man Michael Jackson, through whom the character differences are mediated and to some degree resolved. There is no third party in *Jojo*. *Boy*'s ambiguous resolution has the effect of validating the child's perspective; we come to see the world as he does, to some degree. But in *Jojo*, the narrative follows a more traditional trajectory of disillusioning Jojo with Nazism and teaching him (through love) how to be an adult. In effect, the satire's message is that only some blue-eyed, blond children are stupid enough to believe in Nazism. Or adult caricatures, as all the Nazi characters are. "Caricature has traditionally appealed to a broad audience (unlike satire) because of its relatively simple techniques, and a typical form of caricature is constructed as overstated satirical representations of people's character, looks, and behavior."[43] Thus the satire is ineffective, as it does not implicate the audience enough for them to feel culpable.

The use of a child's perspective (another Waititi leitmotif) in a film about Nazism is nothing new—the Holocaust's horror is such that it can be represented only by someone who does not understand it, as in *The Tin Drum*, *The Boy in the Striped Pajamas* (Mark Herman, 2008), and *Life Is Beautiful* (Roberto Benigni, 1997). Such a device could be satirical—Menippean satire can feature the picaresque adventures of an everyman character, whose gullibility and incomprehension of the outlandish scenes he or she witnesses heightens audience awareness of their incongruity, as in *Gulliver's Travels*, for example.[44] *The Tin Drum* and, to some degree, *Life is Beautiful* fit this model. *Look Who's Back* also pairs Hitler with a series of child-men or women who are oblivious to the main character's evil potential. For this device to be effective, evil has to be believable, but in *Jojo*, none of the Nazis are sufficiently threatening.

All of Waititi's films up to this point (with the possible exception of *Eagle vs Shark*) have been male comedies. In contrast, this film could engage with Waititi's maternal Jewishness, and indeed he has stated, "My film is a love letter to my mother and to all single mothers" (which could also relate to his spouse, Chelsea Winstanley, from whom he has apparently been separated for some time).[45] But Waititi is on unfamiliar ground, with two major female characters and a love story (another narrative mostly absent from his oeuvre).[46] So how do these characters and scenarios fit into the comic narrative? Jojo's mother (Scarlett Johansson) and Elsa, the Jewish fugitive (Thomasin McKenzie) may have some funny lines and scenes, but they are basically serious characters in a conventional narrative: Jojo learns to transfer his childish love of his mother into his adult love of Elsa, a device made less credible by the obvious maturity gap between the two leads (although consistent with Waititi's usual characterization of male-female relations). It's hard for any character to cast off the childish connotations of a name like Jojo. As Jojo becomes more involved with Elsa, Hitler and the cast of funny Nazis fade into the background and romantic melodrama takes over, introducing the uneasy tension between comedy and sentiment noted by reviewers. Melodrama is also arguably the genre most implacably opposed to satire, further blunting the intended message. Such lines as Rosie's "They'll never win. That is the power you have—as long as there is someone alive somewhere, then they lose. They didn't get you yesterday, or today. Make tomorrow the same" typify the platitudes of the second half of the film, which ends with a Rilke quote as far from satire as one could imagine: "Let everything happen to you/ Beauty and terror/ No feeling is final/ Just keep going."

However, the two female leads give strong performances, and this arguably has the effect of broadening the film's appeal, which would have helped its Oscar chances. Elsa and Rosie are continuous with women in Waititi's other films—they're both "ball-busters," literally in Rosie's case, when she floors Captain Klenzendorf with a knee to the groin. Waititi's women are often the "real" men: a scene where Rosie blacks up her neck and chin to look like stubble and delivers a stinging rebuke to Jojo in the persona of his father is one of the most striking in the film. Elsa also uses fear, intimidation, and wit to put Jojo in his place:

JOJO: Tell me everything about the Jewish race.
ELSA: Okay. We're like you but human. Done.

The film also develops the relationship between Elsa and Rosie, culminating in an exchange where Rosie rhapsodizes about being a woman, her speech culminating in the following lines: "You'll go to Morocco, take up lovers and make them suffer, look a tiger in the eye and learn to trust without fear. That's what it is to be a woman." Given that Rosie is to some degree modeled on Waititi's mother, how much can we read into "look a tiger in the eye," as presumably she must have looked Taika in the eye on many occasions? Equally, Waititi might have felt that confronting his mother (clearly a formidable woman, going by his many comments about her and the characterization of Elsie and women in general in his films) was also eyeing a tiger.

Failed Camp?

Almost every Waititi film has a camp aspect to it, from Sakaar in *Thor: Ragnarok*, to antipodean camp in *Wilderpeople*, to men dressing as vampires in *Shadows*, as their favorite animal in *Eagle vs Shark*, and as Michael Jackson in *Boy*. In *Jojo Rabbit*, Waititi tries to make Nazis camp, but arguably it doesn't work. It's not that Nazis can't be made camp—as "Springtime for Hitler" shows. It's just that in most Nazi comedies, the Nazis are either at least partly metafictional (that is, there are characters playing or impersonating Nazis within the diegesis, as in *To Be or Not To Be* [Ernst Lubitsch, 1942], *The Producers* [Mel Brooks, 1967], and *The Great Dictator*) or else they are fish out of water (as in *Look Who's Back*). These strategies put a protective layer of irony around the evil characters—either they are being mixed up with people dressed as Nazis, or they are aberrations. But in *Jojo*, the Nazis are literally Nazis. The Hitler character is imaginary, but he's also Hitler. This lack of a fictive element, or a containment strategy, makes it hard for a critical audience to reconcile the conventional wisdom of Nazi evil with the buffoons we see on screen. Of course, we see evidence of their evil—the death of Frau Betzler, for example. But this feels as if it belongs in a different movie to the one with the Nazis in it. The only time the two worlds come together, in my opinion, is the above-mentioned incident when Frau Betzler "blacks herself up" as Herr Betzler (a German soldier) and berates Jojo. This is the one genuinely threatening moment in the film. It's because Waititi understands scary women. It's also, ironically, a moment of bush camp, because it features

Frau Betzler (Scarlett Johansson) as drag king in *Jojo Rabbit* (2019).

a drag king, a woman impersonating a man. It's not funny, but it is arguably more convincing than the japery of the rest of the film.

Jojo is basically a film of two halves, with a broadly comic opening transitioning somewhat awkwardly into a melodramatic love story. Neither of these halves is particularly satirical—in the first part, the Nazis are too much like caricatures, and in the second half, the comic tone mostly dissolves into sentiment. A satire should make people reexamine their own lives and behavior. However, the film has been popular, and its awards success has raised Waititi's profile. Its message of tolerance for other cultures, however cloyingly expressed, seems timely in contemporary US, where Californian liberalism and Trump authoritarian populism are increasingly at odds.[47] It seems improbable that this standoff will result in a stream of anti-Trump satire, however, as Hollywood cannot afford to alienate US audiences, so *Jojo*'s indirect satire-lite fits the bill perfectly for the time being. Is there something that Waititi can learn from the film's torrid reception? Perhaps that the opinions of film critics are not very consequential.

Conclusion

So far, Waititi's Hollywood sojourn can be deemed a success. Both *Thor: Ragnarok* and *Jojo Rabbit* have been popular, *Ragnarok* was critically well reviewed, and *Jojo* won an Oscar.[1] Waititi's latest coup is cowriting and directing the next *Star Wars* movie.[2] As with Marvel, there's a policy of using "hot" directors to keep the franchise fresh. Both Marvel and *Star Wars* are owned by Disney, who bought LucasFilm in 2012. Disney has followed the three George Lucas–directed prequels of *Episode I: The Phantom Menace* (1999), *Episode II: Attack of the Clones* (2002), and *Episode III: Revenge of the Sith* (2005) with another trilogy of sequels: *Episode VII: The Force Awakens* (J. J. Abrams, 2015), *Episode VIII: The Last Jedi* (Rian Johnston, 2017), and *Episode IX: The Rise of Skywalker* (J. J. Abrams, 2019). Many fans and critics were disappointed with the Lucas-directed prequels, and the director's tinkering with the first three films.[3] As one fan put it, "Has he fulfilled his destiny or destroyed his legacy?"[4] The phrase "the Lucas Effect" sums up Lucas's huge influence on contemporary film, for good or ill, with some arguing that control can destroy creativity, as discussed in the documentary *The People vs George Lucas* (Alexandre Phillipe, 2010).[5]

The Disney takeover could be seen as a new start, and *The Force Awakens* was generally liked by fans and critics,[6] balancing new elements (a female heroine, a bit more casting diversity) with familiarity (reappearances of Harrison Ford, Carrie Fisher, and Mark Hamill, and a plot lifted straight out of the first *Star Wars* film [*A New Hope*, George Lucas, 1977]). However, the next installment, *The Last Jedi*, although critically praised and reasonably successful, attracted the wrath of conservative fans, who objected to the film's "progressivism," including its casting diversity and the irreverent treatment of some of the stalwarts (in particular Luke Skywalker).[7] Director Rian Johnson reportedly commented, "If someone's responding to diversity negatively, fuck 'em," in response to fans who "whine about 'SJWs' [Social Justice Warriors] and take issue with the movie having women and people of color in lead roles."[8] Another analysis made comparison with Gamergate and the backlash to the all-women

Ghostbusters (Paul Feig, 2016) remake.[9] It also pointed out low audience ratings on sites like Rotten Tomatoes and Metacritic. In 2020, *The Last Jedi's* audience rating was 43 percent on Rotten Tomatoes compared with 86 percent for *The Force Awakens*. On Metacritic the ratings were 4.3 vs. 6.8 (out of 10). Both movies were liked by critics, but the audience disparity is quite noticeable, even three years later, although obviously audience ratings can be manipulated. In 2019, Lucasfilm president Kathleen Kennedy was still defending *The Last Jedi*, stating that fans' strong reactions showed their ongoing investment in the franchise.[10] Director of *The Force Awakens*, J. J. Abrams, was brought back for the final sequel, *The Rise of Skywalker*. Abrams did the macho, old-school-style *Star Trek* reboot (2009), ironic since the original *Star Trek* was considered a model of diversity in its day.[11] These controversies could echo political and social divisions in contemporary Western culture as it heads into uncertainty and confusion with peak oil, climate change, pandemics, and increasing economic disparity and instability.

Considering that the film Waititi will be working on is the first of a new trilogy, the recent controversies, the polarized political climate, and Waititi's indigeneity, expectations are very high. He won't be the first Māori in *Star Wars*, however: Temuera Morrison starred as Jango Fett in *Attack of the Clones* and *Revenge of the Sith*, along with smaller parts for Rena Owen and Keisha Castle-Hughes. Dan Taipua writes that Māori as indigenes have had a special connection with the films: "The idea that once sovereign lands are occupied and controlled by the forces of a remote and wealthy empire . . . rings out in the everyday lives of the indigenous nations of America, Kanaka Māoli, the Aboriginal peoples of occupied Australia, and many others."[12] Admittedly, the "Evil Empire" is a feature of almost every sci-fi fantasy film ever made, but Taipua also points out the multicultural storytelling in *Star Wars* films, drawing on Japanese and Italian directors Akira Kurosawa and Sergio Leone, the use of "modified Haitian languages," "Hopi motifs in costume designs," and how "The Force" derives from the Chinese concept of chi or qi.[13] At the same time, he notes that most of this culture has been appropriated uncredited and displayed as exoticism. The recent *Star Wars* spin-off *The Mandalorian* has featured a range of directors, including Waititi for the season finale. The episode features some obvious Waititi touches: extended banter between two Empire soldiers in the opening scene, and a self-sacrificing droid voiced by Waititi. Wit has arguably been in short supply in this franchise, apart from the early films.

Waititi has a penchant for playing aliens, which perhaps speaks to a longer history of links between aliens and nonwhites—Afro-futurism.[14] Apart from Korg in *Thor*, there is an alien character that I have discussed elsewhere, but the link is especially obvious in *Boy*, with its frequent E.T. and Michael Jackson references. Jackson popularized "the robot dance" in 1974, which subsequently became an influence on hip-hop styles such as locking, demonstrated in the kapa haka sequence at the end of the film.[15] Julian Vigo writes of Jackson "blurring . . . the lines between male and female, between black and white and between human and animal."[16] To this we could add Donna Haraway's cyborg categories of organic/ artificial and physical/nonphysical.[17] Both Afro-futurism and Haraway's cyborg explore the potential of sci-fi for resisting hegemony. Looking across Waititi's career, one is struck by the kinds of beings that inhabit his films, and how they often seem to stand on the threshold between worlds: vampires, man-gods, comic heroes, child-men, adult children, masculine women, fantasists, tricksters, robots, aliens, and perhaps most important, those of mixed ethnicity, both indigenous and dias- poric. Another kind of liminality is displayed by the comic performer, continually moving between fiction and real life, via a knowing wink to the audience. The comic challenge invites us to suspend the normal distinctions by which we live and play awhile.

Much of Waititi's comedy is located on blurred boundaries, between serious and nonserious, Same and Other. He plays with ethnicity by adopting a range of masks—Polynesian, Māori, Jew, New Zealander, nonspecific Other, racist. His self-identifications as a "Polynesian Jew" highlights his "Poly"-semy, the ways that he makes links beyond Maori- dom to the wider Polynesian diaspora (as in *Thor*) and beyond that to Jewish comedy.[18] Mockumentary locates humorous play not so much in its action as in the audience's assessment of what is "for real," bearing in mind that fictive/real and serious/nonserious binaries relate in com- plex ways—fiction can be serious or nonserious, as can reality. His insistent use of direct address generates a multitude of effects, ranging from emotional disengagement (the sense that the character is outside the action, commenting on it) or engaging with media in preference to engaging with people (as when characters stare at screens, simultaneously staring at the audience), to quirky awkwardness, where the character's direct address almost seems like an appeal to the audience (Get me out of here!), to performing for the audience, which seems to be about a fantasy of direct connection with an Other who is absent in the diegetic world. It's no coincidence that it's often Waititi himself, or the character he is playing, that we see looking at us (the eye of the Taika), reminding us how his work is rooted in live performance while simultaneously questioning that performance: "This is a joke." The paradox of the eye is that it often stands in for identity (the pun on "I") while itself being only a medium. The eye is both medium and message, empty and full, something and nothing, a voyeur—the eye of the camera.[19] But I think that for Waititi its deepest meaning is social—eye contact is a way of connecting to other beings. From accounts of his childhood onward to his present status as celebrity socialite, it seems obvious that Waititi is a sociable person, but also has the "double consciousness" of the ethnic outsider, who performs his malleable identity according to the situation. His working methods suggests that he enjoys working and playing with others, and he has that "Kiwi" disdain of hierarchy. Waititi's practical joking also questions the boundary between art and life—indeed, there may be a connection between practical joking and NZ's (male) egalitarian ethos, as both aim to deflate pretension (but whose pretension?).[20] Waititi's play with his indigenous Māori identity suggests that rather than simply identifying Māori with New Zealand, he recognizes, with Paul Gilroy or Robbie Shilliam, a more fluid situation where nonwhite identities partake in flows of people and culture across oceans (the Black Atlantic, the Black Pacific) to constitute multicultural societies.[21]

Postcolonial comedy carries a legacy of trauma, not as profound as Gilroy's slavery, but real. This can be articulated in painful comedy, or comedy of embarrassment, which denies the audience the cues that signal levity, so they are left wondering what the appropriate response is. When the atmosphere is tense and uncomfortable, we feel the need to laugh most, so, ironically, painful comedy appears to imitate real life, by generating that kind of suspense, and by using documentary conventions. This is allied to flat or deadpan style: people die in Waititi's films, either off-screen (*Eagle, Boy*) or on-screen (*Shadows, Wilderpeople*). But typically death is dismissed by bathos—for example, Waititi's sermon over Bella's body, with its "two doors," one leading to "nummy treats";

the fastidious Viago's attempted seduction of a victim, resulting in blood "all over my nice clean sheets"; and Nick's trial in *Shadows*, where we expect the worst, because he is responsible for the death of another vampire, but the scene ends with the vampires lamely chanting "shame" at him. The oscillation of tone from serious to trivial is a feature of both comedy and camp. Science fiction can also be camp—witness *The Rocky Horror Show*, written by New Zealander Richard O'Brien, the progenitor of a distinctive local genre of science fiction horror comedy.

Camp is relevant to comedy because it is "failed seriousness"—as, for example, with the Kiwi Bloke, whose reiteration as the dominant discourse of NZ identity became camp partly because of the increasingly obvious contradiction between its rural iconography and the urban reality of most New Zealanders. Camp upsets the equation of masculinity/documentary realism that underwrites settler national identity, turning the Kiwi "practical joker" into a practical joke. Reiterations of the bloke archetype, such as Uncle Hec in *Wilderpeople*, reveal their dependence on Māori, in the figure of Ricky, who, unlike Hec, has the ability to textualize his environment, reversing the historic colonizing textualization of Māori by Pākehā. Heteronormative masculinity is also challenged by gender parody—the women of Waititi's films are more authentically masculine than the men. Men are supposed to confirm their heterosexuality by having sex with women, but in Waititi's films this hardly happens. To be a woman in NZ, you have to be a man, and the same paradox applies to national identity (perhaps with Jacinda Ardern as NZ prime minister, this association is finally starting to unravel). At the same time, Waititi's films work with this gender paradox—arguably, it is the source of much of their humor—rather than attempting to resolve it. Comedy is premised on "a state of conspiratorial irony" between audience and performer, but really challenging social norms would require breaking out of this complicity.[22] At various junctures, I have pointed out how the homosociality of Waititi's work gives rise to questionable ethics and gender conservatism. "Laughter is an important resource for affirming that which is shared in a collective and for affirming experiences that cannot be named without violating social taboos," in this case, the inadmissible continuum between homosociality and homosexuality.[23]

Antipodean camp is a reverse discourse—taking signs of marginality, irrelevance, tedium, and inauthenticity and rearticulating them as constitutive of authentic locality. Waititi says, "At the end of the day, the reality is we're all losers, and we're all uncoordinated. We're the worst of all of the animals on earth, and there's something quite endearing about that."[24] The impassivity of the Kiwi bloke could also connote his obliviousness to the wider world, as in Fred Dagg's catchphrase, "We don't know how lucky we are." The danger of reverse discourse is that if taken literally, it can rebound on the group using it, as, for example, with Waititi's comment, "We Polynesians [substitute Kiwis if you like] are real self-deprecating." A troll could answer, "and with good reason!"[25] It remains a possibility that Waititi will one day make a more overtly political film about race in NZ.

Taika Waititi is now, along with Peter Jackson, NZ's best known and most successful film director. Part of his success seems to be his ability to make popular films without sacrificing his quirky approach. He uses comedy without being defined by it; this gives him more flexibility in his approach. In Bourdieu's terms, he balances the autonomy of art against the heteronomous demands of commerce, and comedy is a mode that demands attention to both aspects, particularly when it combines serious and nonserious modes.[26] Perhaps a defining feature of the present epoch is that the distinction between nonserious and serious has blurred, and that the most prevalent form of comic play is in the hinterland between them. This is a world where Donald Trump can be US president, someone whose actions and words are consequential for billions, but who is simultaneously viewed as a clown, a buffoon, even a postmodern trickster.[27] Another factor in Waititi's success, unlike Trump's, seems to be his ability to collaborate with other people, and Waititi's work displays that sociality, whether through semi-improvised ensemble work on camera or through the multiple ways that his films relate to local and global audiences.

Although Waititi is working overseas, he has maintained considerable involvement in NZ, producing recent films like *The Breaker Upperers* and TV series like *Wellington Paranormal*.[28] Piki Films, the production company Waititi runs with Carthew Neal, produces local Māori/Pasifika content such as Māori Television's animated series *Aroha Bridge* and Pasifika comic Rose Matefeo's 2020 film debut, *Baby Done*, as well as many of Waititi's films. He also appeared in *Poi E*, Tearepa Kahi's 2016 documentary on the song that is central to *Boy*, and *Merata: How Mum Decolonised the Screen* (2018), a documentary on Māori film director Merata Mita by her son Heperi Mita, produced by Chelsea Winstanley (whom Waititi married in 2011 and with whom he has had two daughters): Te Kainga o Te Hinekāhu in 2012, and Matewa Kiritapu in 2015. Waititi continues, through collaborations, to raise the profile of indigenous and Pasifika talent locally and overseas, most recently producing a Native American film, *Frybread Face and Me* (Billy Luther).[29] He is dedicated to developing indigenous film, while also creating entertainment, thus balancing politics with pleasure.

Some questions remain. Will we ever see a convincing love story in a Waititi film? The jury's out on *Jojo Rabbit*. Will a Waititi film ever feature a female lead (perhaps the new *Star Wars* film)? Again, *Jojo* had more central female characters than his previous work, but there was still a feeling that they mostly belonged in a separate world to the comic parts of the film. Can he write male characters who are not, basically, children or buffoons? Or are these actually his strengths? In this light, another potential Waititi project, adapting a 2015 documentary *Next Goal Wins*, about the American Samoa soccer team, feels like a (welcome?) return to familiar ground—Polynesia, presumably a mostly male cast with many familiar faces (Oscar Kightley, David Fane, Rachel House, Rhys Darby), a male bonding theme, and self-deprecating humor (supposedly they were the worst international soccer team ever).[30] A South Pacific *Cool Runnings* (Jon Turteltaub, 1993), it feels like a comfortable compromise between US and Pasifika influences, both of which have also been historically significant in his work, highlighting how Waititi has always interpreted Polynesia in its broadest sense. However, it's possible that *Star Wars* may come first.[31]

Whatever the future may hold for Waititi, he is now part of a Māori/Pasifikan renaissance, from *bro'Town* to Hawaiian indigenous nationalist ukulele player Israel Kamakawiwo'ole; from local comedians like Coco Solid and Rose Matafeo to Waititi contemporaries like Jemaine Clement and Bret McKenzie who now work in Hollywood, to Māori musicians like Six60, who have been packing out stadiums throughout New Zealand. Then there are Hollywood actors like Jason Momoa, Dwayne Johnson, Cliff Curtis, and Kelly Hu, to film directors like Toa Fraser, Tearepa Kahi, Sima Urale, Briar Grace-Smith, and Ainsley Gardiner. The future is brown, and may the Force be with them.

Notes

Introduction

1 "The Art of Creativity, Taika Waititi, TEDxDoha," YouTube, November 4, 2010, www.youtube.com/watch?v=pL71KhNmnls&t=12s.

2 "Top Ten Highest Grossing New Zealand Movies," Flicks, November 1, 2019, www.flicks.co.nz/news/top-10-highest-grossing-new-zealand -movies-ever.

3 Gregory Bateson, *Steps to an Ecology of Mind* (Chicago: University of Chicago Press, 1972), 180.

4 Marianna Keisalo, "'Picking People to Hate': Reversible Reversals in Stand-up Comedy," *Suomen Antropologi* 41, no. 4 (2016): 63.

5 Johan Huizinga, *Homo Ludens: A Study of the Play Element in Culture* (London: Taylor and Francis, 2003); Erving Goffman, *The Presentation of Self in Everyday Life* (New York: Doubleday, 1959).

6 Keisalo, "'Picking People to Hate.'"

7 Don Handelman, "Postlude: Framing Hierarchically, Framing Moebiusly," *Journal of Ritual Studies* 26, no. 2 (2012): 65–77.

8 Keisalo, "'Picking People to Hate,'" 62; Henry Louis Gates, *Signifying Monkey: A Theory of African-American Literary Criticism* (New York: Oxford University Press, 1989), 52.

9 TED, www.ted.com/about/programs-initiatives/tedx-program, accessed May 10, 2020.

10 Andrew S. Horton, *Comedy/Cinema/Theory* (Berkeley: University of California Press, 1991), 4; John Morreall, *Comic Relief: A Comprehensive Philosophy of Humor* (Malden: Wiley-Blackwell, 2011); Alexander Kozintsev, *The Mirror of Laughter* (New Brunswick, NJ: Transaction, 2012).

11 Kozintsev, *The Mirror of Laughter*, 85.

12 Ibid., 89–90.

13 Ibid., 91.

14 Ibid., 94.

15 Ibid., 100.

16 Ibid., 104.

17 Ibid., 98.

18 Ibid., 104

19 Ibid., 99.

20 Henri Bergson, *Laughter: An Essay on the Meaning of the Comic* (Mineola, NY: Dover Publications, 2005), 24–25.

21 Laura Cull, "Performance as Philosophy: Responding to the Problem of 'Application,'" *Theatre Research International* 37 (2012): 22; William Beeman, "Humor," in *Key Terms in Language and Culture*, ed. Alessandro Duranti (Oxford: Blackwell Publishers, 2001), 98.

22 Bergson, *Laughter*, 9.

23 Ibid., 10.

24 Keisalo, "'Picking People to Hate.'"

25 Mary Douglas, "The Social Control of Cognition: Some Factors in Joke Perception," *Man* 3, no. 3 (1968): 365. Kozintsev, *The Mirror of Laughter*, 17.

26 "The Art of Creativity."

27 Morreall, *Comic Relief*, 37.

28 Blake Gopnik, *Warhol: A Life as Art* (London: Penguin, Random House, 2020).

29 Morreall, *Comic Relief*, 37.

30 Tony Deverson, *The Oxford Dictionary of New Zealandisms* (South Melbourne, Victoria: Oxford University Press, 2010), 121; *Flight of the Conchords*, "Drive-By," written and directed by Taika Waititi, 2007.

31 Caleb Moses, Twitter, February 10, 2020, twitter.com/Caleb_Speak.

32 "Short Film Winners: 2005 Oscars," February 19, 2015, www.youtube.com/watch?v=_CGR0T9-Qho.

33 "Taika Waititi stashes his Oscars trophy under the seat in front of him," YouTube, February 10, 2020, www.youtube.com/watch?v=5pdRhhPDR-E.

34 Moira Marsh, *Practically Joking* (Logan: Utah State University Press, 2015), 150.

35 Morreall, *Comic Relief*, 29–30.

36 Ibid., 31.

37 Bergson, *Laughter*, 3.

38 Steve Seidman, *Comedian Comedy: A Tradition in Hollywood Film* (Ann Arbor, MI: UMI Research Press, 1981).

39 Barry Barclay, *Our Own Image* (Minneapolis: Minnesota University Press, 2015); Brendan Hokowhitu and Vijay Devadas, eds., *The Fourth Eye: Maori Media in Aotearoa New Zealand* (Minneapolis: University of Minnesota Press, 2013).

40 *Pulp Comedy*, Series Seven, Episode Three, 2003, *NZ On Screen*, accessed October 17, 2020, www.nzonscreen.com/title/pulp-comedy-s7e3-taika-waititi-2003.

41 Aristotle, *The Poetics of Aristotle*, trans. S. H. Butcher (London: Macmillan, 1902), 13.

42 Jerry Palmer, *The Logic of the Absurd: On Film and TV Comedy* (London: BFI, 1987), 39–44.

43 Ibid.

44 Ibid., 44.

45 Kozintsev, *The Mirror of Laughter*, 4–5.

46 Ibid.

47 Sigmund Freud, "Jokes and Their Relation to the Unconscious," in *Standard Edition of the Complete Psychological Works of Sigmund Freud*, vol. 5, trans. James Strachey (New York: W. W. Norton, 1963).

48 Bergson, *Laughter*, 67.

49 Christopher Vogler, *The Writer's Journey: Mythic Structure for Storytellers and Screenwriters* (London: Boxtree, 1996); Syd Field, *The Definitive Guide to Screenwriting* (London: Ebury, 2003).

50 "Jojo Rabbit Conversation with Taika Waititi Part 1," YouTube, January 31, 2020, www.youtube.com/watch?v=_ro3l9TqBNA.

51 Palmer, *The Logic of the Absurd*, 97.

52 Henry Jenkins, "Anarchistic Comedy and the Vaudeville Aesthetic," in *Hollywood Comedians, The Film Reader*, ed. Frank Krutnik (London: Routledge, 2001), 97.

53 Silas Lesnick, "CS Interview: Hunting for the Wilderpeople with Taika Waititi," July 19, 2016, https://www.comingsoon.net/movies/features/703677-taika-waititi-wilderpeople-ragnarok.

54 Barclay, *Our Own Image*.

55 Andrew Stott, *Comedy* (New York: Routledge, 2005), 148; John Mundy and Glyn White, *Laughing Matters: Understanding Film, Radio and Television Comedy* (Manchester: Manchester University Press, 2012), 4.

56 Andrew Sarris, *The American Cinema: Directors and Directions 1929–1968* (New York: E. P. Dutton & Co., 1968).

57 "Jojo Rabbit Conversation with Taika Waititi Part 1."

58 Sarris, *The American Cinema*, 41.

59 Michel Foucault, "What Is an Author?" *The Foucault Reader*, ed. Paul Rabinow (New York: Pantheon Books, 1984), 103.

60 David P. Marshall, *Celebrity and Power: Fame in Contemporary Culture* (Minneapolis: University of Minnesota Press, 2014), xi.

61 Thomas Elsaesser, "The Global Author: Control, Creative Constraints, and Performative Self-Contradiction," in *The Global Auteur: The Politics of Authorship in 21st Century Cinema*, ed. Seung-hoon Jeong and Jeremi Szaniawski (New York: Bloomsbury Academic & Professional, 2017), 22.

62 Elsaesser, "The Global Author," 28.

63 "Taika Waititi," The Arts Foundation, accessed May 31, 2018, www .thearts.co.nz/artists/taika-waititi.

64 Diels/Kranz, *Die Fragmente der Vorsokratiker*, 2005, I 3B1 (a fragment attributed to Epimenides and quoted by Clement of Alexandria).

65 Elsaesser, "The Global Author," 37.

66 Keisalo, "'Picking People to Hate,'" 62.

67 "Taika Waititi: The real story behind 'that' Oscars gag, and much more . . . Interviews 2009," NZ On Screen, September 22, 2009, www .nzonscreen.com/interviews/taika-waititi-reveals-real-story-behind -that-oscars-gag. People sleeping on maraes is quite normal. The letter writer displays his ignorance of Māori culture.

68 Tess Nichols, "Taika Waititi divides audience as music awards host," *NZ Herald*, November 20, 2015, www.nzherald.co.nz/entertainment/ news/article.cfm?c_id=1501119&objectid=11548559; "Taika Waititi at the VNZMA 2012," YouTube, November 2, 2012, www.youtube.com/ watch?v=fALzDsxB2cw.

69 Taika Waititi, Scarlett Johansson on "Jojo Rabbit," YouTube, February 2, 2020, www.youtube.com/watch?v=F4rJiijl47A.

70 Josie Adams, "Taika Waititi has a long history of good speeches," *The Spinoff*, February 11, 2020, thespinoff.co.nz/media/11-02-2020/taika -waititi-has-a-long-history-of-good-speeches/; Nichols, "Taika Waititi divides audience as music awards host."

71 Nick Perry, *Hyperreality and Global Culture* (New York: Routledge, 1998).

72　Susan Sontag, *Notes on "Camp"* (1964), monoskop.org/images/5/59/ Sontag_Susan_1964_Notes_on_Camp.pdf.

73　Amanda D. Lotz, *Cable Guys: Television and Masculinities in the 21st Century* (New York: NYU Press, 2014), 116.

74　Pākehā is a Māori term, usually used to refer to European settlers. See Michael King, *Being Pakeha Now: Reflections and Recollections of a White Native* (Auckland: Penguin, 1999).

75　"Becoming" is usually associated with Gilles Deleuze, but the concept first occurs in Henri Bergson's *Creative Evolution* (London: MacMillan, 1913), 329–30.

76　Richard Dyer, *Only Entertainment* (New York: Routledge, 1992).

77　Taika Waititi, quoted in "'Boy' Q and A (Part II)," YouTube, February 2, 2010, www.youtube.com/watch?v=l_OkifYQbVl&fea.

78　Roger Ebert, "The New Geek Cinema," Roger Ebert.com, September 27, 1998, www.rogerebert.com/festivals-and-awards/the-new-geek -cinema.

79　*MEDIANZ*, Special Issue on Taika Waititi's *Boy*, 13, no. 1 (2012), medianz .otago.ac.nz/medianz/issue/view/9.

80　See especially Ocean Mercier, "Welcome to My Interesting World: Pōwhiri Styled Encounter in *Boy*," *Illusions* 42 (2010): 3–7, and "Alamein's Encore: Entertainment, Information, Intimacy and Reflection in the *Boy* DVD Director's Commentary," *MEDIANZ* 13, no. 1 (2012): 47–65.

81　Hokowhitu and Devadas, *The Fourth Eye*.

82　Alistair Fox, *Coming-of-Age Cinema in NZ: Genre, Gender and Adaptation* (Edinburgh: Edinburgh University Press, 2017).

83　Quoted in *Merata: How Mum Decolonised the Screen*, dir. Heperi Mita, 2018.

84　Douglas, "The Social Control of Cognition," 372.

85　Jerry Palmer, *The Logic of the Absurd: On Film and TV Comedy* (London: BFI, 1987), 14.

Chapter 1

1　"The Art of Creativity, Taika Waititi, TEDxDoha," YouTube, November 4, 2010, www.youtube.com/watch?v=pL71KhNmnls&t=12s.

2　Arezou Zalipour, introduction to *Migrant and Diasporic Film and Filmmaking in New Zealand*, ed. Arezou Zalipour (Singapore: Springer, 2019), 1.

3 Mike White, "No End of Stories," *North and South* 234 (2005): 76.

4 David L. Reznik, *New Jews: Race and American Jewish Identity in 21st-Century Film* (New York: Taylor & Francis Group, 2012), 2.

5 Alex Denney, "Unknown Mortal Orchestra & Taika Waititi on New Zealand culture," Dazed, April 5, 2018, www.dazeddigital.com/music/article/39590/1/unknown-mortal-orchestra-ruban-nielson-taika-waititi-interview.

6 Leonie Pihama, "Are Films Dangerous? A Maori Woman's Perspective on *The Piano*," *Hecate* 20, no. 2 (1994): 241.

7 Glen Coulthard, "Subjects of Empire: Indigenous Peoples and the 'Politics of Recognition' in Canada," *Contemporary Political Theory* 6 (2007): 437.

8 Torjer A. Olsen, "This Word is (Not?) Very Exciting: Considering Intersectionality in Indigenous Studies," *NORA—Nordic Journal of Feminist and Gender Research* 26, no. 3 (2018): 183.

9 "The Art of Creativity, Taika Waititi, TEDxDoha," YouTube, November 4, 2010, www.youtube.com/watch?v=pL71KhNmnls&t=12s.

10 Keith Sinclair, *A History of New Zealand* (Harmondsworth: Penguin, 1959), 15.

11 Ibid., 34.

12 Not all iwi (tribes) signed. Ranginui Walker, "Rangatiratanga, Kāwanatanga and the Constitution," in *A Land of Milk and Honey?: Making Sense of Aotearoa New Zealand*, ed. Avril Bell, Vivienne Elizabeth, Tracey McIntosh, and Matt Wynyard (Auckland: Auckland University Press, 2017), 26–42; Donna Awatere, *Maori Sovereignty* (Auckland: Broadsheet, 1984).

13 David Green, "Citizenship 1840–1948: British subjects," *Te Ara—the Encyclopedia of New Zealand*, accessed June 12, 2019, www.TeAra.govt.nz/en/citizenship/page-1.

14 Sinclair, *A History of New Zealand*, 142–45.

15 Michael King, *1000 Years of Māori History—Nga Iwi o te Motu* (Auckland: Reed, 1997), 38.

16 Michael King, *1000 Years of Māori History*.

17 Ibid., 100; Michelle Keown, "'He Iwi Kotahi Tatou?': Nationalism and Cultural Identity in Maori Film," in *Contemporary New Zealand Cinema: From New Wave to Blockbusters*, ed. Ian Conrich and Stuart Murray (London: I. B. Taurus, 2008), 197–210.

18 For example, the 100% Pure New Zealand campaign, accessed June 12, 2019, www.newzealand.com/int/; Claudia Bell, "100% PURE New Zealand: Branding for back-packers," *Journal of Vacation Marketing* 14, no. 4 (2008): 345–55.

19 "New Zealand population hits 5 million," RNZ, May 19, 2020, www.rnz .co.nz/news/national/416893/new-zealand-population-hits-5-million.

20 "New Zealand's population reflects growing diversity," September 22, 2019, www.stats.govt.nz/news/new-zealands-population-reflects -growing-diversity.

21 James Liu, "Multiculturalism and Biculturalism in New Zealand: Promises and Regrets," PowerPoint presentation for the Bananas New Zealand Going Global Conference, Auckland, August 18–19, 2007, accessed June 14, 2019, www.goingbananas.org.nz/papers_2007.php.

22 "Taika Waititi," Ethnicity of Celebs, July 3, 2016, ethnicelebs.com/taika -waititi. All biographical information was checked by Robin Cohen.

23 "Taika Waititi: Masterclass," TIFF 2018, YouTube, September 10, 2018, www.youtube.com/watch?v=-5D_9i5Z8lo&t=342s.

24 "Te Ahi Kaa mo 22 o Haratua," RNZ, May 22, 2011, www.radionz.co.nz/ audio/player?audio_id=2489663.

25 Helen Barlow, "That's my boy," *NZ Herald*, March 5, 2010, www .nzherald.co.nz/entertainment/news/article.cfm?c_id=1501119& objectid=10630043.

26 "Taika Waititi: Masterclass."

27 When Māori refer to brothers and sisters, they may mean half brothers or sisters, or cousins. Māori have a broader concept of family (whānau) than the Pākehā nuclear model. Sources that mention Waititi's family have to be read with this in mind: e.g., "Taika Waititi: Masterclass"; Taroi Black, "Woman behind Taika Waititi's success," Maori Television, July 22, 2017, www.maoritelevision.com/news/ national/woman-behind-taika-waititis-success.

28 "Playing Favourites with Taika Waititi," RNZ, June 14, 2014. https:// www.rnz.co.nz/national/programmes/saturday/audio/2599644/ playing-favorites-with-taika-waititi.

29 "Te Ahi Kaa mo 22 o Haratua."

30 "My secret Wellington—Taika Waititi," *Stuff*, December 10, 2014, www .stuff.co.nz/entertainment/film/64001443/my-secret-wellington-taika -waititi.

31 April Henderson, "Maori Boys, Michael Jackson Dance Moves, and that 1984 Structure of Feeling," *MEDIANZ* 13, no. 1 (2012): 77–96.

32 "My secret Wellington—Taika Waititi."

33 Zalipour, introduction, 1.

34 "Taika Waititi: Masterclass."

35 Gregory Bateson, *Steps to an Ecology of Mind* (Chicago: University of Chicago Press, 1972), 180.

36 "Taika Waititi: Masterclass."

37 Taika Waititi, Twitter, June 10, 2014, twitter.com/TaikaWaititi/status/476109559962955776.

38 Barlow, "That's my boy."

39 Conrad Newport, personal communication with author, June 13, 2018.

40 Pierre Bourdieu, *The Rules of Art: Genesis and Structure of the Literary Field*, trans. Susan Emanuel (Cambridge: Polity Press, 1996).

41 "Eagle vs Shark provides the right fit for Loren Horsley," *Herald Sun*, November 20, 2007, www.heraldsun.com.au/entertainment/movies/misfit-the-right-fit/news-story/f91c5e90a8fde23db33ac7bf94afdd64?sv=c592b0e690fd0bc98eb28a897861ba66, accessed July 30, 2017.

42 Russell Baillie, "Interview with Jemaine Clement," *NZ Herald*, August 16, 2007, www.whatthefolk.net/nzherald03.html.

43 "Te Ahi Kaa mo 22 o Haratua."

44 "So You're A Man," Wikipedia, last updated May 22, 2018, en.wikipedia.org/wiki/So_You%27re_a_Man.

45 Victoria University of Wellington, Faculty of Humanities and Social Sciences, Alumni, accessed August 2, 2018, www.victoria.ac.nz/fhss/study/alumni.

46 Billy T. James, born William James Te Wehi Taitoko (1948–91), was arguably NZ's best-known comedian.

47 Baillie, "Interview with Jemaine Clement."

48 "Jemaine Clement & Taika Waititi in Starry Eyed Queenstown," YouTube, December 19, 2009, www.youtube.com/watch?v=xl9uPQEhE50; "Jemaine Clement & Taika Waititi in Starry Eyed," YouTube, February 7, 2010, www.youtube.com/watch?v=qWb5ClhZ9gU&t=1s.

49 Baillie, "Interview with Jemaine Clement."

50 "Jemaine Clement & Taika Waititi in Starry Eyed."

51 "Playing Favourites with Taika Waititi."

52 Te Ahukaramū Charles Royal, "First peoples in Māori tradition—
    Māui," *Te Ara—the Encyclopedia of New Zealand*, accessed May 22,
    2019, www.TeAra.govt.nz/en/first-peoples-in-maori-tradition/page-3;
    Henry Louis Gates, *Signifying Monkey: A Theory of African-American
    Literary Criticism* (New York: Oxford University Press, 1989).

53 Francis Till, "*The Untold Tales of Maui* at The Silo," *NZ Herald*, Decem-
    ber 7, 2003, www.nzherald.co.nz/lifestyle/news/article.cfm?c_id=6&
    objectid=3538066.

54 "The Living Room—Series One," NZ On Screen, 2002, accessed Octo-
    ber 19, 2020, www.nzonscreen.com/title/the-living-room-flight-of
    -the-conchords-edinburgh-festival-2002?video_ref=6262. Waititi
    did in fact accompany the Conchords on the trip, doing their lights,
    see the documentary "Frodo Is Great . . . Who Is That!!?" YouTube,
    September 3, 2019, www.youtube.com/watch?v=l_YQN4hKmF4.

55 "The Living Room—Series Two, Episode Ten," NZ On Screen, 2004,
    accessed October 18, 2020, www.nzonscreen.com/title/the-living
    -room-series-two-episode-ten-2004. The Gunter Schliemann charac-
    ter is very similar to Waititi's stand-up persona.

56 "Taika Waititi: Masterclass."

57 "Taika Waititi," The Arts Foundation, accessed July 28, 2018, www
    .thearts.co.nz/artists/taika-waititi.

58 "Taika Waititi: The real story behind 'that' Oscars gag, and much
    more . . . Interviews 2009," NZ On Screen, September 22, 2009, www
    .nzonscreen.com/interviews/taika-waititi-reveals-real-story-behind
    -that-oscars-gag.

59 Joel McManus, "How a cult Dunedin film gave Taika Waititi his big
    break," The Spinoff, April 15, 2018, thespinoff.co.nz/media/15-04
    -2018/how-a-cult-dunedin-film-gave-taika-waititi-his-big-break/.

60 Marc Fennell, "Taika Waititi: Boy Gone Wild," The Feed, May 31, 2016,
    www.sbs.com.au/news/the-feed/taika-waititi-boy-gone-wild.

61 *Two Cars, One Night* presskit, New Zealand Film Commission, accessed
    May 9, 2020, www.nzfilm.co.nz/sites/default/files/2017-11/Two_Cars
    _One_Night_Press_Kit.pdf.

62 "Playing Favourites with Taika Waititi."

63 "The Living Room—Series Two, Episode Ten."

64 Lee Schweninger, *Imagic Moments: Indigenous North American Film*
    (Athens: University of Georgia Press, 2013), 1.

65 Both *Two Cars* and *Tama Tū* received a "short film production investment" of $70,000. For "feature film production investment," *Eagle vs Shark* received $1,661,169; *Boy* and *Shadows* received $250,000 each, and *Wilderpeople* received $2,000,000 (note: these figures don't include festival travel or script development), accessed May 9, 2020, www.nzfilm.co.nz/funding-and-support/funding-overview/past -funding-decisions?page=1.

66 "Taika Waititi: Masterclass"; Zalipour, introduction, 15, quoting the NZFC Feature Film Development Funding Guidelines 2014, 3.

67 Emiel Martens, "Maori on the Silver Screen: The Evolution of Indigenous Feature Filmmaking in Aotearoa/New Zealand," *International Journal of Critical Indigenous Studies* 5, no. 1 (2012): 2–30.

68 Michael Scott, *Making New Zealand's Pop Renaissance: State, Markets, Musicians* (Burlington, VT: Taylor & Francis Group, 2013), 1.

69 "Catherine Fitzgerald: The art of film producing ... Interviews—2017," NZ On Screen, June 30, 2017, www.nzonscreen.com/interviews/ catherine-fitzgerald.

70 "Taika Waititi: The real story."

71 Ibid.

72 Jo Smith and Ocean Mercier, "Introduction to the Special Issue on Taika Waititi's Boy," *MEDIANZ* 13, no. 1 (2012): 11, medianz.otago.ac .nz/medianz/article/view/23.

73 Ocean Mercier, "Close encounters of the Māori kind—Talking interaction in the films of Taika Waititi," *MEDIANZ* 10, no. 2 (2007): 42, medianz.otago.ac.nz/medianz/article/view/64.

74 Kahurangi Waititi, "Māori documentary film: Interiority and exteriority," *MAI Review* 1 (2008), Intern Research Report 6, www.review.mai .ac.nz/mrindex/MR/article/viewFile/116/116-584-1-PB.pdf.

75 Mercier, "Close encounters of the Māori kind."

76 James Belich, "European ideas about Māori—Modern racial stereotypes," *Te Ara—the Encyclopedia of New Zealand*, accessed June 12, 2018, www.TeAra.govt.nz/en/european-ideas-about-Māori/ page-6.

77 Barry Barclay, *Our Own Image* (Minneapolis: University of Minnesota Press, 2015); Mercier, "Close encounters of the Māori kind."

78 Waititi, "Māori documentary film: Interiority and exteriority."

79 "Taika Waititi: The real story."

80 King, *1000 Years of Māori History*, 76; Monty Soutar's *Nga Tama Toa: The Price of Citizenship* (Auckland: David Bateman, 2008) is the leading Māori text on the Battalion.

81 *Tama Tū*, 2005, accessed April 20, 2018, http://tamatu.co.nz/film.html.

82 *Maori Dictionary*, accessed June 12, 2018, maoridictionary.co.nz/search ?idiom=&phrase=&proverb=&loan=&histLoanWords=&keywords=tu.

83 Mercier, "Close encounters of the Māori kind," 45.

84 "Learning experience 3: Hand games Tākaro ā-ringa," accessed June 11, 2018, health.tki.org.nz/Key-collections/Exploring-te-ao-kori/Learning -experiences/Hand-games.

85 *Tama Tū*, 2005.

86 "Taika Waititi: The real story."

87 Ibid.

88 *Tama Tū*, 2005.

89 Antony Easthope, *What a Man's Gotta Do: The Masculine Myth in Popular Culture* (London: Paladin, 1986), 88.

90 Henry Louis Gates Jr., *The Signifying Monkey: A Theory of African-American Literary Criticism* (New York: Oxford University Press, 1988).

91 Mercier, "Close encounters of the Māori kind," 43.

92 *Arab Samurai*, 2007, accessed April 10, 2021, https://www.youtube.com/ watch?v=Yp4uTYTHrLw&list=PLcNwckgc99uaidKVBeXkNqDU889 9lZQoU&index=6.

93 Kimberle Crenshaw, "Mapping the Margins: Intersectionality, Identity Politics, and Violence against Women of Color," *Stanford Law Review* 43, no. 6 (1991): 1241–99.

94 Barbara Bender, "Subverting the Western Gaze: Mapping Alternative Worlds," in *The Archaeology and Anthropology of Landscape: Shaping Your Landscape*, ed. Robert Layton and Peter Ucko (London: Routledge, 1999): 31–45.

95 Kathleen Connolly, "Mapplethorpe, Denzel, and Sidney Poitier: The White Female Gaze and Black Masculinity in Marina Mayoral's 'La Belleza Del ébano' 1," *Afro-Hispanic Review* 37, no. 2 (2018): 59–75.

96 Eleanor Bishop, review of *The Untold Tales of Maui*, *Salient*, March 15, 2004, 41.

97 Jonathan Williams, "New Zealand hit comedy 'Boy' comes to U.S. theaters," Wrestling with Pop Culture, April 6, 2012, www

.wrestlingwithpopculture.com/2012/new-zealand-hit-comedy-boy
-comes-to-u-s-theaters/.

98 Brendan Hokowhitu, Tackling Maori Masculinity: A Colonial Genealogy of Savagery and Sport, *Contemporary Pacific* 16, no. 2 (2004):
259–84.

99 "Locals Only Podcast: Episode 8—Samuel Flynn Scott," Radio Hauraki,
May 28, 2018, www.hauraki.co.nz/music/podcast/locals-only-podcast
-episode-8-samuel-flynn-scott/.

100 Sean Albiez, *Bloomsbury Encyclopedia of Popular Music of the World*
(New York: Bloomsbury, 2017), 11:347–49.

101 W. E. B. Du Bois, *The Souls of Black Folk* (New York, Avenel; New Jer-
sey: Gramercy Books, 1994).

102 Paul Gilroy, *The Black Atlantic: Modernity and Double Consciousness*
(Cambridge, MA: Harvard University Press, 1993); Robbie Shilliam,
The Black Pacific: Anti-colonial Struggles and Oceanic Connection (Lon-
don, Bloomsbury, 2015).

103 Richard Dyer, *White: Twentieth Anniversary Edition* (New York: Taylor
& Francis Group, 2017), 4.

Chapter 2

1 Alistair Fox, Barry Keith Grant, and Hilary Radner, "Introduction: The
Historical Film in New Zealand Cinema," in *New Zealand Cinema:
Interpreting the Past*, ed. Alistair Fox, Barry Keith Grant, and Hilary
Radner (Chicago: Intellect Books, 2011), 39.

2 Jock Phillips, *A Man's Country? The Image of the Pakeha Male—A History* (Auckland: Penguin, 1987), 204.

3 Ibid., 205, 212.

4 "Charles Upham," Ministry for Culture and Heritage, updated May 30,
2018, nzhistory.govt.nz/people/charles-upham. The quotes are from
J. A. B. Crawford, "Upham, Charles Hazlitt," *Dictionary of New Zealand
Biography*, first published in 2000. *Te Ara—the Encyclopedia of New
Zealand*, teara.govt.nz/en/biographies/5u2/upham-charles-hazlitt.

5 Monty Soutar, *Nga Tama Toa: The Price of Citizenship* (Auckland:
David Bateman, 2008).

6 Marysia Zalewski, *Feminism after Postmodernism: Theorising Through
Practice* (Florence, KY: Routledge, 2000), 24.

7 Nick Perry, *Dominion of Signs: Television, Advertising and Other New Zealand Fictions* (Auckland: Auckland University Press, 1994), 46.

8 Keith Sinclair, *A Destiny Apart: New Zealand's Search for National Identity* (Wellington: Allen & Unwin, 1985), 125.

9 R. W. Connell, *The Men and the Boys* (Cambridge: Polity Press, 2000), 40; Matthew Bannister, "Kiwi Blokes: Recontextualising Pakeha Masculinities in a Global Setting," *Genders Online* (2005), https://www.colorado.edu/gendersarchive1998-2013/2005/08/20/kiwi-blokes-recontextualising-white-new-zealand-masculinities-global-setting.

10 James Belich, *Paradise Reforged: A History of the New Zealanders from the 1880s to the Year 2000* (Auckland: Penguin Press, 2001).

11 Arthur Angel Philips, *On the Cultural Cringe* (Melbourne: Melbourne University Publishing, 2005).

12 Philip Core, *Camp: The Lie That Tells the Truth* (London: Plexus Publishing, 1984); Nick Perry, *Hyperreality and Global Culture* (New York: Routledge, 1998).

13 Matthew Bannister, "'Bush Camp'? The Topp Twins and Antipodean Camp," *Australasian Journal of Popular Culture* 4, no. 1 (2015): 3–14; Sarina Pearson, "Pacific Camp: Satire, Silliness (and Seriousness) on New Zealand Television," *Media, Culture & Society* 27, no. 4 (2005): 551–75.

14 Susan Sontag, *Notes on "Camp"* (1964), accessed June 20, 2018, https://monoskop.org/images/5/59/Sontag_Susan_1964_Notes_on_Camp.pdf.

15 Scott Wilson, "Aching to Believe: The Heresy of *Forgotten Silver*," in *Too Bold for the Box Office: The Mockumentary from Big Screen to Small*, ed. Cynthia J. Miller (Lanham, Toronto: Scarecrow Press, 2012), 137–47.

16 Mette Hjort and Duncan Petrie, introduction to *The Cinema of Small Nations* (Edinburgh: Edinburgh University Press, 2007), 1–19.

17 Ibid., 9.

18 Andrew Higson, "The Limiting Imagination of National Cinema," in *Cinema and Nation*, ed. Mette Hjort and Scott Mackenzie (London: Routledge, 2000), 69.

19 Bruce Babington, *A History of the NZ Fiction Feature Film* (New York: Manchester University Press, 2007), 19.

20 "Koromakinga Rautaki Strategic Intentions 2018–2022" Ministry of Culture and Heritage, Wellington, New Zealand, 8, mch.govt.nz/sites/default/files/Strategic%20Intentions%202018-22.pdf, accessed February 8, 2021.

21 Nabeel Zuberi, "Sounds Like Us: Popular Music and Cultural National-ism in Aotearoa/New Zealand," *Perfect Beat* 8, no. 3 (2007): 5.

22 Babington, *A History of the NZ Fiction Feature Film*, 17.

23 Peter Gibbons, "Cultural Colonization and National Identity," *New Zealand Journal of History* 36, no. 1 (2002): 6.

24 Ibid., 6.

25 Ibid., 10.

26 Ibid., 13.

27 Belich, *Paradise Reforged*.

28 Nick Perry, *Dominion of Signs*, 46.

29 James Belich, *Paradise Reforged*.

30 Bannister, "Kiwi Blokes."

31 Perry, *Dominion of Signs*, 41.

32 Friedrich Engels, "Letter to Franz Mehring," trans. Donna Torr, in *Marx and Engels Correspondence* (New York: International Publishers, 1968), 434–35.

33 Immanuel Wallerstein, *The Modern World-System* (New York: Academic Press, 1974).

34 Mark Williams, "A Waka on the Wild Side: Nationalism and Its Dis-contents in Some Recent New Zealand Films," in *Contemporary New Zealand Cinema: From New Wave to Blockbusters*, ed. Ian Conrich and Stuart Murray (London: I. B. Taurus, 2008), 183–84; James Liu, Tim McCreanor, Tracey McIntosh, and Teresia Teaiwa, "Introduction: Constructing New Zealand Identities," in *New Zealand Identities: Departures and Destinations*, ed. James Liu, Tim McCreanor, Tracey McIntosh, and Teresa Teaiwa (Wellington: Victoria University Press, 2005), 13.

35 Bev James and Kay Saville-Smith, *Gender, Culture and Power: Challeng-ing New Zealand's Gendered Culture* (Auckland: Oxford University Press, 1989), 80.

36 Bruce Jesson, *Fragments of Labour: The Story Behind the Fourth Labour Government* (Auckland: Penguin, 1989), 14–21.

37 Ibid., 10; Keith Sinclair, *A History of New Zealand* (Harmondsworth: Penguin, 1959), 274; Jesson, *Fragments of Labour*, 20–21; Dave Itzkoff, "New in Town, Talking Funny," *New York Times*, June 10, 2007, www.nytimes.com/2007/06/10/arts/television/10itzk.html?pagewanted=print.

38 Gordon Mirams, *Speaking Candidly: Films and People in New Zealand* (Hamilton, NZ: Paul's Book Arcade, 1945), 6.

39 Peter Wells, "Glamour on the Slopes," in *Film in Aotearoa New Zealand*, ed. Jonathan Dennis and Jan Beiringa (Wellington: Victoria University Press, 1992), 174–75.

40 Lindsay Shelton, *The Selling of New Zealand Movies* (Wellington: Awa Press, 2005), 81.

41 Jane Campion, "Different Complexions," in *Film in Aotearoa New Zealand*, ed. Jonathan Dennis and Jan Beiringa (Wellington: Victoria University Press, 1992), 95.

42 Quoted in Roger Horrocks, "A Small Room with Large Windows: Film Making in NZ," in *New Zealand Film: An Illustrated History*, ed. Diane Pivac, Frank Stark, and Lawrence McDonald (Wellington: Te Papa Press, 2011), 5.

43 Jo Smith, *Māori Television: The First Ten Years* (Auckland: Auckland University Press, 2016).

44 Horrocks, "A Small Room with Large Windows," 5.

45 See Paul Theroux, *The Happy Isles of Oceania* (Harmondsworth: Penguin, 1992), 7–13.

46 Alex Denney, "Unknown Mortal Orchestra & Taika Waititi on New Zealand culture," Dazed, April 5, 2018, www.dazeddigital.com/music/article/39590/1/unknown-mortal-orchestra-ruban-nielson-taika-waititi-interview.

47 Robert Chapman, "Fiction and the Social Pattern: Some Implications of Recent New Zealand Writing," in *Essays on New Zealand Literature*, ed. Wystan Curnow (Auckland: Heinemann, 1973), 79–80; Frank Sargeson, *Conversation in a Train and Other Critical Writing*, ed. Keith Cunningham (Auckland: Auckland University Press, 1983), 47; Gordon McLauchlan, *The Passionless People* (Auckland: Cassell, 1976), 1, 14.

48 Sandra Coney, *Out of the Frying Pan: Inflammatory Writing 1972–89* (Auckland: Penguin, 1990), 23.

49 Lawrence Jones, "The Novel," in *The Oxford History of New Zealand Literature in English*, ed. Terry Sturm (Auckland: Oxford University Press, 1991), 140; Dennis McEldowney, "Publishing, Patronage, Literary Magazines," in *The Oxford History of New Zealand Literature in English*, ed. Terry Sturm (Auckland: Oxford University Press, 1991), 562.

50　Allen Curnow, *Look Back Harder: Critical Writing 1935–1984*, ed. and intro. Peter Simpson (Auckland: Auckland University Press, 1987), 17.

51　Robin Law, Hugh Campbell, and Ruth Schick, introduction to *Masculinities in Aotearoa/New Zealand*, ed. Robin Law, Hugh Campbell, and John Dolan (Palmerston North: Dunmore, 1999), 15; Phillips, *A Man's Country?*, vii; Bannister, "Kiwi Blokes."

52　Brendan Hokowhitu, "'Educating Jake': A Genealogy of Māori Masculinity," in *Gender, Masculinities and Lifelong Learning*, ed. Marion Bowl et al. (New York: Taylor & Francis, 2012), 51.

53　*Hotere* (2001), NZ On Screen, www.nzonscreen.com/title/hotere-2001/ quotes.

54　James and Saville-Smith, *Gender, Culture and Power*.

55　Will Wright, "The Structure of Myth and the Structure of the Western Film," in *Cultural Theory and Popular Culture: A Reader*, ed. John Storey (Hemel Hempstead: Prentice Hall, 1998), 123ff.

56　R. W. Connell, *Masculinities* (Berkeley: University of California Press, 1995); Jeff Hearn, *Men in the Public Eye* (London: Routledge, 1994).

57　Kai Jensen, *Whole Men: The Masculine Tradition in New Zealand Literature* (Auckland: Auckland University Press, 1996), 3.

58　Phillips, *A Man's Country?*, 282.

59　E. H. McCormick, *New Zealand Literature: A Survey* (London: Oxford University Press, 1959), 130. "Man Alone" was a phrase coined by NZ poet J. K. Baxter in *The Fire and the Anvil: Notes on Modern Poetry* (Wellington: New Zealand University Press, 1955), 70–72, and the title of a John Mulgan novel (Hamilton: Paul's Book Arcade, 1960). See also Stuart Murray, *Never a Soul at Home: New Zealand Literary Nationalism and the 30s* (Wellington: Victoria University Press, 1998).

60　Murray, *Never a Soul at Home*, 131–32.

61　Robert Chapman, "Fiction and the Social Pattern: Some Implications of Recent New Zealand Writing," in *Essays on New Zealand Literature*, ed. Wystan Curnow (Auckland: Heinemann, 1973), 77.

62　Lydia Wevers, "The Short Story," in *The Oxford History of New Zealand Literature in English*, ed. Terry Sturm (Auckland: Oxford University Press, 1991), 229.

63　Frank Sargeson, *Collected Stories* (London: MacGibbon & Kee, 1965), 255.

64 Bill Ashcroft, Bill, Gareth Griffith, and Helen Tiffin, *The Empire Writes Back: Theory and Practice in Post-colonial Literature* (London: Routledge, 1989), 163.

65 Simon During, "Towards a Revision of Local Critical Habits," *And* 1 (1983): 75–93.

66 *Yeah Right: Tui* (Auckland: Hodder Moa, 2005).

67 Rita M. Denny, Patricia L. Sunderland, Jacqueline Smart, and Chris Christofi, "Finding Ourselves in Images: A Cultural Reading of Trans-Tasman Identities," *Journal of Research for Consumers* 8 (2005): 1–10.

68 Ibid.

69 Jacqueline Smart of FCB, quoted on *Campbell Live*, TV3, New Zealand, April 8, 2005.

70 Robin Law, Hugh Campbell, and Ruth Schick, introduction to *Masculinities in Aotearoa/New Zealand* (Palmerston North: Dunmore, 1999), 14.

71 Eve Sedgwick, *Between Men: English Literature and Male Homosocial Desire (New York: Columbia University Press, 1992)*; Anita Brady, "The Transgendered Kiwi: Homosocial Desire and 'New Zealand Identity,'" *Sexualities* 15, no. 3–4 (2012): 358.

72 Lee Wallace, "Queer, Here: Sexuality and Space," in *Cultural Studies in Aotearoa New Zealand: Identity, Space and Place*, ed. Claudia Bell and Steve Matthewman (Melbourne: Oxford University Press, 2004), 67–68.

73 Quoted in *Untouchable Girls*, dir. Leanne Pooley, 2009.

74 Brady, "The Transgendered Kiwi," 355.

75 Bill Pearson, *Fretful Sleepers and Other Essays* (Auckland: Heinemann, 1974), 14.

76 Homi Bhabha, *The Location of Culture* (New York: Routledge, 1994).

77 Bill Ashcroft, Gareth Griffith, and Helen Tiffin, *Key Concepts in Post-colonial Studies* (London: Routledge, 1998), 211–12.

78 Gibbons, "Cultural Colonization and National Identity," 13.

79 Babington, *A History of the NZ Fiction Feature Film*, 19; *Cinema of Unease*—Film (excerpts), 1995, NZ On Screen, www.nzonscreen.com/title/cinema-of-unease-1995.

80 Pearson, *Fretful Sleepers*.

81 Quoted in *Breaking Barriers*, 1993, NZ On Screen, www.nzonscreen.com/title/breaking-barriers-1992.

82 Barry Crump, *Wild Pork and Watercress* (Auckland: Beckett Publishing, 1986).

83 Horrocks, "A Small Room with Large Windows," 13.

84 Martin Blythe, *Naming the Other: Images of the Maori in Film and TV* (Metuchen, NJ: Scarecrow Press, 1994), 94.

85 Stuart Murray, "Once Were Warriors," in *Making film and Television Histories: Australia and New Zealand*, ed. James Bennett and Rebecca Beirne (London: I.B. Tauris, 2011), 60.

86 Ibid., 59.

87 Taika Waititi, quoted in "Boy Q and A (Part II)," Sundance Film Festival, YouTube, February 2, 2010, www.youtube.com/watch?v=l_OkifYQbVl&fea.

88 Ian Biddle and Freya Jarman-Ivens, introduction to *Oh Boy!: Masculinities and Popular Music*, ed. Freya Jarman-Ivens (New York: Taylor & Francis Group, 2007), 6–7.

89 Merata Mita, "The Soul and the Image," in *Film in Aotearoa New Zealand*, ed. Jonathan Dennis and Jan Beiringa (Wellington: Victoria University Press, 1992), 47.

90 Leonie Pihama, "Repositioning Māori Representation: Contextualising *Once Were Warriors*," in *Film in Aotearoa New Zealand*, ed. Jonathan Dennis and Jan Beiringa (Wellington: Victoria University Press, 1992), 191–94.

91 Mita, "The Soul and the Image," 47.

92 Barry Barclay, *Our Own Image* (Minneapolis: University of Minnesota Press, 2015); Trisha Dunleavy and Hester Joyce, *New Zealand Film and Television Institution, Industry and Cultural Change* (Bristol: Intellect, 2011), 98.

93 Barclay, *Our Own Image*.

94 Pam Grady, "Taika Waititi draws on his experience for 'Boy,'" SFGate, March 18, 2012, www.sfgate.com/movies/article/Taika-Waititi-draws-on-his-experience-for-Boy-3410289.php.

95 Blythe, *Naming the Other*.

96 Ibid., 9.

97 Quoted in Sinclair, *A History of New Zealand*, 183.

98 Blythe, *Naming the Other*, 17.

99 Mita, "The Soul and the Image," 42.

100 Marianne Schultz, *Performing Indigenous Culture on Stage and Screen: A Harmony of Frenzy* (New York: Palgrave Macmillan, 2016), 127.

101 The World of Taika, accessed May 18, 2019, worldoftaika.com/taika
-waititi/the-comedian/.

102 *Theatre*, Sydney, December 2, 1912, 37/a. Quoted in Babington, *A History of the NZ Fiction Feature Film*, 34.

103 Mark Derby, "Méliès in Maoriland: The Making of the First New Zealand Feature Films," in *Making Film and Television Histories: Australia and New Zealand*, ed. James Bennett and Rebecca Beirne (London: I.B. Tauris, 2011), 41–42.

104 Letter from Joseph Ward contained in announcement made by the general manager of Universal Film Manufacturing Australasia, May 2, 1929, *The Devil's Pit/Under the Southern Cross*, Drop File, US 1929, the NZ Archive of Film, Television and Sound/Ngā Taonga Whitiāhua Me Ngā Taonga Kōrero, Wellington. Quoted in Schultz, *Performing Indigenous Culture*, 137.

105 Quoted in *Adventures in Maoriland—Alexander Markey and the Making of Hei Tiki* (1985), NZ On Screen, accessed August 12, 2018, www
.nzonscreen.com/title/adventures-in-maoriland-1985.

106 Avril Bell, "Imagining Aotearoa New Zealand: The Politics of National Imagining," in *A Land of Milk and Honey?: Making Sense of Aotearoa New Zealand*, ed. Avril Bell, Vivienne Elizabeth, Tracey McIntosh, and Matt Wynyard (Auckland: Auckland University Press, 2017), 62, emphasis in original.

107 Schultz, *Performing Indigenous Culture*, 8.

108 Ibid., 140.

109 Méliès's *Loved by a Maori Chieftess* features an interracial romance, but Maoriland remains the frame, as there is only one white character.

110 Blythe, *Naming the Other*, 10.

111 Ibid., 11.

112 Ibid., 34.

113 Ibid., 35.

114 John O'Shea, quoted in *Breaking Barriers*.

115 Waititi, quoted in "Boy Q and A."

116 Diane Pivac, "The Rise of Fiction: Between the Wars," in *New Zealand Film: An Illustrated History*, ed. Diane Pivac, Frank Stark, and Lawrence McDonald (Wellington: Te Papa Press, 2011), 65.

117 Jeanette Hoorn and Michelle Smith, "Rudall Hayward's Democratic Cinema and the 'Civilising Mission' in the 'Land of the Wrong White

Crowd,'" in *New Zealand Cinema: Interpreting the Past*, ed. Alistair Fox, Barry Keith Grant, and Hilary Radner (Chicago: Intellect, 2011), 65–81.

118 Babington, *A History of the NZ Fiction Feature Film*, 64.

119 Jo Smith and Annie Goldson, "The Contested Nation: Documentary and Dissent," in *Contemporary New Zealand Cinema: From New Wave to Blockbusters*, ed. Ian Conrich and Stuart Murray (London: I. B. Taurus, 2008), 157–58.

120 Quoted in Mirams, *Speaking Candidly*, 203.

121 Lars Weckbecker, "From Colony to Nation in One Hundred Crowded Years: A Narrative on Civilisation, Progress and Modernity," in *Making Film and Television Histories: Australia and New Zealand*, ed. James Bennett and Rebecca Beirne (London: I.B. Tauris, 2011), 100.

122 Ibid., 102.

123 Hamish McDouall, *100 Essential NZ Films* (Wellington: Awa Press, 2009), 30.

124 Quoted in Babington, *A History of the NZ Fiction Feature Film*, 5.

125 Chapman, "Fiction and the Social Pattern," 79–80; Sargeson, *Conversation in a Train and Other Critical Writing*, 47; McLauchlan, *The Passionless People*, 1, 14.

126 Misha Kavka, Jennifer Lawn, and Mary Paul, *Gothic NZ: The Darker Side of Kiwi Culture* (Dunedin: Otago University Press, 2006).

127 "God's own country," a term used to describe NZ, was the title of a poem published in 1893 by New Zealand resident Thomas Bracken. W. S. Broughton, "Bracken, Thomas," updated May 2014, *Te Ara—the Encyclopedia of New Zealand*, teara.govt.nz/en/biographies/2b35/bracken-thomas.

128 Wilson, "Aching to Believe."

129 Ian Conrich, *Studies in NZ Cinema* (London: Kakapo, 2009), 147.

130 Russell Baillie, "Movie review: *What We Do in the Shadows*," *NZ Herald*, June 19, 2014, "Time Out," 13.

131 "Taika Waititi: The real story behind 'that' Oscars gag, and much more . . . Interviews 2009," NZ On Screen, www.nzonscreen.com/interviews/taika-waititi-reveals-real-story-behind-that-oscars-gag.

132 *Focus on the Audience: New Zealand Film and Television Conference 1993* (Auckland: Onfilm, 1993), 8.

133 Perry, *Dominion of Signs.*

134 Perry, *Hyperreality and Global Culture.*

135 Babington, *A History of the NZ Fiction Feature Film*, 21.

136 Perry, *Hyperreality and Global Culture*, 11.

137 Babington, *A History of the NZ Fiction Feature Film*, 3.

138 Richard Dyer, *Only Entertainment* (New York: Routledge, 1992); Bannister, "Bush Camp?"

139 Judith Halberstam. *Female Masculinity* (Durham, NC: Duke University Press, 1998).

140 Chris Barton, "Where women are real men," *NZ Herald*, February 5, 2005, www.nzherald.co.nz/nz/news/article.cfm?c_id=1&objectid= 10009522; Halberstam, *Female Masculinity*, 57–58.

141 Brady, "The Transgendered Kiwi."

142 Perry, *Hyperreality and Global Culture*, 11, 13.

143 The original stage musical (1973) was called *The Rocky Horror Show.*

144 Barry Keith Grant, "Bringing It All Back Home: The Films of Peter Jackson," in *New Zealand Filmmakers*, ed. Ian Conrich and Stuart Murray (Detroit: Wayne State University Press, 2007), 320–35.

145 Sontag, *Notes on "Camp."*

146 Perry, *Hyperreality and Global Culture*, 13.

147 Dyer, *Only Entertainment*, 138.

148 Richard Dyer, *Heavenly Bodies: Film Stars and Society* (New York: Routledge, 1986), 154.

149 Dyer, *Only Entertainment*, 13.

150 This emphasis on low, populist forms explains why a film like *Desperate Remedies* (1993) isn't antipodean camp, in my view. See Bannister, "Bush Camp?"

151 Ben Dibley, "Antipodean Aesthetics, Public Policy and the Museum," *Cultural Studies Review* 13, no. 1 (2007): 142.

152 Ibid., 139–40.

153 John Wilson, "Nation and government—Nationhood and identity," *Te Ara—the Encyclopedia of New Zealand*, accessed July 26, 2018, www.TeAra.govt.nz/en/nation-and-government/page-9.

154 Grant, "Bringing it All Back Home," 323.

155 "The Most Epic Safety Video Ever Made takes flight," October 23, 2014, https://media.newzealand.com/en/news/the-most-epic-safety-video-ever -made-takes-flight/.

156   Perry, *Hyperreality and Global Culture*, 12; Eric Hobsbawm and Terence
      Ranger, eds., *The Invention of Tradition* (New York: Cambridge Uni-
      versity Press, 1983).

157   Paul Gilroy, *The Black Atlantic: Modernity and Double Consciousness*
      (Cambridge, MA: Harvard University Press, 1993), 87; Stuart Hall,
      "Cultural Identity and Diaspora," in *Identity: Community, Culture,
      Difference*, ed. Jonathan Rutherford (London: Lawrence and Wishart,
      1990), 222–37.

158   "Southern Man Axed," *National Business Review*, November 2, 2012,
      www.nbr.co.nz/article/kiwi-ad-icon-axed-vy-p-131741. However, the
      campaign was revived in 2018 with Māori/Pasifika males in the cast.

159   Carolyn Michelle, "Co-Constructions of Gender and Ethnicity in New
      Zealand Television Advertising," *Sex Roles* 66 (2012): 21–37.

160   Ricki Green, "'Boy' Star James Rolleston Returns in New TV Spots for
      Vodafone's Supernet via DraftFCB NZ," July 22, 2013, campaignbrief
      .com/boy-star-james-rollestin-retur/; "New World Lucky Day Cam-
      paign," Ads of the World, May 29, 2012, https://www.adsoftheworld
      .com/media/film/new_world_lucky_day; Ricki Green, "Lotto's 'Pop
      Gift' via DDB NZ Announced as New Zealand's Favourite Ad at Fair
      Go 2015 Ad Awards," November 12, 2015, campaignbrief.co.nz/2015/
      11/12/lottos-pop-gift-via-ddb-nz-ann/; "Spark Father's Day," You-
      Tube, January 30, 2018, www.youtube.com/watch?v=vfTk5AjlqGE;
      "TSB Bank 'New to Earth' launch commercial by Special Group and
      The Sweet Shop via StopPress," YouTube, September 19, 2011, www
      .youtube.com/watch?v=idrKqL9ZEEw.

161   "Legend (Ghost Chips)—Road Safety," NZ On Screen, 2011, www
      .nzonscreen.com/title/legend-ghost-chips; Steven Elers, "Public
      Information Advertisements: Maori Perspectives" (PhD diss., Auck-
      land University of Technology, 2016), openrepository.aut.ac.nz/
      handle/10292/1016.

162   Natasha Conland, ed., *Judy Darragh: So . . . You Made It?* (Wellington:
      Te Papa Press, 2004).

163   Babington, *A History of the NZ Fiction Feature Film*, 15.

164   Perry, *Hyperreality and Global Culture*, 14.

Chapter 3

1 Lawrence McDonald, "A Book Review of *Film in Aotearoa New Zealand* that Ended Up as an Essay on Film in Aotearoa New Zealand," *Illusions* 21/22 (1993): 59–60.

2 Bruce Babington, *A History of the NZ Fiction Feature Film* (New York: Manchester University Press, 2007), 111; McDonald. "A Book Review."

3 Stuart Murray, *Never a Soul at Home: New Zealand Literary Nationalism and the 30s* (Wellington: Victoria University Press, 1998), 131–32.

4 Dominic Corry, "New Zealand's funniest movies," *NZ Herald*, March 16, 2017, www.nzherald.co.nz/entertainment/news/article.cfm?c_id=1501119&objectid=11820131.

5 Craig Hubert, "Taika Waititi's Inner Child," *Interview*, February 29, 2012, www.interviewmagazine.com/film/taika-waititi-boy.

6 Alex Billington, "Sundance Interview: 'Hunt for the Wilderpeople' Director Taika Waititi," First Showing.Net, February 5, 2016, www.firstshowing.net/2016/sundance-interview-hunt-for-the-wilderpeople-director-taika-waititi/. Emphasis added.

7 Richard Dyer, *Only Entertainment* (New York: Routledge, 1992), 13, 17.

8 Ibid., 18.

9 Ibid.

10 John O'Shea, *Don't Let It Get You: Memories—Documents* (Wellington: Victoria University Press, 1999), 70.

11 Babington, *A History of the NZ Fiction Feature Film*, 108; Laurence Simmons, "Don't Let It Get You: Livin' and Lovin' in NZ's First Film Musical," *Music in New Zealand* 26 (1994): 24–27.

12 Dyer, *Only Entertainment*, 3.

13 Mikhail Bakhtin, *Rabelais and His World*, trans. Helene Iswolsky (Bloomington: Indiana University Press, 1984), 7.

14 Andrew Horton and Joanna E. Rapf, "Comic Introduction 'Make 'em Laugh, Make 'em Laugh!'" in *Companion to Film Comedy*, ed. Andrew Horton and Joanna E. Rapf (Malden, MA: Wiley-Blackwell, 2012), 3–4.

15 Henri Bergson, *Laughter: An Essay on the Meaning of the Comic* (Mineola, NY: Dover Publications, 2005), 3–4.

16 Quoted in Matt Elliott, *Kiwi Jokers: The Rise and Rise of NZ Comedy* (Auckland: HarperCollins, 1997), 34.

17 Babington, *A History of the NZ Fiction Feature Film*, 63–64.

18 Quoted in "Billy T James," NZ On Screen, accessed July 28, 2018, www
   .nzonscreen.com/person/billy-t-james/biography.

19 *Funny As: The Story of New Zealand Comedy*—Episode 3: Tuxedos
   and Trojan Horses, broadcast on TVNZ August 4, 2019, www.tvnz
   .co.nz/shows/funny-as-the-story-of-new-zealand-comedy/episodes/
   s1-e3.

20 Chris Bourke, *Blue Smoke: The Lost Dawn of New Zealand Popular Music,
   1918–1964* (Auckland: Auckland University Press, 2010), 259.

21 Ibid., 310.

22 "New Zealand's first official TV broadcast," Ministry for Culture and
   Heritage, updated December 21, 2016, nzhistory.govt.nz/first-official
   -tv-broadcast.

23 Bourke, *Blue Smoke*, 30.

24 Ibid., 309.

25 Bryan Dawe, quoted in Elliott, *Kiwi Jokers*, 28.

26 Elliott, *Kiwi Jokers*, 21.

27 "Larry Loves Barry," YouTube, accessed October 22, 2020,
   www.youtube.com/watch?v=oik7PeMou9E&list=OLAK5uy
   _kGEIsbUa5UaZqP33bxaysVA_RwHGxVFws&index=15.

28 Quoted in *Funny As: The Story of New Zealand Comedy*.

29 Dyer, *Only Entertainment*, 21.

30 Roger Horrocks, "Alternatives: Experimental Film Making in New Zealand," in *Film in Aotearoa New Zealand*, ed. Jonathan Dennis and Jan
   Beiringa (Wellington: Victoria University Press, 1996), 57–88.

31 Susy Pointon, "The Independents: The Creation of a New Zealand Film
   Industry" (PhD diss., University of Auckland, 2005); *Blerta Revisited*,
   dir. Geoff Murphy, 2001.

32 Horrocks, "Alternatives."

33 McDonald, "A Book Review."

34 Matthew Bannister, "'Bush Camp'? The Topp Twins and Antipodean
   camp," *Australasian Journal of Popular Culture* 4, no. 1 (2015): 3–14;
   Leanne Pooley, *The Topp Twins: Untouchable Girls* (Auckland: Diva
   Productions, NZFC, 2009)

35 Elliott, *Kiwi Jokers*, 89.

36 Horrocks, "Alternatives," 82.

37 "Jemaine Clement: Biography," *NZ On Screen*, accessed July 28, 2018,
   www.nzonscreen.com/person/jemaine-clement/biography.

38 Monika Barton, "Taika Waititi and Ryan Reynolds' new musical collab-
oration delights fans," *Newshub*, May 26, 2020, www.newshub.co.nz/
home/entertainment/2020/05/taika-waititi-and-ryan-reynolds-new
-musical-collaboration-delights-fans.html.

39 John Clarke, quoted in *Beyond a Joke*, 1995, NZ On Screen, www
.nzonscreen.com/title/beyond-a-joke-1995.

40 Waititi, quoted in Billington, "Sundance Interview: 'Hunt for the
Wilderpeople.'"

41 Dyer, *Only Entertainment*, 23. Dyer suggests that both values relate
to "authenticity" (25), and what could be more authentic than
improvisation?

42 Philip Auslander, *Liveness: Performance in a Mediatized Culture* (New
York: Routledge, 1999).

43 *Jon Bridges and David Downs, No. 8 Wire: The Best of Kiwi Ingenuity
(Auckland: Hodder Moa Beckett, 2000).*

44 John Clarke, quoted in *Beyond a Joke*.

45 Barry Crump, quoted in *Beyond a Joke* 1995, NZ On Screen, www
.nzonscreen.com/title/beyond-a-joke-1995; Jock Phillips, *A Man's
Country? The Image of the Pakeha Male—A History* (Auckland:
Penguin, 1987).

46 Richard Dyer, *Only Entertainment*, 23

47 Pointon, "The Independents."

48 Barbara Cairns and Helen Martin, *Shadows on the Wall: A Study of Seven
New Zealand Feature Films* (Auckland: Longman Paul, 1994), 71.

49 "Harry Sinclair: life in L.A.," RNZ, August 20, 2011, www.radionz.co.nz/
national/programmes/saturday/audio/2496145/harry-sinclair-life-in-l-a.

50 Tasha Robinson, "Jemaine Clement and Taika Waititi on their
years-in-the-making vampire comedy *What We Do In The Shadows*,"
The Dissolve, February 13, 2015. thedissolve.com/features/interview/
923-jemaine-clement-and-taika-waititi-on-their-years-i/; Ali
Plumb and Helen O'Hara, "What We Do in the Shadows Interview:
Taika Waititi and Jemaine Clement," *Empire*, April 10, 2015, www
.empireonline.com/movies/features/shadows-interview-jemaine
-clement-taika-waititi/.

51 *Hunt for the Wilderpeople* DVD extras.

52 Jemaine Clement, discussing *Shadows*, quoted in Garry Maddox, "Conchords star Jemaine Clement wings it with vampire comedy What We

Do in the Shadows," *Sydney Morning Herald*, August 29, 2014, www
.smh.com.au/entertainment/movies/conchords-star-jemaine-clement
-wings-it-with-vampire-comedy-what-we-do-in-the-shadows
-20140826-107qej.htm.

53 Ibid.

54 Waititi, quoted in "Te Ahi Kaa mo 22 o Haratua," RNZ, May 22, 2011,
www.radionz.co.nz/national/programmes/teahikaa/audio/2489663/te
-ahi-kaa-mo-22-o-haratua-may-2011.

55 Quoted in Robinson, "Jemaine Clement and Taika Waititi on their
years-in-the-making vampire comedy *What We Do In The Shadows*."

56 Tasha Robinson, "Thor director Taika Waititi on letting his cast 'reboot'
their characters," The Verge, November 7, 2017, www.theverge.com/
2017/11/7/16618930/thor-director-taika-waititi-interview-behind
-the-scenes-improv-chris-hemsworth; Jessica Rawden, "How Much
of Thor: Ragnarok's Dialogue Is Improvised," CinemaBlend, July 25,
2017, www.cinemablend.com/news/1685031/how-much-of-thor
-ragnaroks-dialogue-is-improvised.

57 Dyer, *Only Entertainment*, 22–32.

58 Tom Brown, *Breaking the Fourth Wall: Direct Address in the Cinema*
(Edinburgh: Edinburgh University Press, 2012).

59 Steinlager advertisement, 2012, YouTube, accessed October 19, 2020,
https://www.youtube.com/watch?v=XABnxMyt6H.

60 Blazed—Drug Driving in Aotearoa, 2013, NZ On Screen, accessed October 18, 2020, www.nzonscreen.com/title/blazed-drug-driving-2013/
credits.

61 *Team Thor*, 2016, accessed October 17, 2020, www.youtube.com/watch
?v=6XB0-UFs1al.

62 "The Ordinary Alien" from *Radiradirah*, 2010, TV3, prod. Elizabeth
Mitchell, YouTube, accessed October 16, 2020, www.youtube.com/
watch?v=rNHlXmQQdog.

63 Bergson, *Laughter*.

64 "The Ordinary Alien" from *Radiradirah*, 2010.

65 *Pulp Comedy*, Series Seven, Episode Three, 2003, NZ On Screen,
accessed October 17, 2020, www.nzonscreen.com/title/pulp-comedy
-s7e3-taika-waititi-2003.

66 Ella Shohat and Robert Stam, *Unthinking Eurocentrism: Multiculturalism
and the Media* (London: Routledge, 1994), 182.

67 James MacDowell, "Wes Anderson, Tone and the Quirky Sensibility," *New Review of Film and Television Studies* 10, no. 1 (2012): 6–27.

68 Michael Billig, *Laughter and Ridicule: Towards a Social Critique of Humour* (Thousand Oaks, CA: SAGE Publications, 2005).

69 Bergson, *Laughter*, 35–36.

70 Alexander Kozintsev, *The Mirror of Laughter* (New Brunswick, NJ: Transaction, 2012), 100.

71 Bergson, *Laughter*, 4.

72 Ibid., 17.

73 Ibid., capitals in original.

74 Gilles Deleuze and Felix Guattari, *A Thousand Plateaus: Capitalism and Schizophrenia*, trans. Brian Massumi (Minneapolis: University of Minnesota Press, 1987), 88–91.

75 Billig, *Laughter and Ridicule*.

76 Bakhtin, *Rabelais and His World*, 11.

77 Marianna Keisalo. "'Picking People to Hate': Reversible Reversals in Stand-up Comedy," *Suomen Antropologi* 41, no. 4 (2016): 62–76.

78 Bergson, *Laughter*, 32.

79 Ibid., 25.

80 Ibid., 43, capitals in original.

81 Babington, *A History of the NZ Fiction Feature Film*, 123; James Belich, *Making Peoples: A History of the New Zealanders* (London: Penguin, 2001), 424–36.

82 Quoted in Pooley, *The Topp Twins*.

83 Robyn Longhurst and Carla Wilson, "Heartland Wainuiomata: Rurality to Suburbs, Black Singlets to Naughty Lingerie," in *Masculinities in Aotearoa/New Zealand*, ed. Robin Law, Hugh Campbell, and John Dolan (Palmerston North: Dunmore, 1999), 215–28.

84 "Crumpy and Scotty—Toyota Hilux," NZ On Screen, 1982, www.nzonscreen.com/title/crumpy-scotty-toyota-ad?collection=top-ten-nz-tv-ads.

85 Nick Perry, *Dominion of Signs: Television, Advertising and Other New Zealand Fictions* (Auckland: Auckland University Press, 1994), 55.

86 Brigid Magner, "Crump, Barry," *Te Ara—the Encyclopedia of New Zealand*, last updated November 2012, teara.govt.nz/en/biographies/6c2/crump-barry.

87 Margie Mellsop, quoted in Elliott, *Kiwi Jokers*, 89.

88 "So You're A Man," Wikipedia, last updated May 22, 2018, en.wikipedia
.org/wiki/So_You%27re_a_Man.

89 Dave Itzkoff, "New in Town, Talking Funny," *New York Times*, June 10,
2007, www.nytimes.com/2007/06/10/arts/television/10itzk.html
?pagewanted=print.

90 "Must watch Carlton Dry Beer This is what happened after a few too
many," YouTube, December 13, 2013, www.youtube.com/watch?v=
C7cxKmXNcak

91 "NZTA and Clemenger take NZ's second gold Lion as Cannes wraps
up," StopPress, June 29, 2015, stoppress.co.nz/news/nzta-and
-clemenger-take-nzs-second-gold-lion-cannes-wraps.

92 "Melbourne teams with Flight of the Conchords director Taika Waititi
to produce series of new #HelloBeer spots for Carlton Dry," Campaign Brief, December 12, 2013, www.campaignbrief.com/2013/12/
clemenger-bbdo-melbourne-teams.html.

93 "Melbourne teams with Flight of the Conchords director Taika Waititi."

94 "Blazed—Drug Driving in Aotearoa."

95 Steven Elers, "Public Information Advertisements: Maori Perspectives"
(PhD diss., Auckland University of Technology, 2016), openrepository
.aut.ac.nz/handle/10292/10163.

Chapter 4

1 "Taika Waititi: Masterclass," TIFF 2018, YouTube, September 10, 2018,
www.youtube.com/watch?v=-5D_9i5Z8lo&t=342s.

2 "10 things you need to know about Pasifika peoples in Aotearoa
(dispelling some common myths about the Pacific)," Core Education,
April 2014, blog.core-ed.org/blog/2014/04/10-things-you-need-to
-know-about-pasifika-peoples-in-aotearoa-dispelling-some-common
-myths-about-the-pacific.html.

3 Robbie Shilliam, *The Black Pacific: Anti-colonial Struggles and Oceanic
Connection* (London: Bloomsbury, 2015), 60.

4 Emiel Martens, "Maori on the Silver Screen: The Evolution of Indigenous Feature Filmmaking in Aotearoa/New Zealand," *International
Journal of Critical Indigenous Studies* 5, no. 1 (2012): 8.

5 Michael Bodey, "Universal truths in boy's own adventure," *The Australian*, August 25, 2010.

6 Jo Smith and Sue Abel, "Ka Whawhai Tonu Matou: Indigenous Television in Aotearoa/New Zealand," *MEDIANZ* 11 (2008): 1; Jo Smith, *Māori Television: The First Ten Years* (Auckland: Auckland University Press, 2016).

7 Ilana Gershon, *No Family Is an Island: Cultural Expertise among Samoans in Diaspora* (Ithaca: Cornell University Press, 2012).

8 Steve Neale and Frank Krutnik, *Popular Film and TV Comedy* (New York: Routledge, 1990), 3–4.

9 Rangihiroa Panoho, "The Harakeke—No Place for the Bellbird to Sing: Western Colonization of Maori Art in Aotearoa," *Cultural Studies* 9, no. 1 (1995): 23–24.

10 Robert K. Paterson, "Taonga Maori Renaissance: Protecting the Cultural Heritage of Aotearoa/New Zealand," in *Cultural Heritage Issues: The Legacy of Conquest, Colonization and Commerce*, ed. J. A. Nafziger and Ann M. Nicgorski (The Netherlands: BRILL, 2009), 107–36.

11 *Focus on the Audience: New Zealand Film and Television Conference 1993* (Auckland: Onfilm, 1993), 8.

12 *Funny As: The Story of New Zealand Comedy*—Episode 3: Tuxedos and Trojan Horses, August 4, 2019, www.tvnz.co.nz/shows/funny-as-the-story-of-new-zealand-comedy.

13 Peter L. Berger, *Redeeming Laughter: The Comic Dimension of Human Experience* (Boston: Walter de Gruyter GmbH, 2014), xx.

14 Aaryn L. Green and Annulla Linders, "The Impact of Comedy on Racial and Ethnic Discourse," *Sociological Inquiry* 86, no. 2 (2016): 241.

15 Neale and Krutnik, *Popular Film and TV Comedy*, 4.

16 Caroline Harker, "Humour—Developing a national sense of humour, 1900–1970," *Te Ara—the Encyclopedia of New Zealand*, accessed April 13, 2020, www.TeAra.govt.nz/en/humour/page-2.

17 Chris Bourke, *Blue Smoke: The Lost Dawn of New Zealand Popular Music, 1918–1964* (Auckland: Auckland University Press, 2011).

18 Sander Gilman, *The Jew's Body* (New York: Routledge, 1991), 177.

19 David L. Reznik, *New Jews: Race and American Jewish Identity in 21st-Century Film* (New York: Taylor & Francis Group, 2012), 32.

20 Michael Lerner, "Jews Are Not White," *Village Voice*, May 18, 1993, 33–34.

21 Bambi L. Haggins, "Laughing Mad: The Black Comedian's Place in American Comedy of the Post–Civil Rights Era," in *Hollywood*

Comedians, The Film Reader, ed. Frank Krutnik (London: Routledge, 2001), 171–86.

22 Green and Linders, "The Impact of Comedy"; Reznik, *New Jews*, 2.

23 Green and Linders, "The Impact of Comedy," 245.

24 Nathan Abrams, *The New Jew in Film: Exploring Jewishness and Judaism in Contemporary Cinema* (New Brunswick, NJ: Rutgers University Press, 2012), 13.

25 Henry Bial, *Acting Jewish: Negotiating Ethnicity on the American Stage and Screen* (Ann Arbor: University of Michigan Press, 2005), 3.

26 Jessica Harding, F. Sibley, and Chris Robertson, "New Zealand = Māori, New Zealand = Bicultural: Ethnic Group Differences in a National Sample of Māori and Europeans," *Social Indicators Research* 100, no. 1 (2011): 137–48.

27 Ibid., 139.

28 Paul Spoonley, "Mana Tangata, Mana Tangatarua: Ethnic Identities in Contemporary Aotearoa," in *Mana Tangatarua: Mixed Heritages, Ethnic Identity and Biculturalism in Aotearoa/New Zealand*, ed. Zarine L. Rocha and Melinda Webber (New York: Routledge, 2017), 15.

29 Chan Yul Yoo, "The International Relations of Korea as a Small State" (PhD diss., Johns Hopkins University, 1990), 12.

30 Mette Hjort and Duncan Petrie, *The Cinema of Small Nations* (Edinburgh: Edinburgh University Press, 2007), 9.

31 Mark Bray and Steve Packer, *Education in Small States: Concepts, Challenges and Strategies* (Oxford: Pergamon, 1993), xxiii.

32 Gershon, *No Family Is an Island*, 3.

33 *Ibid.*, 81.

34 Zarine L. Rocha and Melinda Webber, "Introduction: Situating Mixed Race in New Zealand and the World," in *Mana Tangatarua: Mixed Heritages, Ethnic Identity and Biculturalism in Aotearoa/New Zealand*, ed. Zarine L. Rocha and Melinda Webber (New York: Routledge, 2017), 21.

35 "Ethnicity standard classification: Consultation," Stats NZ, November 24, 2019, Wellington, 2. www.stats.govt.nz/consultations/ethnicity-standard-classification-consultation.

36 Reznik, *New Jews*, 36.

37 Harding, Sibley, and Robertson, "New Zealand = Māori," 138.

38 "'Kia ora lady' made Dame Companion," *Stuff*, December 30, 2017, www.stuff.co.nz/national/100070037/kia-ora-lady-made-dame-companion.

39 Janine Hayward, "Biculturalism—Biculturalism in the state sector," *Te Ara—the Encyclopedia of New Zealand*, accessed April 14, 2020, www .TeAra.govt.nz/en/biculturalism/page-2.

40 Gershon, *No Family Is an Island*, 166.

41 Bruce Jesson, *Fragments of Labour: The Story Behind the Fourth Labour Government* (Auckland: Penguin, 1989).

42 Harding, Sibley, and Robertson, "New Zealand = Māori," 145.

43 Ilana Gershon, "Indigeneity for Life: *bro'Town* and Its Stereotypes," *Flow Journal*, May 4, 2007, www.flowjournal.org/2007/05/indigeneity -for-life-brotown-and-its-stereotypes/.

44 Brendan Hokowhitu and Vijay Devadas, introduction to *Fourth Eye: Maori Media in Aotearoa New Zealand*, ed. Brendan Hokowhitu and Vijay Devadas (Minneapolis: University of Minnesota Press, 2013), xx.

45 Mike White, "No End of Stories," *North and South* 234 (2005):76; see also Stephen Turner, "Reflections on Barry Barclay and Fourth Cinema," in *The Fourth Eye: Maori Media in Aotearoa New Zealand*, ed. Brendan Hokowhitu and Vijay Devadas (Minneapolis: University of Minnesota Press, 2013), 162–80.

46 Shilliam, *The Black Pacific*, 68.

47 Maria Amoamo and Anna Thompson, "(Re)Imaging Māori Tourism: Representation and Cultural Hybridity in Postcolonial New Zealand," *Tourist Studies* 10, no. 1 (2010): 35–55.

48 Shilliam, *The Black Pacific*, 51.

49 Ibid., 53.

50 Ibid., 57.

51 Ibid., 65.

52 Ibid., 68.

53 Ibid., 67.

54 Ibid., 69.

55 Ibid., 70.

56 Ibid.

57 *Focus on the Audience*, 8.

58 Stuart Hall, "Cultural Identity and Diaspora," in *Identity: Community, Culture, Difference*, ed. Jonathan Rutherford (London: Lawrence and Wishart, 1990).

59 Martin Blythe, *Naming the Other: Images of the Māori in Film and TV* (Metuchen, NJ: Scarecrow Press, 1994), 19.

60 Adapted from Ronald Hugh Morrieson's novel, published in 1964.

61 Blythe, *Naming the Other*, 251.

62 Sarina Pearson, "Cowboy Contradictions: Westerns in the Postcolonial Pacific," *Studies in Australasian Cinema* 7, nos. 2–3 (2013): 153–64. The inset quote is from Ella Shohat and Robert Stam's *Unthinking Eurocentrism: Multiculturalism and the Media* (London: Routledge, 1994), 12.

63 Tony Mitchell, *Global Noise: Rap and Hip-Hop Outside the USA* (Middletown, CT: Wesleyan University Press, 2001); April K. Henderson, "Māori Boys, Michael Jackson Dance Moves, and that 1984 Structure of Feeling," *MEDIANZ* 13, no. 1 (2012). What is not discussed in Pearson's or Blythe's accounts, however, is the continuity of masculinity—identifying with white American cowboys was also about identifying with images of male power.

64 Blythe, *Naming the Other*, 252.

65 Stephen Turner, "Colonialism Continued: Producing the Self for Export," in *Race, Colour and Identity in Australia and New Zealand*, ed. John Docker and Gerhard Fischer (Sydney: University of New South Wales Press, 2000), 223.

66 Homi K. Bhabha, *The Location of Culture* (Abingdon: Routledge, 2004), 55.

67 Waititi, quoted in Adeline Sire, "Taika Waititi Revisits His Maori Roots in 'Boy,'" *World*, March 30, 2012, www.pri.org/stories/2012-03-30/taika-waititi-revisits-his-maori-roots-boy.

68 Gershon, "Indigeneity for Life."

69 Quoted in *Funny As: The Story of New Zealand Comedy*.

70 Sarina Pearson, "Pacific Camp: Satire, Silliness (and Seriousness) on New Zealand Television," *Media, Culture & Society* 27, no. 4 (2005): 566.

71 Ibid., 557.

72 Ibid., 551.

73 Ibid., 558.

74 Ibid.

75 Matthew Bannister. "'Bush Camp'? The Topp Twins and Antipodean Camp," *Australasian Journal of Popular Culture* 4, no. 1 (2015): 3–14.

76 Pearson, "Pacific Camp," 553.

77 Ibid., 560.

78 Susan Sontag, *Notes on "Camp"* (1964), accessed June 20, 2018, https://monoskop.org/images/5/59/Sontag_Susan_1964_Notes_on _Camp.pdf.

79 Quoted in *Funny As: The Story of New Zealand Comedy.*

80 Ibid.

81 Michelle Keown, "The Politics of Postcolonial Laughter: The International Reception of the New Zealand Animated Comedy Series *bro'Town*," in *Postcolonial Audiences: Readers, Viewers and Reception,* ed. Bethan Benwell, James Procter, and Gemma Robinson (New York: Routledge, 2012).

82 Rees, "Academic slams bro'Town."

83 Emma Earl, "Brand New Zealanders: The Commodification of Polynesian Youth Identity in Television Advertising" (master's thesis, University of Canterbury, 2005), ir.canterbury.ac.nz/handle/10092/1036.

84 Keown, "The Politics of Postcolonial Laughter," 28.

85 Ibid., 35.

86 Ibid., 36; Melani Anae, Lautofa Iuli, and Leilani Tamu, *Polynesian Panthers: Pacific Protest and Affirmative Action in Aotearoa New Zealand 1971–1981* (Wellington: Huia Publishers, 2015).

87 Ray Lillis, "Funny Brown Guys: Comedy and Race in New Zealand," *Metro Magazine: Media & Education Magazine* 154 (2007): 80–82.

88 Quoted in *Funny As: The Story of New Zealand Comedy.*

89 Keown, "The Politics of Postcolonial Laughter," 37.

90 Frederic Jameson, "Fear and Loathing in Globalization," *New Left Review* 23 (2003): 107.

91 Michel Foucault, *The Will to Knowledge: The History of Sexuality,* vol. 1 (Harmondsworth: Penguin, 1978), 101.

92 Henry Louis Gates, *Signifying Monkey: A Theory of African-American Literary Criticism* (New York: Oxford University Press, 1989), 66.

93 Malachi Andrews and Paul T. Owens, *Black Language* (West Los Angeles: SeymourSmith, 1973), 95.

94 Gates, *Signifying Monkey,* 117.

95 Sheila Roberts, "Eagle vs Shark Loren Horsley, Taika Waititi Interview," MoviesOnline, accessed April 20, 2020, www.webcitation.org/ 5qtqS9dM4?url=http://www.moviesonline.ca/movienews_12250.html. Waititi discusses his love of the anime classic *Akira* in Alex Denney, "Unknown Mortal Orchestra & Taika Waititi on New Zealand

culture," Dazed, April 5, 2018, www.dazeddigital.com/music/article/
39590/1/unknown-mortal-orchestra-ruban-nielson-taika-waititi
-interview.

96 Frances Till, "*The Untold Tales of Maui* at The Silo," *NZ Herald*, December 7, 2003, www.nzherald.co.nz/lifestyle/news/article.cfm?c_id=6&objectid=3538066.

97 Jonathan Williams, "New Zealand hit comedy 'Boy' comes to U.S. theaters," Wrestling with Pop Culture, April 6, 2012, www.wrestlingwithpopculture.com/2012/new-zealand-hit-comedy-boy-comes-to-u-s-theaters/.

98 Melanie Wall, "Stereotypical Constructions of the Māori 'Race' in the Media," *New Zealand Geographer* 53, no. 2 (1997): 40–45.

99 Quoted in *Funny As: The Story of New Zealand Comedy*.

100 *Focus on the Audience*, 8.

101 Ray Lillis, "Black Comedy," *Metro: Media & Education Magazine* 12 (2007): 74–78.

102 Rose Matafeo, quoted in *Funny As: The Story of New Zealand Comedy*.

103 All quotes are from *Funny As: The Story of New Zealand Comedy*.

104 *Pulp Comedy*, Series Seven, Episode Three, 2003, NZ On Screen, accessed October 17, 2020, www.nzonscreen.com/title/pulp-comedy-s7e3-taika-waititi-2003; Shohat and Stam, *Unthinking Eurocentrism*, 182.

105 Reznik, *New Jews*, 4.

106 Richard F. Shepard, "Songs and a New Comedian Make Lively Cabaret," *New York Times*, July 11, 1974, www.nytimes.com/1974/07/11/archives/songs-and-a-new-comedian-make-lively-cabaret.html.

107 Ibid.

108 Nathalie Atkinson, "Vampire mockumentary What We Do in the Shadows heading for cult status," *Globe and Mail*, February 12, 2015, updated May 12, 2018, www.theglobeandmail.com/arts/film/vampire-mockumentary-what-we-do-in-the-shadows-heading-for-cult-status/article22956380/.

109 Zarine L. Rocha and Angela Wanhalla, "A History of Mixed Race in Aotearoa/New Zealand," in *Mana Tangatarua: Mixed Heritages, Ethnic Identity and Biculturalism in Aotearoa/New Zealand*, ed. Zarine L. Rocha and Melinda Webber (New York: Routledge, 2017), 33.

110 Philip H. Ennis, *The Seventh Stream: The Emergence of Rocknroll in American Popular Music* (Middletown, CT: Wesleyan University Press, 1992).

111 Max Rashbrooke, "How can NZ close the gap between rich and poor?" RNZ, December 14, 2018, www.rnz.co.nz/news/national/378307/how -can-nz-close-the-gap-between-rich-and-poor; The distribution of wealth by Gini coefficient (where 0 would reflect equality and 1 would reflect the most unequal) is US 0.852, NZ 0.708, "Global Wealth Databook 2018," *Credit Suisse*.

112 Bambi L. Haggins, "Laughing Mad," 180.

113 Ola Sjberg, "Unemployment and Unemployment Benefits In The OECD (1960–1990): An Empirical Test of Neo-Classical Economic Theory," *Work, Employment and Society* 14, no. 1 (2000): 51–76.

114 "Taika Waititi," The Arts Foundation, accessed on February 1, 2021, www.thearts.co.nz/artists/taika-waititi.

115 Abrams, *The New Jew in Film*, 13.

116 Reznik, *New Jews*, 11–12.

117 "An Audience with the King—Part 2," November 16, 2010, www .youtube.com/watch?v=UuYpUtgeGFg.

118 Martens, "Maori on the Silver Screen," 3.

119 Abrams, *The New Jew in Film*, 21.

120 Quoted in *Funny As: The Story of New Zealand Comedy*.

121 Ibid.

Chapter 5

1 Deborah J. Thomas, "Framing the 'Melancomic': Character, Aesthetics and Affect in Wes Anderson's *Rushmore*," *New Review of Film and Television Studies* 10, no. 1 (2012): 99.

2 Roger Ebert, "The New Geek Cinema," Roger Ebert.com, September 27, 1998, www.rogerebert.com/festivals-and-awards/the-new-geek -cinema.

3 Sam Fragoso, "Sundance Review: Taika Waititi's 'Hunt For The Wilderpeople' Starring Sam Neill & Julian Dennison," *IndieWire*, January 24, 2016, www.indiewire.com/2016/01/sundance-review -taika-waititis-hunt-for-the-wilderpeople-starring-sam-neill-julian -dennison-88197/; David Perkins, "What Are the Characteristics of

Taika Waititi's Filmmaking Style?" ScreenPrism, August 25, 2016, screenprism.com/insights/article/what-are-the-techniques-and -characteristics-of-taika-waititis-filmmaking. *Jojo Rabbit* has brought a fresh flood of Anderson comparisons: for example, Justin Chang, "Satirical Nazi Film 'Jojo Rabbit' Treats the Viewer Like A Child," *NPR*, October 18, 2019, www.npr.org/2019/10/18/770938639/satirical-nazi -film-jojo-rabbit-treats-the-viewer-like-a-child.

4   Kom Kunyosying and Carter Soles, "Postmodern geekdom as simulated ethnicity," *Jump Cut*, 2012, www.ejumpcut.org/archive/jc54 .2012/SolesKunyoGeedom/index.html.

5   Andrew Higson, "Film Acting and Independent Cinema," *Screen* 27, nos. 3–4 (1986): 112.

6   Thomas, "Framing the 'Melancomic,'" 100.

7   Ibid., 101.

8   Waititi has mentioned *Punch-Drunk Love* as a favorite. "Why Watch 'Punch Drunk Love': Taika Waititi," YouTube, April 4, 2017, www .youtube.com/watch?v=VgsMcB8-QyA.

9   Andrew Ross, *No Respect: Intellectuals & Popular Culture* (New York: Routledge, 1989).

10 Jesse F. Mayshark, *Post-Pop Cinema: The Search for Meaning in New American Film* (Westport CT: Praeger, 2007).

11 Ross, *No Respect*, 5.

12 Heather Mendick and Becky Francis, "Boffin and Geek Identities: Abject or Privileged?" *Gender & Education* 24, no. 1 (January 2012): 19.

13 J. A. McArthur, "Digital Subculture: A Geek Meaning of Style," *Journal of Communication Inquiry* 33, no. 1 (January 2009): 58–70.

14 Ross, *No Respect*, 5.

15 Pierre Bourdieu, *Distinction: A Social Critique of the Judgement of Taste*, trans. Richard Nice (London: Routledge & Kegan Paul, 1984); Keith Negus, "The Work of Cultural Intermediaries and the Enduring Distance between Production and Consumption," *Cultural Studies* 16, no. 4 (2002): 501–15.

16 Ross, *No Respect*, 5.

17 Mendick and Francis, "Boffin and Geek Identities."

18 Ibid.

19 Henry Jenkins, *Convergence Culture: Where Old and New Media Collide* (New York: New York University Press, 2008); Henry Jenkins, Sam

Ford, and Joshua Green, *Spreadable Media: Creating Value and Meaning in a Networked Culture* (New York: New York University Press, 2013).

20 Ross, *No Respect.*

21 David L. Reznik, *New Jews: Race and American Jewish Identity in 21st-Century Film* (New York: Taylor & Francis Group, 2012), 34–35.

22 William Paul, *Laughing Screaming: Modern Hollywood Horror and Comedy* (New York: Columbia University Press, 1994), 225; Chris Russell, "Now It's Time for a Little Braggadocio: Nerdcore, Rap, Race, and the Politics of Appropriation," in *Geek Rock: An Exploration of Music and Subculture*, ed. Alex di Blais and Victoria Willis (Lanham, MD: Rowman and Littlefield, 2014), 161–75.

23 Laura Mulvey, *Visual and Other Pleasures* (Bloomington: Indiana University Press, 1989).

24 Ibid., 17.

25 Will Straw, "Sizing Up Record Collections: Gender and Connoisseurship in Rock Music Culture," in *Sexing the Groove: Popular Music and Gender*, ed. Sheila Whiteley (London: Routledge, 1997), 7–8.

26 Ross, *No Respect*, 5.

27 Patrick S. Smith, *Warhol: Conversations about the Artist* (Ann Arbor: UMI Research, 1998), 122.

28 Ibid., 8, 20, 25, 34, 44, 53, 59, 88, 100, 105, 122–25, 188, 193.

29 Ibid., 292.

30 Ibid., 295.

31 Ross, *No Respect*, 150. Emphasis in original.

32 Bourdieu, *Distinction*, 31–32. Emphasis in original.

33 Ross, *No Respect*, 145.

34 Phillip Auslander, *Liveness: Performance in a Mediatized Culture* (New York: Routledge, 1999), 20.

35 Jay David Bolter and Richard Grusin, *Remediation: Understanding New Media* (Cambridge, MA: MIT Press, 1999).

36 Jasia Reichardt, "Pop Art and After," in *Pop Art: A Critical History*, ed. Steven H. Madoff (Berkeley: University of California Press, 1997), 18.

37 Ross, *No Respect*, 167.

38 Mayshark, *Post-Pop Cinema.*

39 *Ibid.*, 14.

40 Jeffrey Sconce, "Irony, Nihilism and the New American Smart Film," *Screen* 43, no. 4 (2002): 349–69.

41 Kenneth Turan, "Fade to pitch black," *Los Angeles Times*, November 22, 1998, n.p.

42 Sconce "Irony, Nihilism," 367.

43 Ibid., 365.

44 Ibid., 366.

45 James MacDowell, "Notes on Quirky," *Movie: A Journal of Film Criticism* 1 (2010), warwick.ac.uk/fac/arts/film/movie/contents/notes_on _quirky.pdf.

46 Ibid., 6.

47 Sconce, "Irony, Nihilism," 365.

48 Mark Olsen, "If I Can Dream: The Everlasting Boyhoods of Wes Anderson," *Film Comment* 35, no. 1 (January/February 1999): 17.

49 *Timotheus Vermeulen and Robin van den Akker*, "Notes on Metamodernism," *Journal of Aesthetics and Culture* 2 (2010): 1–14.

50 MacDowell, "Notes on Quirky," 13.

51 Trisha Dunleavy, "Hybridity in TV Sitcom: The Case of Comedy Verité," *Flow Journal* 12 (2008), www.Flowjournal.org/2008/12/Hybridity-In-Tv -Sitcom-The-Case-Of-Comedy-Verite%C2%A0%C2%A0trisha-Dunleavy %C2%A0%C2%A0victoria-University-Of-Wellington%C2%A0/.

52 James Naremore, *Acting in the Cinema* (London: University of California Press, 1988), 115.

53 Henri Bergson, *Laughter: An Essay on the Meaning of the Comic* (Mineola, NY: Dover Publications, 2005), 82.

54 Dunleavy, "Hybridity in TV Sitcom."

55 MacDowell, "Notes on Quirky," 3.

56 Ibid., 5.

57 Ross, *No Respect*, 146.

58 Sconce, "Irony, Nihilism."

59 MacDowell, "Notes on Quirky," 8.

60 Lexi Feinberg, review of *Eagle vs Shark*, CinemaBlend, May 27, 2016, www.cinemablend.com/reviews/Eagle-Vs-Shark-2229.html; Joe Morgenstern, "Kiwi Comedy 'Eagle vs Shark' is Endearing, Odd," *Wall Street Journal*, June 15, 2007, www.wsj.com/articles/ SB118186395464336075; Alex Billington, "Sundance Interview: 'Hunt for the Wilderpeople' Director Taika Waititi," First Showing.Net, February 5, 2016, firstshowing.net/2016/sundance-interview-hunt-for -the-wilderpeople-director-taika-waititi/; Steven Rea, "2 nerdy clerks

find costumes and true love," *Philadelphia Enquirer*, June 21, 2007, www.inquirer.com/philly/entertainment/movies/20070622_2_nerdy _clerks_find_costumes_and_true_love.html.

61 Thomas, "Framing the 'Melancomic,'" 109.

62 Sconce, "Irony, Nihilism," 364.

63 Jason Garrett Lyle, "Social Outcast Cinema: Generic Evolution and Identification in Early 21st Century Teen Film," (PhD diss., Regent University, 2008), 71.

64 Pertti Grönholm, "When Tomorrow Began Yesterday: Kraftwerk's Nostalgia for the Past Futures," *Popular Music and Society* 38, no. 3 (2015): 372–88.

65 Feinberg, review of *Eagle vs Shark*.

66 John Champagne, "Dancing Queen? Feminist and Gay Male Spectatorship in Three Recent Films from Australia," *Film Criticism* 21, no. 3 (1997): 66–88.

67 Sara D'Arcy, "Mourning, Gender Melancholia, and Subversive Homoeroticism in Virginia Woolf's *Mrs Dalloway and Michael Cunningham's The Hours*," *Leitura Flutuante* 4, no. 1 (2012): 43; Judith Butler, *The Psychic Life of Power: Theories in Subjection* (Stanford, CA: Stanford University Press, 1997).

68 Butler, *The Psychic Life of Power*.

69 Tina Law, "National suicide numbers rise three years in a row," *Stuff*, August 28, 2017, www.stuff.co.nz/national/health/96217175/national -suicide-numbers-rise-three-years-in-a-row.

70 World Health Organization, "Suicide rate estimates, age-standardized Estimates by country," last updated July 17, 2018, apps.who.int/gho/ data/node.main.MHSUICIDEASDR?lang=en.

Chapter 6

1 Steve Seidman, *Comedian Comedy: A Tradition in Hollywood Film* (Ann Arbor, MI: UMI Research Press, 1981).

2 Ibid., 5.

3 Frank Krutnik, "Mutinies Wednesdays and Saturdays: Carnivalesque Comedy and the Marx Brothers," in *Companion to Film Comedy*, ed. Andrew Horton and Joanna E. Rapf (Malden, MA: Wiley-Blackwell, 2012), 104.

4 Seidman, *Comedian Comedy*, 124. For a discussion of spirituality in *Boy*, see Ann Hardy, "Hidden Gods—Religion, Spirituality and Recent New Zealand Cinema," *Studies in Australasian Cinema* 6, no. 1 (2012): 11–27.

5 Linda Tuhiwai Smith, *Decolonizing Methodologies: Research and Indigenous Peoples* (London: Zed Books, 2012), 303.

6 Seidman, *Comedian Comedy*, 143–46; Ocean Mercier, "Welcome to My Interesting World: Pōwhiri Styled Encounter in Boy," *Illusions* 42 (2010): 3–7.

7 Sharon Mazer and Te Rita Papesch, "Māori Performance/Cultural Performance: Stages of Pōwhiri," in *Ngā Kete a Rēhua: Inaugural Māori Research Symposium Te Waipounamu Proceedings* (Christchurch: University of Canterbury, 2010), 280.

8 Mercier, "Welcome to My Interesting World."

9 Ibid.

10 Peter Kramer, "Derailing the Honeymoon Express: Comicality and Narrative Closure in Buster Keaton's *The Blacksmith*," in *Hollywood Comedians, The Film Reader*, ed. Frank Krutnik (London: Routledge, 2001), 43.

11 Jo Smith and Ocean Mercier, "Introduction to the Special Issue on Taika Waititi's Boy," *MEDIANZ* 13, no. 1 (2012): 6.

12 Ella Shohat and Robert Stam, *Unthinking Eurocentrism: Multiculturalism and the Media* (London: Routledge, 1994), 182.

13 Smith and Mercier, "Introduction," 1.

14 Leonie Pihama, "A Short Commentary on Boy," *MEDIANZ* 13, no. 1 (2012): 99.

15 Smith and Mercier, "Introduction," 6.

16 Misha Kavka and Stephen Turner, "Boy and the Postcolonial Taniwha," *MEDIANZ* 13, no. 1 (2012): 38.

17 Barry Barclay, *Our Own Image* (Minneapolis: University of Minnesota Press, 2015), ix, 96.

18 Smith and Mercier, "Introduction," 11.

19 David Geary, "Taika Waititi—Boy Wonder!" *MEDIANZ* 13, no. 1 (2012): 16.

20 Seidman, *Comedian Comedy*, 133.

21 Barclay, *Our Own Image*, 79.

22 Mercier, "Welcome to My Interesting World."

23 Alistair Fox, *Coming of Age Cinema in NZ: Genre, Gender and Adaptation* (Edinburgh: Edinburgh University Press, 2017), 198; Richard Dyer, *Only Entertainment* (New York: Routledge, 1992), 3.

24 Matthew DeKneef, "The Kids Are All Waititi: A Conversation with New Zealand's New Indie Darling," *Honolulu Weekly* 22, no. 17, April 25, 2012, 9.

25 Ocean Mercier, "Alamein's Encore: Entertainment, Information, Intimacy and Reflection in the *Boy* DVD Director's Commentary," *MEDIANZ* 13, no. 1 (2012): 47–65.

26 Ibid., 56.

27 Ibid., 47; Dyer, *Only Entertainment*, 22–23.

28 Seidman, *Comedian Comedy*, 64.

29 Henry Louis Gates, *Signifying Monkey: A Theory of African-American Literary Criticism* (New York: Oxford University Press, 1989).

30 Kavka and Turner, "Boy and the Postcolonial Taniwha."

31 Mercier, "Alamein's Encore," 51.

32 Steve Krutnik, "General Introduction," in *Hollywood Comedians, The Film Reader*, ed. Frank Krutnik (London: Routledge, 2001), 7.

33 Seidman, *Comedian Comedy*, 5.

34 Steve Neale and Frank Krutnik, *Popular Film and TV Comedy* (New York: Routledge, 1990), 104–5.

35 Seidman, *Comedian Comedy*, 24–25.

36 Kramer, "Derailing the Honeymoon Express," 47.

37 Krutnik, "General Introduction," 8.

38 Seidman, *Comedian Comedy*, 4–5.

39 Ibid.

40 Matt Rodriguez, "Taika Waititi: The Interview (Boy)." *Shakefire*, accessed February 2, 2012, www.shakefire.com/interview/taika-waititi -the-interview-boy.

41 "Taika Waititi: Masterclass," Toronto International Film Festival 2018, YouTube, September 10, 2018, www.youtube.com/watch?v=-5D _9i5Z8lo&t=342s; Emily Brookes, "Taika Waititi: My father was a gang member," *Stuff*, June 4, 2019, www.stuff.co.nz/entertainment/film/ 113204244/taika-waititi-my-father-was-a-gang-member.

42 Seidman, *Comedian Comedy*, 132.

43 Ibid., 15.

44 DeKneef, "The Kids Are All Waititi."

45 Seidman, *Comedian Comedy*, 7.

46 Philip Drake, "Theorizing Performance in Post-Classical Comedian Comedy," in *Hollywood Comedians, The Film Reader*, ed. Frank Krutnik (London: Routledge, 2001), 191.

47 Ibid., 193.

48 Seidman, *Comedian Comedy*, 6.

49 Matthew Bannister, "Kiwi Blokes: Recontextualising White New Zealand Masculinities in a Global Setting," *Genders* 42 (2005), www.colorado.edu/gendersarchive1998-2013/2005/08/20/kiwi-blokes-recontextualising-white-new-zealand-masculinities-global-setting.

50 Mercier, "Alamein's Encore," 55.

51 Neale and Krutnik, *Popular Film and TV Comedy*, 104.

52 Seidman, *Comedian Comedy*, 124.

53 Neale and Krutnik, *Popular Film and TV Comedy*, 106.

54 Mercier, "Welcome to My Interesting World," 5.

55 Seidman, *Comedian Comedy*, 133.

56 Drake, "Theorizing Performance in Post-Classical Comedian Comedy," 191.

57 Ibid.

58 Seidman, *Comedian Comedy*, 80.

59 Drake, "Theorizing Performance in Post-Classical Comedian Comedy," 190.

60 Ibid., 191.

61 Seidman, *Comedian Comedy*, 124.

62 Ibid., 143, 146.

63 Mercier, "Welcome to My Interesting World," 6.

64 Ibid.

65 Barclay, *Our Own Image*, 59.

66 Ibid., 14–15.

67 April Henderson, "Maori Boys, Michael Jackson Dance Moves, and that 1984 Structure of Feeling," *MEDIANZ* 13, no. 1 (2012): 87.

68 Mazer and Papesch, "Māori Performance/Cultural Performance," 280.

69 Mercier, "Welcome to My Interesting World."

70 Stuart Hall, "Cultural Identity and Diaspora," in *Identity: Community, Culture, Difference*, ed. Jonathan Rutherford (London: Lawrence and Wishart, 1990), 225.

71 "For us to bring 40 people and a crew and sort of boost the population of the town, you know. It was really cool for them. All the crew
became like a big extended family in the town. It was a very lively and
really homely affair. So they were all very supportive. My auntie was
the head caterer and a lot of people I'm related to helped out in the
film. My uncle plays the teacher at the start who's smoking. So yeah,
it's cool to be able to involve the community within the film making
part of it as well." Waititi, quoted in Rodriguez, "Taika Waititi"; Barclay, *Our Own Image*.

Chapter 7

1 Karl Marx, *Capital*, vol. 1, section 1, accessed on February 3, 2021, www
.marxists.org/archive/marx/works/1867-c1/ch10.htm; Rob Latham,
Consuming Youth: Vampires, Cyborgs, and the Culture of Consumption
(Chicago: University of Chicago Press, 2002), 74.

2 Richard Dyer, "Children of the Night: Vampirism as Homosexuality,
Homosexuality as Vampirism," in *Sweet Dreams: Sexuality, Gender, and
Popular Fiction, ed. Susannah Radstone* (London: Lawrence & Wishart,
1988), 64.

3 Marlow Stern, "Anne Rice on Sparkly Vampires, 'Twilight,' 'True
Blood,' and Werewolves," *The Book Beast*, November 23, 2011, www
.thedailybeast.com/anne-rice-on-sparkly-vampires-twilight-true
-blood-and-werewolves.

4 Vampire texts written by women can be read as empowering a female
gaze by eroticizing men, as in slash or fan fiction. See, for example,
Lucy Neville, "'The Tent's Big Enough for Everyone': Online Slash
Fiction as a Site for Activism and Change," *Gender, Place and Culture*
25, no. 3 (2018): 384–98.

5 Robin is not an immigrant, however.

6 Nathalie Atkinson, "Vampire mockumentary What We Do in the
Shadows heading for cult status," *Globe and Mail*, February 12, 2015,
updated May 12, 2018, www.theglobeandmail.com/arts/film/
vampire-mockumentary-what-we-do-in-the-shadows-heading
-for-cult-status/article22956380/; Tasha Robinson, "Jemaine Clement
and Taika Waititi on their years-in-the-making vampire comedy
What We Do In The Shadows," The Dissolve, February 13, 2015,

thedissolve.com/features/interview/923-jemaine-clement-and-taika
-waititi-on-their-years-i/.

7 Ellie Shohat and Robert Stam, *Unthinking Eurocentrism: Multiculturalism and the Media* (London: Routledge, 1994), 189.

8 Brenda Gardenour, "The Biology of Blood-Lust: Medieval Medicine,
Theology, and the Vampire Jew," *Film & History* 41, no. 2 (Fall 2011):
51–63.

9 Anthony Giddens, *Runaway World: How Globalisation Is Reshaping
Our Lives* (London: Profile, 1999), 21.

10 Ibid., 2.

11 Ibid., 19.

12 Ulrich Beck and Natan Sznaider, "Unpacking Cosmopolitanism for the
Social Sciences: A Research Agenda," *British Journal of Sociology* 57
(2006): 20.

13 Anthony Giddens, *The Consequences of Modernity* (Cambridge: Polity,
1990), 139.

14 Giddens, *Runaway World*, 50.

15 Ibid., 46.

16 Ibid., 27.

17 Jane Roscoe and Craig Hight, *Faking It: Mock-Documentary and the Subversion of Factuality* (Manchester: Manchester University Press, 2001), 5.

18 J. R. Jones, "Clement and Taika Waititi want to suck your blood,"
Chicagoreader, February 25, 2015, www.chicagoreader.com/chicago/
what-we-do-in-the-shadows-jemaine-clement-taika-waititi-horror
-comedy/Content?oid=16676536.

19 Ibid.; Gardenour, "The Biology of Blood-Lust," 53.

20 John Corner, quoted in Jane L. Chapman, *Issues in Contemporary Documentary* (Cambridge: Polity Press, 2009), 18.

21 Giddens, *The Consequences of Modernity*, 38; Giddens, *Runaway
World*, 47.

22 Mark Andrejevic, *Reality TV: The Work of Being Watched* (Lanham, MD:
Rowman & Littlefield, 2003).

23 Ibid.

24 Ryan Bishop, *Comedy and Cultural Critique in American Film* (Edinburgh: Edinburgh University Press, 2013), 81.

25 Slavoj Zizek, *How to Read Lacan* (New York: W.W. Norton and Co.,
2006), 8.

26 Giddens, *Runaway World*.

27 Ibid., 5.

28 Beck and Sznaider, "Unpacking Cosmopolitanism," 20.

29 Anthony Giddens, *The Transformation of Intimacy: Sexuality, Love and Eroticism in Modern Societies* (Cambridge: Polity, 1992).

30 Giddens, *Runaway World*, 47.

31 Ibid., 16.

32 Edward Said, *Orientalism* (New York: Vintage Books, 1994).

33 Leshu Torchin, "Cultural Learnings of Borat for Make Benefit Glorious Study of Documentary," *Film & History* 38, no. 1 (2008): 55.

34 Arezou Zalipour, introduction to *Migrant and Diasporic Film and Filmmaking in New Zealand*, ed. Arezou Zalipour (Singapore: Springer, 2019), 22.

35 Ibid.

36 *Iqbal Jogi & Party—Authentic Music of the Snake Charmer*, accessed 29 July, 2018, www.discogs.com/Iqbal-Jogi-Party-Authentic-Music-Of -The-Snake-Charmer/release/2760461.

37 Giddens, *Consequences of Modernity*, 19, emphasis added.

38 Giddens, *Runaway World*, 57.

39 Atkinson, "Vampire mockumentary."

40 Eve Sedgwick, *Between Men: English Literature and Male Homosocial Desire* (New York: Columbia University Press, 1992).

41 Steve Kilgallon, "IT guy turns accidental film star," *Stuff*, June 8, 2014, www.stuff.co.nz/entertainment/film/10127770/IT-guy-turns -accidental-film-star.

42 Giddens, *Runaway World*, 46.

43 Ibid.

44 Ibid., 47.

45 "Red Blooded—Lion Red," NZ On Screen, 1993, www.nzonscreen.com/ title/red-blooded-lion-red.

46 Matthew Bannister, "Kiwi Blokes: Recontextualising Pakeha Mascu-linities in a Global Setting," *Genders Online* 42 (2005), https://www .colorado.edu/gendersarchive1998-2013/2005/08/20/kiwi-blokes -recontextualising-white-new-zealand-masculinities-global-setting.

47 David C. Oh and Doreen V. Kutufam, "The Orientalized 'Other' and Corrosive Femininity: Threats to White Masculinity in *300*," *Journal of Communication Inquiry* 38, no. 2 (2014): 158.

48 Sigmund Freud, "Humour," in the *Standard Edition of the Complete Psychological Works of Sigmund Freud*, vol. 21 (London: Hogarth Press, 1964), 162–63.

49 Joanna E. Rapf, "Comic Theory from a Feminist Perspective: A Look at Jerry Lewis," in *Hollywood Comedians, The Film Reader*, ed. Frank Krutnik (London: Routledge, 2001), 145.

50 "Te Ahi Kaa mo 22 o Haratua," RNZ, May 22, 2011, www.radionz.co.nz/audio/player?audio_id=2489663.

51 Rob Hunter, "32 Things We Learned from the What We Do in the Shadows Commentary," Film School Rejects, July 20, 2015, filmschoolrejects.com/32-things-we-learned-from-the-what-we-do-in-the-shadows-commentary-1a3a4a339681/.

52 Ibid.

53 "Locals Only Podcast: Episode 8—Samuel Flynn Scott," *Radio Hauraki*, May 28, 2018, www.hauraki.co.nz/music/podcast/locals-only-podcast-episode-8-samuel-flynn-scott/.

54 C. Wesley Buerkle, "Adam Mansplains Everything: White-Hipster Masculinity as Covert Hegemony," *Southern Communication Journal* 84, no. 3 (2019): 170.

55 Lynne Segal, *Slow Motion: Changing Masculinities, Changing Men* (London: Virago, 1990), 16–17.

56 Stjepan Mestrovic, *Anthony Giddens: The Last Modernist* (London: Routledge, 2005); Anthony King, "Legitimating Post-Fordism: A Critique of Anthony Giddens' Later Works," *Telos* 115 (1999): 61–77.

57 Zalipour, introduction, 20, 22.

Chapter 8

1   Conan O'Brien, quoted in Lynn Hirschberg, "Heeeere's . . . Conan!!!," *New York Times*, May 20, 2009, www.nytimes.com/2009/05/24/magazine/24Conan-t.html.

2   Susan Sontag, *Notes on "Camp"* (1964), accessed 20 June 2016, https://monoskop.org/images/5/59/Sontag_Susan_1964_Notes_on_Camp.pdf.

3   Nick Perry, *Hyperreality and Global Culture* (New York: Routledge, 1998).

4   Richard Dyer, *Only Entertainment* (New York: Routledge, 1992), 24.

5 Peter Wegele, *Max Steiner: Composing, Casablanca, and the Golden Age of Film Music* (Lanham, MD: Rowman & Littlefield, 2014), 37.

6 Liz Guiffre and Mark Evans, "Sounding Funny: The Importance of Hearing the Joke," in *Sounding Funny: Sound and Comedy Cinema*, ed. Mark Evans and Philip Hayward (Bristol, CT: Equinox, 2016), 8.

7 The Howard Morrison Quartet recording "George, the Wild(er) NZ Boy" became a huge local hit in 1963 despite being banned by NZ radio.

8 "Skux" means cool. "Koretux" is a slang version of Māori word "*koretake*," which means "useless."

9 Sean Albiez, *Bloomsbury Encyclopedia of Popular Music of the World* (New York: Bloomsbury, 2017), 11:347–49.

10 "Taika Waititi Interview—Zimbio Exclusive," YouTube, March 15, 2012, www.youtube.com/watch?v=QUHp16hTp44.

11 Simon O'Hagan, "Debate: If the Seventies Were the Decade Taste Forgot, Why Are We So Keen to Remember Them?" *The Independent*, October 24, 1998, www.independent.co.uk/life-style/debate-if-the -seventies-were-the-decade-taste-forgot-why-are-we-so-keen-to -remember-them-1180468.html.

12 Sontag, *Notes on "Camp."*

13 Maria Pramaggiore and Tom Wallis, *Film: A Critical Introduction* (London: Laurence King, 2005).

14 Anahid Kassabian, *Hearing Film: Tracking Identifications in Contemporary Hollywood Film Music* (New York: Routledge, 2001).

15 Taika Waititi, quoted in Alex Billington, "Sundance Interview: 'Hunt for the Wilderpeople' Director Taika Waititi," First Showing.Net, February 5, 2016, www.firstshowing.net/2016/sundance-interview-hunt -for-the-wilderpeople-director-taika-waititi/.

16 Helen Wong, review of *Hunt for the Wilderpeople*, *The Listener*, April 2–8, 2016, 60–61.

17 Russell Baillie, "Movie review: *The Hunt for the Wilderpeople*," *NZ Herald*, March 30, 2016, www.nzherald.co.nz/entertainment/news/article .cfm?c_id=1501119&objectid=11613732.

18 Steve Newall, "Flicks Review," accessed July 20, 2018, www.flicks.co.nz/ movie/hunt-for-the-wilderpeople/.

19 Nick Schager, "Don't Miss Taika Waititi's Mad Fable 'Hunt for the Wilderpeople' at Tribeca," *Village Voice*, April 20, 2016, www .villagevoice.com/film/don-t-miss-taika-waititi-s-mad-fable-hunt-for -the-wilderpeople-at-tribeca-8533819.

20 Sophie Gilbert, "The Teen Dramas That Reject Modernity," *The Atlantic*, March 4, 2020, www.theatlantic.com/culture/archive/2020/03/ neflix-new-teen-nostalgia-i-am-not-okay-with-this-sex-education -stranger-things/607366/.

21 Rita Felski, "Fin de siècle, Fin de sexe: Transsexuality, Postmodernism, and the Death of History," *New Literary History* 27, no. 2 (1996): 337–49.

22 Graeme Tuckett, "Review: *Hunt for the Wilderpeople*," *Stuff*, March 31, 2016, www.stuff.co.nz/entertainment/film/film-reviews/ 78419677/Review-Hunt-For-The-Wilderpeople; Nigel Smith, "Hunt for the Wilderpeople review: Sam Neill + misfit kid = Kiwi hit," *The Guardian*, January 23, 2016, www.theguardian.com/film/ 2016/jan/23/hunt-for-the-wilderpeople-review-sam-neill-misfit -kid-kiwi-hit; Dennis Harvey, "Sundance Film Review: *Hunt for the Wilderpeople*," *Variety*, January 23, 2016, variety.com/2016/ film/reviews/hunt-for-the-wilderpeople-review-sundance -1201686843/.

23 Quoted in *Legend of Birds*, National Film Unit, 1962.

24 Birdsong also features in classical works by Jenny McLeod, Douglas Lilburn, John Rimmer, and Eve de Castro-Robinson. Glenda Keam, "Attachments to Place: Locative Aspects of New Zealand Art Music," in *Home Land and Sea: Situating Music in Aotearoa/New Zealand*, ed. Glenda Keam and Tony Mitchell (Auckland: Pearson, 2011), 218–33.

25 "40 years of bird calls," RNZ, February 6, 2014, www.radionz.co.nz/ news/national/235343/40-years-of-bird-calls.

26 Eric Hobsbawm and Terence Ranger, eds., *The Invention of Tradition* (New York: Cambridge University Press, 1983).

27 Perry, *Hyperreality and Global Culture*, 12.

28 Stephen Barnett and Richard Wolfe, *New Zealand! New Zealand! In Praise of Kiwiana* (Auckland: Hodder & Stoughton, 1989).

29 "40 years of bird calls." Ruru is a native owl.

30 Richard Holdaway, "Extinctions—Smaller birds, reptiles, frogs, fish, plants," *Te Ara—the Encyclopedia of New Zealand*, accessed June 18, 2019, www.TeAra.govt.nz/en/extinctions/page-6.

31 Tony Mitchell, "He waiata na Aotearoa: Maori and Pacific Islander Music in Aotearoa/NZ," in *Sound Alliances: Indigenous Peoples, Cultural Politics and Popular Music in the Pacific*, ed. Philip Hayward (New York: Cassell, 1998), 26–44; Elizabeth Turner, "What's Be Happen? The Discourse of Reggae Lyrics Thirty Years On," *Sites: New Series* 9, no. 2 (2012): 23–38.

32 Alex Denney, "Unknown Mortal Orchestra & Taika Waititi on New Zealand culture," Dazed, April 5, 2018, www.dazeddigital.com/music/article/39590/1/unknown-mortal-orchestra-ruban-nielson-taika-waititi-interview.

33 James MacDowell, "Notes on Quirky," *Movie: A Journal of Film Criticism* 1 (2010): 8, warwick.ac.uk/fac/arts/film/movie/contents/notes_on_quirky.pdf.

34 Jonathan Broxton, "Hunt for the Wilderpeople—Moniker," Movie Music UK, August 12, 2016, moviemusicuk.us/2016/08/12/hunt-for-the-wilderpeople-moniker/.

35 Hugh Campbell, Robin Law, and James Honeyfield, "What It Means to Be a Man: Hegemonic Masculinity and the Reinvention of Beer," in *Masculinities in Aotearoa/New Zealand*, ed. Robin Law, Hugh Campbell, and John Dolan (Palmerston North: Dunmore, 1999), 166–87.

36 Quoted in Billington, "Sundance Interview," First Showing.net, www.firstshowing.net/2016/sundance-interview-hunt-for-the-wilderpeople-director-taika-waititi/.

37 "Magic What She Do" also appears in *What We Do in the Shadows*, suggesting that the song has some special meaning for the director.

38 Kassabian, *Hearing Film*, 1–4.

39 "Interview with Taika Waititi on making kiwi [*sic*] film 'Boy,'" YouTube, January 24, 2013, www.youtube.com/watch?v=-EsmSgG_NZI.

40 Sontag, *Notes on "Camp."*

41 Perry, *Hyperreality and Global Culture.*

42 Judith Butler, *Gender Trouble: Feminism and the Subversion of Identity* (New York: Routledge, 1990).

43 Jonno Revanche and Justine Sachs, "The colonial critique in *Hunt for the Wilderpeople*," *Overland*, November 1, 2016, overland.org.au/2016/

11/the-colonial-critique-of-hunt-for-the-wilderpeople/; Michael Agresta, "SXSW Film Review: *Hunt for the Wilderpeople*," *Austin Chronicle*, March 12, 2016, www.austinchronicle.com/daily/screens/2016-03-12/sxsw-film-review-hunt-for-the-wilderpeople/; Angie Han, "Review: Taika Waititi's *Hunt for the Wilderpeople* Is a New Childhood Classic," Slash Film, June 24, 2016, www.slashfilm.com/hunt-for-the-wilderpeople-review/; Matt Goldberg, "*Hunt for the Wilderpeople* Review: Fun on the Run," Collider, June 23, 2016, collider.com/hunt-for-the-wilderpeople-review-sundance-2016/.

44 Dyer, *Only Entertainment*.

45 Ibid., 17–18.

46 Sarina Pearson, "Pacific Camp: Satire, Silliness (and Seriousness) on New Zealand Television," *Media, Culture & Society* 27, no. 4 (2005): 560.

47 Tuckett, "Review: *Hunt for the Wilderpeople*."

48 Schager, "Don't Miss Taika Waititi's Mad Fable."

49 Smith, "Hunt for the Wilderpeople review."

50 Han, "Review."

51 Harvey, "Sundance Film Review."

52 Sontag, *Notes on "Camp."*

53 Tuckett, "Review: *Hunt for the Wilderpeople*."

54 L&P (Lemon & Paeroa) is an NZ soft drink; Burger Rings is an Australian brand of snack food.

55 Joelle Dally and Michael Daly, "'Racist' cartoon slammed," *Stuff*, May 30, 2013, www.stuff.co.nz/national/8736295/Racist-cartoon-slammed.

56 Cathy Griggers, "Thelma and Louise and the Cultural Generation of the New Butch-Femme" in *Film Theory Goes to the Movies*, ed. Jim Collins, Hilary Radner, and Ava Preacher Collins (New York: Routledge, 1993), 129–41; Bernie Cook, ed., *Thelma & Louise Live! The Cultural Afterlife of an American Film* (Austin: University of Texas Press, 2007).

57 Nick Perry, *Dominion of Signs: Television, Advertising and Other New Zealand Fictions* (Auckland: Auckland University Press, 1994), 56.

58 Sontag, *Notes on "Camp."*

59 Matthew Bannister, "'Bush Camp'? The Topp Twins and Antipodean Camp," *Australasian Journal of Popular Culture* 4, no. 1 (2015): 3–14.

60 Paula Hore may be a caricature of Paula Bennett, NZ minister of social development from 2008–14, who was criticized for her harsh

treatment of beneficiaries and comments about child poverty (hence her nickname Paula Benefit). Bennett is also Māori, like Rachel House.

61 Public Law 107–110, 2002, accessed June 25, 2016, https://www.govinfo .gov/app/details/PLAW-107publ11.

62 Judith Halberstam, *Female Masculinity* (Durham, NC: Duke University Press, 1998).

63 Matthew Bannister, "'Bush Camp'?"

64 The latter are an obvious influence on Flight of the Conchords' tracks like "Inner City Pressure" (2008).

65 Halberstam, *Female Masculinity*.

66 Bannister, "'Bush Camp'?"

67 Dyer, *Only Entertainment*, 145; Halberstam, *Female Masculinity*.

68 Michelle Ann Abate and Kenneth Kidd, eds., *Over the Rainbow: Queer Children's and Young Adult Literature* (Ann Arbor: University of Michigan Press, 2011).

69 Sontag, *Notes on "Camp."*

Chapter 9

1 Siddhant Adlakha, "'Thor: Ragnarok': Marvel from a Postcolonial Perspective," *Village Voice*, November 10, 2017, www.villagevoice.com/ 2017/11/10/thor-ragnarok-marvel-from-a-postcolonial-perspective.

2 Robert G. Weiner, Robert Moses Peaslee, and Matthew J. McEniry, introduction to *Marvel Comics into Film: Essays on Adaptations since the 1940s*, ed. Matthew J. McEniry et al. (Jefferson, NC: McFarland & Company, 2016), 1.

3 Brian Cogan and Jeff Massey, "'Yeah? Well, MY god has a HAMMER!': Myth-Taken Identity in the Marvel Cinematic Universe," in *Marvel Comics into Film: Essays on Adaptations since the 1940s*, ed. Matthew J. McEniry et al. (Jefferson, NC: McFarland & Company, 2016), 12.

4 Henry Jenkins, *Convergence Culture: Where Old and New Media Collide* (New York: New York University Press, 2008).

5 Jenkins, *Convergence Culture*; Henry Jenkins, Sam Ford, and Joshua Green, *Spreadable Media: Creating Value and Meaning in a Networked Culture* (New York: New York University Press, 2013).

6 Quoted in Peter Bennett, Andrew Hickman, and Peter Wall, *Film Studies: The Essential Resource* (Abingdon, Oxon: Routledge, 2007), 331.

7 Quoted in Bennett, Hickman, and Wall, *Film Studies*, 324.

8 Derek Johnson, "Cinematic Destiny: Marvel Studios and the Trade Stories of Industrial Convergence," *Cinema Journal* 52, no. 1 (Fall 2012): 7.

9 Johnson, "Cinematic Destiny," 7.

10 "Taika Waititi: Masterclass," Toronto International Film Festival 2018, YouTube, September 10, 2018. www.youtube.com/watch?v=-5D _9i5Z8lo&t=342s.

11 Haleigh Fouch, "Taika Waititi Says 'Thor: Ragnarok' Is Taking Some Cues from 'Big Trouble in Little China,'" Collider, March 10, 2017, collider.com/thor-ragnarok-big-trouble-in-little-china/#images.

12 Kristin Thompson, *The Frodo Franchise: How the Lord of the Rings Became a Hollywood Blockbuster and Put New Zealand on the Map* (North Shore, NZ: Penguin Books, 2007).

13 Cogan and Massey, "Yeah? Well, MY god has a HAMMER!," 12.

14 Ursula K. Le Guin, "American SF and the Other," *Science Fiction Studies* 2, no. 3 (November 1975): 209.

15 Cogan and Massey, "Yeah? Well, MY god has a HAMMER!"

16 Justin Chang, "'Thor: Ragnarok' is punchy, predictable and fun in fits and starts," *Los Angeles Times*, November 3, 2017, www.latimes.com/ entertainment/movies/la-et-mn-thor-ragnarok-review-20171103 -story.html.

17 Mikhail Bakhtin, *Rabelais and His World*, trans. Helene Iswolsky (Bloomington: Indiana University Press, 1984), 11.

18 *Ibid.*, 7.

19 Bilge Ebiri, "'Thor: Ragnarok' Shows That Marvel Movies Can Still Hit Where It Counts," *Village Voice*, October 27, 2017, www.villagevoice .com/2017/10/27/thor-ragnarok-shows-that-marvel-movies-can-still -hit-where-it-counts/.

20 Anahid Kassabian, *Hearing Film: Tracking Identifications in Contemporary Hollywood Film Music* (New York: Routledge, 2001).

21 Anjelica Oswald, "'Thor: Ragnarok' has 3 huge surprise cameos you may have missed—here they all are," Insider, November 2, 2017, https://www.insider.com/thor-ragnarok-cameos-2017-11.

22 Adlakha, "'Thor: Ragnarok': Marvel from a Postcolonial Perspective."

23 Bakhtin, *Rabelais and His World*, 17.

24 Ibid., 21.

25 Ibid., 19.

26 Christopher Orr, "The Overdue Comedy of *Thor: Ragnarok*," *The Atlantic*, November 3, 2017, www.theatlantic.com/entertainment/archive/2017/11/thor-ragnarok-review/544871/.

27 Mark Booth, *Camp* (New York: Quartet, *1983*), 18.

28 Bakhtin, *Rabelais and His World*, 11.

29 Ibid., 16.

30 Ibid.

31 Kate Rodger, "Taika Waititi almost steals the show in new Thor: Ragnarok," *Newshub*, October 24, 2017, www.newshub.co.nz/home/entertainment/2017/10/taika-waititi-almost-steals-the-show-in-new-thor-ragnarok.html.

32 Epeli Hau'ofa, *We Are the Ocean: Selected Works* (Honolulu: University of Hawaii Press, 2008), 121.

33 Kevin Jagernauth, "Taika Waititi Explains Why He Bailed on Writing 'Moana,'" Playlist, November 6, 2017, theplaylist.net/taika-waititi-writing-moana-20171106/.

34 D. Stokes Piercy and Ron Von Burg, "Hulk Smash Binaries," *Marvel Comics into Film: Essays on Adaptations since the 1940s*, ed. Matthew J. McEniry et al. (Jefferson, NC: McFarland & Company, 2016), 244.

35 Ibid., 245.

36 Sarina Pearson, "Persistent Primitivisms: Popular and Academic Discourses about Pacific and Māori Cinema and Television," *Journal of the Polynesian Society* 122, no. 1 (2013): 22.

37 Adlakha, "'Thor: Ragnarok': Marvel from a Postcolonial Perspective."

38 "Taika Waititi: Masterclass."

39 Joanna Robinson, "Tessa Thompson on a Decade Defying On-Screen Stereotypes," *Vanity Fair*, November 1, 2017, www.vanityfair.com/hollywood/2017/11/tessa-thompson-thor-ragnarok-westworld-valkyrie-interview-bisexual.

40 Danette Chavez, "Thor: Ragnarok ultimately cut the one scene that confirmed Valkyrie's bisexuality," AV Club, November 1, 2017, www.avclub.com/thor-ragnarok-ultimately-cut-the-one-scene-that-confir-1820047758.

41 Adlakha, "'Thor: Ragnarok': Marvel from a Postcolonial Perspective."

42 Hau'ofa, *We Are the Ocean*, 33.

43 Adrian Acu, "Time to Work for a Living: The Marvel Cinematic Universe and the Organized Superhero," *Journal of Popular Film & Television 44, no. 4* (2016): 195–205.

44 Bruce Babington, *A History of the NZ Fiction Feature Film*, (New York: Manchester University Press, 2007), 9.

45 Thomas Elsaesser, "The Global Author: Control, Creative Constraints, and Performative Self-Contradiction," in *The Global Auteur: The Politics of Authorship in 21st Century Cinema*, ed. Seung-hoon Jeong and Jeremi Szaniawski (New York: Bloomsbury Academic & Professional, 2017), 21–41.

Chapter 10

1 Aja Romano, "The Academy's new member class is a big step for diversity. But there's a long way to go," *Vox*, June 27, 2018, www.vox.com/latest-news/2018/6/27/17507418/the-academy-membership-2018-diversity.

2 Rachel Yang, "The adorable young *Jojo Rabbit* stars just stole everyone's hearts on Oscars red carpet," *Entertainment Weekly*, February 9, 2020, ew.com/oscars/2020/02/09/jojo-rabbit-stars-oscars-red-carpet/.

3 Richard Meadows, "Well-heeled traveller loves Palmy," *Stuff*, August 4, 2011, www.stuff.co.nz/manawatu-standard/news/5387369/Well-heeled-traveller-loves-Palmy; the book is Christine Leunens's *Caging Skies* (Auckland: Random House New Zealand, 2008).

4 Mark Salisbury, "How Taika Waititi made 'Jojo Rabbit': 'He didn't wait for anyone to give him permission,'" *ScreenDaily*, January 4, 2020, www.screendaily.com/features/how-taika-waititi-made-jojo-rabbit-he-didnt-wait-for-anyone-to-give-him-permission/5145919.article.

5 Charlotte Graham-McLay, "'We can make it here': Taika Waititi urges on Indigenous talent after Oscar win," *The Guardian*, February 10, 2020, www.theguardian.com/film/2020/feb/10/taika-waititi-first-maori-oscars-2020-indigenous-new-zealand.

6 Emily Burack, "'Jojo Rabbit' doesn't glorify Nazis, but is a lesson in how hate is taught," *Times of Israel*, October 19, 2019, www.timesofisrael.com/jojo-rabbit-doesnt-glorify-nazis-but-is-a-lesson-in-how-hate-is-taught/.

7 "'Buries the awful truth': Taika Waititi's Jojo Rabbit finds critics divided," *Stuff*, September 10, 2019, www.stuff.co.nz/entertainment/film/115665624/buries-the-awful-truth-taika-waititis-jojo-rabbit-finds-critics-divided.

8 Alissa Wilkinson, Zack Beauchamp, and Allegra Frank, "Taika Waititi's 'anti-hate satire' Jojo Rabbit is up for Best Picture. Should it win?," *Vox*, January 23, 2020, www.vox.com/culture/2020/1/23/21076770/jojo-rabbit-best-picture-oscars-2020-win-lose.

9 Dustin Griffin, *Satire: A Critical Reintroduction* (Lexington: University Press of Kentucky, 1994), 2.

10 David Ehrlich, "'Jojo Rabbit' Is 'Easy Listening' Cinema: Critics Debate the Success of Taika Waititi's 'Anti-Hate' Satire," *IndieWire*, October 28, 2019, www.indiewire.com/gallery/critics-debate-jojo-rabbit/207ba5cd-a2e2-4d1c-a542-5548faa21516-vpc_jojo_rabbit_trailer_desk_thumb-00_01_39_00-still001/.

11 Owen Glieberman, "Film Review: 'Jojo Rabbit,'" *Variety*, September 8, 2019, variety.com/2019/film/reviews/jojo-rabbit-review-taiki-waititi-1203328083/.

12 Patrick Kingsley, "New Zealand Massacre Highlights Global Reach of White Extremism," *New York Times*, March 15, 2019, www.nytimes.com/2019/03/15/world/asia/christchurch-mass-shooting-extremism.html.

13 "Jacinda Ardern on the Christchurch shooting: 'One of New Zealand's darkest days,'" *The Guardian*, March 15, 2019, www.theguardian.com/world/2019/mar/15/one-of-new-zealands-darkest-days-jacinda-ardern-responds-to-christchurch-shooting.

14 "Get all of these monkeys the hell out of our country—now! Heil Donald Trump," quoted in David Neiwert, *Alt-America: The Rise of the Radical Right in the Age of Trump* (New York: Verso, 2017), 8.

15 Human Rights Act 1993, New Zealand Legislation, accessed February 5, 2021, www.legislation.govt.nz/act/public/1993/0082/latest/DLM304643.html?search=sw_096be8ed81901539_threatening%2c+abusive%2c+or+insulting_25_se&p=1&sr=0.

16 Richard Brody, "Springtime for Nazis: How the Satire Of 'Jojo Rabbit' Backfires," *New Yorker*, October 22, 2019, www.newyorker.com/culture/the-front-row/springtime-for-nazis-how-the-satire-of-jojo-rabbit-backfires.

17 Griffin, *Satire*, 27.

18 Massih Zekavat, *Satire, Humor and the Construction of Identities* (Amsterdam: John Benjamins Publishing Company, 2017), 9.

19 "New Zealand mosque massacre suspect Brenton Tarrant flashes 'white power' sign in court, as PM Jacinda Ardern vows 'gun laws will change,'" *South China Morning Post*, March 16, 2019, www.scmp.com/news/asia/australasia/article/3001967/new-zealand-mosque-massacre-suspect-brenton-tarrant-faces; Poppy Noor, "How the alt-right co-opted the OK hand sign to fool the media," *The Guardian*, October 3, 2019, www.theguardian.com/world/2019/oct/03/ok-sign-gesture-emoji-rightwing-alt-right.

20 John T. Gilmore, *Satire* (Florence: Routledge, 2017), 5–6.

21 Fredric V. Bogel, *The Difference Satire Makes* (Ithaca: Cornell University Press, 2001), 42.

22 Burack, "'Jojo Rabbit' doesn't glorify Nazis"; Allen Meek, "Postcolonial Trauma, Child Abuse, Genocide, and Journalism in New Zealand," in *Fourth Eye: Maori Media in Aotearoa New Zealand*, ed. Brendan Hokowhitu and Vijay Devadas (Minneapolis: University of Minnesota Press, 2013), 25–41.

23 Charlotte Graham-McLay, "Taika Waititi says Jojo Rabbit's six Oscar nominations vindicate risks of making 'divisive' film," *The Guardian*, January 13, 2020, www.theguardian.com/film/2020/jan/14/jojo-rabbit-director-taika-waititi-wears-criticism-of-divisive-nazi-parody-as-badge-of-honour.

24 Mark Kermode, "Jojo Rabbit review—down the rabbit hole with Hitler," *The Guardian*, January 14, 2020, www.theguardian.com/film/2020/jan/05/jojo-rabbit-review-taika-waititi-hitler-scarlett-johansson-sam-rockwell; Brian Tallerico, "Jojo Rabbit," *RogerEbert.com*, October 18, 2019, www.rogerebert.com/reviews/jojo-rabbit-movie-review-2019.

25 Burack, "'Jojo Rabbit' doesn't glorify Nazis."

26 Peter Bradshaw, "Jojo Rabbit review—Taika Waititi's Hitler comedy is intensely unfunny," *The Guardian*, December 20, 2019, www.theguardian.com/film/2019/dec/20/jojo-rabbit-review-taika-waititi-hitler-comedy; Armond White, "*Jojo Rabbit* Mocks *Other* People's Fanaticism," *National Review*, October 16, 2019, www.nationalreview.com/2019/10/movie-review-jojo-rabbit-hitler-satire-strained-childish/.

27 Glieberman, "Film Review: 'Jojo Rabbit.'"

28 Robbie Collin, "Jojo Rabbit, review: this feeble, one-note Nazi comedy fails to land a single meaningful blow," *Daily Telegraph*, February 2, 2020, www.telegraph.co.uk/films/2019/10/05/jojo-rabbit-review -feeble-one-note-nazi-comedy-fails-land-single/.

29 Johan Nilsson, *American Film Satire in the 1990s: Hollywood Subversion* (London, Palgrave Macmillan, 2013), 9.

30 Andrea Mendell, "Why Jojo Rabbit's Taika Waititi didn't study Hitler before playing him," *USA Today*, October 21, 2019, www.usatoday .com/story/entertainment/movies/2019/10/21/taika-waititi-defends -jojo-rabbit-explains-his-goofy-hitler/4035233002/; Steve Rose, "Taika Waititi: 'You don't want to be directing kids with a swastika on your arm,'" *The Guardian*, December 26, 2019, www.theguardian.com/film/ 2019/dec/26/taika-waititi-flight-of-the-conchords-thor-ragnarok-jojo -rabbit-nazi-dictator.

31 *Smith & Jones*, "Nazi Generals," Series 5, Episode 5, YouTube, accessed May 11, 2020, www.youtube.com/watch?v=U_Z6tv7cQmM.

32 Benjamin Lee, "Jojo Rabbit review—Scarlett Johansson lifts smug Hitler comedy," *The Guardian*, September 9, 2019, www.theguardian.com/ film/2019/sep/09/jojo-rabbit-review-scarlett-johansson-lifts-smug -hitler-comedy; Collin, "Jojo Rabbit, review."

33 Mark Kermode, "Jojo Rabbit review . . ."; Joyce Slaton, review of *Jojo Rabbit*, accessed February 6, 2021, www.commonsensemedia.org/ movie-reviews/jojo-rabbit.

34 Ehrlich, "'Jojo Rabbit' Is 'Easy Listening' Cinema."

35 Nilsson, *American Film Satire in the 1990s*, 8.

36 Brody, "Springtime for Nazis."

37 Gilmore, *Satire*, 12.

38 Aaryn L. Green and Annulla Linders, "The Impact of Comedy on Racial and Ethnic Discourse," *Sociological Inquiry* 86, no. 2 (2016): 245.

39 Stuart Hall, "The Question of Cultural Identity," in *Modernity: An Introduction to Modern Societies*, ed. Stuart Hall, David Held, Don Hubert, and Kenneth Thompson (London: Blackwell, 1996), 596, 615.

40 Chris Sibley, Carla Houkamau, and William Hoverd, "Ethnic Group Labels and Intergroup Attitudes in New Zealand: Naming Preferences Predict Distinct Ingroup and Outgroup Biases," *Analyses of Social Issues & Public Policy* 11, no. 1 (December 2011): 201–20; Paul Callister,

"Seeking an Ethnic Identity: Is 'New Zealander' a Valid Ethnic Category?" *New Zealand Population Review* 30, nos. 1–2 (2004): 5–22.

41 Zane Small, "Labour MP Tāmati Coffey hits out at NZ media for calling Taika Waititi a 'Kiwi' filmmaker," *Newshub*, February 11, 2020, www .newshub.co.nz/home/politics/2020/02/labour-mp-t-mati-coffey-hits -out-at-nz-media-for-calling-taika-waititi-a-kiwi-filmmaker.html.

42 Mitch Berbrier, "The Victim Ideology of White Supremacists and White Separatists in The United States," *Sociological Focus* 33, no. 2 (2000): 175–91.

43 Nilsson, *American Film Satire in the 1990s*, 48.

44 Griffin, *Satire*, 2.

45 "Taika Waititi and wife Chelsea Winstanley separated," *NZ Herald*, March 14, 2020, www.nzherald.co.nz/entertainment/news/article.cfm ?c_id=1501119&objectid=12316723.

46 "'Jojo Rabbit' Director Taika Waititi Reveals Why He Decided to Play 'Adolf' Hitler | Rotten Tomatoes," YouTube, October 16, 2019, www .youtube.com/watch?v=fYBJHBm7LKY.

47 Rory Carroll, "Trump v Hollywood? Don't expect to see the culture war play out on screen," *Guardian*, January 13, 2017, www.theguardian .com/film/2017/jan/13/donald-trump-hollywood-culture-wars -movie-story-lines.

Conclusion

1 Rotten Tomatoes' critical consensus reads: "Exciting, funny, and above all fun, *Thor: Ragnarok* is a colorful cosmic adventure that sets a new standard for its franchise—and the rest of the Marvel Cinematic Universe," Rotten Tomatoes, accessed May 10, 2020, www .rottentomatoes.com/m/thor_ragnarok_2017.

2 Waititi is cowriting with Krysty Wilson-Cairns, nominated for an Oscar for *1917*. "Taika Waititi to make new Star Wars film," RNZ, May 5, 2020, www.rnz.co.nz/news/national/415828/taika-waititi-to -make-new-star-wars-film.

3 Rotten Tomatoes' critical consensus for *The Phantom Menace* describes it as "Burdened by exposition and populated with stock characters," Rotten Tomatoes, accessed May 10, 2020, www .rottentomatoes.com/m/star_wars_episode_i_the_phantom_menace.

4   Quoted in *The People vs George Lucas* (Alexandre Phillipe, 2010).

5   For two sides of the story, try John Francis Mccullagh, "'The Lucas Effect': When Filmmaking Creativity Goes Unchecked," The Beat, July 5, 2019, www.premiumbeat.com/blog/when-filmmaking -creativity-goes-unchecked/, and Patti J. McCarthy, *The Lucas Effect: George Lucas and the New Hollywood* (Youngstown, NY: Teneo Press, 2014).

6   *Star Wars: The Force Awakens*, Rotten Tomatoes, accessed May 9, 2020, www.rottentomatoes.com/m/star_wars_episode_vii_the_force _awakens.

7   Emily Van Der Werff, "The 'backlash' against Star Wars: The Last Jedi, explained," Vox, updated December 19, 2017, www.vox.com/culture/ 2017/12/18/16791844/star-wars-last-jedi-backlash-controversy.

8   Adam Holmes, "Rian Johnson Drops F-Bomb Over Star Wars: The Last Jedi Hate," Cinema Blend, November 12, 2019, www.cinemablend .com/news/2484567/rian-johnson-drops-f-bomb-over-star-wars-the -last-jedi-hate.

9   Van Der Werff, "The 'backlash' against Star Wars: The Last Jedi."

10 Sarah El-Mahmoud, "Star Wars Boss Kathleen Kennedy Is Still Defending the Last Jedi," Cinema Blend, November 21, 2019, www.cinemablend.com/news/2485373/star-wars-boss-kathleen -kennedy-is-still-defending-the-last-jedi?fbclid=lwAR31Eim -VRd2El5rNUwyBzOEzRvBqVfEwfiphQ4w1Sij1l8hfZgpBBEfwu8.

11 Margaret A. Weitekamp, "More than 'Just Uhura': Understanding Star Trek's Lt. Uhura, Civil Rights and Space History," in *Star Trek and history*, ed. Nancy Reagin (New York: Wiley, 2013), 24–25.

12 Dan Taipua, "Empire and rebellion: What Taika Waititi directing Star Wars means for Māori," The Spinoff, May 10, 2020, thespinoff.co.nz/ atea/10-05-2020/empire-and-rebellion-what-taika-waititi-directing -star-wars-means-for-maori/.

13 Taipua, "Empire and rebellion."

14 Mark Dery, "Black to the Future: Interviews with Samuel R. Delany, Greg Tate, and Tricia Rose," in *Flame Wars: The Discourse of Cyberculture*, ed. Mark Dery (Durham, NC: Duke University Press), 180.

15 David Mansour, *From Abba to Zoom: A Pop Culture Encyclopedia of the Late 20th Century* (Kansas City: Andrews McMeel Publishing, 2005), 403. Then there is Jackson's well-known interest in science fiction,

from *E.T.* (for which he recorded a soundtrack/storybook album) to *Captain Eo* (Francis Ford Coppola, 1986), a 3D science fiction short film starring Jackson cowritten and produced by George Lucas that was shown at Disneyland's Tomorrowland.

16 Julian Vigo, "Metaphor of Hybridity: The Body of Michael Jackson." *Journal of Pan-African Studies* 3, no. 7 (2010): 29.

17 Donna J. Haraway, "A Cyborg Manifesto: Science, Technology, and Socialist-Feminism in the Late Twentieth Century," in *Simians, Cyborgs and Women: The Reinvention of Nature* (New York; Routledge, 1991), 149–81.

18 Taika Waititi, Twitter, June 2, 2018, twitter.com/TaikaWaititi.

19 Christian Quendler, *The Camera-Eye Metaphor in Cinema* (New York: Taylor & Francis Group, 2016).

20 Moira Marsh, *Practically Joking* (Logan: Utah State University Press, 2015). Interestingly, most of the book's examples come from the US and New Zealand.

21 Paul Gilroy, *The Black Atlantic: Modernity and Double Consciousness* (Cambridge, MA: Harvard University Press, 1993); Robbie Shilliam, *The Black Pacific: Anti-colonial Struggles and Oceanic Connection* (London: Bloomsbury, 2015).

22 Kenneth McLeish, *The Theatre of Aristophanes* (New York: Taplinger, 1980), 17.

23 Anna Hickey Moody and Timothy Laurie, "Masculinity and Ridicule," in *Gender: Laughter*, ed. Bettina Papenburg (Farmington Hills: Gale, Cengage Learning, 2016), 226.

24 Taika Waititi, Twitter, June 4, 2018, twitter.com/search?q=%23TaikaWaititi%2C&src=hash.

25 Alex Denney, "Unknown Mortal Orchestra & Taika Waititi on New Zealand culture," Dazed, April 5, 2018, www.dazeddigital.com/music/article/39590/1/unknown-mortal-orchestra-ruban-nielson-taika-waititi-interview.

26 Pierre Bourdieu, *The Rules of Art: Genesis and Structure of the Literary Field*, trans. Susan Emanuel (Cambridge: Polity Press, 1996).

27 Michael Villanova, "The Rise of Trump in Postmodern Times," *International Journal of Baudrillard Studies* 14, no. 1 (2017).

28 There's also the US TV series of *Shadows*, for which Waititi has directed some episodes.

29 Jazz Tangcay, "Taika Waititi to Executive Produce Sundance Labs Film 'Frybread Face and Me,'" *Variety*, October 23, 2020, variety.com/2020/film/news/taika-waititi-frybread-face-and-me-1234814612/.

30 Justin Kroll, "Taika Waititi Sets New Project with Fox Searchlight Before 'Thor 4' (EXCLUSIVE)," *Variety*, August 7, 2019, variety.com/2019/film/news/taika-waititi-secret-project-fox-searchlight-garrett-basch-1203290828/.

31 "Taika Waititi to direct new Star Wars film," Stuff, May 5, 2020, www.stuff.co.nz/entertainment/film/300004418/taika-waititi-to-direct-new-star-wars-film?fbclid=IwAR2kYJzWKqUZaEenTSqqzLlyQggbRA33sySDybdOFo6hOZqyKQTpvsKinLk.

Index

Page numbers in bold refer to figures.

Academy Awards, 6, 13. *See also* Oscars
Adventures of Algy, The (Beaumont Smith), 57
Afro-futurism, 227
Allen, Woody, 1, 12, 94, 111, 146, 147, 180
American Splendor (Shari Springer Berman and Robert Pulcini), 115, 118, 119, 125
Anderson, Wes, 15, 66, 115, 122, 123, 125, 180, 186, 188
Ansari, Aziz, 218
Antipodean camp, 13, 36, 39, 42–43, 229–30; in film, 62–67, 104, 177–93, 223. *See also* camp; queer; transgender
Arab Samurai (Taika Waititi), 33
Ardern, Jacinda, 214, 229
Aroha (Michael Forlong), 60
audience: and comedy, 1, 5, 7, 9, 13, 15, 21, 26, 80–84; film, 60, 132, 138, 148, 149, 193, 195, 213; and film music, 181, 183–86; New Zealand, 1, 70, 71, 74–75, 78, 85–88, 103, 106–7, 112, 219; postmodern/reality TV, 120, 166, 174–75; quirky film, 122–27; and satire, 221–23; studies, 49–50, 106–7; and *Thor: Ragnarok*, 200, 201; Waititi's interaction with live audience, 5, 7, 80–84
Australia, 49, 73, 94, 96, 109, 192, 197, 226

auteurism, 88, 125, 142, 180, 186, 196, 210; as comic, 17–18; as performative self-contradiction, 12–13; and Waititi, 10–13, 17, 18, 113, 121
Avengers, The (Joss Whedon), 195, 198

Baby Done (Curtis Vowell), 230
Back to the Future (Robert Zemeckis), 36, 134, 196
Bad Blood (Mike Newell), 53, 178
Bad Boys II (Michael Bay), 180
Bad Taste (Peter Jackson), 63, 65
banter, 18, 189, 191, 205, 226; in early short films, 30, 33; as masculine, 13, 14, 33, 87, 173; as signifying, 107, 146; Waititi bantering with audience, 4, 81, 84
Barclay, Barry, 10, 22, 54, 60, 78, 112, 144, 157
Bastion Point Day 507 (Merata Mita), 60
Baumbach, Noah, 117
Beek, Jackie van, 167
Bergson, Henri, theory of comedy, 4, 7, 8, 71, 79–83, 85, 88, 123
biculturalism, 15, 20–23, 25, 38, 91–93, 96–103, 108–13
Big Trouble in Little China (John Carpenter), 197
Birch, Thora, 117, 119
Black, Jack, 122

Blackness, 22, 91–92, 99–100, 118, 218
Black Pacific, The, 38, 228
Black Panther (Ryan Coogler), 210, 213
Black Panthers, 100
Black Power, 100
Black Women's Movement, 100
Blanchett, Cate, 198
Blerta, 73
Borat (Larry Charles), 123, 162, 169, 174
Botes, Costa, 41, 42, 60, 61
Boy (Taika Waititi), 1, 9, 30, 32, 38,
    53, 64, 72, 100, 142–60; African
    American influence on, 102, 107–9;
    autobiographical aspects of, 11,
    147, 148, 162; character relations
    (including gender), 47, 51, 54, 160,
    191, 201, 220; as comedian comedy,
    16, 142–60; critical reception
    of, 17, 18, 106, 141–44; director's
    commentary of, 36, 61, 78, 145, 191;
    ending, 158–59; ethnicity in, 92,
    103; Kiwiana in, 66; Māori culture
    and, 112, 142, 157–59; and Michael
    Jackson, 153, 157–59, 159, 186, 221,
    223, 227; setting of, 23, 25, 37, 147,
    148, 178; soundtrack of, 36, 65,
    157–59, 178, 186, 230; visual design
    of, 28
Boy in the Striped Pajamas, The (Mark
    Herman), 221
Braindead (Peter Jackson), 63, 65
Bram Stoker's Dracula (Francis Ford
    Coppola), 162, 163
Breaker Upperers, The (Madeleine Sami,
    Jackie van Beek), 230
Bridge to Nowhere (Ian Mune), 53
Britain, Great, 14, 42, 45, 48, 52, 56,
    62, 97
British Empire, 31, 32, 38, 45, 198
Broken Barrier (John O'Shea), 57, 58, 69
Brooks, Mel, 12, 111, 223
bro'Town (TV3), 15, 28, 65, 74, 92, 96,
    103–8, 231

Brown, Riwia, 101, 109
Brugh, Jonathan, 77, 166, 167
Brunning, Nancy, 29
Buffy the Vampire Slayer (Joss Whedon),
    162
Buscemi, Steve, 119
Bush Cinderella, The (Rudall
    Hayward), 58

Came a Hot Friday (Ian Mune), 85
camp, 18, 36, 63; Australian, 17, 62; bush
    camp (NZ), 42, 62, 190, 223; Pacific,
    42, 103–4
Carell, Steve, 122
carnival, 13, 17, 65, 71, 83, 195–212; and
    Bakhtin, 199, 202–3, 205
Carpenter, John, 178, 197
Carry Me Back (John Reid), 85
Casablanca (Michael Curtiz), 64
celebrity, 11, 78–79, 88, 165, 189, 228
Chaplin, Charlie, 1, 10, 11, 12, 146, 147,
    218
Chappelle, Dave, 96, 218, 220
Christchurch mosque shootings, 214
C. K., Lewis, 2
Clarke, John (Fred Dagg), 72, 73, 75
Clement, Jemaine, 112, 126, 129,
    161, 166, 168, 197, 218, 231;
    improvisation, 77, 86; relationship
    with Waititi, 25, 26, 55, 76
Coco Solid, 106, 231
Coffey, Tāmati, 219
Cohen, Robin, 19, 23, 24, 162, 213, 222,
    223
colonization, 13, 19, 22, 44, 54, 57;
    recolonization, 42–44; reverse
    colonization, 168, 195
colorblindness, 95
comedy: as aggression, 2, 3, 5, 152,
    174; animated comedy, 73, 103–6,
    148, 230; comedian comedy, 7,
    16, 134, 142–60, 220; community
    comedies, 71; critical denigration

of, 10, 69; direct address in, 77, 78-80, 86, 113; of embarrassment, 123-24, 134, 139, 228; ethnic comedy, 17-18, 80, 91-114; film, 10, 71, 74, 77; incongruity theory of, 2, 8-9; joke-based theory of, 2, 8-9, 81-82, 84; Māori, 31, 55, 71-73, 81, 91-114, 144-45; masculinity and, 6, 13, 17-18, 34, 43, 51, 173-75; mockumentary, 14, 25, 42, 43, 60-61, 163-65; morality of, 84-88, 92-93, 112, 173-75, 229; music and, 73-74, 177, 185; narrative structure and, 10, 64, 134, 217; NZ, 6, 10, 13, 15, 25-27, 69-89, 91-114, 177-93; as play, 8-9, 81-84; practical jokes, 2, 5-6, 28, 33, 60-61, 229; relief theory of, 8-9; romantic, 10, 126; satirical, 34, 214-15; silent, 10, 58, 71; stand-up, 2, 78, 81-85, 95, 110; superiority theory of, 8-9, 81, 83, 165; theatrical, 25, 26; TV, 2, 15, 25-27, 34, 96, 217; as unemotional, 6-7, 81, 227. *See also* banter
Cool Runnings (Jon Turteltaub), 231
Cormack, Danielle, 76
Cosby, Bill, 95
Crump, Barry, 53, 75, 85, 184, 189
Crush (Alison Maclean), 60
cultural cringe, 42, 46, 51, 60
Curb Your Enthusiasm (Larry David), 124
Curtis, Cliff, 231

Damon, Matt, 200
Dean Spanley, Toa Fraser, 220
Deer Hunter, The (Michael Cimino), 64
Dennison, Julian, 66, 79, **87**, 178, **184**
direct address, 15, 16, 78-80, 88, 121, 163, 227, 228; breaking the fourth wall, 7, 78, 220; in comedian comedy, 141, 151-52, 157, 219-20; facing camera, 126-29, **128**, **131**, **137**, **191**

documentary, 32, 50, 52, 74, 108, 178, 225, 230; and comedy, 5, 123-24, 228; and mockumentary, 14, 25, 42, 43, 60-61, 163-65, 168; and NZ identity, 14, 43, 58, 59-61, 229; and reality TV, 164-65; and representation of Māori, 53, 59-60, 145
Dogma (Kevin Smith), 200
Don Quixote, 82
Don't Let It Get You (John O'Shea), 69-71
double consciousness, 38, 228
Dracula (Tod Browning), 196

Eagle vs Shark (Taika Waititi), 15, 25, 28, 30, 35, 74, 76, **128**, **131**, **137**, **191**, 197, 221, 223; cinematography of, 126-29; compared to *Napoleon Dynamite*, 126-39; differences, 135-36; ethnicity in, 92, 98, 103, 113; gender and ethnicity, 136-39; interracial romance, 35, 114, 137; mise-en-scene, 134; as quirky film, 64, 78, 80, 115-39; soundtrack, 134
Eketone-Whitu, Te Aho Aho, 142
entertainment: as camp, 15, 17, 62, 64, 67, 69, 177, 187-93; in comedian comedy, 141, 145; industry in Australia, 109; Jewish and African American involvement in, 109-13, 118; in NZ, 70-73, 75, 78, 88, 94, 113, 141, 145, 180, 187-91
Eruera, Taura, 100
essentialization, 98, 99, 101
ethnicity: in comedy, 80, 91-114; mixed, 18, 38, 98, 110, 211, 227; vs. race, 97-98; "substitutable other," 80, 110, 162

fa'afafine, 104
Falling Leaves (Taika Waititi), 34-35
Fane, David, 74, 92, 103, 136

Ferrell, Will, 122
Fields, W. C., 3
Fitzgerald, Catherine, 29
Flavell-Hudson, Darcey-Ray, 66
Fleabag, 7
Flight of the Conchords, 6, 25–26, 74, 86, 218–19
Footrot Flats (Murray Ball), 73
Forgotten Silver (Peter Jackson, Costa Botes), 14, 41, 42, 43, 60–61, 71, 163
48Hours (film competition), 33–34
Fourth Cinema, 10, 31, 54, 78, 112, 160
Frankenstein (James Whale), 196
Fraser, Toa, 231
Frighteners, The (Peter Jackson), 163
Front Lawn, The, 74
Funny As: The Story of New Zealand Comedy (TVNZ), 108–10

Gaoa, Mario, 103
Gardiner, Ainsley, 28, 29, 231
Ghost World (Terry Zwigoff), 115, 119, 121, 125
Gibson, Mel, 215
globalization, 43, 97; in *What We Do in the Shadows*, 16, 161, 162, 169, 175–76
Godfather, The (Francis Ford Coppola), 64
Goldblum, Jeff, 197, 202, **204**
Gondry, Jean-Michel, 37
Gonzalez-Macuer, Cori, 77, 165
Goodbye Pork Pie (Geoff Murphy), 53, 178
Gosling, Ryan, 123
Grace-Smith, Briar, 231
Great Dictator, The (Charles Chaplin), 217
Green Lantern, The (Martin Campbell), 27
Gregory, Dick, 95
Grierson, John, 59
Gries, Jon, 127

Happiness (Todd Solondz), 122
Hard Day's Night, A (Richard Lester), 70
harirū (touching), 14, 157
hauntology, 37, 179
Haynes, Todd, 117
Hayward, Rudall, 57, 58, 71
Heart of the Stag (Michael Firth), 53
Heavenly Creatures (Peter Jackson and Fran Walsh), 63
Heder, Jon, 126
Heinous Crime (Taika Waititi), 34
Hei Tiki (Alexander Markey), 55, **56**
Hemsworth, Chris, 198, **201**, **206**
Hemsworth, Luke, 200
Hess, Jared, 117
Hiddleston, Tom, 198
Hinemoa (Gaston Mélies), 55
Hitchcock, Alfred, 11, 180
Hitler, Adolf, 8, 113, 214–15, 220–23
Hollywood, 43, 79, 115, 119, 133, 170, 197, 210; classical narrative, 10, 17, 54, 146, 148, 158, 180, 185, 196; and ethnicity, 95, 213; impact on Māori, 101; vs. indie film, 12, 15; New Hollywood, 53, 196; parody of, 34, 209; silent comedy, 10; Waititi in, 17, 27–28, 89, 92, 95, 193, 225
homophobia, 35–36, 73, 175
homosexuality, 62, 114, 119, 161, 171, 173, 176
homosociality, 14, 15, 16, 30, 38, 46–50, 61, 85, 88, 163, 171, 191, 201, 229
Hopkins, Anthony, 198, **201**
horror film, 61, 63, 65, 161, 163, 229
Horsley, Loren, 29, 34, 126, **128**, **131**, 138
Hotere, Ralph, 47
House, Rachel, 51, 178, **204**, 231
How Chief Te Ponga Won His Bride (Gaston Mélies), 55
Hu, Kelly, 231
Human Traces (Nic Gorman), 60
Humourbeasts, 26, 113

Hunt for the Wilderpeople (Taika
    Waititi), 1, 28, 30, 72, 75, 78, 79,
    109, 143, 177–93; African American
    influence on, 102; as Antipodean
    camp, 16, 69, 177, 188–93, 217, 223;
    character relations (including
    gender), 47, 53, 86, 184, 188–93, 200,
    229; entertainment and, 69, 192;
    Kiwiana in, 65, 189; Māori culture
    in, 177, 178, 179, 182, 183, 189–91,
    229; setting of, 178–81; soundtrack
    of, 36, 66, 69, 77, 178–81, 184–87,
    197

I Heart Huckabees (David O. Russell),
    125
Improvisation, 76–78
indie film, 12, 15, 115, 116, 139, 177, 184,
    187, 196, 199
indie music, 36–37, 76, 126, 135
indigeneity: globally, 213, 215, 226, 227,
    231; indigenous auteur, 11, 13, 18;
    indigenous comedy, 93, 109, 160;
    indigenous film, media, 10, 28, 38,
    92, 112, 231; and intersectionality,
    21; as Māori, 12, 15, 19, 43, 54, 57, 91,
    99, 102, 105, 168, 228
In My Father's Den (Brad McGann), 60
interracial romance, 35, 39, 54, 57, 69,
    114, 137
intersectionality, 14, 21, 35, 38, 136–37
Interstellar (Christopher Nolan), 209
Interview with the Vampire (Neil
    Jordan), 161, 170, 171
Inuit, 27
invented tradition, 65, 177, 181–83
Iron Man (Jon Favreau), 195

Jackson, Michael, 26, 113; in *Boy*, 65,
    101, 141, 142, 147, 148, 152, 158, 186,
    221, 223, 227
Jackson, Peter, 41, 42, 60, 71, 97, 160,
    197, 230

James, Billy T., 65, 71, 73, 93, 94, 102,
    102, 108; Award, 26; death of, 109
Japanese culture, 33, 103, 151–52, 226
Jazz Singer, The (Alan Crosland), 118
Jewish (cultural identity), 118, 119, 162,
    163, 169, 222; anti-semitism, 162,
    215; comedy, 15, 89, 92–96, 110, 111,
    112, 114, 117, 118, 222, 227; Waititi's
    ethnicity, 11, 12, 14, 15, 18, 21, 24,
    160, 162, 211, 215
Johansson, Scarlett, 222, **224**
John & Pogo (Taika Waititi), 34, **34**
Johnson, Dwayne, 231
Jojo Rabbit (Taika Waititi), 8, 17, 47, 51,
    89, 96, 160, 213–24, **224**, 231
Jubilee (Michael Hurst), 35
July, Miranda, 117
Juno (Adam Reitman), 123, 125, 126

Kahi, Tearepa, 230
kai (eating), 54, 143, 159
Kamakawiwo'ole, Israel, 231
kapa haka (song/dance), 65, 143, 158–59,
    159, 227
karanga (call), 143, 147, 150, 152
Kaufman, Andy, 110
Khan, Chaka, 26
Kightley, Oscar, 103, 105, 190, 231
King, Mike, 108, 112, 113
Kingi, Troy, 191
Kingi's Story (Mike Walker), 35
Kingpin (Mike Walker), 53
Kiwi bloke, 13, 14, 38, 42–52, 72, 75, 85,
    150, 184, 229, 230
Knocked Up (Judd Apatow), 115
koha (gift), 143, 157
Kurosawa, Akira, 226

Lars and the Real Girl (Craig Gillespie),
    123, 125
Laughter, 1–8, 71, 81–83, 123, 229. *See
    also* comedy
Lee, Stan, 197

Legend of Birds (Oxley Hughan), 182
Legend of the Wanganui River (John Feeney), 59
Lelisi, Shimpal, 103
Leone, Sergio, 226
Leota, Jerome, 103
Life Is Beautiful (Roberto Benigni), 221
Linda's Body (Harry Sinclair), 74
Little Miss Sunshine (Jonathan Dayton and Valerie Faris), 123
Look Who's Back! (David Wnendt), 215
Lord of the Rings, The (Peter Jackson), 17, 63, 65, 97, 179, 180, 183, 197
Lost Boys, The (Joel Schumacher), 174
Lou and Simon (Lou Clauson and Simon Meihana), 72
Lounge Bar, The (The Front Lawn), 74
Love at First Bite (Stan Dragoti), 161–62
Loved by a Maori Chieftess (Gaston Mélies), 55
Lovegrove, Brendhan, 81
Lucas, George, 196, 225
Luhrmann, Baz, 62, 192

Magasiva, Robbie, 103
Majorino, Tina, 126
Mandalorian, The, 226
Māori, 14, 15, 17, 18; concert parties/ show bands, 71–72; cultural practices, 30–33; film, 28, 29; history, 21–22; kaupapa Māori, 16; masculinity, 36, 53–54; population, 21–23; sense of time, 30–31; Waititi's ethnicity, 6, 10, 11, 14, 15, 20–21, 22–24. *See also* indigeneity; New Zealand/Aotearoa
Māori Battalion, 23, 30–31, 72, 149, 208
Maoriland, 43, 55, 56, 57, 101
Māori/Pasifika, 17, 62, 66, 70, 179, 182, 189, 230
Māori Television, 46, 92, 101, 230
Maori Today, The (Oxley Hughan), 60
marae (meeting house), 30, 31, 102, 144

Mark II (John Anderson), 35
Marley, Bob, 182–83
Marvel Cinematic Universe, 195–98, 210
Marx Brothers, 16, 141, 146
Marxism, 45, 161
Masculinity, 14, 35, 53, 65, 86, 104, 112–13, 138, 206–7. *See also* homophobia; homosexuality; homosociality; Kiwi bloke; queer; transgender
Matafeo, Rose, 105, 231
Māui, 26
Mauri (Merata Mita), 54
Maxwell, Paora, 9
McKenzie, Bret, 6, 25, 26, 76, 77, 219, 231
McKenzie, Thomasin, 222
Me and You and Everyone We Know (Miranda July), 122
Meet the Feebles (Peter Jackson), 63
Merata: How Mum Decolonised the Screen (Heperi Mita), 231
Mercier, Ocean, 31, 33, 144, 146, 150, 159
Meyer, Russ, 63
Milligan, Spike, 33
Mita, Merata, 18, 22, 54, 230–31
Mitchell, Elizabeth, 103
Moana (Ron Clements, John Musker), 206
Momoa, Jason, 231
Moroder, Giorgio, 178, 183
Morrison, Howard, 70, 71, 94
Mothersbaugh, Mark, 186, 199
Mulheron, Danny, 110
Muppet Show, The, 64
Muriel's Wedding (P. J. Hogan), 17, 62, 136
Murphy, Eddie, 95, 111, 123, 146, 155
Murray, Bill, 122, 124
Museum of New Zealand, The, Te Papa Tongarewa, 64–65

My Lady of the Cave (Rudall Hayward), 58

Naked Samoans, 65, 74, 103
Napoleon Dynamite (Jared Hess), 15, 116, 122, 125, 126–36, 138
narcissism, 27, 79, 138, 141, 205
National Film Unit, 43, 59, 60
Nation of Islam, 100
nebbish, 110, 117
Neill, Sam, 53, 178, **184**, 200
neoliberalism, 22, 23, 43, 98, 99, 164
nerds, 115–39
Neverending Story, The (Wolfgang Petersen), 183
New Zealand/Aotearoa: comparison with the US, 96–103, 110–11, 218; ethnic relations, 13, 16, 17, 18, 19–21, 25, 99–114, 137–40, 218–19, 228–29; film, 1, 36, 41, 46, 52–67, **56**, **58**, 69–71, **102**, 210; history, 14, 21–22, 41–45, 99–101; Māori, 21–23, 26, 36, 38–39, 52, 54–67, 69–73, 86–89, 116, 137–40, 218–19, 228–29; masculinity, 26, 38–39, 41–45, 47–51, 54–67, 85–86, 228–29; national identity, 14, 16, 17, 18, 38–39, 47–51, 55–67, 96–98, 163, 181–93, 228–29; population, 23; as queer, 137–40; style, 6, 10; suicide rate, 139
New Zealand Film Commission, 28, 29, 43
New Zealand Music Awards, 13
New Zealand Wars, 22, 57, 72
Next Goal Wins (Mike Brett, Steve Jamison), 231
Ngatai-Melbourne, Tioreore, 178
Ngā Tamatoa (Young Warriors), 22, 99–100
Ngāti (Barry Barclay), 54
Nokise, James, 109
Nosferatu (F. W. Murnau), 162, 163

O'Brien, Richard, 63, 229
Oceania, 102, 209
Office, The, 27, 123, 124
Once Were Warriors (Lee Tamahori), 28, 34, 36, 53–54, 65, 105, 108, 144
One Hundred Crowded Years (Michael Forlong), 57
Oscars, 213, 219
Other Halves (John Laing), 35
Out of the Blue (Robert Sarkies), 60

Paid in Full (Taika Waititi), 35
Pākehā (settler): anxiety/cultural cringe, 46–51, 52–54, 61; as camp, Kiwiana, 65; and colonization/appropriation, 44–47, 52, 55–57, 105, 229; cultural nationalism, 47; and documentary realism, 59–60; masculinity (*see also* Kiwi bloke); parody of, 51, 60–61; queer, 48–50; racism, 6, 20, 31, 38, 94, 98, 189, 219; in relation to Māori/biculturalism, 14, 20, 21, 22, 38, 39, 54–57, 69–72, 91, 96–99, 137–38, 219. *See also* New Zealand/Aotearoa
Parasite (Bong Joon-ho), 213
Pasifika, 22, 99–105, 205, 209–10, 231
Patu! (Merata Mita), 60
Perfect Love, A (Taika Waititi), 138
performance: in *Boy*, 143, 146, 154, 158, 159; comic performance as negative play, 1–4, 16, 18, 25, 219; live performance and New Zealand comedy, 71–74, 78; New Zealand identity as performance, 42–59, 64–65; as play, 1–11, 199–201; Waititi live, 3–5, 12–13, 81–84, 110
Phoenix Foundation, The, 36, **37**, 135, 145, 178, 186
Pineaha, Kahu, 72
Platoon (Oliver Stone), 64
"Poi E," 65, 141, 143, 147, 158–59
Poi E (Tearepa Kahi), 230

Polynesian Panthers, 22, 100, 105
popular culture, 15, 17, 64, 88, 91, 100, 102, 139; as entertainment, 69–70, 88; intellectuals, 116–20, 175; New Zealand, 49, 67, 182; US, 17, 36, 64, 92, 95, 102, 187, 189
postcolonialism, 47, 49, 52, 141, 177, 195, 215, 228
pōwhiri (welcome), 30, 31, 142–44, 157, 159
Price of Milk, The (Harry Sinclair), 74
Producers, The (Mel Brooks), 223
proletariat, 45, 48, 207
Pryor, Richard, 95
Pulp Comedy (TV3), 80, **82**
Punch-Drunk Love (Paul Thomas Anderson), 116, 119, 122, 123, 124, 125

queer: and carnival, 191–92, 203; drag king, 63, 192, 224, **224**; drag queen, 62, 192; and intersectionality, 136–38; and New Zealand identity, 39, 50–52, 177, 183, 187; and vampires, 161, 169–71
Queer Eye for the Straight Guy, 138
Quiet Earth, The (Geoff Murphy), 53

race vs. ethnicity, 97–98
racism, 6, 20, 31, 38, 94, 165, 185, 189, 198, 219; Give Nothing to Racism advertisement, 79, 218–20, **220**; hate speech, 216; reverse racism, 107, 112, 149, 199, 218–20; in the US, 94, 96, 98, 118, 213
Radio New Zealand, 180, 182
Radiradirah (TV3), 79, **80**
Rain (Christine Jeffs), 60
Revenge of the Nerds (Jeff Kanew), 118
reverse discourse, 107, 229, 230
Rewi's Last Stand (Rudall Hayward), 57
Rock, Chris, 95, 111
Rocky Horror Picture Show, The (Jim Sharman), 63, 142, 203

Rocky Horror Show, The, 229
Rolleston, James, 66, 141
Romance of Hine-Moa, The (Gustave Pauli), 55
Rousseau, Henri, 9
Royal Tenenbaums, The (Wes Anderson), 123, 125
Ruell, Aaron, 127
Runaway (John O'Shea), 52, 69, 85
Running with Scissors (Ryan Murphy), 123
Rushmore (Wes Anderson), 115, 116, 123, 124, 125
Rutherford, Stu, 166, **168**

Safe (Todd Haynes), 121, 122, 127
Sami, Madeleine, 109
Samoa, 92, 97, 103, 104, 105, 107, 109, 132, 136, 231
Sandler, Adam, 117, 119, 122, 123, 124
Sargeson, Frank, 48–49
Scarfies (Robert Sarkies), 27
schlemiel, 110, 117, 119
Schwartzmann, Jason, 112, 115, 117
sci-fi film, 16, 63, 79, 198, 226–27
Seinfeld, Jerry, 81, 96
Shortland, Wassi (Waihoroi), 61
signifying, 106–7, 146
Signifying Monkey, 26, 145
Sinclair, Harry, 74
Sione's Wedding (Chris Graham), 35, 65, 102
Sister Act (Emile Ardolino), 174
Skin Deep (Geoff Steven), 85
Slacker (Richard Linklater), 76
Slade in Full (Taika Waititi), 35
Sleeping Dogs (Roger Donaldson), 53
small nation (state) cinema, 43, 97
Smash Palace (Roger Donaldson), 53, 178, 190
Snakeskin (Gillian Ashurst), 27, 46
Snipes, Wesley, 174
Solondz, Todd, 115

Sons for the Return Home (Paul Maunder), 35
South Park, 103, 215
Speight's beer advertisements, 49–50, 63, 65, 184
Spielberg, Steven, 196
Springbok tour (1981), 60, 101
Squid and the Whale, The (Noah Baumbach), 123, 125
Star Trek, 79, 226
Star Wars, 196, 203, 210, 225–26, 231
stereotypes: in *Boy*, 141, 144, 145, 149; in *bro'Town*, 105–7; ethnic, 28, 30, 34, 35, 38, 88, 93, 96, 99; Nazi, 217; reversing, 107, 229, 230; in the US, 112, 117
Stiller, Ben, 111, 117, 122
Stoker, Bram, 161
Strictly Ballroom (Baz Luhrmann), 17, 136, 192
Superbad (Greg Mottola), 115

taha Māori (Māori Renaissance), 22, 65, 231
Taika's Incredible Show, 27
Tamanui, Zena, 100
Tama Tū (Taika Waititi), 14, 23, 31–33, **33**, 47
Tangata Whenua (Barry Barclay), 60
tangata whenua (people of the land), 52, 100
Team Thor, 79, 197
TEDx, 1–3, 6, 8, 12, 20–21
Te Kanawa, Kiri (Dame), 70
Te Kooti Trail, The (Rudall Hayward), 57
television: as Antipodean camp, 65; comedy, 25, 26; and direct address, 7, 78–80, 120–21; as intermediary between stand-up and film comedy, 96; New Zealand, 46, 65–66, **66**, 72–89, **80**, 103–6, 108–10, 178, 184, 197, 230

television advertisements (by Waititi), 11, 28, 66, **87**, 184, **219**; Give Nothing to Racism advertisement, 79, 219–20; morality of, 15, 86–88. *See also* Speight's beer advertisements
Te Māngai Pāho, 29
Terei, Pio, 93, 109, 113
Terminator, The (James Cameron), 180, 190, 197, 208
Te-Whānau-ā-Apanui, 23, 28, **159**
Te Wiata, Rima, 77, 109, 178, **185**
Thelma & Louise (Ridley Scott), 178, 189
This Is Spinal Tap (Rob Reiner), 174
Thompson, Tessa, **204**, 208–9
Thor (Kenneth Branagh), 195, 197
Thor: The Dark World (Alan Taylor), 195, 200
Thor: Ragnarok (Taika Waititi), 11, 17, 31, 32, 47, 77, 186, 191, 195–212, **201**, **202**, **204**, **206**, 225
Tin Drum, The (Volker Schlöndorff), 216
Tobeck, Joel, 76
To Be or Not To Be (Ernst Lubitsch), 223
To Love a Maori (Ramai and Rudall Hayward), 35
Topless Women Talk about Their Lives (Harry Sinclair), 74, 76
Topp Twins, The, 50, 62, 73, 74, 85, 190
Toy Boy (Julian Arahanga), 35
Toy Love (Harry Sinclair), 74
transgender, 51
transmedia, 195, 196
trickster, 2, 12–13, 18, 26, 145, 199, 219, 230
Trier, Lars von, 12, 13
True Blood, 161, 172
Tuberculosis and the Maori People of the Wairoa District (James Harris), 60
TVNZ, 60
TV3, 26, 27

Twilight (Catherine Hardwicke), 161, 165, 166, 172
Two Cars, One Night (Taika Waititi), 6, 14, 28–31, **29**, 79, 126, 197
2012 (Roland Emmerich), 209

Under the Southern Cross (a.k.a. *The Devil's Pit*) (Lew Collins), 55
Untold Tales of Maui, The, 26, 108
Untouchable Girls (Leanne Pooley), 50, 74
Upham, Charles, 41–42
Urale, Sima, 231
Utu (Geoff Murphy), 53

Vampires (Vincent Lannoo), 173–74
Vampire's Kiss (Robert Bierman), 161
Vampires Suck (Jason Friedberg and Aaron Seltzer), 161
Vamps (Amy Heckerling), 161
Vigil (Vincent Ward), 53

waiata (song), 65, 158
Waihau Bay, 23, 24, 28, 142, 147
Waititi, Taika, **37**, **80**, **82**, **137**, **153**, **157**, **159**, **166**, **220**; biography, 19–21, 23–28; in Hollywood, 17, 27–28, 89, 92, 95, 193, 225; as live performer, 1–13, 81–84, 110

Waititi, Taika (father of Taika Waititi, nickname Tiger), 7, 19, 23, 24, 28, 142, 147
Walk Short (Bill Toepfer), 74
Warhol, Andy, 15, 116, 120–21, 139
Waters, John, 63
Watson, Emily, 119
Wellington Paranormal, 197, 230
whaikōrero (discussion), 143, 152
whakapapa (genealogy), 99, 100, 152, 159
Whale Rider (Niki Caro), 105
Whatarau, Matariki, 108
What We Do in the Shadows (Taika Waititi, Jemaine Clement), 11, 16, 27, 47, 61, 77, 110, 139, 161–76, 197; and addiction, 172–73; and sexuality, 169–74
Wilder, George, 72
Wild Man (Geoff Murphy), 73, 75, 85
Wild Pork and Watercress, 75, 85, 178
Willy Wonka and the Chocolate Factory (Mel Stuart), 202
Winstanley, Chelsea, 222, 231
Wonder Woman (Patty Jenkins), 210

Young Ones, The, 25

Zelig (Woody Allen), 94